THE TIMES
Obituaries
1992

THE
TIMES
OBITUARIES
1992

—

LIVES REMEMBERED

—

Foreword by
ALISTAIR COOKE

—

Edited by
DAVID HEATON AND JOHN HIGGINS

—

Published by The Blewbury Press
Pound House, Church Road, Blewbury,
Oxon OX11 9PY

Jacket design by Peter Medcalf

© Times Newspapers Limited, 1992
ISBN 0 951 8282 1 5 Hardback
ISBN 0 951 8282 2 3 Paperback

Typeset by Avocet Typesetters, Bicester, Oxon
Printed in Great Britain by Biddles Ltd,
Guildford, Surrey

Obiter Dicta by
ALISTAIR COOKE

It was, I believe, Somerset Maugham who confessed to a lifetime's habit of turning, first thing in the morning, to the obituary page. When I first read this, I was shocked at what I took to be a hard-hearted routine typical of an author who, more than most, had profitably marketed a personal brand of cynicism. Today, I can't remember how many years it has been – twenty, at least – since I started the day with the same ritual.

It may be tasteless but it is true to say that it is a pleasure, provided the suddenly dead is not a cherished friend, or you don't, like the man in the H. G. Wells' fantasy, find your name there. The obits offer various satisfactions. Of course, there is the base, secret pleasure of seeing that someone you thoroughly dislike has had it. Also, hardly more creditable, is the sense of seeing a file closed, a piece of history packaged and labelled. But for the rest, and for most of the time, you are offered the privilege of learning, and celebrating, the enormous variety of trades, adventures, gifts, quirks, hobbies and passions that human beings are capable of. I think "wonder" is a truer word than "pleasure". Amanda Ros hit off the feeling exactly in her verse on visiting Westminster Abbey:

> "Holy Moses! Have a look!
> Flesh decayed in every nook.
> Some rare bits of brain lie here,
> Mortal loads of beef and beer."

The pungency of that quatrain, and the nouns I have emphasised (quirks, passions, etc) may cajole innocents who barely scan the obits into thinking they have been missing something all this time. They should be disabused at once, because most obituaries are time charts tempered by respectful prose. (I must say that part of the morning's fun is guessing at the emotions between the lines of the dullest résumés.)

But now comes a break in the long tradition of the statistical, treadmill obituary. And it is a happy thing that the break should be made by a paper that published nothing but the po-faced obit, for the longest time. I must, however, concede that only in *The Times* were the chronicles of upper-crust types supplemented, after a day or two's interval, by warm, sometimes hysterical "appreciations" of the adorable foibles of "Freddy" or "Pudgy", which did at least bring hilarity and mirth to the lesser breeds that read them.

So we have now a new form: an obituary somewhere between Aubrey's *Brief Lives* and the (old) *New Yorker*'s classic profile. Last year, somebody had the wit to compile an annual of them. And what riches! To those of us who don't read novels but, nevertheless, maintain a catlike watch on the human animal, *Lives Remembered* was a delight. As I expect this one will be. One of the unpredicted consequences of this publishing venture, I'm sure, will be a lively concern, on the part of living celebrities in many fields, to trim the cut of their biographical jib, indulge in good works, spread the word of their newfound compassion, generosity, whatever − in the hope of making it in an eventual *Lives*.

On this side of the ocean, on the *New York Times,* for many years there was a journalist who from an early age devoted his life to the proper entombment of the eminent dead. He collected punctiliously down the years every vital, soon to be mortal, fact about the world's great and the good. All that was missing from this bursting file was, of course, the personal touch. He pointed this out to the owners of the *New York Times*. Accordingly, he was sent off on an annual mission, with impressive credentials, to meet and quiz his impending (?) subjects. Foreign secretaries, new ambassadors might have to wait a while in the outer offices of an ageing monarch, but through the years the word of Alden Whitman's stature had spread far and wide and the door was open. In those days, the Pope did not grant exclusive interviews, except to Mr. Whitman. On his way once to accommodate General De Gaulle, he stopped off in London and had lunch at the Athenaeum. Two bishops spotted him and feared that their day had come. There was not a prime minister, a Nobel laureate or a dictactor anywhere who, at the onset of the first sneeze, did not crave an audience with Whitman. Everybody on earth wanted a good notice from this dedicated man.

The appearance of this new form, this new annual, may turn all of us into similar wards of *The Times*'s obit. editor. Anyway, here is plenty, for anyone who has the honesty to admit that next to oneself nothing in life is more interesting than other people's lives. Especially when they're over.

CONTENTS

Contents

DAME JUDITH ANDERSON

Australian actress who moved to America and achieved success in Shakespeare theatre and appeared in 25 films attaining distinction in Cat on a Hot Tin Roof.

JUDITH Anderson will be best remembered for her portrayal of the sinister and ultimately incinerated Mrs Danvers in the Hitchcock film *Rebecca* (1940), for which she was nominated for an Academy Award. But her career was primarily in the classical theatre, with a heavy emphasis on Greek tragedy and Shakespeare and although an Australian she achieved her most enduring success, on stage as well as on film, in America: she is to date the only woman to have played the title role in *Hamlet* at New York's Carnegie Hall. Her portrayal was slated as bloodless by the critics but she won a television Emmy Award in 1954 for her performance in *Macbeth* in a production televised for the American network NBC's "Hallmark Hall of Fame".

The high period in her career began in 1936 when she played Gertrude to Gielgud's Hamlet on Broadway. "Now that I have begun my classical education," she said, "do I dare breathe that I have dreamed of Lady Macbeth and now wish to act her?" A year later she played the part opposite Laurence Olivier at the Old Vic. She was 39 and it was her first appearance in London. Michel Saint-Denis's production was voted puzzling by audiences and on being transferred, to the New Theatre in the West End it languished there. In 1941, however, Anderson's Lady Macbeth opposite the British born Maurice Evans on Broadway was a big success and rated very highly by the critics.

One of her last roles was in 1984, at the age of 86, when she played a grand dame in NBC television's daytime soap-opera *Santa Barbara*, where she also happened to live.

Judith Anderson was born Frances Margaret Anderson. Her father was Scottish by descent, her mother English and she was one of four children. Her first appearance on stage was at the age of 17 in *A Royal Divorce* at the Theatre Royal in Sydney. Then, after a year spent touring Australia in *Monsieur Beaucaire* and *The Scarlet Pimpernel* she moved to America in 1918, and made the rest of her life and career there.

Her Broadway debut was in a stock company at the old 14th Street Playhouse; in 1920, she toured the United States with William Gillette in *Dear Brutus*. By then, critics were already commenting on her "unrestrained" stage style which some were uncharitable enough to define as overacting in the grand manner.

Through the 1920s she played with a series of stock and regional companies until (after a brief return to her homeland in 1927) she succeeded Lynn Fontanne as Nina in O'Neill's *Strange Interlude* on Broadway. Three years later she was Lavinia in O'Neill's *Mourning Becomes Electra* and then, in 1936, Gertrude to Gielgud's Broadway *Hamlet*.

After her stage success as Lady Macbeth she repeated it twice on television during the 1950s, performances described by one local critic as "alternately vibrant, calculating, cruel, regal and pitiful; the intricacy of the characterisation was knitted so faultlessly that it had a thrilling power."

Judith Anderson's other great role was as Medea, most notably in a 1947 production which she invited Gielgud to direct and co-star in as Jason, though he was less than entirely happy with either his production or his performance. She again played Medea in Australia for the opening of the Elizabethan Theatre Trust's first season in 1955 and in Paris at the second Drama Festival, but not in Britain. In 1959 she filmed her Lady Macbeth opposite Maurice Evans but much of her later career on stage met with less success as modern audiences grew disenchanted with her often larger-than-life performances. She appeared in more than 25 films including *Stage Door Canteen, Salome* and *The Ten Commandments* but her films only occasionally achieved the distinction of the 1958 *Cat on a Hot Tin Roof* in which she played Big Mama alongside Burl Ives, Elizabeth Taylor and Paul Newman.

Her post-war stage work included a sinister Miss Madrigal in the first production of Enid Bagnold's *The Chalk Garden* on Broadway (the role later played in London by Peggy Ashcroft), and a 1960 appearance at the Edinburgh Festival as Arkadina in a production of *The Seagull* which marked the stage debut of Tom Courtenay.

Back in America, she took increasingly to solo recitals featuring highlights from her former Shakespearian and Greek triumphs, although when she played one of these "Evenings With" at her own native Adelaide Festival, the local press was distinctly less than ecstatic.

She was created a Dame of the British Empire in the New Year Honours of 1960.

She continued to be active occasionally in films appearing in *Cinderella* (1960) *A Man Called Horse* (1970), *Inn of the Damned* (1974), and *Star Trek III* (1984).

Judith Anderson married twice, first to Benjamin Lehman and secondly to Luther Greene, with both marriages ending in divorce.

Her reputation seems likely to rest on her two major classical performances, notably the Medea of which Rosamund Gilder once wrote "It is pure evil, dark, dangerous, cruel, raging, ruthless. From beginning to end she maintains an almost incredible intensity, yet she varies her mood so constantly and moves with such skill through unexplored regions of pain and despair that she can hold her audience in suspense throughout the evening."

b 10.2.98 d 3.1.92 aged 93

ARLETTY

Arletty (Léonie Bathiat) French actress and unforgettable star of Marcel Carné's screen masterpiece, Les Enfants du Paradis.

ALTHOUGH she had command of a wide range of gifts: popular singer, music hall performer, comic and "straight" stage actress, it is to the underlying melancholy that Marcel Carné discovered in her, that Arletty owes her immortality. Her career was to last into the 1960s, as she paid frequent return visits to the stage where it had begun. But she belonged essentially to the golden age of French cinema, the 1930s and 1940s when masterpieces seemed to flow effortlessly from the Paris studios.

Her apogee was her performance as Garance, the elusive beauty loved so intensely and so much in vain in *Les Enfants du Paradis*. Indeed the world owes to Carné's perceptiveness the discovery of an aspect of her character which might have lain forever buried under the earthy and joyous vulgarity which had been her stock in trade until he took over the direction of her career. In this long, intricate and often enigmatic melodrama she brilliantly sustained the role of the hungered-after woman in a manner which combined world-weary sophistication with a haunting sense of vulnerability. The resulting film, to which her contribution was so germane, is one of the most memorable things to have emerged from the cinema.

Arletty was born Léonie Bathiat into a family and a caste whose outlook and innate vitality was shaped by the streets of Paris. Courbevoie may, in those days have beeen a drab suburb but its people: artisans, shop keepers, office workers, the odd crook and the occasional prostitute, were intensely aware of themselves as Parisians. Céline, a near contemporary, was from Courbevoie. His friend the metaphysical satirist Marcel Aymé, brilliantly caught the wit of its inhabitants in his writings; Edith Piaf evoked their vigorous brand of sentimentality in her songs; Arletty, beautiful and possessed of a somehow uncorrupted street wisdom, remains, quintessentially, their representative.

The Bathiat family was a large one and Léonie's mother was compelled to take in washing to help support it even before her husband was killed in a metro accident in 1916. Léonie had to take a job in an armaments factory, but the Bohemian café life of Paris was her natural métier. It was in one such café that she was spotted by the Cubist painter Paul Gillaume. Entranced by her singular beauty, he sent her to a revue producer. She also picked up work as a model and by the end of the first world war she was earning a living as a chorus girl. She adopted the stage name Arletti, but for some reason deciding that English was more chic than French, changed the terminal "i" to a "y". She learned to sing and her performances on stage brought her a wide circle of admirers, drawn as much by the earthy vitality of her character in revue sketches as by her scantily clad form behind the footlights. She was, after all, in her own words "as thin as a runner bean".

Cinema had at first no use for her. Her great asset, her voice, counted for nothing on the silent screen of those days. Sound remedied that, but the reputation she had made on stage as an essentially light actress, most at home as a prostitute or woman of easy virtue, did not at first go down well in the more serious studios. Nevertheless work eventually came, although her first few films were unmemorable. In the 1930s she worked with the director Jacques Feyder in *Pension Mimosa* and with Sacha Guitry in *Les Perles de la Couronne* and *Désiré*.

But it was not until 1938 – when she was forty – that she began the collaboration with Marcel Carné which was to shape the rest of her life and ensure her immortality. In *Hôtel du Nord* (1938) she played – ironically in view of her earlier difficulties – a prostitute, Madame Raymonde, a kind of Mother Courage of her profession, grumbling her way through a life divided between waiting for custom down by the Canal Saint-Martin and being maltreated by her murderous lover. In *Le Jour se léve* (1939) she played another mistress in a film whose fatalistic and violent mood was heavy with impending war.

Her admirers were by now legion – and unrequited. The Aga Khan wooed her immensely from afar but never got beyond dinner *á deux* in the private dining room of Larue's restaurant. Sacha Guitry, too, made a stupendous effort and was rewarded with as he ruefully noted, "everlasting friendship". For a long time the most admired woman in Paris seemed to have no lover.

Ironically, again, when she did fall in love during the war this paricular species of happiness presented itself in equivocal guise. Her chosen object was a high-ranking officer in the *Luftwaffe*, who was ADC to Goering. He was handsome and Arletty fell for him almost at first glance, with a passion which seemed the more violent for having been so long suppressed.

She was not, of course, the only French actress to have got into bed with the enemy and was personally unrepentant. As she riposted when taxed with her apostasy: "My heart is French but my body is international." Nevertheless the climate of Liberation judged such behaviour harshly and she was charged with collaboration. This charge was subsequently dropped but she spent some time in an internment camp in 1944 and was to find the offence counted against her when she later tried to get work.

Meanwhile *Les Enfants du Paradis* had appeared, astonishing international audiences that such a marvellous film could have been made under the noses of the German occupiers. By the time Arletty played Garance she was actually 46. It was in a sense both the pinnacle and the end of her film career. Already mature to play romantic leads under the merciless scrutiny of the cameras, she returned to the stage where she found some rewarding roles in the Paris productions of plays such as *A Streetcar Named Desire*. She made a few more films, too, including Carné's *L'Air de Paris* (1954) and a version of Sartre's *Huit Clos*.

But in 1963 she was blinded when she administered some medicine to her eyes, thinking it was eye lotion. Although an operation partially restored her sight it thereafter deteriorated again. Nevertheless the publication of her autobiography, *Je Suis comme Je Suis* at the age of 89 brough her renewed popularity and attention. The book took its title from a verse of one of the songs she had sung in her music hall days, and summed up her attitude to life perfectly.

Je suis come je suis,
Je suis faite comme ça,
Quand j'ai envie de rire,
Oui je ris aux eclats

b 15.5.98 d 24.7.92 aged 94

ROBERT BEATTY

Robert Beatty, Canadian actor who played Don Maguire in the television series Dial 999.

IN THE immediate post-war years Robert Beatty's Canadian accent and his craggy good looks were eminently marketable features and for a time he was one of Britain's most familiar actors in films, television, radio and the theatre. In the 1950s, before the acting profession became quite the global village it is today, he was much in demand in Britain to portray Americans. Indeed in addition to transatlantic roles, his dark-brown voice enabled him to tackle Scottish, Irish and colonial parts with ease. He also exuded considerable charm and his tough but gentle features would crinkle up into what was once described as "an audible smile."

Although he probably failed to realise his full potential and never quite managed to translate these attributes into mega-stardom he had a worthy career. He made his greatest impact as Detective Inspector Don Maguire, a Canadian Mountie attached to Scotland Yard in a short-lived television series, *Dial 999*, and capped this, unexpectedly at the age of 78, by a masterly portrayal of Ronald Reagan, capturing precisely the mannerisms and gestures of the American president in a television "docu-drama" *Breakthrough at Reykjavik*.

Robert Beatty was the son of a clothing manufacturer who was descended from the Dr Beatty who was a surgeon on the *Victory* when Nelson was mortally wounded at Trafalgar. His grandfather was an Irish farmer who emigrated to Canada. Beatty acquired a BA at the University of Toronto. His first job was as a cashier at a petrol-filling station in Hamilton but after joining a local amateur dramatic society he decided to train for the professional stage. At 28 he was a late starter but in 1937, on the advice of an aunt, he came to England and enrolled at RADA. After seeing fellow Canadian Raymond Massey in *Idiot's Delight* at London's Apollo Theatre he went backstage and asked for a walk on part. He was taken on as understudy, given a small part and launched on a London stage career.

Having failed to pass an Army medical, Beatty joined the BBC as a newsreader for transmissions to North America and appeared in various wartime stage productions including *The Petrified Forest* at the Globe Theatre and *A Soldier for Christmas* at Wyndhams. In 1945 he appeared in three well-known plays: as Mark McPherson in *Laura* at the St Martin's, Bruce Lovell in *Love From A Stranger* at the Gateway and as Major Joppolo in *A Bell for Adano* at the Phoenix. In 1957 he took over the lead in *The Happiest Millionaire* at the Cambridge Theatre from Wilfrid Hyde White and three years later took over the lead from Sir Michael Redgrave in *The Aspern Papers*.

Beatty began appearing in films in 1938 and had his first big success playing an heroic captain who brought his crippled tanker back to port in *San Demetrio London*. Three years later he had a starring part in *Appointment With Crime* and in 1946 made an impressive appearance with James Mason in Carol Reed's *Odd Man Out*.

In the 1950s he was at his busiest. His films included *Captain Horatio Hornblower RN, The Square Ring, Albert RN, The Gentle Gunman, Tarzan and the Lost Safari* and *Something of Value*. In addition to film and stage roles, he played Philip O'Dell, an Irish private investigator, in a long-running BBC radio series and appeared as "the man with the mike" interviewing people "out and about in London" for the television series *Saturday Night Out*. He also appeared, strikingly, in a haircream advertisement and provided the distinctive transatlantic tones for numerous "voice-over" commercials.

In 1957-58 came his television series *Dial 999*. In spite of its success it ran for only nine months and he was to claim later that it "killed him for ten years" as far as other television work was concerned. "As far as producers were concerned I was Maguire of the Mounties and that was that."

Certainly he worked less from then on but he turned in an effective portrayal of the first Lord Beaverbrook alongside Richard Burton's Churchill in *Walk With Destiny* for television and was featured in the films *A Space Odyssey* (1968) and *Where Eagles Dare* (1969). After appearing in *Superman III* (1983) came his most critically successful portrayal of President Reagan in *Breakthrough at Reykjavik*.

Robert Beatty was a genial, unassuming workaday actor with none of the self-importance that affects some others of the craft. Asked, following his successful portrayal of President Reagan, whether it had engendered within him any statesman-like thoughts or desires, he replied simply: "I learned my lines and I delivered them."

Robert Beatty was married four times: the first, a wartime marriage, lasted three months; the second to a BBC secretary, lasted 18 years; the third to Princess Obolensky lasted five years. His final marriage was in 1975. He was declared bankrupt in 1978. He leaves a son from his second marriage.

b 19.10.09   d 3.3.92   aged 82

CURT BOIS

German stage and screen actor who moved to the US to avoid Nazism and appeared in some 46 Hollywood pictures but returned to Germany in 1950 to enjoy new success.

THE active career of Curt Bois spanned 80 uninterrupted years, from his stage debut in 1908 to his final film appearance in Wim Wenders's *Wings of Desire* in 1987. After his father abandoned the family, Curt Bois's mother married the playwright Albert Bernstein-Sawersky, who encouraged the precocious show-business careers of his step-children. In 1908 Curt made his professional debut as Heinerle in Leo Fall's operetta *Der fiedel Bauer*. His film debut was practically simultaneous, since his "Heinerle-duett", with Greta Dierkes, was recorded by an early sound film system and shown in cinemas a few days after the premiere.

By his early twenties he was a star in Berlin variety and cabaret and recorded a number of songs, some of them composed for him by Mischa Spoliansky and Friedrich Holländer. As a character comedian he appeared in productions by Reinhardt and Piscator and in 1928 had a particular success in Hugo Thimig's production of *Charley's Aunt* at Vienna's Theater in der Josefstadt.

In February 1933, seeing the rise of Nazism, Bois and his first wife, the soubrette Hedi Ury, left Germany. Their search for a new home took them through Vienna, Prague, Paris, London and New York, where Bois's excellent command of English brought work in several Broadway shows. By 1937 he had arrived in Hollywood, where many of his Berlin acquaintances had preceded him. Like other one-time European stars, Bois was happy to play supporting roles and he became practically indispensable where a camp hairdresser or dress designer was required. Between 1937 and 1950 he appeared in 46 Hollywood pictures, ranging from *Golddiggers of Paris* and *The Hunchback of Notre Dame* to *Cover Girl, Joe Palooka Meets Humphrey* and *The Lovable Cheat*. Max Ophüls's *Caught* gave him one of his best roles.

In 1950 Bois returned to a divided Berlin and chose the East. His last stage appearance in Germany, in 1932, had been as Khlestakov in *The Government Inspector*. He chose the same role for his first appearance in his homeland after 17 years, at the Deutsches Theater. He enjoyed new success as Puntilla in Brecht's own production of *Herr Puntilla und sein Knecht Matti*, and in 1955 repeated the role in Alberto Cavalcanti's film version. In the East, too, he resumed his career as film director with an adaptation of his own stage production of the Berlin burlesque *Ein Polterabend*.

Dissatisfied with the roles available in East Berlin, in 1954 Bois moved to West Germany, only to find himself boycoted in the ugly political atmosphere of the period. After three years, however, he enjoyed outstanding success in a series of leading roles, including Androcles and Argan.

In *Wings of Desire* Wim Wenders cast Bois, now tiny and withered but with bright eyes behind his large spectacles, as the spirit of Berlin. It was an appropriate swansong to a career which ornamented Berlin show business through so many generations.

b 5.4.01   d 25.12.91   aged 90

MARLENE DIETRICH

Marlene Dietrich, screen and stage actress and cabaret entertainer.

Though we all might enjoy
Seeing Helen of Troy
As a gay cabaret entertainer
I doubt that she could
Be one quarter as good
As our legendary, lovely
Marlene.

THUS Noël Coward, introducing Dietrich to a London nightclub audience at the Café de Paris in 1954 by which time the star was well into her fifties and a second career. In her first career she had conquered the screens, first as Lola in *The*

Blue Angel. Others have taken the role of Heirnrich Mann's temptress, on screen and on stage – a version is about to open on Shaftesbury Avenue. But none could match Dietrich. Hollywood seized her and Paramount turned her into a star. She became synonymous with the erotic: no one could light a cigarette more sensuously than she or tell, in the huskiest of voices, the boys in the backroom what they should have. Unlike most actresses who are compelled to evolve with age the image of Dietrich, once established, was amplified rather than altered as time went on. The insolent, ironic style of her youth did at one point mellow into approachability, but it re-emerged in maturer form to haunt her later performances on the screen and in cabaret. But the soul of

'An insolent youthful style mellowed in maturity'

the Dietrich secret, a quality which kept crowds queuing for her one-woman shows at an age when such a thing came to seem almost preposterous, was something, perhaps, more fundamental. Reduced to its simplist terms, Dietrich's appeal was, indeed, sex appeal. But it was a sex appeal which involved not merely the face, the million dollar legs and the air of Do Not Touch, which were all part of the armoury. Essentially, it embodied the idea of the eternal woman and like Garbo – whose occupation of the same position at MGM Paramount imported her to challenge – it began with beauty of an order calculated to overwhelm the senses, suspending criticism of the roles (frequently in Dietrich's case tawdry ones) represented by the actress. The crowds who later flocked to see and hear the septuagenarian Dietrich came not to judge the performance but simply to be part of the ambience it created.

The biggest mystery about Dietrich was, for a long time, her date of birth. This was carefully concealed and suggestions for the date ranged from 1894 through to 1912. Then the secret came out when an East German clerk located in his registry and somewhat tactlessly published the entry relating to the birth of one Maria Magdalene (hence the contraction Marlene) Dietrich on December 27, 1901, in the suburb of Schöneberg.

Marlene Dietrich was born Maria Magdalena, the second daughter of an officer in the Prussian police and a mother who came from a well-known family of Berlin jewellers. She grew up against a background of clenched social and financial respectability. A year or two after her birth Dietrich's father died and her mother married another military man, Edouard von Losch, who was killed on the Russian front in the closing weeks of the first world war, leaving his widow and her daughters in severely straitened circumstances. But her mother strenuously supported her daughter's intense desire to be a performer and she in turn remained proud of her Prussian ancestry.

By 1919 Dietrich, was enrolled in the Berlin Hochschule für Musik, since it was thought she had a future as a violinist. Damage to her wrist put an end to that idea, and she soon afterwards auditioned for Max Reinhardt. But he gravely doubted her acting ability and her first attempt was not successful. For some time after that she worked as a chorus girl in a touring company before he eventually gave her small roles at the Deutsches Theater.

While there Dietrich, like many of her contemporaries, also began to play small roles at the UFA studios.

It was in 1922, though she often denied it, that she made her debut at the age of 21 as a maid in *The Little Napoleon*. For the next seven years she divided her time more or less equally between the theatres of Berlin and its film studios: on stage, guided by Reinhardt, she worked in Shaws's *Misalliance* and *Back to Methuselah*, establishing a local reputation second only to that of Elisabeth Bergner who once remarked: "If I were as beautiful as Marlene, I wouldn't know what to do with my talent."

The success of *The Blue Angel* in Berlin confirmed rather than created Dietrich as a star in Germany: a year earlier she had already been sharing German movie-magazine covers with Garbo. But internationally it was the film in which she was born, and which was to characterise her forever. "What happened to you before *Blue Angel*?" she was once asked at a Hollywood press conference. Dietrich, who was never renowned for courtesy when dealing with the press replied curtly and none too accurately, "Nothing".

Paramount immediately signed her to a two-picture deal and she moved to California with von Sternberg, sending only some months later for the husband and daughter with whom she had started her family in Berlin during the late 1920s.

Her first American picture was *Morocco* (1930) for which Paramount made her lose 33 pounds in weight. Thereafter she appeared in films ranging from such von Sternberg classics as *Blonde Venus* (1932) and *The Scarlet Empress* (1934) through the considerably less impressive *Garden of Allah* (1936) to George Marshall's great western *Destry Rides Again* (1939). But it became increasingly clear that with von Sternberg's determination to end their partnership in the middle 1930s the focus of Marlene's interest in cinema became blurred. Her last film with von Sternberg was *Devil is a Woman* (1935).

So when the war came, it was with a kind of relief that she went off around the world on extended army concert tours, beginning to work as a singer with live audiences that were to occupy more and more of her time in the second half of her career. She had rejected an offer by Hitler — the only person she ever "hated" she said in her 1979 memoirs — to return to Germany and become a star of the Nazi-controlled film company UFA, and in 1937 she took United States citizenship.

During the second world war she participated in the US war effort by keeping the troops' moral high as a singer in benefit performances for the US army's welfare services in North Africa,

Italy and other European war theatres. This first work as a singer with the live audiences was to occupy more and more of her time in the second half of her career. Quite extraordinarily it was her version of a German first world war soldiers' song, "Lili Marlene" that propelled it to fame, in spite of the initial attempts of both British and American army authorities to have it suppressed as subversive. Her version of the song eventually made it popular on both sides of the fighting lines. "Falling in Love Again" was another huge wartime success, as popular with German PoWs as it had been with American GIs.

After the war, an affair with Jean Gabin led her back to the cinema for *Martin Roumagnac*, but from now on her films were to get fewer and further apart. Her next venture was Billy Wilder's *A Foreign Affair* (1948) a hard-edged comedy of postwar Berlin. In 1950 she starred in Alfred Hitchcock's *Stage Fright* and Henry Koster's *No Highway* (1951).

But between the films she had begun to develop a cabaret talent second to none. Cocteau once said that her beauty was its own praise, and Hemingway, a lover of blondes in general and Dietrich in particular, noted: "her voice alone could break your heart". Beyond the heartbreak was the expression of an immensely theatrical talent for going out alone on stage and holding an audience with all the power of a great dramatic actress that many of her songs, from "Lili Marlene" of the second world war to "Where Have all the Flowers Gone?" of the Vietnam conflict, required.

Although she worked once with Hitchcock, once with Kramer and most memorably with Orson Welles in *A Touch of Evil* (1958), few directors were able to follow in the footsteps of "Svengali Jo" von Sternberg. So she took to travelling more and more alone on solo cabaret. Her last cameo role was in *Just a Gigolo* in 1976.

The "Marlene" of the 1930s, a German-American creation of von Sternberg and some excellent lighting cameramen, was gradually translated into "Dietrich", a somewhat tougher and lonelier figure who, around the world, learnt the greatest of all theatrical lessons: waste nothing. Money, time and herself were all exquisitely preserved against need, and, although sometimes cold to frosty and distant before the footlights, she passed again and again that final test of stardom – the ability not just to do something, but to stand there.

Her war activities tarnished her reputation in Germany, where she was regarded as a traitor long after hostilities ceased. When she returned to West Germany in 1960 for a series of performances, she found that the image of her wearing an American uniform was still livid in the minds of many Germans.

Her homecoming was marred by bomb threats, pickets carrying signs in English that read "Marlene Go Home" and editorials calling her a "traitor". Despite a unanimously acclaimed performance with two encores and 11 curtain calls, she said she would never return.

Towards the end of her career, in concert seasons for the West End and New York and Australia through the middle 1970s, she would take centre stage, an elderly German lady with a slight limp swathed in acres of white fur. She was Dietrich, a constant reminder of the survival of the human spirit and of endurance. She was a theatrical Mother Courage without Brecht, belonging – with Lotte Lenya and Edith Piaf and precious few others – to a band of dramatic singers who had spanned much of the century. Having her sing to you was not unlike being entertained by the Statue of Liberty. Her greatest achievement was perhaps to evoke memories and the past and then to transcend them.

As the years went on her one-woman show with its battery of the old, irresistible songs, "Lili Marlene", "Falling in Love Again" and "Honeysuckle Rose", established her beyond the reach of any criticism that might have accrued to her films. Audiences that included large numbers of women – to whom she had an appeal as electrifying as she did to men — packed in to see her wherever she appeared. In a way, her image regained its pristine Sternbergian remoteness (although, owing to her creator's lack of charity to her in his autobiography, she did for a while stop alluding to his contribution to her early success).

As she passed 60 and then 70, an older generation went to see her out of nostalgia for an age of elegant and beautiful women that seemed to have departed, while their children were fascinated anew by the timeless distillation of the experience of being a woman she communicated. In the end, perhaps, the act was more and more in the nature of a carefully planned assault on the emotions, meticulously orchestrated, calculatingly lit and evocatively dressed.

But nobody minded. The idea of the woman who had been a close friend of Cocteau and Remarque, of whom Hemingway had characteristically remarked: 'The Kraut's the best thing that ever came into the ring'', had long outlived its physical embodiment.

By the time the famous legs did fail and Marlene Dietrich fell on stage and broke a thigh bone in Sydney on September 29, 1975, she had passed unassailably into the legends which it is Hollywood's peculiar power to create.

She retired to her home on the Avenue Montaigne in Paris. Like Callas and Garbo before her, she shunned publicity and declined interviews, especially from those trying to chronicle her life in one or other of the media. "No one will ever trespass on my private world," she said and she kept to her word.

The Dietrich image was well preserved elsewhere. In 1947 she was awarded the Medal of Freedom, the highest US decoration for civilians, for her contributions to the American war effort, and made French Chevalier of the Légion d'honneur in 1951 and Officier of the Légion d'honneur in 1972.

Dietrich leaves her only child, a daughter Maria born in 1925 to the husband, Rudolph Sieber whom she had married a year earlier and to whom she remained distantly married until his death a decade ago in California.

b 27.12.01   d 6.5.92   aged 90

DENHOLM ELLIOTT

Stage and screen actor who will be remembered for The Cruel Sea *and* Alfie, *among many films.*

ONLY occasionally did Denholm Elliott command top billing either in the theatre or on film, but he regularly stole the show. As he grew older he took pride in being a masterly supporting actor on screen, totally relaxed and confident inside his character, which more often than not had an element of the seedy or the guilty – and sometimes both. When he played the boozing journalist in *Defence of the Realm* (1986) it was almost possible to smell the whisky coming off him. In Alan Bennett's *A Private Function* a couple of years earlier he personified all that was corrupt and greedy in postwar Britain.

Denholm Elliott made the best use of his face, which quite early on became lined. He once described it himself as having a ravaged look: "lived-in" might have been a politer expression. It could have been used for many characters from Graham Greene, although it rarely was.

Elliott played the police inspector in *The Heart of the Matter* and in a few short stories adapted for televison, but otherwise his only major Greene role was in *The Return of A. J. Raffles*, a play which did not provide one of the RSC's better nights at the Aldwych. Elliott, though, always did have a good line in gentlemen cads.

The turning point in his film career was probably *Alfie* in 1966, in which he played a back street abortionist. The strength of this performance when Elliott was in his mid forties – often a difficult age for an actor – anchored him amidst the dirty mac brigade. Thereafter, when the script called for someone with a few guilty secrets, a bit dishevelled, somewhat down on his luck then the casting director was apt to say "Send for Denholm".

He, too, a few years earlier had been down on his luck, drinking heavily and trying to piece together his career again. At one point, after successes in the verse plays of Fry and Eliot, he had been seen as a probable "gentleman actor" in the Gielgud tradition. It did not work out that way. He had a dismal time at Stratford-on-Avon, professionally and privately, complaining that pub conversation there tended to revolve around alternative interpretations of Malvolio in Act III. H. M. Tennent, the ruling West End management of the day, appeared little interested in him and the new pack of kitchen-sink actors, performing in a rather different style, were snapping at his heels.

In the cinema things were hardly better: early in Elliott's career Korda had put him on a handsome 15-year contract at £5,000 p.a. and then made little use of him. Denholm Elliott needed *Alfie*, which helped him establish a corner in the roles he was to play best: characters with a glass in the hand, a strand of lank hair hanging over the right eyebrow and a few nasty secrets lurking somewhere. Possibly a touch of rebellion, too.

There was more than a streak of rebelliousness in Elliott's character, much of which stemmed from his unhappy childhood. His family was upper middle class, but his father, a KC, was murdered by terrorists in Palestine. He disliked his time at Malvern College and had a few sharp things to say when the school was foolish enough to invite him back for prize-giving day. He was sufficiently disturbed to become a kleptomaniac before trying his hand as an actor at RADA – surprisingly, a recommended therapy then. Even there reports on Elliott were not good.

Wartime service in the RAF might have come as a relief – he was a gunner in Group Captain Leonard Cheshire's squadron – had he not been shot down over the Baltic and forced to spend three years as a PoW in Silesia.

Confinement at least gave him a chance to prove that he *could* act. He set up a company drawn from his fellow prisoners and took a number of leading roles himself, ranging from Eliza Doolittle to Macbeth.

After release Denholm Elliott had no doubts about his future. In his RAF uniform he auditioned for the Amersham repertory company and was engaged on the spot. His still boyish good looks won him a part in *The Guinea Pig* (1946) as a prefect and then he attracted the eye of Laurence Olivier, who was due to play the amorous Duke in Christopher Fry's *Venus Observed* at the St James's. Olivier teasingly told Elliott that he was really "not quite aristocrat enough" for the role of the Duke's son, but engaged him nonetheless. The two actors were to remain great friends.

More Fry followed, this time an Anouilh adaptation, *Ring Round the Moon*, in which Denholm Elliott took over the Paul Scofield double role on Broadway. He began to be associated with "serious drama". There was T. S. Eliot's *The Confidential Clerk* (1954) and immediately afterwards an involvement with the avant-garde seasons Peter Hall put on, first at the Arts and then at the Phoenix. Elliott impressed in *South* by Julien Green, an early theatrical foray into homosexuality, and had one of his few really jolly roles as Kilroy in Tennessee Williams's experimental *Camino Real*, directed by Hall.

This work was dovetailed with considerably less demanding, but financially much more rewarding screen appearances. His debut was in a forgotten film, *Dear Mr Prohack*, based on Arnold Bennett. But *The Sound Barrier* and a recommendation from David Lean brought him the Alexander Korda contract. On the set of *The Cruel Sea* he met his first wife, Virginia McKenna, although the marriage was to last only three years.

Towards the end of the 1950s the Elliott career began to run out of steam and when the work offers did not come in he drank heavily. A season at Stratford in 1960 brought little acclaim and some dull roles. Most of Elliott's appearances in classical drama were to be in America, where he flirted briefly with Lee Strasberg's Actors Studio. It is the West End's loss that he was hardly ever seen there in glossy revivals of Chekhov and Ibsen, two playwrights made for him, although there was a mightily impressive Judge Brack (*Hedda Gabler*) at the Royal

stealer, which earned him the much-quoted show business quip "Never act with children, animals or Denholm Elliott". He specialised, both in the cinema and on television, in tipplers with a kind of dissipated charm and a few guilty secrets. Once when asked how he chose his scripts, Denholm Elliott replied that he opened them midway through and if he found a few characters he would not mind having a drink with in a pub then he went back to the beginning.

Denholm Elliott's re-won success, which included a useful partnership with Denis Potter (*Blade on the Feather*, *Brimstone and Treacle*) and quantities of other roles on TV, meant that his appearances on stage became fewer. Peter Nichols's *Chez Nous*, about the tribulations of the English middle class in the Dordogne, at the Globe gave him a chance again to shine in comedy. His last West End play was David Mamet's *A Life in the Theatre* (Haymarket) three years ago.

Denholm Elliott could be difficult. He had fits of depression and periods of elation when he would roar off in full gear on his motorbike across Europe. In a flamboyant profession he was a man who usually preferred to sit on the sidelines, glass of vodka in hand, observing others. He knew his own capabilities and knew, perhaps too that he lacked the willpower to realise all of them. He used his voice, he used his face, especially that seen-it-all-before expression that transferred so well to the screen. In the past decade the British cinema has not been exactly strong but Denholm Elliott appeared in a high proportion of its best films.

He is survived by his second wife, Susan, to whom he had been married 30 years, a son and a daughter.

b 31.5.22   d 6.10.92   aged 70

Court. And it was his loss that he himself never became a star or a true box-office draw, which was within his potential. He admitted that he was not very good at pushing others, including some of lesser talent, out of the way. He tended to be somewhat dismissive and cynical about himself, especially when talking with fellow actors at the Garrick bar.

His career was retrieved through the cinema. Clive Donner's *Nothing But the Best* (1964), with a Frederic Raphael script, led the way back in giving Elliott a meaty cad role. *King Rat* took him to Hollywood and proved his exceptional ability to play the flawed and even corrupt. And then came *Alfie* to put the stamp on the new Elliott career. Thereafter he became the regular scene-

JOSE FERRER

American actor and director who won an Oscar in 1951 for his performance as Cyrano de Bergerac, *a role he also played on stage and on television.*

TO THE public at large the name of Jose Ferrer has long conjured up two images: Cyrano de Bergerac and Toulouse Lautrec in John Huston's film *Moulin Rouge*. Both roles involved prodigies — and quantities — of make-up. Rostand's hero needed a nose spectacular enough for his whole life to centre upon it and Toulouse-Lautrec in *Moulin Rouge* required a normal-sized actor to appear about four feet tall on screen. That Ferrer succeeded memorably in both these roles gives some idea of the sort of actor he was: flamboyant, actorly, full of tricks and definitely larger than life even when spectacularly smaller.

He had a long and varied screen career and won his Oscar despite the overall stodginess of the 1950 film version of *Cyrano de Bergerac*. But he was really too bravura to be wholly at home in films, which always seemed rather to cramp his style. Curiously, when he came to direct in the theatre and cinema he was much more sober and meticulous, making good, solid stage successes and films that were interesting and serious rather than thrillingly original.

On stage he was something quite different. In the years before he became a star he gained a reputation simply for versatility and reliability. Once he was a headliner and his name started appearing above the title of the play he could be relied upon for fireworks. He never hesitated to try out new and newsworthy things: in 1960 he sang the title role in Puccini's *Gianni Schicchi* at the Santa Fé Opera Festival and in 1965 he played the mime role of Dr Coppelius in the ballet *Coppélia* in Palm Beach.

He was christened Jose Vincente Ferrer de Otero y Cintron, son of a wealthy lawyer. The family moved to New York when he was a child and he originally intended to be an architect. But while studying architecture he discovered the pleasures of university dramatics and instantly decided that he had found his true vocation. His first professional appearance was in a showboat on Long Island in 1934. The next year he joined Joshua Logan's stock company, thereby beginning a personal and professional association which continued until Logan's death. In 1935 he reached Broadway, in the humble guise of Second Policeman in *A Slight Case of Murder* and little by little he was noticed as a capable all-round performer. His first major success also came via Logan. He took on the title role of Brandon Thomas's *Charley's Aunt* at the Court Theatre in 1940 in a revival originally intended for Walter Slezak. Ferrer himself recalled that Slezak was none too pleased with the success he had on the opening night. It was a role Ferrer revived on several subsequent occasions.

At this time he also began to direct on stage and underlined his versatility by taking over from Danny Kaye in the long-running Cole Porter musical *Let's Face It*, and then immediately afterwards playing Iago to Paul Robeson's Othello. In 1946, he toured an ambitious repertory of plays starring himself, including *Richard III, Cyrano de Bergerac* (for the first time), and William Archer's creaking but enjoyable melodrama *The Green Goddess*. Later in the year he brought his Cyrano to Broadway. It seemed only logical that when Maxwell Anderson's *Joan of Arc* was being adapted as a starring vehicle for Ingrid Bergman, Ferrer should be brought to Hollywood to play the Dauphin.

Unfortunately, the film proved a costly flop.

But he was soon called back to appear in three films: as a crazed hypnotist in *Whirlpool*, a sick Latin American dictator in *Crisis*, and as Cyrano in Stanley Kramer's reverent version of the Rostand, evidently devised entirely as a showcase for Ferrer's much praised stage performance.

In 1950 he had a big stage success as the manic actor/manager in a revival of *Twentieth Century* and produced and directed the dramatic success *Stalag 17* and the two-handed comedy, *The Fourposter*. In 1952 he directed and starred in *The Shrike*, Joseph Kramm's overheated drama of a savagely vindictive wife and the husband she drives close to insanity. This was another of his biggest successes, revived in repertory at City Centre with Ferrer's old favourites Cyrano, Richard

III and that "Aunt" created by Brandon Thomas. *The Shrike* was later filmed, with Ferrer again starring and directing.

On screen his career at this time was no less rewarding. Apart from *Moulin Rouge* he appeared as the fallible preacher in *Miss Sadie Thompson* with Rita Hayworth, *The Caine Mutiny* and *Deep in my Heart*, where he played the composer Sigmund Romberg. The first film he directed was *Cockleshell Heroes*, in which he also starred – some thought over-prominently. Undeterred by such criticism he continued in quick succession with *The Great Man, I Accuse!* (Ferrer as Dreyfus), *The High cost of Loving*, *Return to Peyton Place* and the second version of the Rodgers and Hammerstein musical *State Fair*.

By 1962 when he appeared in the all-star cast of *Lawrence of Arabia* his film career had really peaked, and though he continued to appear regularly on screen throughout the Seventies he tended to be one of many veterans playing small roles in big movies like *The Greatest Story Ever Told, Ship of fools, Voyage of The Damned* and *The Swarm*.

Ferrer was an actor held in reverence by the sort of audience that likes to see the wheels going round; with him, acting was something that not only had to be done, but had to be seen to be done.

Chichester saw his Cyrano in 1975 and he later became rather fond of the Sussex Festival, being last seen there in a musical version of Ionesco's *Rhinoceros*.

He was married four times, his wives including the actress Uta Hagen and the singer, Rosemary Clooney of "Me and My Teddybear" fame. The first three marriages were dissolved and apparently Ferrer was not well pleased in the late Eighties to see himself portrayed by the pop singer Tony Orlando in *Rosie*, a television biography of Rosemary Clooney which placed most of the blame for her mental breakdown on his philandering. Two of his six children are actors.

b 8.1.12   d 26.1.92   aged 80

DAME GWEN FFRANGCON-DAVIES

Dame Gwen at the Tate in front of the painting of her

An actress whose career spanned 80 years. Her partnership with Sir John Gielgud in 1924 in Romeo and Juliet *went into theatrical history. Nearly forty years later she was playing with Peter Hall's Royal Shakespeare Company during its first London season.*

GWEN Ffrangcon-Davies made her first stage appearance as "a Fairy" in *A Midsummer Night's Dream* in April, 1911, and was last seen in a Sherlock Holmes television adventure just after Christmas. Her career was therefore,

alongside that of Athene Seyler, the longest and most distinguished of character actresses this century and her death has brought down one of the great pillars of classical acting in our time. No one who saw the BBC television documentary of a few years ago, in which, already well into her nineties, Miss Ffrangcon-Davies instructed a group of teenage drama students in the art of being Juliet and, in the process, became younger than all of them, could doubt that hers was a remarkable talent.

Born in London, she was the daughter of a Welsh choral singer who was said to have taken the name Ffrangcon from a Welsh beauty spot to add to his more prosaic Davies. Early in her career she was instructed by *The Times* that the hyphenated result was "far too un-wieldy" for theatre posters, advice she seems to have ignored for the remainder of the century. Her stage debut at Her Majesty's in *A Midsummer Night's Dream* was followed by several first world war tours in everything from Shakespeare to the operetta *The Arcadians* and it was as a singer that she had her earliest successes in such choral dramas as *The Immortal Hour* and *The Birth of Arthur* at the Glastonbury Festival and later the Old Vic.

By 1921 she was at the Birmingham Rep playing leading roles in J. M. Barrie's *Quality Street* and *The Admirable Crichton*, and two years later scored her first great London success creating the roles of Eve and the Newly Born in the first production of Shaw's *Back to Methuselah*. In 1924 she played Juliet to Gielgud's first Romeo, though their great partnership did not get off to the easiest of starts as he later recalled.

"I had seen her in *The Immortal Hour* and the beauty of her acting and singing enchanted me — those lovely, stylised movements of her hands and her high, clear voice seemed to belong to another world as she glided through the forest, hardly seeming to touch the ground . . . but the Gwen who appeared at our first *Romeo* rehearsal was very different, wearing an old dress and a business-like overall: her face was no longer pale, and she was brisk and impulsive in her movements. As we were introduced she looked at me strangely and then said: 'Thank God.' She went on to explain that she had seen me 'as that wretched butterfly poet in *The Insect Play*' and was appalled at the idea of my becoming her Romeo . . . It was a nasty shock to my vanity to find that my performance had affected her so unpleasantly.''

Happily, however, they triumphed as Romeo and Juliet, not only at the Regent in London but also, more surprisingly perhaps, at the London Coliseum where they reprised the balcony scene on a variety bill several months later. Gwen Ffrangcon-Davies was to enjoy two other great triumphs with Gielgud at ten-year intervals, as the Queen to his Richard of Bordeaux in 1932 and as Gwendolyn in his 1940 revival of *The Importance of Being Earnest*. Less successfully, they also starred together in a 1942 *Macbeth*. In the intervening years, she had also enjoyed considerable acclaim through the 1930s as Elizabeth Browning in the long-running *The Barretts of Wimpole Street*, where her rather long face and plaintive eyes perfectly suited the valiant spirit in the sick body of a sweet young woman.

In 1942, after several wartime tours with Gielgud and others, she and her lifelong companion, the actress Marda Vanne, went out to Vanne's native Johannesburg to set up the first major classical theatre company in South Africa, one much admired by Noël Coward when he was out there on tour and saw them in a production of his own *Blithe Spirit*. Returning to England in 1947, she played the Mother in Terence Rattigan's ill-fated *Adventure Story* and then joined the 1950 Stratford season to play Portia, Katharine in *Henry VIII*, Regan, and to succeed Peggy Ashcroft as Beatrice in *Much Ado*. She toured extensively for the British Council before making an unusual break into comedy for Donna Lucia in the John Mills *Charley's Aunt* revival. At the Lyric, Hammersmith, in 1954, she was a memorable Ranevskaya in *The Cherry Orchard* and

two years later a founder-member of the Royal Court in their opening production, *The Mulberry Bush*, from which she went immediately into T. S. Eliot's *The Family Reunion*.

Again she replaced Peggy Ashcroft, this time in *The Chalk Garden* and created Mrs Callifer in Graham Greene's *The Potting Shed* before her last great critical success in 1958, as Mary Tyrone in O'Neill's *Long Day's Journey Into Night*. This role won her the *Evening Standard* award for best actress.

As well as being in at the beginning of George Devine's English Stage Company at the Royal Court, Gwen Ffrangcon-Davies was also a founder of Peter Hall's Royal Shakespeare Company, which she joined at the Aldwych in 1961 for the queens in *Ondine* and *Becket*. Two years later, well into her seventies, she made her Broadway debut as Mrs Candour in *The School For Scandal* and was back at the Haymarket in 1965 for *The Glass Menagerie* and at the Court in 1970 for *Uncle Vanya*.

Always a little too theatrical for great film or television success, she remained into her eighties a tower of strength on stage and when she came out of retirement in 1988 for the master class on the playing of Juliet, it was one of her asides to a young and nervous drama student that came as a breathtaking reminder of the historical tradition she represented. "Don't worry, my dear," she told her: "I know how frightening this is: I had to audition as Juliet for Ellen Terry."

Hers was a tough generation for classical actresses of theatrical grandeur, perhaps the toughest: all her life she had to compete for the great roles against Sybil Thorndike, Edith Evans and Peggy Ashcroft and it is arguable that they very often were the winners. Yet she retained a craggy authority and the ability to break the audience's heart on those rare moments, as when playing Mary Tyrone, when she let the façade crack to reveal inner torment.

She was created DBE in 1991.

b 25.1.1891   d 27.1.1992   aged 101

BENNY HILL

Comedian and talented impressionist who became a cult figure and was revered by his showbusiness peers.

BENNY Hill's humour was drawn from a number of sources, including music-hall and the silent cinema. He excelled both in mime and in clever word play. He also made great use of outrageous characterisation, employing all the worst and funniest of national traits from cross-eyed Orientals to belligerent Bavarians and could transform himself at will from a bashful choirboy into a lascivious lout. He was the first British comedian really to harness the facilities of television to advance the art of comedy beyond the music hall stage without resorting to the dependence on the strong story-lines of the modern cinema. He pioneered the visual techniques of split screens and multiple appearances, playing all four members of the *Juke Box Jury* panel in one innovative 1961 take-off and in another taking 50 parts in one comedy playlet.

In essence Benny Hill animated for the small screen the bawdy tradition of the seaside postcard, with its jokes about bottoms and bosoms and hen-pecked husbands leering at pretty girls displaying their suspenders and stocking-tops.

He was often criticised by the more po-faced sectors of society for vulgarity and the ''sexist'' nature of his sketches, falling foul of the Broadcasting Standards Council and Mrs Mary Whitehouse and her campaign to clean up television. Nor did his penchant for scantily clad girls endear him to some of the more ardent feminists. He argued cogently, however, that in his sketches it was the men who lost their dignity rather than the women. Benny Hill never swore. Nor did he chase the girls in his sketches. The girls chased him. Whatever his critics said, for much of the viewing public both at home and abroad he was, year after year, just about the funniest man on television. He eventually became something of a cult figure in America and was revered by many of his showbusiness peers as one of the all-time masters of visual comedy, alongside Chaplin and Laurel and Hardy.

Benny Hill's persona was that of a plumpish man with a moon face, a mischievous grin and the bearing of an overgrown schoolboy. The dirty joke and the rude rhyme were an essential part of his act, although they were usually conveyed by innuendo. The audience was left to pick up the double meaning while Hill protested wide-eyed innocence that anyone could misinterpret what he was saying. Hill was a master at leading his audience into naughty thoughts before

ending with a perfectly innocent line. ''Two bishops in a bed. Which one wears the nightdress?'' he would ask, then add: ''Mrs Bishop.''

He was a talented impressionist and one of the first comedians to make a feature of sending up other television shows. He also evolved his own comic characters, among them the lisping impresario, Fred Scuttle; Mr Chow Mein, the Chinaman with an accident-prone grasp of the English language; and the black-wigged madrigal singer, Herbert Fudge. He would play as many as 30 parts in one show. Hill took great delight in word play, showing great originality in his use of tongue-twisters and outrageous puns. But he believed that television humour should be primarily visual and many of his sketches were entirely without dialogue, comprising a non-stop succession of gags speeded up by the camera and delivered to tinkling piano accompaniment after the style of the silent film.

Hill wrote his own scripts, at first in collaboration with Dave Freeman and later alone; he composed the music for his shows: and he was virtually the director as well, spending hours on one routine to perfect its pace and timing.

Benny Hill was born Alfred Hawthorne Hill of working class parents in Southampton. His interest in showbusiness may have come from his father, a former circus performer. After attending Taunton's School — where he was taught English by Horace King, later Speaker of the House of Commons — he left early, and was a weighbridge clerk in a coal yard, served in Woolworth's and became a milk roundsman. In his spare time he played the drums in a dance band. While still only 16 he was a property boy and played small parts in a touring revue, later becoming stage manager. He got his first chance to appear on stage at the East Ham Palace. The comedian's stooge failed to appear one night and Hill went on in his place.

He developed as a performer in troop concerts during the second world war. He joined the army in 1942, serving for five

Benny Hill with Sue Upton during rehearsal at Thames TV Studios (1980)

years, the last of which he spent appearing in "Stars in Battle Dress". After leaving the army he went into variety, a tough but invaluable training ground. In a summer show at Margate he was straight man to Reg Varney, the cockney comedian later to star in *The Rag Trade* and *On the Buses*. In the immediate post-war years he made more that 200 broadcasts, performing on such shows as *Midday Music Hall, Starlight Hour, Anything Goes* and *Henry Hall's Guest Night* as well as at least one Royal Command performance. Early television success came when he was chosen to compere a forces show from the Nuffield Centre in the early 1950s. He was an immediate success with viewers, and within two years he had been given his own series, winning his first television personality of the year award in 1954.

Benny Hill was shrewd enough to realise that television performers can easily be over-exposed and outstay their welcome and he deliberately restricted himself to a handful of shows a year. In doing so he risked the opposite danger, that the public would forget him, but this never happened.

Once he was established his style and his routines varied little but he had an unfailing grasp of popular taste and even when he had been away from the screen for a long period he was able to pick up exactly where he left off. Scantily-clad girls — known as Hill's Angels — were a fixture of the productions, usually displaying their stocking tops or their cleavage before the either mischievously lustful or mischievously innocent gaze of Hill and a cast of supporting character actors which he seldom changed. In addition to writing his own scripts he composed comic songs, several of which became hits, in particular "Ernie (the Fastest Milkman in the West)". The show's finale was almost always a speeded-up chase sequence in which Hill was pursued by a melée of women in varying states of attire, police, irate husbands and assorted animals and children, to the accompaniment of the Benny Hill theme tune.

Between 1968 and 1988 he made about 70 of these one-hour productions for Thames Television. The programmes were rarely out of the top ten ratings, winning the Bafta best comedy award in 1971, and were enormously popular worldwide, being transmitted in such unlikely places as Angola, China and Russia. During the 1970s Hill was one of the few British comedians to be successful both in America and Europe. Compilations of sketches from his television shows were screened from coast to coast in the United States and enjoyed huge ratings.

Thames Television, however, was eventually cowed by the so-called anti-sexist lobby into dropping the comedian from its schedules. He was distressed by this snub. Recalling the moment, he said it happened at 10 am and he was out of the building by ten past. After more than 20 years it would have been nice, he added, to have had a "pat on the back". He was later to remark that in one "alternative comedy" act on television he had counted 91 swear words; yet he would get into trouble simply for: "looking at a girl and saying: 'Oh her dumplings are boiling over!' " During the following three years Hill made only one television programme – for American audiences.

Early in his career, in the 1950s he appeared in two West End revues, *Paris By Night* and *Fine Fettle* but he then abandoned the theatre completely. In the 1960s he was in several films, among them *Those Magnificent Men in Their Flying Machines, Chitty Chitty Bang Bang* and *The Italian Job.* Like other television comedians, though, he had less impact on the larger screen. In 1964 he made a single excursion into Shakespeare, playing Bottom in a television production of *A Midsummer Night's Dream.*

Unlike many fellow comedians Benny Hill never appeared to be weighed down by the responsibility of being funny. He enjoyed his craft, was a perfectionist in its practice but avoided taking himself too seriously. He was a cultivated man with wide interests. He travelled extensively and spent much time in France, speaking French with ease, as well as some German and Spanish. He had a reputation for being unfailingly courteous and caring. He never married and did his best to keep his private life private. In response to the perpetual enquiries, resulting from the fact that he was so often surrounded by pretty girls, he said he had had three serious attachments and in each his proposal of marriage had been rejected.

Despite being one of the highest paid entertainers in Britain, Hill lived simply. He had a London flat and a modest house in his home town of Southampton. He never owned a car and did his own shopping in the local supermarket. His passion was travel and wherever he went he was on the look-out for some quirk of human behaviour that could be worked into a gag for his next show.

b 21.1.25   d 20.4.92   aged 67

FRANKIE HOWERD

A stand-up comedian who was the master of the sexual innuendo and bawdy one liners.

FRANKIE Howerd was born to be funny. His forlorn, elongated face, like a bloodhound that had mislaid its bone, the expressive bushy eyebrows, the loose, uncoordinated limbs plus a lightning wit, sustained him for almost 50 years as one of our foremost post-war comedians. His secret was that he appealed to all sections of society. His bawdy one-liners, his ability to extract sexual innuendo from the most innocent seeming remark with a purse of the lips or a lift of the eyebrow, were guaranteed to convulse his countless housewife fans of a certain age. Yet time and again throughout his career he was taken up or "rediscovered" by a new generation, including the more thoughtful who saw something deeper in his shrewder side-swipes at life.

Howerd's highly-strung insecurity as a stand-up performer was with him all his life and showed itself in a nervous stammer on which he quickly learned to capitalise. Many of his enduring catch phrases quoted nationwide were the result of this hesitancy. They were delivered as imaginary interruptions of some joke or humorous narrative: "Ah yes . . . Well . . . No. lis-sen! . . . No. don't laugh . . . titter ye not . . . it's wicked to mock the afflicted . . ." and so on. And if the joke didn't get the laugh he anticipated, he would draw himself up in mock high dudgeon and roar: "Please yourselves!" At other times he would exhort his audience to loosen something and enjoy a good titter. "Let us not go home titterless," was another of his cries.

On stage, Frankie Howerd, a long time favourite of the Queen Mother, was a comic of the old school who believed that the well tried lines were those best loved by his devoted audience, although they were usually sprinkled with new material being given a trial. It was a different story with radio, at which he excelled, and also, to some extent, his solo appearances on television when he would go to infinite pains to ensure there was fresh material. Nevertheless, he had his favourite jokes. Typical was the one about two young mothers with new babies who meet on the street.

"One mother looked at the other's baby and said, 'Oh isn't she small.' And the other mother replied, 'Oh, well, you see, I've only been married a fortnight!' "

Frankie Howerd was born Francis Alick Howard — he was later to change his name to Howerd — the eldest son of Sergeant Frank Howard, Royal Artillery. The actual year of birth was a secret confided only to his passport. He and his

family moved to Eltham, Kent, when his father was posted to Woolwich, southeast London. He was educated at Gordon School and Shooter's Hill Grammar School and as a tall, thin, shy 13-year-old he became a Sunday school teacher. He first became interested in showbusiness when he successfully starred in his church dramatic society's production of Ian Hay's *Tilly of Bloomsbury*.

His ambition to go on the stage stayed with him in spite of a disastrous RADA audition, and he bided his time working as an office clerk until he was called up for the war in 1940, training as a gunner. He was to sum up his stock-in-trade at that period of his life as, ". . . born of natural shortcomings and weaned on necessity during those years at Shoeburyness."

He failed to get into the entertainment corps ENSA (Entertainment National Service Association) or, as another wartime comic Tommy Trinder once described it, Every Night Something Awful, but ended his war service, after the cessation of hostilities, running a concert party touring north west Germany. On demobilisation and with the unwavering encouragement of his mother and his sisters, he persevered as a funny man until in 1946 he was squeezed onto the bill of a revue at the Sheffield Empire as "Frankie Howerd, the Borderline Case."

He began to develop his uniquely individual style of narrative or what he called his "one-man situational comedy" rather than the conventional reeling off of a string of unrelated jokes. The first catch phrases also emerged: "I was a-mazed!" . . . "Not on your Nellie!" and "What a funny woman!" And when referring to his supposedly deaf piano accompanist, "Poor soul — she's past it!"

At this stage he achieved national fame on radio in the popular *Variety Bandbox* where yet another of his phrases, "Ladies and gentle-*men*" was born. He was soon topping the bill of the still flourishing variety theatres and in 1949 he appeared at Buckingham Palace; the following year

Frankie Howerd, OBE

he was on the bill of his first Royal Variety Performance. Recruiting Eric Sykes and Galton and Simpson – who later wrote *Steptoe* and *Hancock's Half Hour* – as his scriptwriters, his career took off and remained airborne for much of the next decade with more radio, annual pantomime and trips abroad entertaining the troops, including one to Korea in 1952. He starred in films like *The Runaway Bus, An Alligator Named Daisy, Jumping for Joy, The Lady-killers, Further Up the Creek* and *Watch It Sailor*.

Frankie Howerd was not the world's greatest ad-libber and relied heavily on his scripts so that an appearance on the popular quiz show *What's My Line?* proved disappointing. But a television revival of *Tons of Money* proved successful and he scored a West End triumph at the Prince of Wales Theatre in 1953 starring in the revue *Pardon My French*, which ran for 759 performances. In 1955 he starred as Lord Fancourt Babberley in *Charley's Aunt* at the Globe followed two years later with another stage winner playing Bottom in *A Midsummer Night's Dream* at the Old Vic.

But his every-shaky confidence was sapped in 1958 when the lavish and costly musical *Mister Venus* closed in London after only 17 days and recovery was not helped when he suffered a painful riding accident soon after. There followed the first of the slumps that were to occur during his career when in 1960–62 he counted himself lucky to land a pantomime booking. Things brightened in 1963 when a new generation discovered him on the television satire show *That Was the Week That Was*. It was said that the producers wanted him as an exhibit of the last of the old music hall comics. Instead, the canny Howerd outwitted them by putting together a cracker of an up-to-the-minute routine and stole the show. He landed the roles of Prologus and Pseudolus in the hit American musical set in ancient Rome, *A Funny Thing Happened on the Way to the Forum*, which ran in the West End for two years. During that time he kept his name in front of the wider public with two radio series and the occasional television special.

He starred on Broadway in 1968 at the Ethel Barrymore Theatre, as John Emery Rockefeller in *Rockefeller and the Red Indians*, and in the early 1970s appeared in pantomime at the London Palladium. More films followed including *The Great St Trinian's Train Robbery* and *Up Pompeii*, which was a spin-off of his double-entendrè-laden television series in which he played the mournful slave Lurcio. At first the leery nod-and-wink innuendoes caused some protest but his saucy music-hall delivery won over the pruder viewers and it became cult viewing, running to two series, both repeated. The even broader sequel *Whoops Baghdad* was less successful. He was never afraid to experiment outside his field; he even tried opera, playing the drunken jailer Frosch in *Die Fledermaus* at the London Coliseum in 1982 as well as taking roles in Gilbert and Sullivan's *Trial by Jury* and *HMS Pinafore*. He played a number of Royal Command performances and was made an OBE in 1977. In 1986 he starred in a revival of *A Funny Thing . . .* at the Chichester Festival and in the West End.

Frankie Howerd was accident prone. In 1987 he fell while walking in the countryside, injuring his leg and a surgeon warned him he might have to spend the rest of his life on crutches. He once fell from the balcony of his hotel while admiring the view. In the 1990s he became the darling of the new generation of alternative comedy fans in another resurgence of his fluctuating career. He was persuaded to do a show at Barking town hall, which he found packed with young people eager for his autograph, and last year he made a so-called rap record which climed the pop charts.

A lifelong bachelor, Howerd was a close friend of the film actress Joan Greenwood for many years and was engaged in his adolescent years to a girl he first met at school, although it came to nothing.

Frankie Howerd was a complex personality nursing a mixture of doubts, some depression coupled with a powerful sense of ambition and deep philosophical integrity. He took his humour seriously and had put together a fine collection of books on the subject at his Kensington home. Beneath the insecurity that troubles many stand-up comedians because they dare to presume to amuse an audience on their own, Frankie Howerd enjoyed his success. Once asked for his favourite memory he replied: ''It hasn't happened yet.''

b 17.3.21 d 19.4.92 aged 71

LAURA KENDAL

Actress mother of Felicity and Jennifer who formed with her husband a touring company which enthusiastically took Shakespeare to the Indian hills.

IN ADDITION to rearing her two actress daughters – Jennifer, who died in 1984, and Felicity Kendal – Laura Kendal had a pivotal role in the Shakespearian touring company she and her husband, Geoffrey, ran in India and which was immortalised in the film *Shakespeare Wallah*. As well as being the company's leading actress, she designed the sets and costumes, making extraordinarily effective use of limited resources. She also had to be mother not only to her daughters – both of whom served their acting apprenticeships in the company – but also to the young and often inex-perienced company members.

During a wartime ENSA tour the Kendals fell in love with India and returned a year after the war with their own company. The tour was cut short by the struggles of India's independence. But in 1953 the Kendals and Shakespeariana were back and the company did not disband until the 1960s. Thereafter Geoffrey and Laura continued to tour with two-hander shows. As late as 1985 they were a main attraction at a theatre festival in Bombay.

The company took Shakespeare to the Indian hills in the way that Sybil Thorndike and Lewis Casson took Macbeth to the Welsh valleys, bringing the English classics to two generations of Indians. While Geoffrey drummed up the bookings in schools throughout India, she made sure the company arrived at each destination looking immaculate, despite having sometimes travelled Indian rail, third-class.

With dusty benches rather than couches, broken lights and inadequate fans, train conditions were likely to have arrested the enthusiasm of all but the most determined western travellers. The venues were often many miles from the railway station, entailing a further journey, with the wardrobe baskets and portable props, by country bus or lorry. The charge for admission was one rupee (about 8p) and it was sufficient to sustain the cost of a 12-strong company. They depended for their audiences mostly on undergraduates and discovered that Indians had an insatiable appetite for Shakespeare.

The novelty of a band of Europeans appearing with wigs and swords in areas where previously the only Englishmen seen were tax collectors and police superintendents may have accounted for some of their success. But Shakespeare was the main attraction. Tamils, Madrasis, Bengalis and Punjabis, who were first introduced to the plays as a subject to be mastered before passing the Senior Cambridge examination – a necessary scholastic achievement for a government clerkship – yielded happily to Shakespeare when it was brought to their town by such an adventurous English company.

Born and brought up in the Lake District, as was Geoffrey, the young Laura Liddell was already a well regarded actress in the Edward Dunstan touring company when the future couple met. In his autobiography, *The Shakespeare Wallah*, Geoffrey describes the first time he saw her at a rehearsal: "She had a pointed chin and a round face, deep brown slanting eyes and a retroussé nose that made her look almost oriental, and an air of enormous vitality . . . Never had I seen a more lively woman, or a more interesting actress. Laura was incredibly individual and made every part she played intriguing . . ."

Laura could well have made a successful career on her own in the West End, but she resolved when they married in 1933 that their marriage should be a partnership as well, and thereafter they never worked separately. She shared with Geoffrey a love of adventure, and the two embarked on the hazardous life of running an unsubsidised touring company, taking Shakespeare around England and Ireland, and finally to India and the Far East. They played in village halls and maharajahs' palaces, from the Himalayas to Travancore. Once their lorry of costumes and props was swept away in a flood in Assam, but undaunted they continued their tour of the tea plantations. Both Geoffrey and Laura were brought up in the tradition that the show must go on, and they had an intense love and enthusiasm for Shakespeare which sustained them in the near impossible conditions brought by heat, monsoons, plagues of mosquitoes and, on one occasion, an earthquake. A generation of Indians in their middle years remember their first taste of Shakespeare with the Kendals in the school halls of Doon, St Paul's or Loretto Convent. Indeed, the Kendals greatly contributed to the continuing love of Shakespeare in India today.

The Kendals' elder daughter, Jennifer, remained in India after her marriage to the film actor Shashi Kapoor. Her death in 1984 came soon after her highly acclaimed return to acting in the film *Chowringhee Lane*. This was a tremendous blow for the family, and the festival at the Prithvi Theatre in Bombay a year later was dedicated to Jennifer.

Geoffrey and Laura Kendal flew out to India last year to receive the Sangeet Natak Academy Award for services to the arts in India from the president of India, the first foreigners to be given this honour. Laura Kendal's final visit to India, the land that became her second home, was made when her ashes were taken there by her husband.

b 8.5.08 d 5.2.92 aged 83

GINETTE LECLERC

French actress who portrayed 'bad girls' in films produced during the German occupation.

ONE glance at Ginette Leclerc in Henri-Georges Clouzot's film *Le Corbeau* and one instinctively knew she was what movie circles called, in those days, a "bad girl". Dressed in a negligee, she lounged on a bed, a cigarette between painted lips, polishing her toe nails: this was Denise, the town cripple, though she never let any physical impediment stand in the way of her sexuality.

Produced during the Occupation for Continental Films, an off-shoot of the German company UFA, *Le Corbeau* (1943) describes a town, under siege from a poison pen, steadily disintegrating into malice and hysteria. The Resistance viewed Clouzot's tale as sabotage of France's good name and they extracted revenge during the purges that followed the Liberation. Clouzot and the screenwriter were banned from cinema work; Leclerc, along with her co-star Pierre Fresnay, spent time in prison.

Leclerc's trademark had always been earthy, uncomplicated sex appeal, though most films from her debut in 1932 onwards looked no further than the immediate surface. The surface, indeed, was beguiling: hair often gathered in a heavy fringe, a succulent mouth cradling dazzling teeth, saucer-shaped eyes set in a face dancing with quick expressions. Like her rival screen vamp Viviane Romance, Leclerc had little solid theatrical training: she was essentially born under the arc lights.

Ciboulette (1933), based on Reynaldo Hahn's operetta, required her to sing and dance – she could do both well, and sometimes performed in cabaret and music hall; other early films used her merely as the saucy girl perched on an old gentleman's lap. But discerning directors soon rewarded her with better parts.

Next, Marcel Pagnol gave her the title role in his comedy *La Femme du boulanger* (1938), alongside the great, scene-stealing Raimu. True to type, Leclerc deserted her husband for a handsome shepherd, prompting the baker to go on strike. The film's friendly depiction of Provençal manners found a wide audience in France and abroad.

After the troubles of the purges, Leclerc worked less in the cinema: time, in any case, was taking its toll of the vamp image. But the Paris theatre welcomed her special talents: she appeared successfully in Tennessee Williams's *Cat On a Hot Tin Roof* and in Sartre's *La Putain respectueuse* (the author particularly relished her performance).

Future film assignments remained mostly routine, though she flourished under Max Ophuls's direction as a lady of pleasure in *Le Plaisir* (1951). In a last fling with controversy, she joined the surreal dance of love and death that was Walerian Borowczyk's *Gozo, L'Ile d'Amour* (1968), and took a small part (a brothel madame, naturally) in Joseph Strick's verson of Henry Miller's *Tropic of Cancer* (1969).

An autobiography, *Ma Vie privée,* appeared in 1963.

b 6.9.12   d 1.1.92   aged 79

ROBERT MORLEY

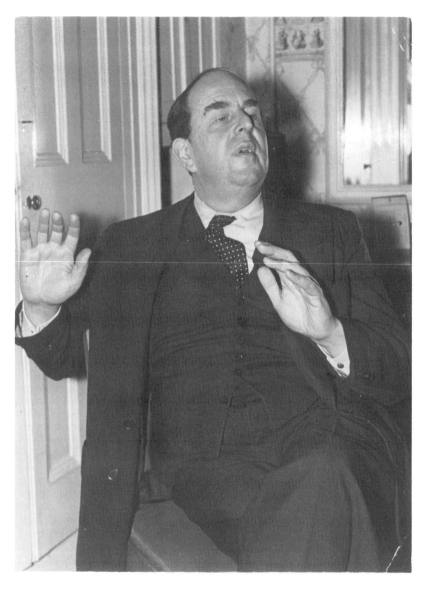

Robert Morley, CBE, stage and film actor, playwright and author, veteran of television advertisements and one of the last of a breed of "gentleman players".

FEW qualitites are more likable than the ability to give the impression that one is enjoying oneself hugely; few leading actors have integrated this quality more infectiously into their style than Robert Morley. His triumph was to make self-indulgence look like a discipline: the area in which he was really disciplined was in choosing his parts. Actors like Charles

Laughton and Lee J. Cobb found it impossible to say no to the chance of playing roles like King Lear. Morley was content to remain one of the heavyweight champions of light comedy. On stage the personality he exuded was much the same as that recognised by those who knew him. Morley made no attempt to be one of the great masters of disguise. What he projected, over the footlights, to the cinema audience and to those who switched on to watch his remarkable television commercials, was very much an extension of his off-stage self.

From the first of his several characterisations of Oscar Wilde (at the Gate in 1936) he was not out of the limelight for long. Most of his roles seemed to have been selected — as most of his plays, collaborations and adaptations were written — to provide him with a series of comic opportunities to range between righteous outrage, endearing eccentricity and amiable bluster. He could change gear very amusingly between pathos and irascibility, stubbornness and gentleness, and he could erect the trivial into the monumental. It was in 1954 that he appeared in *Hippo Dancing*, which he adapted very freely from André Roussin's Paris comedy — and he made something quite unforgettable out of Hippo's fury at car-drivers who reversed in his drive.

Robert Morley was the son of Major Robert Morley and his wife Gertrude Fass, the daughter of a South African businessman. He was not happy at school, attending numerous private establishments in England, Germany, France and Italy before going to Wellington College. This was not an experience which improved his equanimity. In later life he remarked of Wellington's muscular environment: "I was compelled to play games. I believe the ball, with the exception of the wheel, was the greatest single disaster of mankind."

His father's intention was that he should have a diplomatic career, but he went to RADA and after a period selling vacuum cleaners door-to-door, an experience he always claimed was the best possible training for an actor, he made his first professional appearance on the stage at Margate, two days after his 20th birthday, in *Dr Syn*. His London debut was as a pirate in *Treasure Island* at the Strand in 1929, and he then worked as assistant stage manager on a tour of *And So To Bed*. Norman Marshall employed him for a season at the Festival Theatre, Cambridge, in 1933 and called him "as unpromising an actor as I have ever seen". Nevertheless he cast Morley in the lead in *Oscar Wilde*, and he made such a success in the part that he repeated it on Broadway in 1938. Meanwhile he had written a play, *Short Story*, in which Marie Tempest had appeared in 1935, and he had played Louis XVI in the film *Marie Antoinette*.

Before being produced in London, his second play, *Goodness How Sad!*, was tried out at Perranporth, Cornwall, in a theatre he founded with Peter Bull. He scored an enormous success as Sheridan Whiteside in the American comedy *The Man Who Came To Dinner*, which opened at the Savoy in December 1941 and ran for 709 performances. The ensuing provincial tour took him into 1943, and in 1944 he toured in his own play *Staff Dance*.

In 1945 he had another big success as the Prince Regent in Norman Ginsbury's play *The First Gentleman*, which ran in the West End for over a year, and he collaborated with Noel Langley on *Edward My Son*, which provided him with another very long run. He opened in the play at His Majesty's in May 1947 and, after it had run for 787 performances, he played the part on Broadway in September 1949, afterwards touring Australia and New Zealand in it.

Returning to England in 1950 he opened in a play which was to run for even longer — André Roussin's *The Little Hut*, directed by Peter Brook. Despite Brook's predictable clash of temperament with Morley, the production notched up 1,261 performances. The second of the three Roussin plays he did, *Hippo Dancing*, was the first that he adapted himself. It was produced at the same

theatre as *The Little Hut*, the Lyric, and ran for 443 performances, thanks to Morley's performance. The third Roussin, *Hook, Line and Sinker*, also adapted by Morley himself, followed in 1958 at the Piccadilly. For this Joan Plowright was wooed away from the Royal Court by dint of persistent persuasion, flowers, boxes of chocolates and promises of rehearsals in the South of France. Morley had to make one entrance, sopping wet, having been pushed into a river. Seeing him, she had to swoon, dropping the tray she was carrying, and he picked everything up. But at one matinee, as soon as she dropped the tray, he swooned on the sofa,

saying "You pick them up this afternoon. I'm too tired."

By then he was involved in management. In 1956 he had co-presented (with H. M. Tennent) *A Likely Tale* at the Globe and played a leading part. Then, as a member of the Robin Fox partnership, he was jointly responsible for presenting a number of comedies, including *Hook, Line and Sinker* and *Six Months Grace*, which he wrote in collaboration with Dundas Hamilton. He directed *The Tunnel of Love* in 1957 and *Once More, With Feeling* in 1969.

In 1967 he starred in Gielgud's production of Ustinov's *Half Way Up the Trees* and rewrote so many of his own lines that Gielgud was apprehensive about Ustinov's reaction. Fortunately he was directing the New York production which was in rehearsal simultaneously and on returning to London made no objection to the rescripting. Alan Ayckbourn's 1970 play *How the Other Half Loves* was also changed by Morley's steamroller personality. At Scarborough, in the original production, the characters had all been of roughly equal importance. Morley afterwards told Ayckbourn: "I've left a trail of richer but sadder authors behind me."

Occasionally he was said to think he ought to have been a better actor, or, at least, a more serious one: certain performances (as Oscar Wilde; as Louis XVI; as Holt in his own play *Edward My Son*) suggested to some critics that one day here could be a Falstaff, perhaps even a Lear. But when the offer did come from Peter Hall to play Falstaff at Stratford he avoided it, not perhaps out of fear or laziness, but because of the conviction that he wouldn't enjoy it and that therefore nor would the audience.

He continued acting into his eighties: "not many easier ways of making a living than acting", he would say. It was characteristic of the many humorously self-depreciating statements he made about both himself and the acting profession. Among other examples were: "Anyone who works is a fool. I don't work: I merely inflict myself on the public"; and:

"It is a great help for a man to be in love with himself. For an actor it is absolutely essential." Of the world and human affairs in general he declared: "You can get along if you really believe there are two things necessary for salvation: money and a lively acceptance of the likelihood of the improbable happening."

He appeared in scores of films, often offering good, well acted cameos that were not allowed to dominate the script. Among these were roles in Shaw's *Major Barbara* (1940), *The African Queen* (1951), John Huston's *Beat the Devil* (1953), *Around the World in Eighty Days* (1956), *Doctor in Trouble* (1970), *Song of Norway* (1970), *Who is Killing the Great Chefs of Europe?* (1978), *The Human Factor* (1979) and *High Road to China* (1982). As the years went by and the personality increased in rotundity as well as orotundity, Morley was increasingly in demand on the other side of the Atlantic whenever Hollywood wanted a specimen of the inimitable British gent with an ample girth, rolled umbrella and a quiverful of recognisably cisatlantic prejudices. Yet he brought to films an impressive – and precious – quality, as he had done on stage, where he was capable of turning an evening which threatened to be fragile into something safe and comfortable, merely by his presence on stage; on screen his presence could, likewise, rescue a wretched script and salvage triumph from disaster, to the relief of many a director who had thought the game was up.

In America, too, he commanded huge audiences for his appearances on chat shows, audiences who savoured his love of gilded conversation. Among his later successes on British television was his performance as a war correspondent in the ITV series *War and Remembrance*.

He also had a late flowering in television commercials, notably the hugely successful British Airways advertisements in which he represented the desire for comfort demanding (and of course getting) satisfaction. Indeed, his last appearance was on television in 1991 where he was Father Christmas in a commercial for Sainsbury's. It was a role which took him full circle; his very first part had been in the same role in a children's pantomime at Folkestone in 1916.

Morley wrote as easily as he acted. Besides his eight plays there were five books of reminiscences and an autobiography, all unmistakably bearing the mark of Morley. He was a prolific journalist, writing regular food and travel columns for *Punch* over a period of fifteen years. Food, drink and travel were all near to his heart and he was a member of Bucks and the Garrick. He always professed to be a socialist, with the proviso, of course, that these material comforts were never to be far from hand.

In 1940 he married Joan Buckmaster, daughter of Gladys Cooper by her first husband, Captain Herbert Buckmaster. There were two sons, one of whom is Sheridan Morley the drama critic, and a daughter.

Morley was created CBE in 1957. Subsequently, in 1970, he was offered a knighthood but he refused the honour. Stage knighthoods, he felt ought only to be given to the great exponents of the classical stage and not to light comedians like himself. It was characteristic of the innate modesty and truth to himself of a man whose stage and screen persona – not to mention his many published statements – might have suggested something quite the reverse. Finally, Robert Morley was a tremendous racegoer – and enjoyed best those engagements which were near a decent race course. Indeed, he would have been sorry just to have missed the great flat race of 1992; he died on the morning of Derby Day.

b 26.5.08   d 3.6.92   aged 84

ANTHONY PERKINS

American screen and stage actor, who will always be identified with Norman Bates, motel owner extraordinary and killer in Alfred Hitchcock's film Psycho.

ANTHONY Perkins never shook off the mantle of Norman Bates, the homicidal schizophrenic in *Psycho* (1960). He was cast in the film partly because he needed to complete his studio contract and could be signed for a reasonable fee: Hitchcock planned the entire project as an exercise in low-cost film-making. But Hitchcock also knew that Perkins's nervous persona ideally matched the Bates character as developed by Joseph Stefano from Robert Bloch's novel – a diffident young man, interested in birds and taxidermy, who lived with his mother's skeleton in a Gothic mansion looming behind a rundown motel.

Any guests the Bates Motel might attract tended to be stabbed to death with a knife by Norman dressed in his mother's clothes. In the film's most celebrated scene, which has become one of world cinema's best known sequences, Janet Leigh met her sudden end while showering in cabin number one. Those stopping over in isolated American motels have been in the habit of looking behind the shower curtain ever since.

When Hitchcock came to shoot the scene, Perkins was in New York preparing for a Broadway opening, so Bates's shadow outside the shower curtain was suggested by a stand-in. In all other respects that shadow clung to Perkins for the rest of his life.

Distaste for the psychotic roles he was constantly being offered drove him to Europe for much of the 1960s, though by the early 1980s he had reached a rapprochement with Norman Bates, reprising the role in *Psycho II* (1983), a lively account of Bates's adventures on release from a mental hospital.

Three years later Perkins made his cinema directing debut in *Psycho III*, gearing the film less towards Hitchcock aficionados than the booming teenage market for "slasher" films. "I imagined to myself that Norman Bates was directing the movie thereby simplifying my task."

From birth Perkins had been earmarked for stardom: his father, the stage actor Osgood Perkins deliberately gave him a seven-letter first name so that it would balance his last name on a theatre marquee. Osgood was not able to give him a great deal more. He died when Anthony was five and the boy was brought up by his mother, who was a dominating influence in his life. Anthony Perkins admitted this in direct fashion, describing her as a strong woman and saying that "we were more like lovers than mother and son."

Possibly as an escape route Perkins followed his father and took up acting. In 1947, aged 15, he was already touring in summer stock productions. Five years later, while a student at Columbia University, he won a small Hollywood part in *The Actress* after hitch-hiking to Los Angeles during one vacation. Broadway followed in 1954 when Elia

Kazan invited him to replace John Kerr as the sensitive teenage hero of Robert Anderson's *Tea and Sympathy*. "The kid's all right," Hollywood mogul Samuel Goldwyn was supposed to have said on catching his performance, "but he's seen too many Jimmy Stewart movies."

Goldwyn was only half right. Perkins soon carved out his distinctive terrain: his thin, sensitive features, quivering with uncertainties, gave him a little-boy-lost quality, which appealed to a large female fan club – plus a number of males as well. Elia Kazan might have turned him down for being insufficiently macho for the James Dean part in *East of Eden*, but on his return to Hollywood he won a Best Supporting Actor nomination for his role as Gary Cooper's son, a troubled Quaker in William Wyler's *Friendly Persuasion* (1956). He played a jittery sheriff in *The Tin Star* (1957) and the troubled baseball player Jim Piersall in *Fear Strikes Out* (1957). He stamped such characters with an intense, quivering passion perfectly suited to his wiry physique; one film critic wrote, accurately, that he resembled "a shy, highly-strung greyhound". But it was Hitchcock's *Psycho* that established him among Hollywood's most accomplished and off-beat young leading men.

There was more to Perkins's talents, however, than the ability to portray neurotics. In the year of *Psycho* he took the leading role on Broadway in Frank Loesser's *Greenwillow*, a musical idyll of America's rural past; in the 1970s he frequently lent his voice to Ben Bagley's series of recordings spotlighting neglected Broadway songs. He also collaborated with the composer-lyricist Stephen Sondheim on the script for a chic film thriller, *The Last of Sheila* (1973).

Before then Anthony Perkins had spent some years living in Paris, trying his luck, none too successfully, in the European cinema. Almost inevitably he found himself playing the innocent opposite a major femal star: Ingrid Bergman in *Aimez-vous Brahms?* and Melina Mercouri in *Phaedra*. Among the more interesting of these generally misguided European ventures was *The Trial*, directed by Orson Welles, in which he played Joseph K. The two clashed over motivation – Welles thought Kafka's hero guilty of the nameless crime. Perkins considered him innocent – but the actor still made a strong impression. Perkins said of himself that he was good at "the boxed-in, the narrow, the limited".

Yet his career overall remained stuck in a rut, dogged by the audience's reluctance to forget Norman Bates. His own youthful appearance did not help. ("There's nothing I can do about it," he complained in 1966. "Make-up runs off my face like spaghetti"). Back in America, he maintained his theatre connections, directing numerous shows, appearing in Neil Simon's *The Star-Spangled Girl* (1966) and, following in distinguished footsteps, acting the psychiatrist in Peter Shaffer's *Equus* (1975). He also created bizarre character parts in scattered films until the *Psycho* sequels brought him back in the limelight in the 1980s. Perkins received unwanted publicity in 1984 and 1989 when he was fined for importing small amounts of cannabis into Britain; then, in 1990, it was disclosed that he had contracted the AIDS virus.

After long years as a reclusive bachelor, Perkins married the fashion-photographer Berinthia "Berry" Berenson, sister of the actress Marisa, in 1973. There was a fifteen year age gap between them but the marriage appeared highly successful. They had two sons.

b 4.4.32   d 12.9.92   aged 60

JOAN SANDERSON

Joan Sanderson, television comedy actress and veteran of such series as Please Sir!, Rising Damp *and* Upstairs Downstairs.

SMALL screen battleaxe *par excellence*, whether it was as a schoolmistress bossing her pupils in *Please Sir!* or as a ward sister striking fear into the hearts of her unfortunate charges in *Never Say Die*, Joan Sanderson brought to television the formidable qualities which had earlier served her well on stage in such roles as Shakespeare's Goneril. Even in a series such as *Fawlty Towers* she was able to steal a scene from John Cleese in a prolonged and bitter diatribe about the shortcomings of a view from a hotel window. Never did the hapless hotel proprietor encounter such an intransigent guest.

As time went on she took to playing grannies, though these were seldom aged parents of the benign type. Thus, in *After Henry*, first seen on television in 1987, having been a very successful radio show some years before, she played the interfering old mother to Prunella Scales's widow, herself the harassed mother of a working teenaged daughter. The tyrannical bite had gone out of the role, but the sheer scale of the nosiness which she provided wore down the other protagonists in the series just as effectively as the earlier, more overt, aggression.

Joan Sanderson was the youngest of five children, four daughters and a son. Her father was the director of an Anglo-Dutch import-export company. They were a talented family and at home amateur theatricals were a frequent occurrence, even if it meant staging *Hansel and Gretel* in the bedroom using the bed as a makeshift stage. Her first experience of the professional theatre was being taken to see variety at the Bristol Hippodrome. Although she did not much like school, good drama teachers nurtured an appetite for the stage and she got a scholarship to RADA and embarked on a career in rep just before the war.

She met her husband, Greg, in the wings at Wimbledon Theatre where they were both touring in *Hattie Stowe*. While both touring in rep at Buxton they got married in 1948.

During the early part of the war she played in rep: "five o'clock performances so people could get home before the bombing started", as she later recalled, and subsequently travelled abroad entertaining the forces with ENSA. Immediately after the war she made her West End debut in *See How They Run*. Other roles included some formidable Shakespearean women in a Stratford-upon-Avon season: the vengeful Queen Margaret in *Richard III*, Goneril in *King Lear* and the bitter Constance, Duchess of Brittany, in *King John*. Later she did a season with the Old Vic company in many classical roles as well as acting in *The Mousetrap*.

All this indicated a workmanlike career in the theatre until the advent of television comedy offered her the kinds of roles that were to give her a much wider exposure. She made her name as the spinster schoolmarm Doris Ewell in *Please Sir!* which was first shown on ITV in 1969. It was the first of a succession of roles in which schoolchildren, sons-in-law and hen-pecked husbands were among those who felt the rough edge of her tongue. *Upstairs Downstairs, Fawlty Towers, Ripping Yarns* and *Me & My Girl* all provided vehicles for her in bossy, interfering parts.

This television success took her increasingly away from the stage, though she was back on the boards in 1978 at the Greenwich Theatre and later on tour in *Semi-Detached* with Leonard Rossiter. The following year she played the part of Clara Soppitt in *When We Are Married* at the National Theatre and she followed this with *Pygmalion* at the Churchill Theatre, Bromley. Her last stage appearance was during the successful run of *Anyone for Denis?* at the Whitehall Theatre in 1981. The play later translated successfully to television.

In later life she confessed that she did not much miss the theatre, whose long runs militated against the comfortable home life she so much enjoyed. Needless to say, in real life she was at the opposite pole from the battleaxe-like parts in which she so much revelled in her professional life, and was noted for her keen sense of fun.

She is survived by her husband, Gregory.

b 24.11.12   d 24.5.92   aged 79

LORD CHESHIRE, VC

Wartime bomber pilot, founder of the Cheshire Foundation Homes for the disabled and co-founder with his second wife, Sue Ryder of the Ryder Cheshire Mission for the Relief of Suffering.

LEONARD Cheshire held the two highest awards, for valour and for merit, which are in the gift of a British Sovereign. He won the Victoria Cross in 1944 as an RAF pilot with "a record second to none in Bomber Command . . . placing himself invariably in the forefront of the battle". The Order of Merit, with which he was invested in 1981, marked the many years he spent in peacetime devoted, with religious fervour, to the welfare of disabled people.

The Cheshire Homes for the disabled are his monument. From faltering beginnings in a single house in 1948, after a previous self-help scheme for ex-servicemen had failed, the Cheshire Foundation expanded almost exponentially. Today there are more that 270 homes in Britain and in 50 countries abroad, caring for the physically handicapped and the incurably ill. Cheshire's meeting with (and subsequent marriage to) Sue Ryder in 1956 gave added impetus to his work. She was already renowned for her tireless work on behalf of the victims of Nazi savagery in Europe through her Sue Ryder Foundation. When the pair married their complementary interests found a natural expression in the establishment of the Ryder Cheshire Mission for the Relief of Suffering, operating from centres all over the world.

His peacetime work notwithstanding, it was important to Cheshire to be remembered as one of those who fought in the RAF to preserve the values he held to be important. The culmination of his war could not have been more dramatic. He was official British observer of the dropping of the world's second atomic bomb, at Nagasaki on August 15, 1945. That preview of Doomsday, which separated his two lives, had a profound impact on a seasoned bomber pilot who was also a devout and thoughtful man. A mystical dimension was added to his complex character.

The atom bomb, he wrote later, had the effect, first, of "catapulting him into pacifism"; pacifism attracted him briefly because it "appeared to offer a simple, unequivocal solution and appealed to high ethical prinicples". He then turned his back on pacifism, and on unilateral disarmament as a way of achieving peace, because he "just could not make it fit the real world in which we live". He saw the rest of his life as an attempt to achieve the kind of peace to which the key exists only in men's hearts.

Geoffrey Leonard Cheshire spent his childhood in Oxford where his father, Geoffrey Chevalier Cheshire, was bursar of Exeter College from 1919 to 1933 and subsequently Vinerian Professor of Law and Fellow of All Souls from 1944 to 1949. Leonard Cheshire was educated at Stowe and Merton College, Oxford, where he read jurisprudence and, in 1936, enrolled in the University Air Squadron. In 1939 he was granted a permanent commission in the RAF. He joined No

102 Squadron, Bomber Command, in June 1940.

His Bomber Command career was a unique calendar of courage. The VC he received in 1944 was awarded, unusually, not for a single act but for four years of valour, during which he had already won the DSO and two Bars and the DFC.

Later he was to recall how, while at Oxford before the war, watching Hitler's progress, he had become aware "that something evil and dangerous was abroad". If that was so, it may be said that for four years he devoted himself to a crusade to eradicate that evil with high explosive. An earlier ambition to be a fighter pilot was replaced with an almost fanatical conviction that bombers provided the key to victory over Hitler. Raid after raid he flew over the Ruhr, the north German ports and Berlin. He volunteered for missions when it was not his turn, and even while he was assigned temporarily as a flying instructor.

He found time to write a book, *Bomber Pilot*, which became a best-seller. Promotion came swiftly, to captain of aircraft, to flight commander, to squadron commander. At the age of 25 he was the youngest group captain in the service, commanding the bomber station at Marston Moor. But this took him away from operations and he insisted on reverting to the rank of wing commander so that he could return to a flying command – of 617 Squadron.

This was the legendary squadron which, a few months earlier had earned the nickname "Dambusters" after its daring low-level attacks on the Eder and Möhne dams. Under Cheshire it now developed a technique of precision bombing by dropping marker flares from a height of a few hundred feet on individual targets which were then attacked by a larger force. This development was typical of the relentless search for operational improvement which characterised this highly reflective flier.

It was "Micky" (later Air Chief Marshal Sir Harold) Martin who first suggested to Cheshire that dive-bombing

at low level was the only guaranteeable way of marking a target accurately. When Cheshire had perfected this hazardous procedure he had to prove to his superiors that it would work. Sir Ralph Cochrane, AOC 5 Group, somewhat apprehensively gave him the go-ahead for a raid on the Gnome-Rhône aero engine factory at Limoges. It was known that there was a night shift of French women at the works and Cochrane warned Cheshire that if even one of these was killed there would be such a furore that the prime minister would rule out any further low-level marking.

After briefing his aircrews with intense care, Cheshire made several runs over the factory at low level to warn the workers before the markers were dropped. As a result the workers were able to get to shelter, after which the raid proceeded, completely destroying the factory without one French casualty. A message was later passed by the Gnome-Rhône girls via the resistance to the squadron, thanking the crews for their consideration and for the accuracy of their bombing.

The success of this raid led to Churchill authorising others on targets in France and opened the way for attacks on V-weapon sites in northern France and on submarine pens. In a strategic air offensive which has in recent years been so harshly criticised for its ineffectiveness, these precision raids stand in sharp relief.

Finding, in spite of these successes, that the Lancaster made an unsatisfactory dive-bomber, Cheshire relentlessly badgered his superiors for a more suitable aircraft and, after a personal interview with Sir Arthur Harris, extracted from him the promise of two Mosquitoes for 617 Squadron. With these aircraft and, when it later became available, with the Mustang, 617's marking and bombing achieved an accuracy that was out of all proportion to that of the RAF at large and which was the envy of the Pathfinders. From then on, Cheshire led all 617's raids from the front, in his Mustang, marking the target himself "on the deck".

On the eve of D-Day the squadron used its precision techniques to confuse enemy radar in what was described as the RAF's greatest spoof operation. Metallic strips, known as "window", were dropped in a complex and meticulously planned pattern to create the effect to German radar of a convoy moving in the Pas de Calais area. The operation had to be timed perfectly so that the clouds of metal strips, dropped in advance of each other at precise intervals by successive waves of aircraft gave the impression of a steady approach of shipping at a speed of nine knots. Any aberration would have given the game away. In the event the phantom armada was clearly visible on German radar and had the effect of diverting the attention of coastal and fighter defences away from the real invasion force heading into the beaches of Normandy 150 miles to the south-west. Indeed, as the "convoy" came within range the German guns in the Pas de Calais hurled salvoes of radar-aimed 12-inch shells at the clouds of descending tinsel.

One of 617's last missions under Cheshire's command was the destruction of the third, and potentially most destructive of Hitler's *Vergeltungswaffen*, the V3. This was a nest of long range guns in subterranean tunnels, protected by a thick concrete shelter and designed to be able to pour 600 tons of explosives a day on London with deadly accuracy. From his Mustang Cheshire himself marked the spot and the 12,000lb Barnes Wallis-designed "earthquake" bombs of 617 made sure that the V3, at least, never featured in anger in the history of the V-weapons. Shortly afterwards Cheshire flew his 100th mission, at which point his AOC, Cochrane, told him that it was time to come off operations. Cheshire spent the last part of the war in India and was then attached to the Joint Staff Mission in Washington. From there he went to the Pacific to watch the A-bomb. He reported personally on that mission to Attlee, by then prime minister. He then retired from the RAF.

After several false starts in civilian life – he had, at various times, projects to grow mushrooms in disused tunnels, to fly orchids from the Caribbean to New York and to build a modern *Mayflower* and sail to an uncharted island and settle there with a band of comrades – Cheshire gathered around him a number of equally unsettled ex-servicemen. They formed a self-governing community at his Hampshire family home, Le Court, near Liss, where the intention was that they would work together on altruistic principles.

But Cheshire's health broke down and when he recovered and returned to Britain from convalescence in Canada the community had disintegrated leaving him with debts of £18,000. Cheshire sold the surrounding land to pay his most pressing debts and while considering what to do next heard that a former member of the failed community, an ex-airman, was dying of cancer. Cheshire borrowed a bed, took him in, nursed him and cooked for him. Next a bedridden woman of 95 with no one to care for her came to his notice. She became his second "patient" and he borrowed another bed, took her in and looked after her, too, performing all the necessary menial tasks himself.

The old man eventually died. Cheshire sat with him until he drew his last breath and the experience had a profound effect on his naturally religious nature. He contacted his local Roman Catholic priest, took instruction in the faith and four months later joined the Roman Catholic church. In the meantime, under its own volition his hospital was growing, as more and more incurables knocked at the door, the halt, the lame and the dying. A strange spirit infused the place; patients helped where they could in chores such as sewing and darning. Those few who were mobile enough to get about unaided polished the floors, shuffling about with rags on their feet. Nurses and students volunteered what time they could spare to supplement these efforts.

Financially the place lived from hand to mouth, though through the appeal of the Cheshire name donations kept at least trickling in and from week to week bills somehow got paid. From being a sort of doss-house, gradually Le Court became transformed into a real home, where human wrecks discarded by society were able to regain their self respect. An important financial breakthrough came when Cheshire secured backing from the company that had been so important in the wartime aircraft industry, Vickers. The Cheshire Foundation was gradually established as a major charity. As so often in such cases, the greater the fame of the enterprise, the larger the donations became; the gratefully received anonymous cheques for five and ten pounds of the early days becoming in time, bequests of tens or even hundreds of thousands of pounds from industry or from wealthy Middle Eastern potentates.

In 1956 Cheshire's work expanded in new directions after he met Sue Ryder, who at that time had already earned a name for her charitable work in Poland among survivors of concentration camps after the war. Their joint work included

setting up a centre in India. She, too, was a convert to Roman Catholicism. In 1959 they married and their joint mission for the relief of suffering was formed to undertake projects – which did not lie within the scope of their previously existing foundations. Missions were established in India, Nepal, Tanzania, Australia and New Zealand to cater for sufferers from TB, leprosy and mental handicap. In the United Kingdom the Ryder Cheshire volunteer scheme offered help to housebound people to improve the quality of their lives.

He was made a life peer in 1991 and was also a Knight Grand Cross of the Order of St Gregory the Great.

The marriage to Lady Ryder was his second, a wartime marriage to an American actress, Constance Binney, having ended in divorce. There were a son and a daughter of the second marriage.

b 7.9.17   d 31.7.92   aged 74

AIR COMMODORE EDWARD DONALDSON

Air Commodore Edward Donaldson, CB, CBE, DSO, MFC and bar, former holder of the world air speed record and later air correspondent of The Daily Telegraph.

TEDDY Donaldson was among the most famous pilots of his generation – and one of its most notorious air passengers. He was shot down nine times during the Battle of Britain. But he brought down 11 enemy aircraft in return, a tally which, as he pointed out, left him in credit. His official "bag" was only ten because no-one could trace the 11th he laid claim to. The wreck was discovered years afterwards, however, in the spot which he had pinpointed off Dover.

He could claim with some justice to have taught the United States Air Force how to fight. He crossed the Atlantic in 1941 to help set up four US air gunnery schools and to train pilot instructors in air combat. Among his pupils was Senator Barry Goldwater who was to remain one of Donaldson's lifelong friends. In January 1943 Donaldson produced his *Notes on Air Gunnery and Air Fighting* which was used as a textbook for nearly 20 years.

Then in 1946 he hit the headlines when he set a new world air speed record, breaking the previous one held by the Germans by nearly 150 mph, when he flew a Meteor-IV at 616 mph over the Channel near Littlehampton. Yet Teddy Donaldson was an unnerving airline passenger. A classic example of a man who knew too much, he thought the worst of any sudden vibration and gloomily passed on his views to those around him.

He left the RAF in 1961, rejecting an 11th hour offer of promotion in favour of becoming air correspondent of *The Daily Telegraph*. He drove down Fleet Street in a chauffeur-driven staff car with flag flying for his interview with Lord Hartwell, to continue his second career with similar panache.

Fleet Street, not short of its own characters, quickly welcomed this flamboyant *émigré* from Whitehall — with his monocle, anecdotes and piercing laugh. He moved around London by motor scooter, his old flying helmet identifiable in the traffic.

But his travelling tastes out of town were more exotic. After a stroke in 1977 (which led to his second retirement a year later) he confessed under medical examination to owning an E-Type Jaguar. "At what speeds do you drive?" asked the doctor, bent over his notepad. "Well, it cruises nicely at 123 mph," Donaldson said. The doctor quickly told him to get rid of it.

He was born, the third of four brothers in Malaya, where his Scottish father worked for the civil service as a judge. Donaldson senior died young, however, leaving his wife, also a Scot, to return to this country with her children. Young Teddy was educated at King's School, Rochester, and Christ's Hospital, after which he want to McGill University in Canada.

When he signed up in 1931, the RAF was somewhat nonplussed to discover that Donaldson had studied agriculture. But he quickly dispelled any doubts about his aptitude by winning the RAF firing trophy within two years and repeating the performance 12 months later. In 1937 he led the RAF aerobatic team through impressive performances at the Hendon and Zürich air displays and one year later was given command of 151 Hurricane squadron, based at North Weald.

He led the squadron during the Battle of France and in the subsequent fighting over the Channel, shooting down a variety of enemy aircraft in some hectic combat. In one day, May 17, 1940, he shot down two Stuka dive bombers and damaged a third, and on the following day he destroyed an Me 110 long-range fighter. Four days later he claimed two more Stukas and by the end of the fighting over the beaches had a share in a Ju 88 and another Me 110 to his credit. He was awarded his DSO for these feats and for the leadership of the squadron.

With the Battle of France over and Luftwaffe attacks on shipping in the Channel intensifying, 151 Squadron was heavily engaged again, after the briefest of respites from action, and again on one day in June, Donaldson shot down two aircraft, this time Me 109 fighters. Another Me 109 fell to his guns in mid-July. After being shot down in the early part of the Battle of Britain he was rested from operations.

It was the end of his combat career. But he had much useful wartime service to offer to the RAF and was appointed chief instructor at No. 5 flying training school before crossing the Atlantic to pass on his expertise to the Americans.

In later years he commanded the Air Cadet Corps and Combined Cadet Forces from 1949 to 1951; this was followed by appointment to RAF Fassberg, West Germany, from 1951 to 1954. He was promoted air commodore in 1954 and served as deputy commander Air Forces Arabian Peninsula from 1956 to 1958, then as commandant of the RAF Flying College, Manby, before retiring.

He was still flying as an air correspondent. He was once so dismissive of the American Starfighter — an aircraft actually dubbed "the widowmaker" by the (postwar) Luftwaffe pilots who flew it — that the makers threatened to sue him (on the grounds that he had lost them a contract) unless he flew it himself — a condition to which he immediately agreed.

Teddy Donaldson was married and divorced three times. He is survived by two daughters from his first marriage and a son from his second.

b 22.2.19 d 2.6.92 aged 80

ADMIRAL OF THE FLEET LORD FIELDHOUSE

Commander-in-chief of the task force which recaptured the Falkland Islands after they had been seized by Argentina in 1982 and was later Chief of Defence Staff from 1985 to 1988.

LORD Fieldhouse was a sailor who reached the top of his profession as First Sea Lord and Chief of Naval Staff from 1982, and as Chief of Defence Staff from 1985.

For long his reputation was that of a staff man and in senior appointments he had tended to be thought of as something of a "Whitehall warrior". But this was hardly just as he had had good operational commands all the way up the line and in 1982 he came suddenly before the public as commander-in-chief of the task force which was charged with the recovery of the Falkland Islands after they had been invaded by Argentina in April. As such he was in charge of all the air, sea and land forces in the South Atlantic which he was able to control by satellite communications without having to leave his underground command headquarters at Northwood. In this vital role he much impressed the prime minister, Mrs Thatcher, who went frequently to his headquarters to be briefed by him on the progress of the campaign.

The development of a brigade group 8,000 miles from home made the Falklands operation a highly complex one. Much might have gone wrong against an enemy who was numerically superior, was fighting on his own doorstep and had the inestimable advantage of being able to operate under the umbrella of land-based air cover. That, in spite of some setbacks, the occupying forces had had enough and were ready to surrender by June 15 was a credit to Fieldhouse and planning which, though it owed much to strenuous improvisation, functioned almost as if the campaign had been long foreseen and meditated in detail.

John David Elliott Fieldhouse was the son of Sir Harold Fieldhouse who was secretary of the National Assistance Board from 1946 to 1959 and rose from humble beginnings to be a major and influential figure in the establishment of the State welfare system during and after the second world war. John Fieldhouse joined the Royal Navy as a cadet in 1944 and served as a midshipman in the East Indies fleet in 1945–46. He volunteered for submarine service in 1948 and became the commanding officer of HMS *Acheron* in 1955. He was already marked out as an officer of promise and underwent extensive training in the newly-established department of nuclear science at Greenwich which culminated in the award of a post-graduate degree in 1961.

The Royal Navy at this time was beginning the deployment of nuclear-powered submarines, which was to be much enhanced by the decision, in December 1962, to procure a submarine-based deterent force based upon the American Polaris weapon system. Fieldhouse became the commanding officer of the first British nuclear-powered submarine, HMS *Dreadnought*, in 1964. After a spell as the executive officer of an aircraft carrier, HMS *Hermes*, he was promoted captain in December 1967 and became the first Squadron Commander (SM 10) of the Polaris submarine squadron.

A string of important appointments followed, including command of the Nato Standing Naval Force (Atlantic) in 1972–3, and it was no surprise when he was selected for early promotion to flag rank in January 1975. He became Flag Officer, Submarines (which carried with it a parallel Nato submarine command appointment in 1976 and Controller of the Navy and a member of the Admiralty Board in 1979. This was the period during which both the development of new surface ships, including frigates and the new class of light aircraft carrier and a replacement for the Polaris submarines were matters of high policy. Apart from the strategic questions that were involved about what sorts of ships and what sorts of functions should be selected from a wide range of technological possibilities, the increasing cost of weapons material in a period of high inflation and deepening recession made the settlement of policy highly contentious.

The economic uncertainties of escalating costs and the political environment, in which there was more extensive questioning of Britain's future as a nuclear power, were only partially alleviated by the determination of the new Conservative government in May 1979 to give a higher priority to defence matters. Fieldhouse was a convinced advocate of

Trident, selected by the government as a successor-system to Polaris, early in 1980.

He had become Commander-in-Chief, Fleet, in the summer of 1981, but with the Argentine invasion of the Falklands at the end of March 1982 he became the commander-in-chief of the task force which was dispatched immediately. He sat in the middle of the web in his shore headquarters at Northwood and was the operational director of what was undoubtedly a brilliantly improvised campaign.

The operational plans, for local sea control of the Falkland Island area for the assault and land campaign that would follow if force had to be used to expel the Argentines, had to be devised under the emergency conditions which required a constant interchange between headquarters and the senior officers of the component forces. And then the plans had to be carried out. This involved taking political as well as military factors into account, which also meant a constant flow of advice and communication between London, the command centre at Northwood and the forces in the field. Fieldhouse's principal function in this respect was to provide clear directives to the operational commanders and shield them from the "clutter" of unnecessary detail which modern communications can invite; but at the same time to provide comprehensive information to the Chief of Defence Staff and, through him, to the cabinet group that was in effect the War Cabinet, that would enable broad policy decisions to be made effectively.

Fieldhouse's plan of campaign envisaged four main objectives, to be achieved in phases: the establishment of a sea blockade round the Falklands; the repossession of South Georgia; the gaining of air and sea supremacy throughout the battle area and the eventual repossession of the islands. There were setbacks, notably the loss of some warships and a container ship which carried vital supplies, while there were also casualties among soldiers when two transports were bombed. But that the war plan's goals were all inexorably accomplished after a campaign which from day one of the Argentine aggression lasted only ten weeks was greatly to Fieldhouse's credit and added much to his reputation in professional circles.

The experience added weight to his very strong claims to become the Chief of the Naval Staff in due course and he was appointed First Sea Lord in 1982, having been created GBE for his services during the Falklands operation as well as the GCB, which was the normal award for his rank and appointment. His time as First Sea Lord was naturally preoccupied by the analysis of what lessons had been highlighted in the first campaign against a substantial opponent which the Royal Navy had fought for a quarter of a century; but it was also heavily flavoured by the taste of vindication which the Falklands brought to the navy, after its utility and organisation had been challenged by the secretary of defence, Sir John Nott, in 1981.

Fieldhouse's experience as an operational commander made him an obvious choice as Chief of the Defence Staff in 1985. But it still required a major break with tradition to enable this to happen. Since its creation the post of CDS had been rotated between the three services on the principle of "Buggins's turn". The army in the person of Field Marshal Sir Edwin Bramall had the job and in 1985 it was the RAF's turn, in the person of the Chief of the Air Staff, Marshal of the RAF Sir Keith Williamson. But the high regard in which the government of Mrs Thatcher held Fieldhouse went against the RAF's nominee and, out of turn, the sailor became the CDS. In the event the appointment was doubly appropriate. With the defence reorganisation of 1982 and 1984 the post carried added operational responsibilities for which Fieldhouse was admirably well qualified.

In retirement from his service career Fieldhouse was a consultant to Vosper Thorneycroft (UK) Ltd and in 1990 he became chairman of the White Ensign Association. He was made a life peer in 1990.

He married, in 1953, Margaret Ellen Cull. They had one son and two daughters.

b 12.2.28　d 17.2.92　aged 64

Lord Fieldhouse with the two captains of the Polaris submarine HMS Repulse *(1986)*

ADMIRAL
SIR GUY GRANTHAM

Admiral Sir Guy Grantham, GCB, OBE, DSO, former governor of Malta.

THE governorship of Malta looked like a glittering prize for Guy Grantham in 1959, proper reward at the end of a distinguished career in the Royal Navy. Having just missed being appointed Britain's First Sea Lord, he could contemplate three graceful years — the first admiral for a century and a half to be thus honoured.

Events, however, were to take an unexpected twist. Shortly before the Granthams landed in Valetta, Malta's Labour government under the volatile Dom Mintoff resigned after rejecting a British proposal over the island's future.

The constitution was suspended, a state of emergency declared, and Grantham found himself having to govern in fact as well as in name for the next three years. This he did until Borg Olivier's Nationalist Party won the general election of 1962 and steered the country towards independence two years later.

Grantham's guidance and commonsense while at the helm were held to have contributed in no small measure to the peaceful outcome.

Time and again throughout 40 years in the Royal Navy, he had found himself stationed in the Mediterranean. He was captain of the flagship *Cleopatra* during the second battle of Sirte on March 22, 1942, when the 15th cruiser squadron under Admiral Sir Philip Vian fought off a far stronger Italian force to protect a crucial convoy bound for Malta.

This was the action, described by Churchill in a congratulatory signal as a "naval episode of the highest distinction", in which Vian made brilliant use of a smokescreen to shield the convoy. While the merchantmen were able to make their getaway, the British cruisers dodged in and out of the smoke, taking on the far more heavily armed Italians. Grantham was on *Cleopatra*'s bridge when it was struck by a six-inch shell which killed 15 men and silenced the ship's radio. He survived, however, to receive a glowing report from Vian and to be appointed a Commander of the Bath — an unusually high recognition for one of his rank.

He had already had a dangerous and distinguished war. Promoted captain in December 1937, he had served on the staff of the C-in-C Mediterranean, Admiral Sir Dudley Pound, until Pound was made First Sea Lord — and insisted on Grantham returning to the Admiralty with him as his naval assistant.

Grantham said later that he found it so difficult to get away from Pound that he eventually searched out a suitable officer in the building and talked him into taking over the job.

Meanwhile Grantham managed to get command of the new light cruiser *Phoebe* which he sailed first in the Home Fleet then back to the Mediterranean. There *Phoebe* took part in the hazardous evacuation of British troops from, first, Greece and later, Crete. For this Grantham was awarded his DSO

He left *Phoebe* when she was damaged by a torpedo while operating off Tobruk and had to go for repairs to the United States. She was sent a signal before she sailed which read: "Romans, Chapter 16, Verses 1 and 2: 'I commend unto you

Phebe our sister . . . that ye assist her in whatsoever business she hath need of you; for she hath been a succourer of many and of myself also.' "

Grantham was transferred briefly to act as a naval liaison officer with the Eighth Army, before taking command of his next ship, the light cruiser *Naiad*, in January 1942. This first brought him into close contact with Vian as flag captain and chief staff officer.

Two months later, however, *Naiad* was torpedoed and sunk by a U-boat near the entrance to the fleet harbour at Alexandra. Grantham, like Vian, had to swim for his life, while helping other crew members in the water, until he was picked up exhausted half an hour later. Vian transferred his flag to *Cleopatra*, taking Grantham with him.

In 1943 Grantham was given command of the aircraft carrier *Indomitable* which provided air cover for the allied landings in Sicily. When the carrier was later hit by a torpedo Grantham's prompt action in sealing off the lower decks was held responsible for saving her from sinking.

He then joined Vian's staff again, and was mentioned in dispatches (for the second time during the war) for his part in the allied landings at Salerno. The landings also brought him to the attention of General Montgomery who was to become an admirer and a friend. He saw out the war, however, at the Admiralty as director of plans, a post which took him to the allied conferences at both Yalta and Quebec.

Despite his illustrious career, "Grannie" Grantham, as he was known throughout the fleet, had nearly left the Royal Navy as a young man. He was born in Lincolnshire, the son of a farmer from Skegness who gave his name "Charles Fred Grantham" to the town's first lifeboat. For years his horses pulled the boat into the water.

Young Guy went to Rugby, then to the Royal Naval College, Osborne, as a special entrant, aged 18. He served as midshipman in the battleship *Monarch*, from whose decks he witnessed the surrender of the German fleet after the

first world war. He was a sub-lieutenant on the royal yacht *Victoria and Albert* and the cruiser *New Zealand*, flagship of Admiral of the Fleet Lord Jellicoe on a round-the-world voyage in the early 1920s.

After specialising in submarines in 1923 his first appointments were to the exotic but by no means wholly successful boats *M1* and *X1*, the first of which had been fitted with a 12-inch gun while the latter was the biggest boat built for the navy at that time. He served in the battle cruiser *Hood* (1926–7), then was given his first command, of the submarine *H44*.

He was promoted lieutenant-commander during his next job, on the instucting staff at Dartmouth, then found himself sports officer in *HMS Nelson* at the time of the Invergordon Mutiny. In 1933 he was promoted commander at the early age of 33.

After the second world war he found himself back in the Mediterranean as chief of staff to the C-in-C. In 1951, he became vice-chief of the naval staff in Whitehall, then C-in-C Mediterranean as a full admiral in 1954 in succession to Lord Louis Mountbatten. It was in that capacity that he commanded the naval operations during the Suez crisis of 1956. In 1957 he began his final appointment as commander-in-chief Portsmouth.

He was said to have been the navy's choice to succeed Mountbatten again in the following year as First Sea Lord. But Mountbatten who moved up to become Chief of the Defence Staff threw his not inconsiderable influence behind the claims of Sir Charles Lambe. If Grantham was disappointed, he did not show it.

He was a family man and, in his youth, had been accomplished in several sports, including rugby, at which he was an effective prop forward. He was also a fine ocean-going yachtsman.

Guy Grantham's wife Beryl, whom he married in 1934, died last December and he is survived by two daughters.

b 9.1.00　d 8.9.92　aged 92

ADMIRAL
SIR DAVID HALLIFAX

Admiral Sir David Hallifax, KCB, KCVO, KBE, Constable of Windsor Castle and former Chief of Staff to Lord Fieldhouse.

HOWEVER badly things seemed to be going in the Falklands War, the calm reassuring voice of David Hallifax was like aspirin to the hard-pressed commanders of the British Task Force.

As Chief of Staff to Admiral Sir John Fieldhouse, Commander-in-Chief Fleet, Hallifax was in day-to-day control of his headquarters. There, in the underground bunker at Northwood, Middlesex, he ensured the smooth running of the joint-service operation which was crucial to the task force's success 8,000 miles away. No small measure of the ultimate credit should go to him.

To those embattled in the South Atlantic, he also seemed a perfect interlocutor. It was Hallifax whom they usually addressed when they came through on the secure telephone link, and

his dry humour was a stimulating tonic.

This laid-back style had always belied an incisive mind. As a young officer on the Royal Navy's torpedo and anti-submarine (TAS) course, he had celebrated its termination prematurely. On the morning after the night before, he arrived late for the final gruelling three-hour paper on applied mechanics – and left the examination room half-way through, looking frail and ashen-faced. Nonetheless, when the results came through, his name topped the list.

His very entry to the Navy had been late. Anxious not to limit his options, his naval family had sent him not to Dartmouth but to Winchester. Since he was born in Plymouth, however, the son and the grandson of British admirals, there had never been any serious doubt over his destiny. "It was," as he once put it, "hereditary."

His family had its share of sadness, however, when his father, a vice-admiral serving in the Middle East during the war, was shot down and killed while flying home on leave over North Africa.

Young David joined the Navy as a special entrant in 1945 and, after a tour as a midshipman in the cruiser *Kenya* in the West Indies, served for two years on a minesweeper in the late 1940s, helping to clear mines from the eastern Mediterranean. He commanded a motor torpedo boat in British waters before taking the specialist TAS course in 1954. Two years later he was at Suez serving in the tank landing ship *Salerno* which transported a Royal Tank Regiment to the canal zone. In 1959 he was sent to the Army staff college at Camberley.

He was back in the Caribbean in the early 1960s, as TAS officer with the second frigate squadron, based on HMS *Whirlwind*. Among his achievements was the formation of a ship's steel band, known as "Jim's Tins" which once performed on the radio in this country.

Hallifax commanded the battle-class destroyer *Agincourt*, 1964–65, captained one of the larger county-class destroyers, HMS *Fife*, in 1973–75, then did a tour at the Ministry of Defence as director of naval operational requirements before becoming flag officer of the first flotilla – a position once held by his father. From there he went to Northwood in 1980.

He left his Chief of Staff job shortly before the final victory at Port Stanley to become Deputy Supreme Allied Commander Atlantic in Saclant's headquarters at Norfolk, Virginia.

After an unusually high profile tour in the United States he returned to the Ministry of Defence where he filled in time for 12 months working on a study of ship design at the time of the great controversy over the "short-fat ship" versus the "long thin one". Then, at the start of 1986, he began his final job as commandant of the Royal College of Defence Studies in Belgrave Square.

He left the navy at the end of 1987 and early the following year was made constable and governor of Windsor Castle, a largely honorary appointment which involves acting as the Queen's representative in and around Windsor.

He was the first admiral to be given the post after a succession of retired Army and RAF officers.

Tragedy was shortly to overtake him, however. In July 1989 his younger son Matthew, aged 21, was one of four Edinburgh University students drowned when their dinghy capsized in a squall while crossing at night between two islands off the coast of Donegal. David Hallifax was deeply affected by the loss.

Then last year doctors diagnosed motor neuron disease, which forced him to retire from his post at Windsor earlier this summer. This was not before the Queen personally visited his quarters at Windsor to bestow on him his third knighthood, that of the KCVO.

David Hallifax was an expert sailor who belonged to the Royal Yacht Squadron and had sailed in the Admiral's Cup. He is survived by his wife Anne, whom he married in 1962, and by one son and a daughter.

b 23.9.27   d 23.8.92   aged 64

AIR VICE-MARSHAL DESMOND HUGHES

Air Vice-Marshal Desmond Hughes, CB, CBE, DSO, DFC and two bars, AFC, was one of Britain's fighter aces in the Second World War.

DESMOND Hughes was the most decorated living member of the Battle of Britain Fighter Association and one of the most successful night fighter pilots of the last war. To the press he was "Hawk-Eye" Hughes, a hero in the same mould as "Cat's Eyes" Cunningham, whose exploits helped to keep British spirits high. By the end of the fighting in Europe, still one month short of his 26th birthday, he had been credited with shooting down 18½ enemy aircraft. The "half" was a shared Ju-88.

But at one time Hughes must have counted himself lucky just to have survived the desperate air battles of 1940. During the last week of August, shortly after his 264 squadron had been moved from Lincolnshire to Hornchurch, Essex, it lost nine air gunners, five pilots, one commanding officer, an acting CO injured and two flight commanders shot down. At one point the most experienced pilot left was a pilot officer not yet 21.

On one occasion when the squadron was "scrambled" after a raid, there were only two crews left with serviceable aircraft. Hughes just managed to take off from the badly cratered airfield to fend off an approaching force more than 30 strong. At 12,000 feet, however, the control tower radioed: "Terribly sorry old boy — they've turned away." The sorrow was not shared by Hughes and company.

He had had the misfortune to be assigned to a squadron of Defiants — an aircraft which won few admirers. Its rear gun turret made it slow and vulnerable to anything other than an undefended bomber. As most of the enemy raiders were escorted, Defiant crews had the odds stacked against them.

"The fact was we were out-turned, out-climbed and out-gunned by the Messerschmitt 109," Hughes later wrote. He became involved in converting the Defiants to a night-fighter role, to which they seemed better adapted. His DFC was won on the night of March 12, 1941, when he and his gunner, Sergeant Fred Gash, shot down a He-111.

Hughes moved to No 125 Beaufighter squadron in 1942 and in June bagged the squadron's first victim. Later that year he also became the first (or one of the first) to take his pet dog on a sortie. His mongrel Scruffy, dressed in flying overalls for warmth, survived the mission, only to be killed by a WAAF truck driver shortly afterwards.

In January 1943 Hughes was posted as a flight commander to No 600 squadron in North Africa. He won the first bar to his DFC in February and a second in September as, one by one — and sometimes by as many as three in one day — his tally of enemy aircraft accumulated.

He subsequently served in Sicily and Italy, then was given command of No 604 Mosquito squadron which became the first night fighter unit to be based on the continent after D-Day. Now a wing com-

mander in rank, he was awarded the DSO in March 1945 and next year was offered a permanent commission.

Desmond Hughes belonged to that youthful generation whose futures were reshaped by the second world war. Born in Donaghadee, near Belfast, the son of the director of a linen firm, he went from Campbell College to Pembroke College, Cambridge, to read law. He joined the university air squadron in 1938 and the RAF at the outbreak of the war.

He served on the directing staff of the RAF Staff College, Bracknell, between 1954 and 1956, after which he was personal staff officer to the chief of the air staff, then Air Chief Marshal Sir Dermot Boyle, for two years. Between 1959 and 1961 he was station commander at Geilenkirchen in West Germany. In 1962-64 he was director of air staff plans at the Ministry of Defence and ADC to the Queen.

As commandant of the RAF College, Cranwell, between 1970 and 1972 he supervised the Prince of Wales's flying training and presided over the college's 50th anniversary celebrations. He also had the responsibility for overseeing the reorganisation of officer training, which partly involved phasing out the old three-year cadetship and introducing the university graduate entry.

After two years as senior air staff officer at the Near East Air Force headquarters in Cyprus, Desmond Hughes retired in 1974. He was made a deputy lieutenant of Lincolnshire in 1983.

A fine sportsman all his life, he played on the wing for London Irish RFC after the last war. Two years ago he marched with Battle of Britain crews past Buckingham Palace to commemorate the battle's 50th anniversary. But Hughes himself was a quiet and modest man who talked little in later life about his own war.

He is survived by his wife Pamela, daughter of the conductor and composer Julius Harrison, and by two of their three sons.

b 6.6.19   d 11.1.92   aged 72

MAJOR-GENERAL
ABRAR HUSAIN

Indian General who was imprisoned by Japanese on the Solomon Islands, who later joined the Pakistani army when the country was partitioned.

ABRAR Husain was the senior Allied officer to whom the Japanese forces occupying New Britain in the Solomon Islands surrendered in 1945.

As the son of a distinguished family who had been educated at the Lamartinhiere School and Calvin College, Lucknow, he had been in the first batch of "emergency" officers to be commissioned from the Indian Military Academy in July 1940 and joined the 2nd Battalion, 10th Baluch Regiment, a regular battalion that was sent to Malaya and fought well in the disastrous campaign which ended with surrender and imprisonment in Singapore.

The British officers of the unit were sent to work on the Burma-Siam railway. Pressure was brought to bear on the Indian officers to join the Japanese-sponsored "Indian National Army" and encourage their men to do likewise. Three Indian Officers, of whom Abrar was the youngest, refused to have anything to do with the INA, but they encouraged a fourth to join as he was going to die if he did not receive proper medical treatment. He, later, kept the battalion up to date with Singapore news and what he knew of the rest of the world. The INA got very few recruits from 2/10 Baluch.

The Japanese decided to make an example of Abrar Husain and, in December 1942, sent him off with a party of 150 Gurkha "recalcitrants" to New Britain in the Solomon Islands as prison labour. The group found that food and supplies of any sort were even harder to come by than they were in Singapore, so Abrar taught his Gurkhas to steal to survive, a way of life unnatural to them. By 1945 the Japanese were starving, too, and turned to cannibalism.

In September 1945 it became apparent from the demeanour of their guards that something had happened and the news filtered out that Japan had surrendered, so Abrar, the senior allied officer in New Britain, demanded the surrender of the Japanese forces on the island. After some tricky and shifty negotiations, he got it.

All was far from well, however. Communications were non-existent and New Britain was not high on the list of allied priorities. The last that had been heard of Abrar Husain and his Gurkhas had been when they had been shipped out of Singapore. Ships carrying prisoners were known to have been sunk in the Pacific and so little hope was held out for their survival.

But in December 1945 an Australian force arrived at New Britain and were astonished to find it in allied hands, even if the commander and his men were skeletons in rags carrying Japanese weapons. The Gurkhas were shipped back to India and a large number of Chinese, who had been prisoners since 1937, were returned to China while air passage was arranged for Abrar back to Lucknow. On the recommendation of the Australians Abrar was appointed MBE.

In February 1946 he rejoined his battalion in Karachi, where it had been reformed by his fellow prison inmate, Lieutenant Ismail Khan. The British officers returned from leave in the United Kingdom in March and Abrar was promoted captain and then major in rapid succession.

When independence (and partition) came in 1947, Abrar had no doubts about his sympathies. He opted to go where his men, Punjabis and Pathans, were going – to Pakistan. In 1948 he passed the staff college examination and went to general headquarters as a staff officer. In 1952 he returned to the staff college as an instructor. In 1956 he went back to GHQ as brigadier in charge of staff duties and in 1965 he was promoted major-general in command of the 6th Armoured Division, a somewhat fancifully entitled force which was really merely an armoured brigade reinforced by an infantry brigade. However, in the 1965 war with India this force repulsed the main Indian attack, on the salient between Sialkot, the Ravi River and the Jammu border, which was said to have been carried out by an armoured, a mountain and two infantry divisions.

Two years later Abrar had a minor heart attack, from which he rapidly recovered, and went back once more to the staff college, this time as commandant. But he then had a serious disagreement with GHQ, resigned and turned his talents to industry.

For some time he managed a paper mill but in 1974 he was chairman of the Cement Corporation, one of the biggest companies in Pakistan. But it was not to last. In 1975 he had a very serious stroke on his right side and was unable to speak or to write or, for a time, to walk. Nursed by his beloved wife (a sister of his old colleague, Ismail), he bore his disabilities with fortitude and continued to play a great part in the affairs of his closeknit family until a bad fall a few days before he died. Abrar was a quietly-spoken man with immense inner strength who is remembered with respect and affection.

b 1917   d 15.3.92   aged 74

AIR MARSHAL
SIR GEORGE JONES

Air Marshal Sir George Jones, KBE, CBE, CB, DFC, Australia's last surviving first world war ace and architect of his country's Pacific air defence in the second world war.

GEORGE Jones took charge of Australia's ailing air force in its darkest hour in 1942. Singapore had fallen, Darwin was under aerial bombardment and Japanese forces were poised to sweep south. With quiet confidence Jones fought for the equipment and personnel he needed to organise an air defence network stretching from the south Pacific island of Bougainville westwards to Borneo. From a starting point of 12 poorly equipped squadrons, the RAAF had, by the end of the war, 53 squadrons operating in the Pacific theatre which Jones firmly believed could defeat Japanese air forces alone.

Jones is thought to have been the very last second world war air force commander. A man of quiet humility, he came from a poor background, with little formal education. He worked his way through the ranks from a private, and went on to influence the development of the RAAF until the 1950s. He was the youngest of eight children and his father, an unsuccessful gold miner, died from a fall shortly after George was born.

Leaving school at 14, he moved to Melbourne where he became a motor mechanic.

During the first world war Jones fought as a private in the Australian Imperial Forces' 9th Light Horse Regiment at Gallipoli — the battle that is held to have first bound together Australia as a nation. After moving to No 13 Squadron of the Imperial Camel Corps, he joined No 1 Squadron of the fledgling Australian Flying Corps where he qualified as a pilot. He ended the war, aged 22, as a captain with No 4 Squadron, having flown 113 missions and with seven kills.

Jones was awarded the DFC for shooting down two German planes over France in one action. Despite being badly wounded in the back during an attack on German troops, he returned to action late in 1918 to record two further kills before the Armistice.

Following an attempt to settle down as a motor mechanic in Victoria, Jones returned to the RAAF in 1921 as a test and training pilot. He qualified at the RAF Staff College, Andover, but his urging to develop an Australian aviation industry in the years before the second world war was ignored.

In 1939 he fought another bureaucratic battle against RAF moves to redirect RAAF air crew to the European theatre, which Jones, then head of RAAF training, saw as weakening defences at home. His appointment as RAAF Chief of Air Staff in 1942 saw the beginnings of the turnaround and the crucial decade of change.

His call for Australia to build its own aircraft was finally realised with the construction of the De Havilland Mosquitoes from 1943 and, later, Vampire jet fighters. He was made a CBE in 1942, a CB in 1943, and was knighted in 1953.

Before retiring in 1952, he had commanded the RAAF efforts in the Berlin air lift, Malayan campaign and the Korean War. He also established the Empire Training Scheme in Australia.

b 22.11.96   d 24,8.92   aged 95

CAPTAIN
COLIN McMULLEN, DSC

Gunnery officer of HMS Prince of Wales *both when she fought the* Bismarck *and during her last and fatal sortie against the Japanese.*

LAST December saw the 50th anniversary of the sinking of the battleship *Prince of Wales* and the battlecruiser *Repulse*; it was a disaster whose impact on himself Winston Churchill has graphically recorded: ". . . I put the telephone down. I was thankful to be alone. In all the war I never received a more direct shock . . . how many efforts, hopes and plans foundered with these two ships. As I turned over and twisted in bed the full horror of the news sank in upon me . . ."

Colin McMullen was gunnery officer during the *Prince of Wales*'s short but eventful life which started in May 1941 with the interception of the German battleship *Bismarck* in the Denmark Strait between Greenland and Iceland.

Almost at the outset of the engagement the battlecruiser *Hood*, darling of the Royal Navy, was sunk with almost all hands. Nevertheless, despite teething troubles with her main armament, a new system not yet tested in war (indeed she had put to see with some Clydeside mechanics still on board), the *Prince of Wales* inflicted two vital hits on the *Bismarck* though the significance of these was not immediately appreciated in the atmosphere of gloom which pervaded the British force in the aftermath of *Hood*'s swift destruction.

One of the battleship's 14-inch shells had ruptured *Bismarck*'s fuel tanks, causing an oil leak and thus reducing her radius of action. This led the German admiral, Lutjens, to abort his commerce raiding mission into the Atlantic and attempt a return to a Western French port, such as St Nazaire or Brest, for repairs. This decision led to her ultimate destruction since a Swordfish from the aircraft carrier *Victorious* later crippled her rudders, thus bringing her to bay. McMullen was mentioned in dispatches for his part in the handling of the *Prince of Wales*'s main armament during the battle.

After taking Churchill to Newfoundland for his historic Atlantic Charter meeting with President Roosevelt, the *Prince of Wales* was soon in action again in the successful support of a Malta convoy. Next, at the decision of Churchill, she was sent to the Far East with the battlecruiser *Repulse* as a counter to the rising Japanese threat to Malaya. Alas, the aircraft carrier which had been intended to be part of this task force was damaged and could not accompany the capital ships. They were thus horribly vulnerable to air attack.

In the event, on December 10, 1941,

while attempting to intercept Japanese transports in the South China Sea they were attacked by Japanese bombers and sunk after a two-hour battle in which the air defences of both ships were overwhelmed. *Repulse* sank first, at 1230 hrs, and when, after enduring the assault for almost an hour longer, the *Prince of Wales* succumbed too, McMullen was the last to leave her, swimming off the bridge as the ship rolled over and sank.

Educated at Oakley Hall and Cheltenham College, McMullen joined the Royal Navy in 1925. He specialised in gunnery and was serving in the cruiser *Aurora* at the outbreak of war. Following his return from Singapore in 1942 he took part in the ill-fated Dieppe raid. He was awarded the DSC for his part in an operation which, while it resulted in heavy casualties to the attacking force, nevertheless provided experience which was afterwards put to good effect in the Normandy landings.

McMullen then became an escort group commander, responsible for the safe and timely arrival of slow convoys to and from Gibraltar. On leaving the Western Approaches in 1944 he spent the remainder of the war in command of Home Fleet destroyers, gaining a bar to his DSC for his work on Russian convoys.

Several interesting appointments followed in the post-war period including command of the Rhine Flotilla, Captain Minesweepers Mediterranean – where he organised the search for the crashed Comet airliner off Elba – and Commodore Inshore Flotilla. In this command he sailed with 25 ships as a back-up to the abortive Suez operation. He also served as a commodore at Nato headquarters in Paris where he lived in some comfort and convenience on board his Dutch barge, moored on the Seine in the heart of the city.

On his retirement from the Royal Navy in 1958 he exchanged his barge for a more manageable yacht and successfully combined a new career as a marine consultant with his lifelong passion for offshore cruising. Although a founder member of the Royal Naval Sailing Association, he always sailed under the burgee of the historic Royal Cruising Club of which he was commodore from 1972 to 1977. He was also a three-times winner of the club's most coveted cruising award. He made his last trans-Atlantic voyage in his seventies and was still skippering his wooden sloop *Saecwen* well into his eighties.

He is survived by his wife Gillian and their daughter. One of his two sons, who both predeceased him, was the well-known off-shore racing yachtsman Mike McMullen who was lost at sea in 1976.

b 12.3.07   d 8.2.92   aged 84

APPRECIATION

THAT great seaman, "Colin Mac" – "Skipper" to many – endeared himself to people without trying, and this quality, coupled with his great professional competence gave him outstanding qualities of leadership. The writer was privileged to see this demonstrated in 1944 when Colin took command of a Fleet destroyer, the ship's company of which was war-weary. His personality had the ship on its toes again in a short time and watching him achieve this was an object lesson.

His dry, droll sense of humour was very near the surface.

In an Arctic storm in January 1945 his ship, HMS *Scorpion*, was hove-to for two days and battened down. At midday the dim light revealed a giant wave, even bigger than the rest, bearing down upon the ship. Those with him on the open bridge were daunted, to put it mildly, and looked at Colin Mac for comfort. They were not disappointed; he beckoned them to him, apparently to shout some orders above the screaming wind. In an exaggerated Long-John-Silver-West-Country voice he bellowed: "Marrrk my worrrds – it don't blow like it used to." Long before the laughter subsided, the ship had bobbed up and over the giant wave.

A.G.F.D.

CAPTAIN ANTONIO MARCEGLIA

The Italian naval officer who in 1941 took his "human torpedo" into the harbour of Alexandria and put out of action the British battleship HMS Queen Elizabeth.

THE raid on Alexandria, carried out during the night between December 18 and 19, 1941, was the most brilliant operation credited to the Italian Navy during the second world war. The attack, with three human torpedoes each mounted by two men with breathing apparatus, succeeded in putting out of action the battleships *Valiant* and *Queen Elizabeth*. It was supremely typical of a service which was as ingenious, daring and courageous in small scale actions involving a few individual officers, as it was mismanaged and self-defeating in fleet actions controlled directly by the *Supermarina* in Rome.

The three human torpedoes were dropped by the submarine *Scire* just outside the port of Alexandria, the eastern base of the Royal Navy's Mediterranean fleet. Under water and in darkness, surfacing occasionally to check their course, the three "maiali" (or "pigs"), as the Italians called them, each moved towards its target.

One, commanded by Luigi Durand de La Penne (see page 61), released its 500 pound warhead beneath the hull of the battleship *Valiant*. Lieutenant de La Penne and his navy diver, Emilio Bianchi, were immediately captured by the *Valiant*'s crew and put deep inside the ship as an encouragement to reveal exactly where they had placed their charge. But they kept silent until it exploded at dawn. The battle ship was out of action for six and a half months.

The second "maiale," with Lieutenant Vincenzo Martellotta and navy diver Mario Marino, failed to find an aircraft carrier in harbour and placed its warhead under an 8,000 ton tanker. They were soon captured after landing on shore.

The "maiale" ridden by Captain Antonio Marceglia and navy diver Spartaco Schergat was the most successful of the three. They found the *Queen Elizabeth*, dropped their charge underneath and beached their "maiale" hours before the warhead exploded. The 32,000 tonne *Queen Elizabeth*, Admiral Andrew Cunningham's flagship, was seriously damaged and put out of action for a year and a half.

The crippling of the two British capital ships influenced the balance of sea power in the Eastern Mediterranean, although the Italians failed to take advantage of the situation.

But for Marceglia and Schergat events after the attack were almost as exciting as the attack itself. Having abandoned their "maiale" on an isolated beach they took off their diving suits and rolled up the sleeves of the uniforms they were wearing underneath to hide the Italian insignia. Taking advantage of the fact that their uniforms were very similar to those of the French navy, they wandered around Alexandria harbour for some time until they found the railway station.

Their plan was to reach Rashid, 40 miles east along the coast, where it had been agreed that an Italian submarine would surface for three successive nights to take them off. They tried to pay for their train tickets with British pound notes with which they had been supplied. But they discovered that their intelligence service had blundered and that pounds sterling were not legal tender in Egypt. They changed their money with a street corner moneychanger and took the train to Rashid where they booked into a hotel and set about looking for a small boat. But the next day they were stopped by an Egyptian patrol that arrested them and turned them over to the British.

After the attack Admiral Cunningham said: "One cannot help but admire the sangfroid of these Italians." Winston Churchill was also impressed and ordered the Royal Navy to work along similar lines. The "chariots", the British version of the "maiali", were duly developed but

failed in an attempt to attack the German battleship *Tirpitz* in a Norwegian fjord.

Antonio Marceglia was born in Istria, today part of Yugoslavia. He grew up in Trieste and after three years in the Naval Academy and a two-year naval engineering course at Genoa University was commissioned as an officer in the Naval Engineers.

After the war Marceglia left the navy and worked for a time on salvage operations in the Mediterranean. In 1954 he took a job at the Fincantieri shipyards in Venice of which he became first managing director and then president before he retired. It is to his credit that the Venice shipyard is the only one of those originally controlled by the state-run Fincantieri which has been successfully privatised recently.

b 28.7.15   d 14.7.92   aged 76

WING COMMANDER ROGER MAW

Wing Commander Roger Maw, who designed and built the wooden vaulting-horse used by his fellow prisoners-of-war in one of the most ingenious escapes of the second world war.

THE Wooden Horse escape by prisoners-of-war at Stalag Luft III in Sagen, Germany, became one of the classic stories of the second world war. Inspired by Homer's story of how the Greeks used a wooden horse to infiltrate the city of Troy, the Stalag Luft III PoWs conceived the idea of using a vaulting-horse as a visual and psychological cover for the digging of an underground escape route out of Stalag Luft III.

The camp carpenter declined to participate in the project, on the grounds that his equipment had been obtained on trust from the German authorities and was vital for the maintenance of camp moral. So Maw — who had studied carpentry at school, had once built a three-wheel car and was a constant source of make-shift gadgetry in the camp — was recruited to construct the vaulting-horse.

Using scrapwood, pieces of Red Cross food-parcel crates and the ends of beams surreptitiously sawn from the roofs of huts, he built a vaulting-frame which stood 4ft 6ins high and had a base covering an area of 5ft by 3ft. It was carried out each day to a point close to the camp perimeter wire and then used – in full view of the guards – ostensibly to improve the fitness of the prisoners. But while the prisoners' "athletics team" performed their gymnastic routines, jumping and somersaulting on and over the vaulting-horse, fellow PoWs – hidden one by one in the horse – were secretly tunnelling to freedom underneath. They painstakingly dug their way towards the outside world before returning to the horse, ready to be carried back to their huts, minutes before the exercise period ended. The soil they removed as they tunnelled was meticulously collected and stored alongside the men as they were carried back. It was then either buried under the floorboards of their huts or conveyed in pockets, socks and handkerchiefs to be scattered about the camp compound. They used Maw's tools. He, meanwhile, had fashioned a replica set of tools to display and fool the guards.

Three prisoners managed to escape before the tunnel was discovered by the Germans: Flight Lieutenants Oliver Philpot and Eric Williams and Captain Michael Codner. Maw himself and the other members of the escape committee remained in the camp for another three years until liberated by the British in 1945.

The Wooden Horse escape inspired a book of the same name by Eric Williams, published by Collins in 1949, in which Maw features under the name of "Wings" Cameron. Williams later wrote the screenplay for the 1950 film directed by Jack Lee, starring Leo Genn, David Tomlinson and Anthony Steele with a cast of supporting actors which included Peter Finch and Bryan Forbes.

Roger Hargreaves Maw, a slightly built man with a moustache, was the son of a Lincolnshire landowner. He was educated

at Westerleigh School, St Leonard's on Sea, and Oundle. Having learned to fly as an RAF reservist in 1927, he joined 503 Squadron flying Fairey Fawn biplane light day bombers. He served in India for three years, returning to Britain in 1936 and joining 18 Squadron. The following year he joined 105, an Oudax squadron, and then became an instructor at No 3 Flying Training School. After staff appointments in Nos 20 and 23 Groups in 1940, he joined No 142 in 1941 and later that year became commander of 12 Squadron Wellingtons at Binbrook. In 1942 he took command of 108 Squadron in the Western Desert but in August was shot down. He bailed out but injured his leg as he landed. After surviving in the desert for three days he was captured by the Germans and taken to Stalag Luft III.

He was a striking figure in the camp, decked out in a bright yellow shirt with a large red neckerchief, grey flannel trousers, Egyptian sandals and pink socks. These were the clothes he was wearing when he was shot down.

"I thought I'd dress like a foreigner so that I wouldn't be noticed if I had to bail out," he explained. "But I must have dressed as the wrong sort of foreigner."

After the war he returned to Lincolnshire and farmed at Welton, near Lincoln, before retiring to the Wolds village of Walesby.

He leaves a widow, Janet, and three children, Michael, Jocelyn and Tessa.

b 24.6.06   d 19.8.92   aged 86

BRIGADIER PETER MOORE

Brigadier Peter Neil Moore, DSO and two Bars, MC, a specialist in laying minefields at El Alamein who later fought in Yugoslavia and Korea.

AS HIS three DSOs and his MC suggest, Peter Moore was a man of immense courage, a great leader and a dedicated soldier, who should have risen to three or four star rank had it not been for an unfortunate clash of personalities in the latter half of his career. A quiet, very modest man with acute battle insincts, he was less at home in jobs requiring a measure of diplomacy than in those demanding forthright, determined leadership.

Educated at Clifton College, the Royal Military Academy, Woolwich, and Trinity Hall, Cambridge, he was commissioned into the Royal Engineers in 1931; joined the Bombay Sappers and Miners in 1935; and saw active service in Waziristan. He left India in 1940 for Egypt as Staff Captain "Q" in the 7th Indian Brigade of 4th Indian Division and took part in the opening phases of the Eritrean campaign in early 1941.

Posted to the 2nd Armoured Division in the Western Desert, he was captured by the Germans during Rommel's first surprise offensive in April 1941. He managed to escape with the help of Bedouin tribesmen after barely four days as a prisoner of war. He won his MC during the desert operations that summer.

He had a natural aptitude for desert fighting, a flair for mine warfare, and an enthusiasm for blowing up disabled German tanks before their excellent recovery crews could save them. He commanded the 1st Field Squadron of the 1st Armoured Division in the battles of Gazala in the summer of 1942 and was wounded just before the fall of Tobruk.

But he was back in action again with his squadron in time to play a very full part in the desperate defence of the Alamein line in July, when he excelled in nightly forays to lay new minefields and strengthen existing ones. It became a standing joke amongst his men that anyone displeasing the sergeant-major would be detailed as the officer commanding's scout car driver.

The poacher turned gamekeeper in the preparation for the final battle of El Alamein. Moore was made responsible for devising the sapper drills for breaching the six successive belts of mines protecting the German positions. He did this by forming and commanding the 8th Army's highly successful minefield clearance school.

In the battle itself he commanded the 3rd Field Squadron in the 10th Armoured Division. In the midst of the armoured battles fought to break out from the minefield lanes he surprised and drove the German crew off one of the dreaded 88mm guns with his sub-machinegun and destroyed it with one of the explosive charges he always carried in his scout car for tank destruction. He was awarded his first DSO for his services at El Alamein.

His second DSO came for his work with the Yugoslav partisan forces in Slovenia from 1943 to 1945 where he was an outstanding member of Fitzroy Maclean's mission to Marshal Tito. It was partly on his advice that the decision was taken to give all-out support to Tito and to jettison Mihajlocić. He had a genius for adjusting to Partisan life and won the Partisans' respect through his successful operations with them, such as the demolition of the strategically important Stampetov bridge.

His third DSO was awarded in Korea where he commanded the 28th Field Engineer Regiment in the Commonwealth Division, one squadron of which was Canadian. The flavour of his extraordinary gifts as a sapper commander comes through in the citation: "Lieutenant-Colonel Moore's courage is a byword throughout the whole division. Never once has he committed a sapper to any task until he was personally satisfied that it was reasonable and every step taken to ensure success. Wherever there has been danger, there has been Lieutenant-Colonel Moore."

The tragedy of Moore's career was his appointment as commander of the Commonwealth Brigade in Malaya in 1957. His experience with Commonwealth troops in Korea suggested that he was just the right man for the job, but two factors were to tell against him. He had to compete with the Gurkhas, whose silent movement, enormous patience and very sharp marksmanship gave them a higher success rate and fewer casualties than Moore's British, Australian and New Zealand troops, despite his relentless drive and exacting standards.

The other factor was a personality clash, which developed between himself, a ''Pommy brigadier'', and the commander of his Australian battalion. With a tendency to be overdemanding and uncompromising in his standards, he showed that, *perhaps*, he did not have the sureness of touch for higher command. Sadly, that "perhaps" was enough to halt his further promotion.

He retired from the army in 1963. By then he was married and had a growing family to educate, so he started a new career as an administrative grade civil servant in the Ministry of Agriculture and Fisheries.

In 1976 he joined Reading University as a careers research officer and correspondence course tutor in maths and science subjects.

He married Rosemary Stokes in 1953, when he was 42. She and their two sons and three daughters survive him.

b 13.7.11   d 23.7.92   aged 81

ADMIRAL LUIGI DURAND DE LA PENNE

Italian naval officer who led the human torpedo attack on the port of Alexandria, Egypt which crippled two British battleships Valiant *and* Queen Elizabeth.

LUIGI de La Penne was Italy's most popular and widely-admired hero of the second world war and earned almost as much respect and admiration from his enemies as he did from his compatriots. In 1945, after Italy had joined forces with the allies, King Umberto went to Taranto to present de La Penne with an Italian medal for military valour. Senior British and American naval officers were present at the ceremony held by the quayside, and when the King was about to give de La Penne the medal he hesitated a moment, turned to Admiral Charles Morgan who had commanded HMS *Valiant* which de La Penne had badly damaged three and a half years earlier, and said: "Perhaps you would care to . . ." And Admiral Morgan pinned the medal to de La Penne's breast.

Luigi Durand de La Penne had enrolled as a cadet in the naval academy in Leghorn, and as soon as he was com-

The Royal Navy battleship HMS Valiant

missioned as a midshipman he joined the special unit which was already training with the "maiale", or "pig" for underwater attacks against shipping in harbours. The "maiale" was a seven-metre-long torpedo with controls for a two-man crew sitting astride. This crew guided the torpedo with its explosive charge through the harbour defences and under the enemy ships. The success of the Italian human torpedoes prompted the Royal Navy to develop its own devices, called "chariots", which were later used, unsuccessfully, to try to attack the German battleship *Tirpitz* in a Norwegian fjord.

Lieutenant de La Penne was the senior officer in the attack on Alexandria during the night of December 18-19, 1941. He steered his "maiale" through the harbour defences but when he came close to the battleship *Valiant* he lost control and the torpedo dropped to the seabed. His companion, Emilio Bianchi, became ill after hours under water and swam to the surface, while de La Penne painfully manhandled the torpedo under *Valiant*'s keel. Both de La Penne and Bianchi were captured when they surfaced and put deep below the battleship's waterline to

encourage them to reveal the timing and exact position of the explosive charge. The charge was set for 6am, but it was only at 5.50am that de La Penne asked to speak to Admiral Morgan and advised him to abandon ship because ten minutes later it would blow up. Morgan evacuated his crew and at 6.06 *Valiant*'s bottom was torn open by over 600lbs of explosive. The ship began listing and slowly settled into the mud of the harbour. A few minutes later the battleship *Queen Elizabeth*, attacked by another human torpedo, suffered a similar fate.

De La Penne was sent to a prisoner of war camp in India. But he returned to Italy after his country made peace in September 1943 and fought with the allies against the Germans until the end of the war.

De La Penne retired from the navy in the early 1950s having reached the rank of admiral. He was subsequently elected an MP in five successive Italian parliaments, first with the Christian Democratic Party and later with the Liberal Party.

Luigi Durand de La Penne leaves his widow, Leri and a son, Renzo.

b 11.2.14   d 17.1.92   aged 77

CHRISTOPHER SILVERWOOD-COPE

Christopher Siverwood-Cope, wartime escaper, diplomat, overseas director of the CBI, 1968–80, and historian.

KIT Cope's life was characterised by unfailing strength of character in the face of wartime danger and hardship and physical handicap in later years. It was a life of remarkable variety and enterprise which the rigours of wartime imprisonment – and maltreatment at the hands of the Gestapo – may have made more difficult but could do nothing to subvert. Permanently injured though his health was by his wartime experiences, it did not prevent him from enjoying post-war careers in the Foreign Service and as a vigourous head of the CBI's overseas directorate, based in Europe. He held the latter post at a time when British membership of the EEC was, first, very much on the agenda and then became a reality; as such Cope was at the centre of discussions with, and surveys of, British businesses as they geared up to meet the challenges consequent upon membership. Finally, in retirement, Cope was able to indulge himself in research on aspects of history which interested him, and he wrote two books.

The son of an English father and an American mother, he was educated at Malvern and Magdalen College, Oxford, where he read history. Twelve months after his arrival in Oxford, war was declared. He promptly volunteered for the Royal Artillery and by March 1940 he was in France with the British Expeditionary Force as a subaltern.

Captured during the BEF's retreat to Dunkirk, he eventually found himself in the large camp at Laufen near Salzburg, where conditions were particularly unpleasant. Staightaway he stood out as a man of outstanding integrity and intellect. Transferred to another camp at Posen (now Poznan) early in 1941, he escaped with three friends. With the help of a local Polish resistance organisation they made their way to Warsaw, where they were sheltered by various Polish families while plans for their further travel were being worked out.

Unfortunately during this time he caught typhus, which was endemic in eastern Europe, and for several weeks he was gravely ill. He would probably have died if a Polish doctor and her daughter had not provided medical help and skilled nursing at great personal risk.

Early in 1942 while convalescing he and his friends were arrested and found themselves in Gestapo hands. There they remained, enduring extremely severe treatment and appalling conditions as the Gestapo tried to discover who had been hiding them. Eventually in November 1942, by which time the Gestapo had become convinced they could learn no more from them, the group were given back their prisoner-of-war status and sent to Colditz.

As might be expected, Cope made many new friends at Colditz, but he never quite recovered his health. Indeed, he was due to be repatriated in May 1944 on medical grounds because of the severe condition of his left leg, an after-effect of his typhus. But he was removed from the group at the very last minute, apparently because of Gestapo concern about his knowledge of what he had seen in Warsaw. During his movement by the Gestapo to and from their headquarters, he had had one of the earliest first-hand British experiences of the horrifying beginning of the Holocaust among the Polish Jews in the Warsaw Ghetto and its prison area.

After repatriation at the end of the war he joined the Foreign Service. He and his wife, a former Wren, had a rewarding round of diplomatic assignments in Paris, Rome, Ottawa and the Foreign Office, before going to Budapest shortly before the 1956 uprising, where events provided painful echoes of his wartime years in Warsaw. Subsequent posting to the Hague and to the UK delegation in Geneva, with special responsibility for relations within the European Free Trade Association (EFTA) advanced his career along promising lines.

However, in 1968 he responded to an invitation from the Confederation of British Industry to become director of what is now its international affairs directorate. Twenty years in the Diplomatic Service had equipped him admirably for the move to the CBI, which he served with distinction. He played a key role during the 1970s in the campaign to prepare British businesses for the challenges and opportunities of membership of the European Community, being the architect of a major CBI study analysing the issues and showing where the benefits lay. As the arguments pro and con Britain's entry heightened during the early 1970s he remained convinced that membership was

vital to the country's commercial future in the 1980s and beyond.

He also travelled the world for the CBI to meet business leaders in many coutries and to try to improve trading relations, and he was a tireless lobbyist for British business in Whitehall, at Westminster, in Brussels and in the London embassies of the UK's main trading partners.

His time with the CBI included a momentous return visit to Colditz in 1972 with the ready co-operation of his East German hosts. But in 1975 the pace told, and he suffered a major stroke during an Anglo-American seminar at Eastbourne, organised by the CBI, ironically on the day of the successful referendum on UK membership of the Common Market. Due almost certainly in part to the effects of his wartime illness, he was left with little control of his left leg and left side. This kept him for some months in hospital, but did not dampen his committment to the CBI. His bedside became a hospital office and soon he was back at work with a stick.

At the age of 61 he took early retirement and turned his mind to a meticulously researched study of the mediaeval kingdom of Burgundy – *Phoenix Frustrated* (1987) – a subject little covered by professional historians in previous years. This successful venture into a favourite field gave him perhaps as much satisfaction as any of his previous achievements, and he had just completed a further book on the factual background to the Arthurian legend before he died.

He leaves his widow, Bettina, and a son. Another son died in 1967.

b 24.7.19   d 30.4.92   aged 72

COLONEL
FRED TILSTON, VC

Canadian soldier who won the VC at the Hochwald on March 1, 1945.

ONLY a year ago, Fred Tilston, at 85, was walking the battlefields and military cemeteries in France, Germany and the Netherlands on his artificial legs. A companion was unwise enough at one site, soggy with rain, to complain about getting his feet wet. "Ah!" said Tilston, his one eye twinkling, "That's a problem I don't have to face!"

Tilston's VC exploit was really a first world war operation translated to the second world war. On March 1, 1945, at the Hochwald, this man who "never would make an officer" led his company across 500 yards of open ground with no tank support, just behind a creeping barrage. Wounded in the head, he charged into the enemy trenches, firing his Sten gun from the hip. Silencing a troublesome machine gun with a grenade,

he led his men into the wood where he received his first leg wound.

In hand-to-hand fighting, his company heavily outnumbered and depleted, Major Tilston consolidated a position that was never retaken, and was hit in the other leg. As the result of that action, he lost both legs and an eye – a heavy enough price even for a VC.

Nudging 40, he should not have been at the sharp end, especially as he had taken a bullet near the heart during training in 1941, and then barely survived in 1944, when his jeep struck a mine.

Tilston went from college to Toronto University, where he began what was to be, with the interruption of war, a brilliant pharmaceutical career. A reasonable sportsman with a passion for music, he was known to colleagues and friends as a quiet and amiable companion. He did well professionally with Sterling Products, of Windsor,

Ontario, up to the outbreak of the second world war, when he was commissioned into the Essex Scottish of Toronto, taking up his post in England in 1941. He always expressed bitter regret at missing the Dieppe raid because of his first wounding.

Sharp of eye, and sharp of mind and tongue, although never malicious, Fred Tilston remained a delightful companion, full of good stories and anecdotes, and a good listener when others were stimulated into yarning. On a visit to England some years ago, he was asked on radio what he supposed to be "the main characteristic in a man who is going to win the Victoria Cross". Tilston grinned, his single optic alive with humour and full appreciation of the situation. "Inexperience!" he replied.

When his original military examiners came to the conclusion that Fred Tilston "would never make an officer", they doubtless had in mind his reputation for mild behaviour and an irrepressible sense of fun, leading them to believe that he would never be capable of giving an order, or receiving one seriously. Although he often found it difficult to keep a straight face when listening to the weird and wonderful stories presented by soldiers who had overstayed leave or committed other minor misdemeanors, nonetheless, he was the sternest of men when confronted by the rare incident of meanness or pilfering, and no one could have led, inspired and controlled his men in action with tighter command.

Tilston returned to Sterling Products, in 1946, as vice-president in charge of sales, and he was president of Sterling Drug from 1957 to 1970. He was honorary colonel of the Essex and Kent Scottish Regiment and a supporter of the Canadian militia and the Canadian Legion.

Tilston's wife, Helen, whom he married in 1946, predeceased him. He leaves an adopted son.

b 11.6.06   d 23.9.92   aged 86

LT. JOHN WARREN

John Lynton George Warren, GM, won his George Medal when long range gun shells fell on Dover.

LIEUTENANT John Warren, a young officer in the so-called "Baby Buffs", the young soldiers' battalion of the Royal East Kent Regiment, was at a Dover cinema in March 1942 when the port was hit by a salvo of 380mm shells from the long range guns of the German *Batterie Todt*, located in the Pas de Calais.

As the cinema was evacuated, he ran through the blackout towards Market Square where crowds were gathering outside the smouldering ruins of the Carlton Club, the Conservative Party headquarters in the town. Several members were already dead, but one woman was still trapped inside, beneath tons of masonry.

Warren, a short wiry rugby wing three-quarter, was just small enough to wriggle through a gap in the smoking building. While a fellow subaltern, Ronald Brownrigg (now a retired Church of

England canon), held on to his legs, he burrowed his way ten feet into the rubble. Boys from the regiment, many of whom had joined up from a local reform school, helped pass him two car jacks which Warren used to prop up a beam which was threatening to suffocate the woman.

He then lay by her side for five perilous hours, wiping her face and injecting her with morphia under shouted instructions from a doctor up above, while rescue teams, guided by Warren, struggled to free them.

Next morning at Old Park barracks, he was carpeted for being late on the parade ground — much to the subsequent chagrin of the adjutant, who first learned of the drama on reading the local newspaper. But Warren's bravery was later rewarded with the George Medal and the "Carlton Club Incident" has been given its place in the long history of Dover.

Shortly afterwards, Warren was posted to the Western desert with The Buffs' 4th battalion, only to be captured in the following year while taking part in the ill-judged British diversionary expedition to the Greek island of Leros.

Imprisoned in Oflag 79 near Brunswick, he threw his energies into organising a unique charity. Arguing that their conditions were no worse than those being suffered by young people at home, he and fellow prisoners-of-war collected £13,000 in promissory notes and improvised cheques, most of which were honoured by the men on their release.

The fund went to the National Association of Boys' Clubs which, after challenging the British public to match the PoWs' generosity, used the proceeds to found the celebrated Brunswick club in West London. Warren always retained his close interest in the venture.

Warren commanded a boy soldiers' unit after the war and briefly toyed with the idea of signing on — before leaving the army as a major in 1947 and beginning an entirely different career.

Born at Battle in Sussex, he had left King's School, Bruton, as soon as possible and become a bank clerk — then considered a safe profession with sound prospects. But he disliked that even more than he did school and joined the army on the outbreak of war, almost with relief.

So in 1947 he became a farmer. After 12 months gaining experience on an uncle's farm in Sussex he went to Shuttleworth agricultural college in Bedfordshire, where he became the first president of the union and founded a students' magazine he christened *The Furrow*. He then worked for some time as a farm manager in Lincolnshire before inheriting, in 1955, a 200-acre farm in the River Wey valley which had been in his family for 200 years.

There he built up a herd of 100 pedigree Jerseys and he was at one time chairman of the Southern Jersey Cattle Society. He also became deeply interested in conservation, partly through the River Wey Trust. He restored a number of 17th century aqueducts and water meadows on his own land and fought for the preservation of local commons and heathland. He had been driving home from a National Trust meeting when he was fatally injured in a motor accident.

Ten years ago he sold most of his land and partly retired, to write his own book *River Running By* and spend more time on public work for, among others, local schools and the boy scouts. The heir to a long family Methodist tradition, he was also appointed national coordinator of the 1988 celebrations to mark the 250th anniversary of John Wesley's conversion.

A bachelor until his mid-forties, he fell in love with a young schoolmistress, Marion Mackenzie, who came to preach in his local chapel. He courted her with fresh farm cabbages on his milk round, so successfully that they were married in 1967. John Warren is survived by her and by their son.

b 19.4.21   d 3.10.92   aged 71

AIR VICE-MARSHAL BRIAN YOUNG

Air Vice-Marshal Brian Pashley Young, CB, CBE, South African airman who rose to become commandant-general of the RAF Regiment.

THE second world war was only a few months old when Brian Young baled out from his blazing Hurricane over Belgium, after being hit by a burst of fire from a Messerschmitt 109. The good news was that he landed in British lines, the bad news was that the British army shot him.

One soldier wounded him three times with a machine gun while another threw a grenade which was to leave him with a permanent scar on one side. Only when they drew near did one of them cry out: "My God, he's British." Young, barely conscious, managed to reply: "No, actually I'm South African." But the worst day of his young life was not yet over. The ambulance rushing him to catch a hospital ship to England was caught in an air raid on entering the port. Young was thrown from the top bunk while other injured servicemen fell on top of him. When the raid was over and rescue teams arrived, he was found to be the only one still alive.

Severely burnt, he spent the next two years in hospital at Basingstoke where he met his future wife, a trainee nurse. That he did not lose the use of his hands was due to the pioneering treatment of his surgeon Sir Harold Gillies, who forced his patients to keep exercising their muscles. Though desperately painful it led to his almost complete recovery.

His peripheral vision was slightly impaired, however — not enough to ground him but enough to end his days with Fighter Command. Instead, he was posted to 422 squadron, a Canadian Coastal Command unit in Northern Ireland, operating Sunderland flying-boats against U-boats in the Atlantic.

Once more Young narrowly escaped with his life. Directed to a target at the limit of the aircraft's range, then ordered to wait while a bomber arrived, he only just managed to get back, his fuel tanks virtually empty. He spent 1944 operating over Aden and the Gulf, based on the island of Masirah, then saw out the war at the staff college in Haifa.

Brian Young had always dreamed of being a pilot. A lawyer/farmer's son from Natal who could speak Zulu almost before he could manage English, he went to Michael House School, then won one of two scholarships for South Africans at the RAF College, Cranwell. He was not even among the official candidates, but when one of these dropped out he turned up for the examination in his place and persuaded the authorities to accept him. He had already proved himself a leader and sportsman at school and held the South African schoolboys' record for the quarter-mile.

During 1936–38 at Cranwell, however, he not only won the Sword of Honour but displayed an unexpected talent for writing poetry. His three-stanza poem called "Flight", written in 1937, has become a familiar part of RAF literature and has been frequently published and broadcast.

He moved to Bomber Command in 1951, later commanding a V-bomber force of Valiants at Gaydon. During 1958–60 he was group captain (operations) at Bomber Command headquarters near High Wycombe where he continued to be closely associated with the nuclear threat and Britain's strategic deterrent.

A similar theme ran through his next posting at Nato's military headquarters (Shape) near Paris, where he found himself working on the allied response to a nuclear strike. In an attempt to get across his message at one lecture he let off a thunderflash inside the hall, following this with pictures of a nuclear burst. The effect was so graphic and nerve-wracking that a visiting French general stormed out and ruled that it should never be tried again.

His career, until then that of a high flier, seemed to stall at that point, however. Already an air commodore, Young was to move up only one more rank – a source of disappointment to him. He became assistant chief of staff (intelligence) in London before being given command of the unglamorous Central Reconnaissance Establishment. Then, in 1968, he was made finally commandant-general of the RAF Regiment, staying in the job for five years before retiring.

On leaving the RAF he accepted a post as a Department of the Environment planning inspector, which he filled for ten years. He also acted as technical assessor during the inquiry into London's new City Airport.

Brian Young's schoolboy athleticism remained with him throughout his life. He ran the quarter mile and 100 yards for the RAF and played rugby for the RAF and Wasps. He was on the wing for Wasps when they won the Middlesex Sevens in 1948 and was captain in 1950–51.

At the age of 54 he took part in the services' annual Nijmegen marches, covering 25 miles a day for four days in weather so hot and humid that several men died. He overtook those half his age to get back in time to take the salute at the final march-past.

Brian Young is survived by his wife, Pat, and by their three sons and two daughters.

b 5.5.18   d 26.7.92   aged 74

COLONEL MAURICE BUCKMASTER

Colonel Buckmaster with Mrs Odette Hallowes GC

Colonel Maurice Buckmaster, OBE, head of the "independent French" or F section of the Special Operations Executive from 1941 to 1945.

AS Spymaster of the French Section of the Special Operations Executive it was Maurice Buckmaster's task to organise the activities of the British agents sent to spy, carry out sabotage and recruit resistance groups in occupied France. This had to be done without the advantage of being able to make use of such Frenchmen as succeeded in escaping from France, for although the SOE worked alongside the Free French movement they were entirely separate. It was regarded as remarkable that the SOE was able to find more than 150 British officers whose French was good enough for them to be passed off as Frenchmen and who had, at the same time, the courage and capacity for such hazardous tasks. Among the more famous of SOE's recruits were Odette Hallowes, who was tortured by the Germans and awarded the George Cross, and Violette Szabo, who received a posthumous George Cross after being tortured and shot by the Germans in Ravensbruck in 1945.

Every care was taken to ensure that the individual agents knew only what was necessary to enable them to carry out their particular task. Buckmaster alone had to contrive to know, from London, what was going on in every district of France. There was no easy system of passwords to establish camaraderie between one agent and another. Although the special agents themselves undertook many specific jobs of sabotage, they sought, on the whole, to get the French to work for themselves, thereby enabling them to fight for their self-respect as well as their freedom, while at the same time the agents showed, by their presence, that they were willing to share the peril and to aid them to do the utmost with arms and other materials. Nearly everywhere the response was magnificent – the great problem became how to control them.

The cost of the SOE's cloak and dagger activities was high. Out of some 400 agents operating under Buckmaster's command in more than 80 networks, 117 were killed, many of them being tortured beforehand.

Years after the war Buckmaster and the SOE came under attack at home. Accusations were made in 1958 that the SOE had been run in an amateurish manner, that it was infiltrated by German intelligence, that it suffered betrayals which led to the arrest of many men and women, and that these shortcomings had been deliberately concealed. Buckmaster responded by saying that the SOE was no more amateurish than many other wartime units. He confirmed that the Germans had penetrated one important *reseau* but only one. He described as

monstrous and categorically denied the allegation that 47 British agents had deliberately been dropped to the Germans to distract their attention from other undercover operations.

Maurice James Buckmaster was educated at Eton and made an early intellectual mark by teaching French to those only a few years younger than himself who were trying to pass Common Entrance. This natural talent for languages was to set the pattern for the rest of his life. As a young man he worked on *France-Soir* and then, from 1923–29, for the merchant bankers J. Henry Schroder & Co before becoming publicity manager, then manager of the Ford motor company's French operation and, from 1936–39, head of its European department.

When the second world war began he was commissioned into the Intelligence Corps and was one of the last officers to be evacuated from the French coast near Dunkirk. His linguistic skills – he had by then perfected German – made him a natural candidate for the highly specialised work of the SOE into which he was co-opted, first as a staff officer in F Section and then as head of the Belgian section and, from December 1941, as head of F Section.

His knowledge of France and the French, his gift of leadership, immense energy and enthusiasm, instinctive love of people and, ultimately, his extraordinary capacity for achieving what he believed to be right, made him an extremely effective leader of what was a critical area of operations and proved to be one of the greatest thorns in the side of the Nazis. It was said that Hitler so reviled Buckmaster that he had put him as the third person on a target list if the German invasion of Britain had gone ahead.

Buckmaster's critics complained that he found it hard to delegate, had no first hand experience of the clandestine life of his agents and favoured some agents above others. He certainly had favourites and was equally highly regarded by them. Buckmaster was that sort of man.

His fierce and sometimes

uncompromising loyalty to his own people could at times upset and irritate the military establishment. He was four rungs down the SOE ladder of command and the SOE system was such that officers, like Buckmaster, who commanded "country sections" had to be left to make most of their own decisions about men and measures, within broad outlines laid down from above, and often in dangerous ignorance of each other's doings.

One of the sections with which he had to liaise, representing the Gaullists, regarded F Section as a tiresome rival. Indeed, de Gaulle was openly critical of F Section. But the SOE maintained F's separate identity, in spite of de Gaulle's protests.

Such political ripples undoubtedly contributed to the fact that the OBE was the sole British honour accorded to Buckmaster, inadequate recognition of his contribution to the war effort. The French were later to make him an officer of the Légion d'Honneur and streets were named after him in France.

Running any of the SOE sections was an intensive and 24 hour a day task. By the summer of 1944, in spite of a determined effort by the Gestapo to suppress them all in the previous winter and spring, about half of the *reseaux* were still operational. Their strength and breadth of operation caused severe disruption to vital German military movements to the north at the time of the D-Day landings and they gave invaluable assistance to the advancing allied armies.

After D-day all SOE's forces in France were amalgamated under General Koenig, who had Buckmaster as one of his three chiefs of staff. Following his demobilisation, Buckmaster returned to work for the Ford motor company – this time in Britain – and became head of the company's public relations department, serving a number of chief executives before moving to London where he became a public relations consultant. His love affair with France continued and in 1961 he was invited by the governing body of the Champagne industry to represent them in London. He held this post until the early 1980s.

Buckmaster appeared as himself in Herbert Wilcox's film *Odette* in which Anna Neagle played the leading role. Their friendship lasted the rest of her lifetime. He published two books on the Resistance, presenting F Section's work in semi-fictionalised form; indeed, while he was happy and at ease to talk about certain aspects of his work during that critical period of history, he maintained a reluctance to reveal any "secrets".

Failing health prevented him travelling to Annecy for the unveiling, in May 1991, of a memorial to the Resistance attended by the Queen Mother, who wrote a note reflecting her personal sadness at his absence. It was a personal touch that reflected the affection felt for Buckmaster by the royal family during the second world war.

From his first marriage he had a son and two daughters and he married again in 1944, a marriage that was to last more than 40 years until he was widowed in 1988. There were no children of this marriage.

Although a man of his time, Buckmaster had that rare quality of inspiring affection and respect, none less than among the young French people he met at the annual Resistance reunion in Paris.

b 11.1.02   d 17.4.92   aged 90

LT COMMANDER
HAROLD HARVEY

Harold Harvey, a lifeboat inspector whose bravery in the rescue of crew from a stricken Greek freighter off the Welsh coast in 1966 won him a gold medal.

HAROLD Harvey's courage and initiative won him the unusual honour of the RNLI's gold medal for gallantry. The distinction is so rare that it has been conferred only nine times since the end of the second world war. The service for which Harvey earned his resulted in the award of two of those nine gold medals. It was for the rescue of the crew of the Greek motor vessel *Nafsiporos*.

The *Nafsiporos* was reported in difficulties in the Irish Sea on the morning of December 2, 1966. Harold Harvey, the inspector of lifeboats for the north-west, happened to be in Holyhead when the report came through. With the agreement of the crew, he joined the Holyhead lifeboat whose coxswain was Thomas Alcock. A severe north-westerly gale, force 10, was blowing and gusting to force 11. Because of flying spindrift visibility was down to 500 yards.

Two other lifeboats, those stationed at

Douglas in the Isle of Man, and Moelfre in Anglesey, were also called out. When the Holyhead and Moelfre lifeboats approached the *Nafsiporos* she was seen to roll up to 35 degrees either side of the vertical. She was pitching so much that her forefoot bilge keels and propellor were, in turn, clear of the water. She could not be brought up into the wind. A Russian timber vessel, the *Kunkurley*, managed to get a towline aboard her but, because of the tremendous strength of the wind and the sea conditions, attempts to bring the *Nafsiporos* head to wind were unsuccessful and the tow parted.

By this time there was no longer enough sea room for any attempt to be made to reconnect the tow. The *Nafsiporos* scraped close past the Ethel Rock Buoy and dropped her port anchor, but it failed to hold. She continued to drag until she fetched up less than a quarter of a mile from the rocks. Here the depth of the water was only about six fathoms.

While waiting for the *Nafsiporos* to be brought to her anchor the Holyhead lifeboat had been hove to less than a quarter of a mile off her port quarter. Coxswain Alcock, in command of the Holyhead lifeboat, brought her round the stern. The *Nafsiporos* then gave an extreme roll to starboard. Her counter crashed heavily on the port quarter of the lifeboat causing considerable damage. Coxswain Alcock had to go full ahead and hard to starboard to avoid any further damage.

The starboard boat of the *Nafsiporos* was hanging vertically from the after davit and the jumping ladder, down which the crew would have to come, was only about half a boat's length abaft the hanging boat. At this stage Coxswain Alcock asked Harold Harvey to take command, a decision which was stated in the official report to demand both physical and moral courage on his part.

Late in the afternoon Harold Harvey shaped up for the final run in. Four survivors were taken aboard. Then, just after the fifth survivor had followed them, the falls of the ship's boat parted and the boat came crashing down. Harvey, foreseeing this danger, had kept the lifeboat's engine astern and they were put at full throttle. The alarm was shouted and the men on the deck of the lifeboat just managed to jump aft before the ship's boat crashed down on the deck. The ten other members of the *Nafsiporos*'s crew were rescued by the Moelfre lifeboat in an equally hazardous operation for which Coxswain Richard Evans was also awarded the RNLI's gold medal. . he *Nafsiporos* was eventually towed to safety by the Dutch tug *Utrecht*.

Harold Harvey was in the service of the RNLI from 1952 to 1973. He had earlier served as an observer in the Fleet Air Arm where he saw service on Russian convoys and in the Mediterranean.

His is survived by his wife, Margaret, by his daughters, Imogen and Madelaine, and by a son, Mark.

b 17.9.20   d 23.8.92   aged 71

KATE TER HORST

Kate ter Horst "the angel of Arnhem".

KATE TER HORST, a gifted, determined and courageous Dutch woman, won a unique place in the hearts of the 1st British Airborne Division through her heroism during the nine days of desperate action in September 1944 to secure the Arnhem Bridge.

The affection in which she was held was demonstrated by the many veterans of the battle who visited her every year, to whom she was known as "the angel of Arnhem".

Kate Arriens was the daughter of a Dutch naval officer. Married in 1930 to a lawyer, Jan ter Horst, she came in 1941 to live in the old pastor's house at Oosterbeek, a small town to the west of Arnhem. It was this house which quickly became a British medical post when the airborne troops landed on September 17, 1944, at the start of the Battle of Arnhem.

Her husband was cut off from the house by the fighting but she remained there with her five children throughout the eight days of the battle. The house was badly damaged in the ferocious fighting; one shell went straight through it. But in the basement she ministered continuously to the wounded and dying: more than 200 lay packed on the floor at any one time. She shared everything she had with them. At the height of the fighting she read aloud Psalm 91, " I will say of the Lord, He is my refuge and my fortress . . .'', a scene portrayed movingly by Liv Ullman in the film *A Bridge Too Far*. When the battle was over more than 50 British soldiers were buried in a grave in her garden and she and her children were forced to leave their home immediately with one small cart load of possessions. But some years later the horror of the battle returned tragically when her eldest son jumped from a tree in her garden on to an unexploded mine and was killed instantly.

Kate ter Horst was a revered participant each year at the commemoration of the Battle of Arnhem initiated by her husband, as mayor of Oosterbeek, and by General Urquhart, who had commanded the 1st Airborne Division throughout the battle.

The veterans, from general to private soldier, who came to see her year after year had a special place in her heart. Her profound spiritual strength, which had carried her through the ordeal of the battle of Arnhem, was felt by all who knew her. She was a person of great modesty, but was intensely proud of the honorary OBE which had been awarded to her.

b 6.7.06   d 21.2.92   aged 85

Kate ter Horst with Prince Charles

MICHAEL LEES

Michael Lees, SOE officer and Serbophile.

MICHAEL Lees went directly from school into the second world war and the rest of his life was to be determined by the experience. He came of a Dorset landed family with a military tradition. He was the grandson of Sir Elliott Lees, Bt, a former MP for Oldham. His own father's career was cut short by premature death on service in Nigeria, and he was brought up by his mother, a Yorkshire Radcliffe.

After education at Ampleforth, Michael Lees joined the Dorset Yeomanry and in India transferred to a parachute battalion which was then sent to the Middle East. In Cairo he heard about the Special Operations Executive and wangled himself into that organisation with its promise of exotic and unregimented action. In June 1943, at the age of 22, he parachuted into Yugoslavia as leader of a mission to the Chetnik guerrillas commanded by General Mihailovic. He was meant to replace an SOE officer captured by the Bulgarians, who occupied much of Serbia on behalf of the Germans. Within 48 hours of landing his mission was almost wiped out by Bulgarians who savagely murdered some of his men as they lay wounded.

Lees's force was reconstituted and ordered to attack the Nis-Salonika railway, a vital German link. At this time Mihailovic's commanders were under orders not to undertake actions which might result in further heavy reprisals against Serb civilians but to await the day of a national rising. Despite this, Lees persuaded the commanders in his area to support him in blowing up two long sections of the line, and in the derailment of six trains.

Lees was then hampered by the failure of SOE to drop him the supplies he needed. Britain had decided to withdraw support from Mihailovic and switch it entirely to Tito's Partisans. It was an action which Michael Lees criticised bitterly. In December 1943 he was ordered to suspend operations and pull out with all his fellow officers from the Mihailovic operation. SOE did not want him in Yugoslavia any longer. But it was to be five nerve-wracking months before most of them were evacuated.

At SOE headquarters in Italy, Lees met Gwen Johnson, a FANY officer, and two months later married her in Bari cathedral. After the honeymoon he parachuted into Piedmont to join Italian guerrillas. After seeing some brisk action he was asked to escort two delegates from the Piedmontese liberation committee with an urgent report for the allies. Air pickup was impossible so Lees set out to lead the party into France over the Maritime Alps and across the line where Germans were fighting Americans. On the way he wiped out a German artillery post, and nearly stumbled into a minefield. But he got the delegates safely into allied territory − and out to Italy.

In January 1945 Lees parachuted on his third mission − to an Italian guerrilla division in the Appennine mountains west of Reggio Emilia. For the next two months he helped to prepare the division for the spring offensive, fighting off German and Italian fascist attempts to destroy it. In March he planned and led an attack on a German army corps HQ in a villa at Albinea. For this his Italians were joined by an SAS detachment commanded by Major Roy Farran, complete with piper. The attack was successful but Lees was brought down by four bullets on the staircase of the villa. Severely wounded and unable to walk, he was hidden for several days in a barn before the Italians could get him back into guerrilla territory, using an ox-drawn manure cart with a false bottom. He was picked up from a mountain terrace by an Italian pilot in a captured Storch spotter-plane and finally brought to a British hospital in Naples.

Lees was twice recommended for the DSO and once for the MC, but no award was made, nor was he promoted major. A series of operations failed to restore a severed sciatic nerve, and for the rest of his life he suffered disability and pain. He went into business and became managing director of an international company in London, but in 1971 his disability forced him into early retirement. He then took up cattle and fruit farming in Ireland.

In 1950, during one of his recurrent spells in hospital, Lees had written an account of his SOE missions and in 1986 it was published as *Special Operations Executed*. Researching to check details, he consulted SOE files in the Public Record Office and was so incensed by what he found out about Yugoslavia that he embarked on what became his last mission. Like many of the liaison officers with the Chetnik Serbs he had always felt that they had been unfairly treated, and that Mihailovic had been first let down, then abandoned in favour of Tito, and finally branded as a traitor by the British.

Lees now believed he had documentary evidence which proved how this came about. It formed the basis of his next book, *The Rape of Serbia: The British Role in Tito's Grab for Power*. Its thesis is that Tito was able to seize power and impose communism on Yugoslavia for 45 years because of the British support he was given. Lees also argued that Churchill was persuaded into giving that support on the basis of one-sided information. The main sufferers under Tito were the Serbs who had remained loyal to their king and to the allies until the Chetniks were crushed and Mihailovic was executed. Because it involved the overturning of an account of history that had held official sway for 40 years, and called into question the judgment of certain British protagonists, no British publisher would accept the book. It was published in America in 1990.

The book was translated and published in Yugoslavia and became a best-seller. On a promotional tour Lees was fêted by grateful Serbs of all ages – from veteran Chetniks to young anti-communists who still see in Mihailovic a martyr-hero to inspire them in their struggle against the Milosevic hardliners. With Yugoslavia locked once more in civil strife, Lees took his stand unquestioningly alongside the Serbs, whom he feared were about to be let down again by the British. Virtually single-handed he set out to redress the general partiality of the British media for the Croats. He began a campaign of letters to the press, to government ministers and officials; he addressed meetings in Canada and in Britain, and helped to organise a lobby at Westminster.

Although his health was deteriorating Lees went to the Serb enclave of Krajina to visit the front together with his wife Gwen. In the past two months he had appeared in four BBC television programmes, two to plead the case for the Serbs in the current crisis, and two to put across his view of how Tito bamboozled Churchill.

Lees spent the day he died at his desk intent on his crusade. He had brought to it the great force of personality, the single-mindedness and the courage which had characterised his life. It is not given to many men to die happy in fighting a cause first embraced in youth.

b 17.5.21   d 23.3.92   aged 70

COMMANDER SIR CLIVE LOEHNIS

Commander Sir Clive "Joe" Loehnis, KCMG, former director of the Government Communications Headquarters (GCHQ).

JOE Loehnis (the "Joe" dated from his childhood) was associated with the growth of GCHQ during the cold war when advances in technology enabled a significant expansion in signals intelligence.

But he learnt his craft during the hot war, when the Germans not the Russians were the enemy, in the Admiralty's Operational Intelligence Centre (OIC). He was deeply involved there in the Ultra operation, under which German signals tapped out on their Enigma machines were intercepted and decoded. The Ultra programme has often been described as the greatest secret in the war after the atomic bomb.

He began in the OIC's subsection handling the naval intercepts, a crucial factor in the Battle of the Atlantic against Hitler's U-boats. But he was later promoted an assistant to the director,

liaising between the OIC and Bletchley Park, site of the government's Code and Cipher School (GC and CS), where some of the country's most brilliant analytical minds were engaged in successfully decrypting the signals.

His reputation as a rising star was evidenced in 1944 when he accompanied the director of naval intelligence, the head of Bletchley Park and his own counterpart at Bletchley, Harry Hinsley (later Professor Sir Harry Hinsley, the official historian of intelligence during the war) on a world tour. The quartet visited the Middle East, India, the Far East, Australasia and the United States to plan how best to switch intelligence resources to the Pacific as the war in Europe gave precedence to that against Japan.

A secondary purpose of their talks, however, was to look at the long-term potential of signals intelligence — all of which was to prove valuable for Loehnis. Although demobilised in 1945, he was immediately re-employed by the Foreign Office when the GC and CS moved from Bletchley Park to Cheltenham and was reconstituted as GCHQ. He rose to become its deputy director in 1952 and next its director, 1960–64. He then retired, but later served on the Civil Service Selection Board as deputy chairman between 1967 and 1970.

Joe Loehnis (his forbears fled to Britain from Austria during the Napoleonic Wars) would probably have succeeded in any one of a dozen professions. The son of a barrister at the Inner Temple who died when about to take silk and when Joe was only two years old, he won a scholarship from his preparatory school to Winchester, but turned it down in favour of joining the Royal Navy.

He was educated at the naval colleges of Osborne and Dartmouth and, as a midshipman shortly after the first world war, served in HMS *Renown* on a tour of the Far East with the then Prince of Wales, the future King Edward VIII. He then qualified as a signals officer, doing well enough to be chosen for an advanced "dagger" signals course at Greenwich and went on to serve as flag lieutenant to the commander-in-chief Atlantic in the battleship *Nelson*.

He retired early from the navy in 1935, however. Six years previously he had married Rosemary Beryl Ryder, whose father was the youngest son of the Earl of Harrowby. With a young family to look after, Loehnis like many a young officer, had tired of life at sea with its long periods of separation.

With another retired naval officer, Anthony Kimmins, he went into film production. But after turning out B feature "movies" for two or three years, employing some of Hollywood's less celebrated stars, his signals experience prompted the Admiralty to recall him. It was 1938, the year of Munich, and events were to chart the subsequent course of his career.

Despite his technical knowledge, skills and experience, Loehnis's chief contribution to British intelligence was made through his administrative ability. A short but broad-shouldered man, his cool, easy, economical style had a reassuring influence on Whitehall during some of the most difficult years in Eas-West relations. He divided his time between Cheltenham and London, commuting by car to and from his apartment in Belgravia.

Joe Loehnis, who was knighted in 1962, is survived by his wife and by one son and a daughter.

b 24.8.02   d 23.5.92   aged 89

THOMAS OTTEN PAINE

American head of NASA who was responsible for putting the first man on the moon.

THE FIFTEEN months between March 1969, when he was chosen to head the National Aeronautics and Space Administration, and July 1970, when he resigned, were a time of glory for Thomas Paine. The Apollo programme soared into space, Neil Armstrong became the first human being to set foot on the moon, and an America immersed in the agony of Vietnam at last had something to cheer about. Paine had been lucky. All the preparatory work for the moon mission had been done by his predecessor, James Webb. But with the election of President Nixon in November 1968 Webb had been forced to step aside for a Republican appointee, and Paine, who had been appointed as deputy administrator earlier that year, got the job. Lacking political credentials, he had not been Nixon's first choice, but he proved to be a wise one, handling both his scientists and engineers and the agency's relations with Congress with equal skill.

Even before the historic moon-walk, Paine was making ambitious plans for the future. He envisaged the shuttle programme, a monster space-station, and manned trips to Mars before the turn of the century. He was also an enthusiastic advocate of international cooperation in space, fostering contacts with European and Soviet scientists.

Once the lunar goal had been achieved, however, the purse-strings began to tighten. The Nixon administration announced that it would be chopping NASA's budget by $500 million in 1971, and it must have seemed to the 48-year-old Paine that his grandoise ideas were unlikely to get support. He resigned "for personal reasons" after a 20-minute meeting with the president in the Western White House at San Clemente.

Paine went back to work for the General Electric Company, which he had left to take up his government appointment, and was promptly made a vice-president. He stayed there until 1976, then joined the Northrop Corporation from which he retired in 1982. The son of a naval architect, Paine gained a bachelor's degree in engineering from Brown University and was then commissioned in the US Navy shortly after America entered the second world war. He volunteered for submarine service, qualified as a deep sea diver, and took part in seven war patrols ranging from Indonesia to the coast of Siberia. It was, he said later, an indelible experience: "We were the last of the corsairs, and the life of an Oriental pirate is given to few people. We were part of the tooth-and-claw simplicity of the sea."

In 1946 Paine married and went to graduate school at Stanford University, where he received a master's degree and a Ph.D in physical metallurgy. He joined General Electric as a research associate in 1949, and although the company's rigid hierarchy was alien to his temperament, constant promotions kept him there. In 1963 he was put in charge of the company's think-tank and there demonstrated his ability to mediate between a bunch of disorderly deep-thinkers and the nervous executives at head office. It was a talent that got him noticed; exactly what NASA needed. And it led him, if only intellectually, to the stars.

Thomas Paine is survived by his wife, two sons and two daughters.

b 9.11.21   d 4.5.92   aged 70

GIORGIO PERLASCA

Giorgio Perlasca, Italian livestock agent and businessman who saved the lives of thousands of Hungarian Jews during the second world war.

IT WAS his record as an enthusiastic fascist and a fighter for Franco in the Spanish Civil War, together with his sense of humanity and bravery, that enabled Giorgio Perlasca to rescue, from his base in Budapest, at least 5,000 Jews from deportation to Hitler's gas chambers between 1944 and 1945.

Like the Swedish diplomat Raul Wallenberg, Perlasca provided Jews who were about to be deported with false papers to enable them to escape from Nazi persecution and find refuge in a neutral country. Unlike Wallenberg, he was not a real diplomat, and while Wallenberg's fame has been magnified by his mysterious disappearance in Soviet custody, Perlasca returned to a life of obscurity in Italy after the war.

Giorgio Perlasca was born into a middle-class Catholic family in Como. A youthful admirer of Mussolini, he served as a volunteer with Italian forces in Abyssinia before fighting for Franco in the Spanish Civil War. But the introduction of racial laws in Italy and the alliance with Hitler's Germany destroyed the last residues of his fast waning admiration for the Italian dictator. Having been called up by the Italian army in 1938, he soon found himself at odds with his superior officers, and was discharged after a couple of months.

Perlasca then devoted his energy to cattle trading, working for a while in Yugoslavia and subsequently in Hungary. After the fall of Mussolini in July 1943, Perlasca was interned as an enemy alien in a camp near the Austrian border but three months later escaped and returned to Budapest. There he was able to use his service in the Spanish Civil War to claim the protection of the Spanish embassy in Budapest. He returned the favour by helping the embassy with its programme of assistance to Hungarian Jews.

Spain, along with other neutral states such as Sweden, Switzerland, Portugal and the Vatican, was active in protecting Jews claiming any link to a neutral country. They were provided with refuge in safe houses and papers so that they could leave Hungary.

Such efforts were much needed. Of the 825,000 people considered to be Jews living on Hungarian territory, 565,000 perished in the Holocaust between 1941 and 1945. Perlasca is credited with personally saving around 5,200, and some 25,000 emerged from the safe houses of the neutral embassies in Budapest at the end of the war.

After the departure of the Spanish envoy to Budapest in November 1944, Perlasca simply stepped into his shoes and, with the aid of an embassy seal which had been left behind, passed himself off as the new Spanish consul in order to continue providing protection to Jewish refugees. It was a miracle that the imposter was not unmasked, but the impossibility of direct communication between Budapest and Madrid was certainly an advantage.

Perlasca has described how the representatives of the neutral countries, including himself and Wallenberg, would visit the Budapest railway station to attempt an 11th hour rescue of those about to be deported.

On one occasion, Perlasca said, he and Wallenberg succeeded in snatching two 12-year-old boys, identical twins, from no less a person than Adolf Eichmann. Perlasca dragged them out of a queue of deportees and bundled them into the Spanish embassy car.

The fake Spanish consul "Jorge" Perlasca succeeded in representing his adoptive country in Budapest for six weeks until January 16, 1945, when Soviet troops entered the city. After the last embassy car broke down Perlasca would march through the streets of Budapest accompanied by a policeman carrying the Spanish flag.

After the war Perlasca lived in almost total obscurity until a group of Holocaust survivors succeeded in tracking him down to his home in Padua in 1989. Following this he was honoured by Israel and received official recognition for his actions in the United States, Spain and Hungary.

When he visited Jerusalem to receive the tribute of the Israeli government a woman approached him and presented him with a single rose. With it was a note reading "You saved two members of my family and with them my faith in human kind, a faith which was disappearing."

Perlasca himself gave a modest explanation of his wartime choices. "I could not bear the sight of people being branded like animals. I could not bear to see children being killed. I think it was this, I don't think I was a hero. I saw people being killed and, simply, I could not bear it. I had the chance to act and I acted. Anyone would have done the same thing in my place."

b 31.1.10   d 15.8.92   aged 82

MARKOS VAFIADES

Markos Vafiades, who fought with ELAS partisans against the Germans in occupied Greece and subsequently commanded the communist forces in the Greek civil war of 1946-49.

MARKOS Vafiades, or "General Markos" as he was known in his soldiering days, fought with the communist ELAS resistance to German occupation of Greece during the war years and then took command of the communist armies in their attempt to ensure that Greece remained with the communist fold. Highly successful in the first undertaking, in the second he and the communists were totally defeated. But it was a close-run thing. Only copious American aid to the nationalist forces in the wake of alarmed British warnings to the USA about the extent of communist success, and the sealing off of their Yugoslav havens by a Tito who had by then fallen out with the Russians, turned the tide in 1947 when everything seemed to be going the communists' way. Thereafter exile in the Soviet Union was Markos's lot, an increasingly uncomfortable experience as Soviet gratitude for his efforts for the cause wore thin. Eventually Vafiades was allowed to return to Greece where he

served as a socialist member of parliament until his death.

Markos Vafiades was the sixth of seven children of a teacher in one of the Greek cities of Asia Minor. He received a decent elementary school education but was orphaned at the age of 14 when he moved to Istanbul, taking odd jobs to support his two sisters. He came to Greece as a refugee in 1923 in the aftermath of the Asia Minor disaster – the Greek invasion of Turkey that cost Greece enclaves on the Ionian coastline which had been Greek for more than 2,500 years. Vafiades obtained work as a tobacco labourer in the north-eastern city of Kavalla.

He joined the Greek communist party (KKE) while still in his teens and was appointed to the central committee of the party's youth movement. During the 1930s he was several times sentenced to imprisonment and internal exile before and during the right wing dictatorship of General Ioannis ("Little John") Metaxas. When, in April 1941, the Germans invaded Greece, Vafiades was enjoying one such period of exile at Gavdhos, Greece's southernmost island, off Crete. He escaped and joioned the ELAS communist resistance movement. He was soon appointed political leader of the Macedonian Command Committee in his capacity as a central committee member of the KKE.

The first communist attempt to seize power in Greece was defeated in December 1944 with the help of British troops who had moved into Greece as the Germans pulled out, with the aim of preserving the country as a predominantly western interest. This was a concession Churchill had extracted from Stalin, in exchange for a recognition of Soviet rights over Bulgaria and Romania, in the bargaining between the three allied leaders over the apportionment of post-war spheres of influence.

The second attempt to seize power, which led to the 1946-49 civil war, opened with the formation of the Greek Democratic Army, the communist successor to the partisan ELAS. Appointed its commander, Vafiades adopted the title "General Markos" and provided strong and able leadership. By September 1946 he had set up communist outposts in northern Greece from which to launch hit and run attacks — tactics which he to some extent based on his study of their usage by Mao Tse-tung during the revolutionary struggle in China. He was, perhaps rightly, convinced that they provided the sole hope of eventual victory for the communists in Greece.

The communist movement appeared to be well on the way to victory early in 1947 when economic difficulties forced Britain to warn the Americans that it would have to discontinue military aid to the Greek government and withdraw its troops. The United States responded with the Truman Doctrine, the pledge by President Harry S. Truman of assistance to "free peoples against movements seeking to impose on them totalitarian regimes".

A conflict developed between Vafiades and the Greek communist party leader, Nikos Zachariades, who forced him, against his better judgment, to abandon his successful hit and run tactics for conventional warfare in the open field. When this led to military reverses Zachariades was able not only to accuse him of being an incompetent but also to charge him with being a British agent. Vafiades was dismissed from all his posts and expelled from the communist party in 1948. Tito now withdrew the asylum in Yugoslavia to which the communist forces had been accustomed and Albania and Bulgaria were also denied to them. Zachariades launched a desperate all-out final attack in Greece but was defeated at the battles of Gramos and Vitsi on the Greek side of the Albanian border in the summer of 1949, and the civil war was over.

Vafiades fled to Albania where, for some months he was under house arrest in the Albanian capital. Eventually he was allowed to go to the Soviet Uniion in 1949, but did so virtually in disgrace, having fallen out with his own party and labouring under the twin stigma of being variously an agent of British and Yugoslav intelligence. Since, by then, Tito was Stalin's *bête noir* for having taken Yugoslavia out of the Soviet bloc, these were difficult times for Vafiades and like-minded Greek communists who had taken refuge in the USSR. Following Stalin's death in 1953, Markos and his companions were rehabilitated at the sixth congress of the Greek communist party, which now excluded Zachariades. But the fear of successive Greek centrist and right wing governments still ensured that Vafiades and his fellow exiles received no invitation home. Vafiades spent the next 34 years working as a watch repairer in a provincial township, under the name Vassili Ivanovic Kuliev. Indeed, as the years went by there were about 25,000 Greeks, many of them children of the original exiles, in the Soviet Union, concentrated mainly on the Uzbek capital, Tashkent, where they kept up their culture and traditions.

However, in 1983, with the socialist (PASOK) party of Andreas Papandreou in power, Markos was amnestied with other communists and he returned to Greece on March 25, the anniversary of Greece's declaration of independence from the Ottoman empire in 1921. He wrote his memoirs in two volumes and, though never joining the socialist party, was elected in 1989 as an independent member of the Greek parliament on the PASOK ticket.

Vafiades was a man who could always raise a smile for public scrutiny but was nevertheless often bitter at heart. In a final television interview last December he was still declaring his faith in communism as an ideology, blaming the policies of Mikhail Gorbachev for the dissolution of the Soviet Union. Yet he recognised that the Greek communists had only themselves to blame for their defeat, acknowledging that it would have been wiser if they had participated in elections in 1946.

Married in 1956, he is survived by his wife and a son, Vladimir, who are still living somewhere in the former Soviet Union.

b 28.1.06   d 22.2.92   aged 86

GERT BASTIAN

Gert Bastian, the former Bundeswehr general who was found dead with his companion Petra Kelly, co-founder of the German Green Party, at their Bonn home. Like her, he had been a deputy in the Bundestag.

THE recruitment of such a figure as Major-General Gert Bastian to the ranks of the Greens in the wake of his dismissal from the German army in 1980 added a quite unlooked-for species of authority to the party's cause. He was not a man with a long history of bellyaching and self doubt, but a disciplined senior officer who had commanded 'Panzer forces against both the Russians and the Americans in the second world war. His appearance in the van of Green activity naturally acted as a magnet to many who were not convinced that there was not something slightly irresponsible about the party or who were suspicious that it represented communist subversion. To hear a high-ranking Nato officer exposing the apparent fallacies in the alliances's defence policy stilled many doubts.

His subsequent election to the Bundestag gilded this lily, while his taking up appointment as the Greens' representative on the parliamentary defence committee gave the party a respectability which it could hardly have looked for (and which many of its members could not stomach). This honeymoon was short. Within a year Bastian had left the Greens to sit as an independent, claiming that the party's policies were too one-sided and anti-American to be plausible. However, his relationship with Petra Kelly survived this parting of the political ways, and they remained devoted to each other.

Gert Bastian had been a soldier from his earliest youth. He had volunteered for the Wehrmacht at the age of 16 and after training was sent to the Russian front. He was wounded twice before being transferred to the Western front. By 1945 he was commanding a company in an armoured pioneer battalion.

Returning to Munich after the war, he joined the conservative Christian Social Union (CSU) while working a bookbinder's apprenticeship. But his heart remained very much with military matters and the formation of the Bundeswehr in 1956 gave him a chance to continue his army career. He rose rapidly and was promoted major-general in 1976 and given command of the 12th Panzer Division at Veitshöchheim near Würzburg. Welcoming a thousand new recruits to his division, he exhorted them to serve their fatherland with honour and obedience.

It was not long before he was thinking rather differently. As the deployment of a new generation of American medium-range missiles on German soil was mooted in the wake of the Soviet installation of the SS-20, he came to feel that Germany would become the atomic battlefield and its extinction would be the price of halting any Warsaw pact invasion. He felt that his fellow officers were blind to this, mesmerised by the apparently decisive capabilities of the new weapons, and that, anyway, Nato could withstand a conventional attack without need to resort to the "flexible response". He doubted, too, that the USSR truly wanted to export Marxist-Leninist revolution.

Had these doubts remained a matter of exchanges between fellow officers in the mess, nothing might have become of them, or of Bastian. But when he voiced them on a platform at a meeting of young socialists in March 1979 they received extensive press coverage. His resignation was demanded but the defence minister stood by him. Bastian next sent him a memorandum criticising the proposed deployment of the missiles. The memo was leaked and in the ensuing furore he was compelled to resign.

Bastian got in touch with other anti-nuclear campaigners and soon met Petra Kelly whose influence on him was to be profound and enduring. They drew up a joint appeal to the German government not to deploy the missiles and it was eventually signed by two million people. Exchanging his army uniform for the sunflower badge of the Greens, he appeared with her on public platforms, drawing the opprobrium of his old army colleagues for whom he was a traitor and a communist. But for Bastian, what had begun as a professional and military disagreement on policy was now an idealogical position from which there was no retreat.

The apogee of his — and the Greens' — fortunes was the election of 28 of their number to the Bundestag in the German elections of 1983. But the divisions which soon after rent the party tested his loyalty — and his sense of justice — beyond the limits. Thereafter he bacame more and more disillusioned with the party, though continuing to share Kelly's intense faith in the rectitude of its original ideals.

The manner of their deaths — it appears that he shot her and then killed himself — is tragic, but it cannot eclipse their share in an achievement that has made Germany the standard bearer for ecological conservation among the developed nations of the world.

b 26.3.23   d 12.10.92   aged 69

MENACHEM BEGIN

Menachem Begin, former prime minister of Israel (1977–1983) and Nobel Peace Prize winner (1978).

FROM Soviet labour-camp inmate, militant zionist — whose men blew up the King David Hotel in Jerusalem in July 1946 — to Nobel Peace Prize winner for the peace-treaty he signed between Israel and Egypt in 1979, Menachem Begin played a defintive role in the formative years of Jewish state and in the world events of his time. The massacre of 250 Arabs by his Irgun forces at the village of Deir Yassin in 1948 changed the demography of the newly partitioned Holy Land and the hanging by his men of two British sergeants was credited with

doing more than anything else to break British determination to continue its role in Mandated Palestine. Later, he averted a civil war between rival Jewish forces by belatedly accepting the authority of Israel's first prime minister, David Ben-Gurion, after the Irgun arms ship, *Altalena*, was blown-up by Israeli artillery off Tel Aviv (while he was aboard). He subsequently bowed to the democratic process; and after nearly 30 years running a tiny political grouping on the exteme right of the political spectrum won reward for his patience, gaining power in 1977 as prime minister. It was his unquestioned commitment to the widest perception of *Eretz Yisrael* (the land of Israel) that enabled Begin to carry all but the most uncompromising of his followers with him when in 1979 he relinquished Israel's vast tracts of conquered land in the Sinai and signed the Jewish state's first, and so far only, peace-treaty with a neighbouring country. But it was his lack of vision and weakening command that was primarily responsible for Israel's failure to develop and build upon that first peace. And then, in what proved to be the evening of his political career, he proved unable to restrain the adventurist policies of Ariel Sharon, his defence minister, and General Rafael Eitan, his chief of staff, in launching the fullscale invasion of Lebanon in 1982.

Menachem Begin, who lost his parents and a brother in the Nazi holocaust, was driven by twin forces: an unswerving determination never again to see Jews betrayed to slaughter and a cast iron belief in their destiny to reclaim all their ancient homeland.

As unfailingly courteous in private as he could be vituperative in public, Begin was a slight, fastidious individual with angular features and poor eyesight. He was also a stickler for protocol and, in contrast to most of his casually dressed countrymen, was seldom seen unless smartly dressed in a dark suit and tie. He came to symbolise for much of the world the hard and uncompromising face of Zionism, determined to ensure the security of the Jewish state in its historic or biblical frontiers and seemingly indifferent to any suffering that this might cause to non-Jews.

Menachem Wolfovitch Begin was the son of a convinced Zionist and grew up in the turbulent and often anti-semitic atmosphere of interwar Poland. He was educated first at a Mizrachi (religious Zionist) elementary school, later at a Polish goverment high school, and finally at Warsaw University where he took a degree in law, although he never practised it.

Throughout his life he was an Orthodox though not strictly observant Jew in the religious sense. He insisted on kosher food and refused to write or to use wheeled transport on Saturdays, but did not attend synagogue every day, or even every sabbath, and made no secret of the fact that he listened to the radio on the sabbath.

At the age of 15 he joined Betar, the Zionist youth movement founded by the "Revisionist" leader, Vladimir Zeev Jabotinsky (1880–1940), who insisted on the necessity of a Jewish state embracing both banks of the Jordan and on force as the only credible means to achieve this end. Begin became his most passionate disciple and this led to his first clash with the British in 1937 when he was imprisoned for leading a demonstration against the British embassy in Warsaw to protest at British policy in Palestine. Two years later he was appointed by Jabotinsky as head of Polish Betar, the largest section of the world movement.

After Nazi Germany and Soviet Russia had divided Poland between them in 1939, Begin was arrested by the Russians and sentenced to eight years' correctional labour as "an element dangerous to society". However, after three months in a labour-camp in the far north of Russia – an experience he later described in the book *White Nights* – he was released under the Stalin-Sikorski agreement of 1941 and allowed to join the Polish army formed under General Anders and sent by the Allies to the Near East.

Although working in Jerusalem from May 1942, he was released from the army – ostensibly for propaganda work in the United States – only in late 1943. Soon afterwards he assumed command of the Irgun Svai Leumi (National Military Organisation) – the Revisionist underground – and on February 1, 1944, he proclaimed its revolt against British rule.

Once the war in Europe ended, things changed. The Haganah – the mainstream Jewish defence force – proposed a joint resistance campaign against British rule, and Begin accepted. This lasted until July 1946, when the Irgun blew up the King David Hotel in Jerusalem, the headquarters of British administration, killing 91 people including 28 British, 41 Arabs and 17

Jews. The intention had apparently been to humiliate the British rather than to cause so many casualties, but a telephoned warning did not reach the British in time. The Jewish Agency, which through the Haganah command had tried to get the operation postponed, promptly denounced it and ended the united resistance, concentrating thereafter on diplomatic methods to hasten the end of British rule.

From then on the Revisionists fought a lone and increasingly vicious battle with the British, retaliating for the flogging and execution of their own members by responding in kind. After a British military court sentenced two 17-year-old Irgun members to 15 years imprisonment and 18 lashes with a heavy cane, a British major and three NCOs were captured and flogged; and on July 30, 1947 two British sergeants were formally hanged. The British put a £10,000 price on Begin's head, describing him as an "irresponsible fanatic thirsting for personal power," but were never able to capture him.

After the hanging of the British sergeants Begin turned his attention to the danger of Arab resistance to the creation of the Jewish state. His greatest "achievement" on this front was the massacre of Arab villagers at Deir Yassin, on the outskirts of Jerusalem, on April 9, 1948. Although he always denied that such a massacre had taken place (in spite of detailed eye-witness accounts, mostly from Jews) Begin did not scruple to claim the credit for its effect: the panic flight of most of the Arab population from what was to become Israeli territory.

On the proclamation of the state of Israel in May 1948 Begin emerged from the underground and signed an agreement with the provisional government, providing for the merger of the Irgun into the national army.

Thereafter Begin was a politician. He quickly transformed the Irgun into a political party, the Herut (freedom) movement, and emerged as a formidable speaker both in Parliament and at public meetings. Yet to begin with he spoke only for a small minority of Israelis – 11.5 per

cent in the 1949 elections, falling to 6.6 per cent two years later. His party was to lose eight consecutive elections before coming to power in 1977.

But as the 1950s and 1960s wore on, Begin began to acquire respectability. In 1965 his party formed Gahal, an electoral block with the Liberal Party, as a united opposition; and on the eve of the Six Days War in 1967 he joined the national unity government formed by Levi Eshkol, becoming deputy prime minister. After Eshkol's death he remained in office under Golda Meir, but resigned in August 1970 when Israel first formally accepted the principle of a negotiated peace involving withdrawal "from territories occupied in the 1967 conflict."

Golda Meir retired exhausted in the spring of 1974. In the three years that followed it became apparent that the Labour Party, after a quarter of a century in power, had lost both its grip and its sense of direction. Plagued by a succession of corruption scandals, it appeared to more and more Israelis, especially those of North African or Asian origin (by now roughly half the population), as the vehicle of a smug and patronising aristocracy, almost exclusively European and based on the kubbutzim and the nationalised industries. Begin, although European himself, never talked down to the "oriental" Jews and so came to be seen by many of them as a champion of the underdog against the self-serving governing clique. His intransient nationalism also appealed to most of them.

In the elections of 1977, Yitzak Rabin was forced to renounce the leadership of the Labour Party after the disclosure of financial irregularities involving his wife and the Likud campaign, ably organised by the former air force hero Ezer Weizmann, swept Begin to victory in spite of a recent heart attack.

Begin swiftly made it clear that he was determined to establish permanent Israeli control of "Judea and Samaria" (the West Bank of Jordan) by lifting restrictions on Jewish settlement there.

His arrival in power effectively doomed President Carter's efforts to reconvene the Geneva peace conference of 1973, with a view to obtaining peace involving a Palestinian "homeland" on the West Bank. In July 1977 in Washington Begin had the first of many clashes with Carter on the settlement issue, and refused to budge.

Begin had accepted President Carter's invitation to a summit conference with Sadat at Camp David in September 1977, but went there fully prepared to resist American pressure. He and the Egyptian leader never established an easy personal relationship and virtually all the negotiating at Camp David was done indirectly through the Americans. It took Carter 12 days of patient, often extremely tense argument to get Begin to agree to put the withdrawal of Israeli settlements from Sinai to the Knesset, since it was clear that this was a *sine qua non* for peace with Egypt – though even then Begin was not prepared to *recommend* the withdrawal of settlements, in one of which he had actually promised to make his home after retirement.

Sadat on his side accepted the proposal for autonomy in the West Bank and Gaza, but only as a five-year transitional solution. This left the door theoretically open for ultimate Israeli withdrawal, but also enabled Begin to avoid waiving Israel's claim to sovreignty. The form of autonomy was to be negotiated between Israel, Egypt and Jordan, with possible Palestinian and Jordanian delegations, (but Jordan had not been consulted about this, and in fact refused to take part). Carter believed that he had secured Begin's agreement to freeze Israeli settlement activity during the transitional period. It turned out, however, that Begin had only promised a moratorium of three months while the Egyptian-Israeli peace treaty was being finalised.

Despite an atmosphere soured by this misunderstanding, the Camp David accords were widely hailed as a major breakthrough (or, among Arab nationalists, as a sell-out) and the following month Begin and Sadat were jointly awarded the Nobel peace prize.

The peace treaty between Egypt and Israel was signed, after much further haggling and a personal shuttle between Egypt and Israel by President Carter, in Washington on March 26, 1979. Begin faced some fierce opposition to it within his own party but his authority, combined with the support of a large majority in the country, was sufficient to force it through and to enable the final, most controversial phase of withdrawal from Sinai three years later.

By mid-1980 Begin had lost both his foreign and his defence ministers – Dayan and Weizman, the two most independent-minded members of the government and the most committed to the idea of broadening the peace by giving real autonomy to the inhabitants of the West Bank and Gaza. Begin gave the foreign ministry to Yitzhak Shamir the former leader of the Stern Gang, an extremist off-shoot of the Irgun and by that time a hardline Herut member who had refused to support the Camp David accords. He kept the defence portfolio in his own hands. The "peace process" marked time and public attention was diverted to economic policy where things were not going too well as Begin failed to back the finance minister, Yigal Hurvitz, against other members of the cabinet.

To many observers the prime minister appeared to be fading fast and heading for certain defeat in the 1981 general election. But the approach of another election campaign seemed to stimulate a new flow of adrenalin. In January 1980 Hurvitz resigned and was replaced by Yoram Aridor, whose extravagant reflationary policies brought real, if shortlived, benefits to many Israelis. Begin for his part rallied support with a furiously nationalistic campaign in the course of which he publicly abused the leaders of France and West Germany, talked himself to the brink of war with Syria over the deployment of missiles in Lebanon's Bekaa valley, and sent Israeli bombers to destroy a nuclear reactor in Iraq.

The government was only just re-elected: in alliance with the religious parties, Likud had an overall majority of two. But it was enough. Ariel Sharon, who as agriculture minister had been the driving force of Jewish settlement in the occupied territories, now became defence minister and, with the chief of staff, General Rafael Eitan, began planning a new war in Lebanon aimed at demolishing the Palestine Liberation Organisation – the main focus of resistance in the occupied territories – and, they supposed, ensuring Israel's lasting strategic supremacy in the area by humiliating Syria and wresting Lebanon from her control.

It took Begin and Sharon some months to convince their colleagues that the moment had come for a full-scale invasion of Lebanon: on four occasions in the first five months of 1982 they were dissuaded by American pressure. On the last occasion, in May, the cabinet agreed that the next attack on Jews or Israelis anywhere in the world would be treated as a *casus belli*. Accordingly when the Israeli ambassador in London was shot on June 3 (in fact by a Palestinian splinter group violently hostile to the PLO leadership), the Israeli airforce was sent to bomb Palestinian targets in southern Lebanon and in Beirut. The PLO, which had observed a ceasefire on the Israeli-Lebanese frontier since the previous July, reacted – as expected – by renewed shelling of northern Israel. On June 5 Israel's ground forces poured into Lebanon.

He did little to check the successive stages of the operation as it unfolded, except – again under strong American pressure – to halt the intensive bombing of Beirut in mid-August. Apparently Sharon and Eitan took many key decisions without consulting him – including the fateful one to send Phalangist irregulars into the disarmed Palestinians camps of Sabra and Chatila on September 16 which resulted in the massacre of hundreds of Palestinian refugees – but he was always ready to defend their actions after the event.

Begin never expressed any public remorse for what had happened to non-Jewish civilians as a result of his actions and policies. "*Goyim* kill *goyim* and they blame the Jew" was his comment on the international outcry after the Sabra-Chatila massacre. Only under extreme pressure from the entire Israeli establishment did he consent to the appointment of a commission of inquiry into Israeli responsibility for the affair.

During the summer of 1983 Begin sank into a deep depression which eventually made it impossible for him to continue as prime minister. This was no doubt partly the result of his wife Aliza's death but above all because of the lengthening list of Israeli casualties caused by the war in Lebanon, which his government had begun but seemed unable to finish.

Begin announced his intention to resign on August 28, a few weeks after his 70th birthday. He remained officially prime minister, though refusing to speak to anyone but close relatives and personal staff, until October 10 when Yitzhak Shamir finally took over. So deep was Begin's melancholia that it was not until December 10, after a skin complaint which had prevented him shaving responded to a new treatment, that he felt able to move out of his official residence.

For a year after his resignation Begin remained in almost total seclusion. Last year, in a full interview given to mark the 40th anniversary of the founding of the Irgun Zevai Leumi, he recalled with pride his decision to launch the Israeli air-raid against Iraq's nuclear reactor, which he said had been vindicated by the events in the Gulf. The hardest decision of his career, he said, had been to order the hanging of the British sergeants. "But after that cruel act there were no more hangings of Jews in the land of Israel."

Menachem Begin leaves a son, Binyamin, a Herut member of the Knesset and two daughters, Hassia (named after his mother who was murdered by the Nazis) and Leah.

b 16.8.13   d 9.3.92   aged 78

WILLY BRANDT

Willy Brandt, chancellor of West Germany from 1969 to 1974 and before that governing mayor of West Berlin from 1957 to 1966.

WILLY Brandt was one of the outstanding German statesmen of the post-war years, who played a leading role in re-establishing links between West Germany and the countries of the Soviet bloc. He had first come to prominence as mayor of West Berlin, which he came to symbolise at a time when it was under threat. He then turned to national politics, led the Social Democrats to power in Bonn and, through his *Ostpolitik*, transformed West Germany's external relations.

He was also a man who stirred the imagination of people both in Germany and abroad. He was the only German statesman of his time who could lay a wreath at the concentration camp at Buchenwald, and fall to his knees in the Warsaw ghetto, without striking a false note. When he went to Erfurt for his first meeting with the East German leadership he was all but mobbed by crowds of East Germans. He was cheered to the echo by the Norwegians when he went to Oslo to try to persuade them to join the European Economic Community (though they later rejected his advice).

The reason for this appeal lay in his warm and idealistic temperament and in the fact that, as a man who had resisted the Nazis and been forced to flee for his life, he had clean hands. It meant that as well as building bridges to the East through his policy of détente he did his country another great service. He was able to persuade those West European countries, like Norway, which had the greatest grounds for mistrusting all things German, to accept West Germany as an ally and a friend.

In West Germany itself his anti-Nazi record brought him the hatred of many older Germans who somehow confused his activities with a kind of treason. But he retained throughout his life the ability to appeal to young people, along with the thin skin which meant that, even after years in the Bundestag, he was easily hurt. Towards the end of his life, his ideals were reflected in the work of the Brandt Commission on relations between the industrialised countries of the "North" and the developing ones of the "South". Brandt was an active chairman of the commission and was disappointed when its report, which called for a massive transfer of resources from "North" to "South" had so little effect. Brandt was awarded the Nobel Peace prize for his *Ostpolitik* in 1971.

Willy Brandt was born in Lübeck on the Baltic to Martha Frahm, a 19-year-old salesgirl. He was christened Herbert Ernst Karl Frahm and never knew his father, who did not marry his mother. His illegitimacy never troubled him and certainly did not hold him back, but Adenauer's unworthy gibe in the 1961 election campaign about "Herr Brandt, alias Frahm" drew from its victim a display of seething contempt which it richly deserved.

The main influence in his early life was his maternal grandfather, a farm worker and casual labourer and committed SPD (Sozialdemokratische Partei Deutschlands) supporter who imbued him with political ideals almost from the cradle. He won a scholarship to the distinguished Johanneum Gymnasium (grammar school) at 13 and it was not long before his teachers noticed his political dedication. One told his mother: "Keep your son away from politics. The boy is gifted . . . politics will ruin him." But he joined the SPD *Arbeiterjugend* (workers' youths) at 16 and the party proper a year later.

His sponsor on the latter occasion was Julius Leber, the local SPD leader and a newspaper editor who became the second surrogate father in the life of Herbert Frahm. From this moderate but committed socialist, the young man learned to recognise the magnitude of the threat Hitler and his Nazis represented to Germany and her neighbours.

The robust young Frahm was soon embroiled in the brawls between the brownshirts and the forces of the left. One of the fracas in which he was involved led to him and a number of others being charged with manslaughter, but it was established to the satisfaction of the court that he had not been close to the scene of the death of a demonstrator and he was therefore acquitted.

Frahm remained active and in 1931, impatient with the excessively, in his view, moderate policies being pursued by the SPD, he joined a revolutionary Marxist breakaway group called the Socialist Workers' Party. He and Leber fell out over this, but a year later Frahm returned to the fold and he began to write articles for his re-discovered mentor. The name "Willy Brandt" first appeared at this time as a *nom de plume*.

Adolph Hitler became the chancellor in January 1933. The following month saw a massive protest demonstration in Lübeck in which his friend Leber, on bail after having been arrested and beaten up by the Nazis and banned from taking an active part, delivered a statement: "Freedom." Brandt never saw him again as he found it expedient soon after the rally to flee for his life to Norway. Brandt fled again, from occupied Norway to neutral Sweden, soon after the German

invasion and spent the rest of the war in Stockholm.

Discarding the name Frahm altogether now for that of Brandt, the exiled socialist took up full-time journalism. During the war, he ran a small Norwegian-Swedish news agency, having become by this time fluent in Norwegian and a Norwegian citizen. He had also married his first wife, Carlotta, a Norwegian (they parted in 1944 and were subsequently divorced). He had contact with such German resistance to Hitler as existed within the Reich.

After the war he went to Berlin as press attaché to the Norwegian military mission with his temporary major's commission in 1946. A year later, he took out German citizenship again in his native city and re-joined the SPD. The party very soon made him the representative in Berlin of its executive early in 1948, and that is where he stayed and rose to national fame.

The world first sat up and took notice of him in the wake of the Soviet intervention in Hungary late in 1956, when Brandt, by then president of the Berlin House of Representatives, personally defused dangerous scenes in which enraged mobs of West Berliners seemed set to storm into the Soviet sector of the divided city. In 1957 he was elected mayor and his calm in the face of the Khrushchev ultimatum at the end of 1958, when the Soviet Union demanded that all Berlin was made a ''free city'', consolidated his reputation. He became a symbol of his divided city and a world figure.

In 1961 Brandt was adopted by the SPD, desperate for someone of stature to put up against the commanding figure of Konrad Adenauer as its candidate for chancellor in the West German federal election. On August 13, 1961, while Brandt was campaigning in Lower Saxony, his adopted city was physically divided and sealed off overnight by the Berlin Wall. Returning home to rally his fellow-citizens, Brandt was acutely disappointed at the low-key response, as he felt it to be, of the West in general and the Americans in particular. But President Kennedy's dramatic visit to the city in 1963, when he identified himself with the beleaguered half-city, reconciled Brandt to the United States.

The 1961 election campaign was an unscrupulous one, with frequent use being made of ''bastard mayor'' gibes and the like. But the SPD improved its percentage of the poll by almost five per cent over 1957. So Brandt was the only conceivable choice as candidate for 1965, by which time he was chairman of the SPD as well, a position he was to hold for a good 20 years. A second failure in that hard campaign disappointed him, however, and made him ill with heart trouble. He swore he would never stand again.

With the help of his *éminence grise*, Egon Bahr, Brandt lost no time in launching his *Ostpolitik* of reconciliation with the Soviet Union and the Soviet-dominated countries of Eastern Europe, all of which had suffered at the hands of the Nazis. The first step was to establish diplomatic relations with Romania at the beginning of 1967. This was the first move in this direction since relations had been formalised with the Soviet Union in 1955, and showed the pragmatism which Brandt was to adopt.

Brandt stood for the chancellorship again in 1969 in an election in which the SPD once more narrowed the gap between itself and the CDU. The CDU fell short of an absolute majority, and Brandt persuaded the new, left-liberal leader of the FDR, Walter Scheel, to join him in coalition. The shift of partner by the small liberal party brought the SPD leadership of a government in Germany for the first time since before the second world war. Brandt became chancellor.

Strongly supported by Scheel, who became foreign minister, Brandt proceeded to give a strong new impetus to his *Ostpolitik*. There were three main areas of activity: the establishment of a *modus vivende* with East Germany, the normalisation of relations with Poland, and the negotiation of a treaty with the Soviet Union on the renunciation of force. As far as East Germany was concerned, the first results were seen on March 19, 1970, when Brandt went to Erfurt in East Germany for a summit meeting with Herr Willi Stoph, the East German prime minister – the first meeting of its sort since the foundation of the two states. Brandt received an ecstatic welcome from thousands of East Germans and laid a wreath at Buchenwald.

On December 7, 1970, Brandt went to Warsaw to sign a treaty with Poland. This declared that the Oder-Neisse line constituted the western frontier of Poland and affirmed ''the inviolability of their existing frontiers now and in the future''. On this occasion, too, there were emotional scenes when Brandt laid wreaths at the tomb of the Polish Unknown Soldier and at the monument commemorating the Jewish uprising in the Warsaw ghetto. The image of the West German chancellor on his knees in atonement for the Holocaust caught the world's imagination.

Brandt's most significant change of course, however, had been in negotiations with the Soviet Union. In August 1970 he and Scheel had visited Moscow and signed a treaty agreeing that both sides would "refrain from the threat of force or use of force in any matters affecting security in Europe and international security, as well as in their mutual relations". In the new climate created by this success, Brandt again visited the Soviet Union in September 1971 for talks at Yalta with Brezhnev.

All this and the accompanying Berlin Agreement between the three Western allies and Russia set the seal on West Germany's emergence as a political power. Brandt had been fond of saying that his country was "an economic giant but a political pygmy". By embedding West Germany in Nato and the EEC, Adenauer had provided half the political equation; Brandt completed it by normalising relations with the Soviet bloc as far as it was possible to do so in his time. West Germany might occupy only half the pre-War Reich, but it was no longer half a state. The two Germanies entered the United Nations simultaneously but separately.

Not the least of Brandt's contributions to peace had been his decision to sign the Nuclear Non-Proliferation Treaty. When he became Chancellor, this had been a controversial issue in West Germany for three years, with strong opposition from the right. But in November 1969, he signed the treaty, expressing the hope that it would lead to further arms control and disarmament.

During those years, he also maintained his strong belief in the importance of the Atlantic Alliance, despite the fact that much of his attention was given to West Germany's eastern neighbours. He continued to support the concept of a united Europe and helped to ease Britain's difficulties as it made its way to membership of the European Community.

He ran into stiff opposition to his *Ostpolitik*, however, from within West Germany, particularly from the Christian Democrats and their Bavarian allies, the CSU. In 1972 Brandt was forced to contrive the first premature election in West Germany's brief history because of opposition to the treaties with the Soviet Union and Poland. He made *détente* with the Soviet bloc the central issue of the campaign and led the SPD to its most resounding victory in more than a century.

Despite this famous victory, however, and the crowning of his *détente* programme thereafter, Brandt's customary post-electoral depression took longer than ever to lift. Within six months observers were writing him off, and within a year and a half he had resigned. It was a poignantly brief lapse of time between the zenith and the nadir of his career. The occasion of Brandt's resignation was the discovery that one of his closest advisers Gunther Guillaume, had been an East German "plant", itself an unfortunate and ironic development.

His resignation prevented another far more trivial scandal coming to light at the time, arising from Brandt's lifelong weakness for attractive young women. Brandt considered braving a vote of confidence over Guillaume, for whose treachery he did not feel morally responsible. But his old rival Herbert Wehner, then SPD floorleader, insisted that he should quit. It was also the last straw for a man who had lost the will to rule. Those closest to him, including his second wife, Rut, also a Norwegian, whom he had married in Berlin in 1948, knew that he had wanted to go long before it happened, and that it would have come about in any case.

Brandt remained chairman of the SPD, serving as a useful shield for his successor, Helmut Schmidt, whose pragmatic policies as chancellor always tended to irritate the party's increasingly volatile left wing. Brandt's own contribution to Schmidt's electoral victories in 1976 and 1980 was crucial, although even the long-serving chairman's appeals for unity began to lose their impact soon after the latter poll. World recession, the stagnation of the West German economy and consequent social strains paralysed and divided the coalition with the FDP and exhausted the SPD, which was clearly tired of office devoid of ideas and divided against itself by 1982, when it was abandoned by the FDP.

If the party that had been his life-long cause proved disappointing to him in his declining years, Willy Brandt went on campaigning for peace and working for democratic socialism worldwide as chairman of the Socialist International, despite a heart attack in 1978 and a second divorce and his third marriage, to the much younger Brigitte, a year later. He was a changed man with a new lease of life, acquired in time for the 1980 campaign.

At home, Brandt used his continued holding of the SPD party chairmanship in a bid to restore the party's fortunes by espousing causes close to its left-wing or the emerging Green party. This policy of appeasing the Greens, which alienated the FDP, proved to be a disastrous mistake. Helmut Kohl won three elelctions in a row in 1983, 1987 and 1990 against an SPD which had marooned itself on the left. Chief of the cause espoused proved to be the fierce controversy generated in Germany during 1983 over Nato's decision to deploy intermediate range nuclear missiles. Brandt addressed the monster Bonn rally of that year, organised by peace groups (he had already committed the party against the missiles). But when he insisted he had not become anti-American or anti-Nato he was booed.

Brandt's final stepping down from his SPD post, after holding it for 23 years, was painful. Not due to do so until 1988, he made a surprise announcement that he would quit in March, 1987 — carried out the following June — after the party had revolted over his decision to name a young Greek as the SPD's first press spokeswoman, who was not even a party member. The appointment looked like a self-willed gesture from an old man losing his grip.

The dramatic events of the autumn of 1989, particularly the end of the Berlin Wall, brought the former governing mayor of Berlin back, however, once again into the national limelight. Even there, though, the role he naturally assumed as "Patriach of German Unity", proved to be only short-lived. It was the right-wing Alliance for Germany, driven by Chancellor Kohl, which resoundingly won the East German elections in the following March.

Like many others, Brandt had been overtaken by the swift-moving results of Gorbachev's decision to relinquish the Soviet Union's military hold over Eastern Europe. He had believed progress could only be gained by small steps and increased contacts between Germans. In 1988 Brandt had described the pledge on reunification in the Federal German Constitution as "a living lie". He was proved wrong, and his words came back to haunt him.

True as always to his *Ostpolitik*, Brandt, during East Germany's 1990 election campaign, made a moving gesture by going personally up to the Oder-Neisse frontier with Poland and publicly declaring: "I came here to tell you that this frontier is final." His role in the first all-German federal election in December 1990 was less prominent. With typical good grace Brandt did all he could to avoid overshadowing the ill-fated SPD chancellor candidate Oskar Lafontaine, who survived a crushing defeat at the polls.

Brandt's was a complex character. An emotional and sensual man, he was easily hurt. He was also prone to lengthy bouts of melancholia. But he could display vitality and stamina when his mood was right, working well into the small hours day after day. In later life, he became a genial and philosophical figure.

Brandt is survived by his third wife, Brigitte, whom he married in December, 1983. He had a daughter from his first marriage, and three sons from his second.

b 18.12.13   d 8.10.92   aged 78

LORD BRIGINSHAW

Lord Briginshaw was general secretary of the National Society of Operative Printers, Graphical and Media Personnel (Natsopa) from 1951 to 1975 and one of the more militant voices in the deliberations of the TUC.

RICHARD Briginshaw was, in his day, one of the more radical left-wing trade union leaders and as such he played a major role in the many trade union disputes which afflicted Fleet Street, particularly in the 1960s and 1970s. These disputes were vigorously, not to say ruthlessly, prosecuted in an era of weak newspaper managements which would rather pay periodic Danegeld than confront the enemy. As a result Briginshaw and his members became some of the country's best paid workers.

Briginshaw was a fierce opponent of incomes and trade union legislation by both Labour and Conservative governments; and he was consistently hostile to the idea of Britain's joining the European Community. He became president in the 1960s of the Forward Britain Movement, the most left-wing of the groups opposing membership. In this capacity he wrote a number of pamphlets and addressed hundreds of meetings up and down the country. When Britain did join the community he became a joint founder of the Get Britain Out Campaign.

Within the printing industry, he was a believer all his life in a single printing union, and he appeared to have brought about a big step in that direction when, in the late 1960s, he negotiated a merger between his own union, The National Society of Operative Printers and Assistants, as it then was, and the larger National Union of Printing, Bookbinding and Paper Workers. He became joint secretary of the resulting Society of Graphical and Allied Trades (Sogat).

But printing union leaders make uneasy bedfellows, and Briginshaw himself who was a natural autocrat who liked to have the last word on even the smallest matter on which he was involved. So after disagreements, recriminations and threats of legal action, the two sections fell apart;

and the joint union was only reconstituted after Briginshaw had retired.

His retirement was itself clouded by scandal, when he and two colleagues were sued by the union for sums of money outstanding on property transactions which he claimed had been undertaken to protect funds from possible seizure under industrial relations law introduced in the early 1970s. After a high court hearing Briginshaw and his co-defendants subsequently agreed to pay a sum of money to the union.

Richard William Briginshaw grew up in south London and started work as a printer's devil at 14. But he studied economics and law in his spare time and earned a diploma from University College London. At one time or another he worked in the machine room of almost every office in Fleet Street, the stronghold of Natsopa. In 1938 he became secretary of the London machine branch − the youngest official in the union − but his career was interrupted by six years in the army, mostly in India and the Middle East, and three years back at his trade before election as a national officer in 1949. He was elected general secretary in 1951.

In 1967 he published a pamphlet proposing a state-owned printing corporation to provide plant and facilities for publications to compete with privately-owned newspapers. A couple of years later he brought off the merger with the NUPBPW, with two autonomous divisions each retaining its general secretary. It did not work and fell apart. But the rancour subsided and in his last year of office Briginshaw presided over a new TUC printing industry committee. In 1982 the merger was resumed on the more organic basis he had originally preferred.

During the Heath government of 1970−74, Briginshaw was one of its most adamant union opponents. When the TUC agreed to talks with the government in 1972, Briginshaw as a member of the economic committee refused to take part. Natsopa's own operations were little affected by changes in the law, but

Briginshaw's imagination was fired and he embarked on the ill-starred manipulation of union funds which ended in the courts 10 years later.

Briginshaw and his co-defendants insisted that various property transactions under their names and the movement of funds to Switzerland, had been approved by the executive in accordance with union policy, solely to protect the funds, with no intention of fraud or personal gain. Eventually the case was settled on confidential terms for a "substantial sum" in 1982.

By this time Briginshaw had completely retired from public life after serving on the council of the Advisory, Conciliation and Arbitration Service (Acas), the British Overseas Trade Board and the British National Oil Corporation. After his busy career of authorship on behalf of the Forward Britain Movement, his final fling was another pamphlet, *British Oil: the Big Sell-out*, when he left BNOC in 1979. He was also a member of the court of Cranfield Institute of Technology and, although he was a powerful advocate of socialist education, was for six years a governor of Dulwich College.

He became a life peer in 1974, following it up a year later by denouncing the House of Lords and declaring that he would work for its abolition.

Briginshaw was a tall, vigorous man, who was fond of painting, music and swimming, and had a way of making provocative statements followed by a firm, half-smiling stare from behind his heavy spectacles. As an industrial negotiator, he was an accomplished "wheeler-dealer", who regarded industrial disruption as a routine tactical weapon, but was cautious about deploying it.

He made a point of being well turned out, and was said to have spotless "negotiating shoes" always at hand in his car to put on before going to a meeting.

Lord Briginshaw is suvived by five sons and a daughter.

b 1908   d 28.3.92   aged 83

LORD BROXBOURNE

Lord Broxbourne, Sir Derek Walker-Smith, Bt. as he will be most familiarly remembered, was formerly a Conservative minister under both the Eden and Macmillan administrations.

LORD Broxbourne was a compelling advocate whether he was appearing in the courts, in the Commons or at Conservative party conferences. He held various ministerial posts under Eden and Macmillan but he will be remembered chiefly as Sir Derek Walker-Smith, an outstanding opponent of Britain's membership of the European Community. He fought against entry with skill, tenacity and wit, always commanding respect and always losing the important votes.

His father was Sir Jonah Walker-Smith, one-time borough engineer at Barrow-in-Furness and city engineer at Edinburgh, who was director of housing at the Ministry of Health – his son's future ministry – before being elected Conservative MP for Barrow. From him Broxbourne inherited his fascination with politics and life-long interest in housing. He was educated at Rossall and at Christ Church, Oxford, where he became secretary of the Union and took a first in modern history. In 1934 he was called to the Bar at the Middle Temple.

His pre-war years were a time of relentless activity. He had written his first novel while still an undergraduate and he proceeded to combine the beginning of a promised legal career with the authorship of six other books, including biographies of three famous lawyers, Lord Reading, Lord Darling and Sir Edward Clarke. He was also part-author of a play and editor of the *English Review*. He contributed regular articles to the old *Sunday Dispatch* and stood unsuccessfully for the London county council.

Although Broxbourne was a strong supporter of Chamberlain's foreign policy he came to realise that war was inevitable. After service in the Inns of Court OTC he obtained a territorial commission in the gunners and pursued his part-time military career with customary enthusiasm. He grew a vast handle-bar moustache and insisted on learning to ride under a particularly demanding corporal in the Life Guards, an experience which he always maintained was good training for the rigours of political life. He ended the war as a lieutenant-colonel and an MP. He had been chosen to contest the safe Conservative seat of Hertford, which he duly won in 1945. This election, which saw the beginning of his political career, marked the end of his father's, for Sir Jonas Walker-Smith lost his seat at Barrow.

In the Commons Broxbourne was soon spotted as a promising newcomer. His legal mind proved useful in harassing the Labour governments. He was elected to the 1922 committee of Tory backbenchers, later becoming its chairman. He had to wait until 1955, however, before obtaining office. He had just won the Herts East constituency when he was appointed parliamentary secretary to the Board of Trade by Eden. A year later he became economic secretary to the board. A year later he became economic secretary to the Treasury and by 1957 he was minister of state at the Board of Trade. He did not spend long there before Macmillan made him minister of health. This was a significant post but did not carry cabinet rank. Broxbourne had to maintain his ministry against Labour attacks but during the Macmillan years there was none of the adversarial atmosphere over the health service which developed later.

He was responsible for the Mental Health Act, a measure which was widely approved as marking a new and more rational approach to mental illness. During this time the hospital building programme was expanded at a respectable rate, polio vaccination achieved notable success and pay and conditions in the health service were reorganised and largely accepted without major

disruptions. It was a useful if unspectacular contribution but by 1960 he had had enough.

Broxbourne saw little prospect of obtaining cabinet office and he wanted to make money at the Bar while there was plenty of time. He had made a considerable sacrifice in 1955 when he entered the government and gave up his practice in the unglamorous but highly rewarded field of town planning and local government. Macmillan made no effort to keep him. He appreciated the financial realities and it also gave him the opportunity to bring Enoch Powell back into the government at Broxbourne's ministry. So he sent the retiring minister his best wishes and, always lavish with hereditary honours, included a baronetcy as well.

Macmillan would have done better to keep Broxbourne in his government. Although the Whips knew him as a good party man they also knew they could not rely on him where principle was involved. There were instances when he had defied them in the past. Now he found his great cause – opposition to British membership of the European Community. Within months of returning to the back benches he was in full revolt against entry, supported notably by Robin Turton and Peter Walker. In the summer of 1961, just before the House rose, he made the outstanding speech in the two-day debate on entry. He followed this with another appeal at the party's autumn conference. It drew tremendous applause but little actual support and was defeated on a show of hands. It was the same story at the Llandudno conference a year later. Few who heard it will forget the impression made by his speech which was both emotional and closely reasoned, even mischievous at times. But Macmillan, not present, recorded in his diary that "the conference has rejected the Turton-Walker-Smith amendment on the Common Market by an overwhelming majority – only fifty or so out of 4,000 voting for it", and added: "It was therefore in a happy mood that I left for Llandudno".

Broxbourne was not downcast. He did not think Macmillan's happiness would last. Though he no longer trusted the prime minister he had plenty of trust in De Gaulle; and the general, with his veto, duly obliged him.

But the pro-Europeans, of course, were not beaten. Wilson and then Heath revived their hopes. The anti-marketeers responded with all their usual spirit and all their usual results, losing all the major debates, notably at the 1969 Tory conference in Brighton. By 1972, when Broxbourne voted against his government in the House on the second reading of the European Communities Bill, even the loyalties of his patient constituency association were tested. His executive committee condemned his action and an effort was even made to prevent his adoption for the next general election but this came to nothing. He was, after all, a good constituency MP.

When Britain eventually entered the community he caused some surprise by accepting nomination for the European Parliament at Strasbourg. It was generally thought that he would go there as a wrecker but in fact he proved a highly responsible MEP. Although still believing that British entry involved a damaging loss of sovereignty he also believed that Britain could not withdraw honourably from a treaty into which it had entered and he argued that it could not, in law or in property, release itself from its commitments. He thought Britain's good faith, its respect for treaty obligations and its pledged word were all at stake and he left no doubt about where he stood. From 1975 until he left Strasbourg in 1979 he was chairman of the parliament's legal committee. When he went to the Lords he made an unsuccessful attempt through his Human Rights and Fundamental Freedoms Bill to incorporate the European Convention on Human Rights into Britain's domestic law.

Broxbourne left the Commons in 1983, accepted Mrs Thatcher's offer of a life peerage and remained active in public life, speaking in the upper house, writing to the newspapers and maintaining his interest in his special subjects, particularly house building. From 1973 to 1978 he had been chairman of the National House Building Council. His later speeches were predictably less fierce than his earlier efforts as a party warrior and an anti-marketeer but they were still effective. He once quoted Macaulay's definition of oratory: "Reason penetrated and made red hot by passion". This was no bad description of Broxbourne's own style in his campaigning days.

He was married in 1938 to Dorothy Etherton of Rowlands Castle, Hants. She survives him with their two daughters and their son, John Jonah Walker-Smith.

b 13.4.10   d 22.1.92   aged 81

BARONESS
EWART-BIGGS

Baroness Ewart-Biggs, Opposition Whip in the House of Lords, whose husband was murdered by the IRA when he was British ambassador in Dublin in 1976.

JANE Ewart-Biggs was driving along Birdcage Walk on her way to the Foreign Office in 1976 when she turned on her car radio and heard that her husband, who had taken up his post as British ambassador in Dublin only 12 days before, had been blown up by a land-mine. A week later she fought back her grief to tell the Irish people on television: "I feel no bitterness, there is no hatred in my heart." But what remained was a determination to do all she could to end the Irish tragedy and to spend the rest of her life working for the causes in which her husband believed.

In the process she emerged as a considerable figure in her own right. She worked for the Irish people's peace movement, founded by Mairead Corrigan and Betty Williams; she toured the United States in an attempt to stop American money going to the IRA; she joined the Labour Party and, after being created a life peer, she was a front-bench spokesman and Opposition Whip in the House of Lords.

Felicity Jane Randall was born into an old Army family. But her father, Major Basil Fitzherbert Randall, died when she was three months old and her mother spent the rest of her life in mourning. Her mother's example was one factor which made Lady Ewart-Biggs particularly anxious not to retire into widowhood after her own husband's death.

She had married Christopher Ewart-Biggs, already regarded as a future ambassador, in 1960. She had doubts about her fitness to be the wife of a rising young diplomat. She had left school at 16 and was in her own words "a jolly little secretary at the Savoy." In fact, she proved a popular and effective figure during their posts at Algiers, Brussels and later in Paris, where they lived for nearly five years when he was minister under three ambassadors. They were delighted at the move to Ireland. Christopher Ewart-Biggs had time to give only one press conference in Dublin before he was murdered.

Before her own death Lady Ewart-Biggs said: "Everybody deals with loss in a different way. I dealt with it by becoming more involved in politics and in the sort of causes in which he was interested." She instituted the Christopher Ewart-Biggs Literary Prize as a memorial to him. She led marches of the people's peace movement in Ireland and Britain. She worked briefly for the Savoy Hotel group again, but decided she would be better employed on lecture-tours in the United States. Then she joined the Labour Party. This surprised many of her friends. But her husband, though confined by diplomatic protocol, had been an intellectual socialist and she decided that Labour had a tradition of compassion which appealed to her.

She worked at ward level, then tried to

become a candidate for the GLC and the European Parliament, but failed to get selected. But in 1981 she was nominated by Labour for a life peerage. This was not a gesture to the widow of a man murdered in the service of the state but a recognition that she would make a good working peer. Though she was surprised at the offer it came at the right time. She had worked as hard as she could for peace in Northern Ireland for five years and she felt she was ready to move on. Her elevation was warmly welcomed. Baroness Sharples, who sat on the Conservative benches and whose own husband had been murdered by terrorists in Bermuda in 1973, lent her the robes she needed when she was introduced.

Her maiden speech was on Europe – a cause which had engrossed her for most of her adult life. She was quickly absorbed into the life of the Upper House, even swimming for the Lords against the Commons. She spoke frequently and was noted for the amount of preparatory work she put into her speeches. Her industry was rewarded by successive appointments – spokesman on home affairs, overseas development and consumer affairs before becoming an opposition Whip. She published two books of memoirs: *Pay, Back and Follow* and *Lady in the Lords*.

Lady Ewart-Biggs was a tall striking woman, with strong features to match her spirit.

Shortly before her death she married a close friend of long standing. Kevin O'Sullivan. She is survived by her son and two daughters.

b 22.8.29   d 8.10.92   aged 63

Speaking at the Northern Ireland Women's peace rally (1976)

WILLIAM REES-DAVIES

Former Conservative MP who enjoyed living life to the full.

FOR 30 years William Rees-Davies was one of the most colourful members of the House of Commons. His private life could best be described as animated. His legal career was controversial and his personal appearance was dramatic. His habit of sweeping through the corridors of the House in a black cloak caused him to be known as Dracula. His misfortune in losing an arm during the war resulted in another nickname: Billy the One-Armed Bandit.

He was the only son of Sir William Rees-Davies, a Chief Justice of Hong Kong who was briefly a Liberal MP. Rees-Davies was educated at Eton where he was Victor Ludorum and played for the cricket XI. At Cambridge he gained his blue for cricket and read history and law at Trinity College. He was called to the Bar by the Inner Temple in 1939 but volunteered almost immediately for active service and was commissioned in the Welsh Guards. The loss of his right arm in 1943 saw him resuming his legal career, however, and politics started to play an increasingly important part in his life.

He was adopted as Conservative candidate for South Nottingham and fought it unsuccessfully in the general elections of 1950 and 1951, though in his second election he brought the Labour majority down to 482. In 1953 he won the safe Tory seat of the Isle of Thanet in a by-election and he represented the constituency and later the new West Thanet seat until 1983. In the House he proved to be more rakish than effective though he was before his time when he introduced a Bill to reform the gaming laws. He also tried to ban ultra-sexy advertisements. He was chairman of the all-party tourist committee from 1970 to 1974 and also served on the select committees on anti-discrimination and on divorce in marriage.

His life outside politics attracted more attention from the press. It also drew increasing criticism from his constituents. Soon after he entered the House he was suspended from practice as a barrister for six months as a result of unprofessional conduct when he showed witnesses a transcript of evidence after it had been directed that this should not be done. He was also suspended from practising at the Bar for another six months in 1980 for an incident in which he absented himself from a case.

There was yet another controversy about his absence when he failed to appear at Kent Assizes as he was speaking at a women's luncheon club in his constituency at the point when he should have been making the final speech for his client. There was also a clash with a judge at the Central Criminal Court which resulted in the jury being discharged as the judge said he felt so strongly about Rees-Davies's conduct that it would be wrong for him to continue trying it.

In his personal life he had more troubles with the law. He was ordered to pay damages to an American oil man to whom he let a flea-infested dwelling. Two families who rented his villa in Corfu were awarded damages because it was dirty and damp. After he left the House he was banned for driving for three years and fined £150 for a third drink-drive offence.

But his experiences with the law were not always unfavourable. In 1980 he was awarded £2,484 damages after he had been knocked down by a car near the House of Commons. And he wrote a Conservative Political Centre pamphlet, *The Conquest of Crime*, which was well regarded in its day. He was not re-selected by his constituency party for the 1983 general election. He fought the decision in the courts but it was ruled that the newcomer, Roger Gale, had been properly selected.

He married in 1959 Jane Manders; they had two daughters. . he marriage was dissolved in 1981; in 1982 he married Sharlie Kingsley.

b 19.11.16   d 8.1.92   aged 75

APPRECIATIONS

MY FATHER Billy Rees-Davies had the rare gift of oratory developed in his days as Head of Pop at Eton, the Pitt Club and debates at Cambridge and could always be relied upon to add wit, colour and controversy to the House.

At the Bar he was a highly regarded criminal lawyer and also became a national expert in town and country planning law. He took Silk (Queen's Counsel) in 1973.

One of the youngest head of chambers he successfully defended many hardened criminals. Former colleagues, clients, opponents and his judges all have a story to tell about him. He'll be remembered as a wonderful orator, famed for his cross-examination techniques and his closing speeches which (delivered without a note) rarely failed to charm and sway juries.

Above all, however, he loved life — women, parties, racing, art and antiques were his passions. No one knew how to enjoy life better.

Oonagh Rees Davies

Billy Rees-Davies's obituary omitted a delightful story told to me by my pupil-master, Judge Krikler. Billy, whose client had been found guilty by an Old Bailey jury, had embarked on a dangerous plea in mitigation of sentence. He started to concede what a terrible life of crime his client had adopted. The prisoner in the dock, via his solicitor, tried to pass Billy a note. He stopped and looked round.

"I understand my client wishes to pass me a billetdoux," said Billy to the judge, (who I think was Judge King-Hamilton).

"Much more likely to be a Billy don't," observed the judge.

Stephen Hall-Jones

THERE was a side to Billy Rees-Davies's character which I remember with affection, and I am sure others feel likewise. He could be a most amusing companion, and he and his first wife, Jane, were the most generous of hosts. He suffered severe and continual pain following the loss of his arm. He bore his affliction with great courage.

I never heard him complain once. Finally, though it must be said he was somewhat unpredictable, as an advocate he could be absolutely first class. As a very young junior I heard him cross-examine an experienced prison doctor upon the issue of insanity in a murder trial in front of Mr Justice Slade at the Central Criminal Court. I have never forgotten it. It was one of the finest cross-examinations I have ever heard.

Robin Simpson, QC

PHILIP HABIB

American diplomat and special envoy whose work behind the scenes was largely instrumental in bringing about the Camp David peace agreement between Egypt and Israel.

PHILIP Habib was nothing if not a professional. A man who shunned publicity and avoided reporters whenever possible, he worked his way up from the lowest ranks of the diplomatic corps to become an indispensable element in the execution of United States foreign policy.

He was renowned for his hard work and the number of hours he put in, but in some ways he did not fit in with the popular image of the career diplomat. His language could be forceful and basic. Henry Kissinger once described him as "rough, blunt, direct, as far from the striped pants image as it is possible to be". But he was a gourmet and may perhaps have been content to die in the Burgundian village of Puligny-Montrachet.

Of Lebanese descent, Habib grew up in Brooklyn and worked for a time as a shipping clerk in a local sheet metal factory before enrolling at the University of Idaho. He graduated in 1942, joined the US Army and was admitted to the doctoral programme at the University of California at Berkeley after being demobilised in 1946 with the rank of captain.

His PhD was earned in 1952 with a dissertation on the somewhat unlikely subject of the economics of the lumber industry, but by that time Habib had already begun his career in the foreign service. He served as third secretary at the US embassy in Canada from 1949 to 1951 and went on to hold posts in New Zealand, Trinidad, the State Department and Korea, before going to Saigon in 1966 as chief political adviser to the ambassador, Henry Cabot Lodge.

It was in Vietnam that Habib's career began to take off. Widely considered to be the State Department's most knowledgeable expert on south east Asia, he was chosen in 1967 to head an interdepartmental task force to study the political situation in the war-ravaged country and was credited with persuading President Lyndon Johnson to restrict the bombings of North Vietnam.

When the Paris peace talks began in 1968 Habib was a logical choice for the US delegation, and its nominal leaders, W. Averell Harriman and Cyrus R. Vance, began to rely heavily on his negotiating skill. He worked virtually round the clock, and when Harriman and Vance were replaced by Henry Cabot Lodge and Lawrence Walsh after the election of President Nixon, Habib, who was impervious to political change, stayed on.

Habib served for the next three years as US Ambassador to Korea, becoming assistant secretary of state for East Asian and Pacific affairs in 1974. In this role he was openly critical of the repressive regimes in the Philippines and South Korea, going further than any other American official in his censure of President Ferdinand Marcos and President Park Chung Hee. Nonetheless, he argued that both nations were vital to America's "security interests".

In May 1976, when President Gerald Ford made him under secretary of state for political affairs, Habib shifted his attention to the Middle East. Jimmy Carter retained him in the post after taking office in January 1977, and Habib worked tirelessly to persuade the Egyptian president, Anwar Sadat, and the Israeli premier, Menachem Begin, to meet together under American auspices at Camp David. The resulting peace agreement was the crowning achievement of the Carter presidency, and of Philip Habib's diplomatic career.

Always a workaholic, Habib overtaxed himself in his search for a new political alignment in the Middle East, and early in 1978 he suffered a massive heart attack – his second in six years. After a long period of recuperation he retired from the foreign service and remained inactive until 1981 when President Ronald Reagan called on him to help defuse the explosive situation in Lebanon.

Once again, Habib was on his travels, commuting constantly between Beirut, Damascus, Jerusalem and Riyadh. An expert poker player, he remained optimistic that reason would prevail, and for a while his shuttle diplomacy did seem to lessen the tensions in the region. But constant flare-ups repeatedly aborted efforts and in the end even Philip Habib had to admit defeat.

Habib was replaced by Robert McFarlane in 1983 as President Reagan's special peace envoy in the Middle East. "Personal reasons" was the phrase given for the change, but it was clear that Habib's history of heart problems was a major factor.

Nonetheless he was to be recalled to the Reagan colours a number of times during the 1980s. He was special envoy to Central America and even at one point tried to bring Britain and Argentina together for negotiations over the future of the Falklands.

Diplomatically, Habib straddled the world: in 1986 he was even sent to assess the elections in Manila. But the greatest successes of the Brooklyn boy of Lebanese extraction were based on the Middle East.

b 25.2.20   d 26.5.92   aged 72

PIOTR JAROSZEWICZ

The former prime minister of Poland, was found murdered near Warsaw with his wife.

PIOTR Jaroszewicz rose to prominence under Edward Gierek, who was party leader during the 1970s, and was closely associated with the "dash for growth" policies of those years. As early successes were followed by increasing difficulties, it was Jaroszewicz's unenviable task to announce unpopular measures such as the food price increases of 1976, and then, in effect, to take the blame.

Jaroszewicz was born in Nieswiez, in Warsaw province. He was educated at the Free University in Warsaw, and like his father became a teacher and then headmaster of a secondary school. After 1939 Jaroszewicz worked as a teacher in the USSR, and it was at this time (in 1943) that he joined the Polish Army. He completed an officer's course and then fought the whole way from Lenino to

Berlin, being promoted to colonel and becoming the army's deputy head of political and educational affairs.

Late in 1945 he became deputy minister of defence (a post he held until 1950); he was also promoted to major-general and later lieutenant-general. In 1950 he became a deputy chairman of the state economic planning commission and then, from 1952 until 1970, deputy chairman of the council of ministers, a post he held simultaneously with being minister of the coal industry (1954–56) and permanent Polish representative to Comecon and a member of its executive committee (1955–70).

Jaroszewicz joined the Polish Workers Party (in effect the Communist Party) in 1944, and was a delegate at its first congress. He became a member of its successor, the Polish United Workers Party, and of its central committee from the party's foundation in December 1948. He became a candidate member of the ruling political bureau in 1964 and a full member in December 1970 at the same meeting at which Gomulka was replaced by Edward Gierek. Three days later he became chairman of the Council of Ministers, or premier, a choice that appeared to reflect Soviet support, his long experience in the state and economic machines and the fact that he had not associated himself with any particular faction in the leadership of the time.

Gomulka's departure had been precipitated by a series of food price increases, made public – with some ineptitude – just before Christmas. The result was industrial unrest in the Baltic ports. The new party leader, Gierek, accompanied by Jaroszewicz, went immediately to meet the striking workers and won their confidence. The increases were cancelled, a two-year price freeze was announced, and an ambitious bid was launched to restructure the Polish economy based upon the high rates of investment, foreign borrowing and rising real incomes.

Briefly, in 1973, Poland had the third highest growth rate in the world; and real incomes rose by 40 per cent in five years. In the end the strategy proved unsustainable; the cost of servicing the foreign debt rose rapidly, there was a sharp increase in the subsidies that were required to maintain price stability and exports failed to increase to the extent that had been expected. In 1976 it was Jaroszewicz's unenviable task to announce an "adjustment."

On June 24 he informed the Sejm (Polish parliament) that special allowances would be paid to low-earning workers and pensioners, with higher prices for farmers, in order to balance new and far higher retail prices for food. The increases were certainly substantial. Meat was to rise by 76 per cent in price, sugar by 100 per cent and butter and cheese by at least a third.

There was an immediate reaction: work stopped all over the country, strike committees began to be established, and men from the Ursus tractor plant in Warsaw blocked the main east-west railway line and tore up the tracks. In Radom workers marched to the city centre, besieged the party headquarters and then broke into them. Meat and sausages were passed to the crowds outside with shouts of "Red bourgeoisie!", and then the entire building was set on fire.

Jaroszewicz was forced to step down as prime minister and lost his position in the Politburo; he failed to secure re-election to the Central Committee. His son's reputation for the way he dealt in foreign cars added to his unpopularity.

In 1981 he suffered the humiliation of a formal expulsion from the party for his policy mistakes and disregard of criticism. He was later arrested and held from December 1981 until December 1982, while a commission determined whether or not he should be formally prosecuted. Jaroszewicz did not subsequently return to political life, and his final years were spent as a pensioner.

b 8.10.09   d 2.9.92   aged 82

SIR GLYN JONES

Sir Glyn Jones, GCMG, MBE was the last governor of Nyasaland and the first governor-general of independent Malawi.

GLYN Jones made his sympathy for African advancement crystal clear to segregationist elements of the white colonial establishment in Nyasaland when he resigned as patron of the colony's Zomba Gymkhana Club because of its continued refusal to allow Africans to become members. The ban, he said, was offensive to the dignity of the people whose goodwill was necessary for a happy and peaceful development of the territory.

The year was 1961 when the winds of change had only recently begun blowing through colonial Africa. Jones had just been promoted from chief secretary of Nyasaland to governor and was to play a key role in the British colony's transition to independence as Malawi. It

was a difficult period. Nyasaland was weak and landlocked, one of the poor relations of Britain's imperial past. After four decades living abroad Hastings Banda, a mercurial figure, had been recalled to lead his country and was determined that the new African state should break free from the white-dominated Federation of Rhodesia and Nyasaland. He was also at odds with many of Nyasaland's own politicians and with most of the trends of pan-African opinion and was a far from popular figure in Salisbury, the federal capital.

Easing the strained relations between the federal government and the Banda administration in Zomba, the Nyasaland capital, was the first big task facing Jones and his difficulties were increased by the existence of an entrenched white expatriate population which saw any recognition of the realities of power as "giving in to black nationalism".

In the face of these difficulties Jones managed to set an example to the expatriates and to win the trust of Doctor Banda to such an extent that it was the Malawian leader himself who requested that he should be appointed the first governor-general of the newly independent country. His closeness to the Malawian leader did not win him unanimous approval, however, Nyasaland opposition leaders accused him of having become a "private secretary" to Dr Banda and called for his resignation. It was with some sorrow that Jones watched in retirement as the Malawian leader's rule became increasingly dictatorial, but he retained Dr Banda's trust and some years ago put it to use by persuading the increasingly reclusive African leader to agree to participate in a televised interview.

Glyn Smallwood Jones was educated at King's School, Chester, and at St Catherine's Society (as the college then was), Oxford. He entered the Colonial Service in 1931 as a cadet in Northern Rhodesia (later to become Zambia) and spent his whole service there until his transfer to Nyasaland. He served as a district officer from 1933 until 1951 when he became commissioner for native development.

In 1972 Glyn Jones was appointed as deputy chairman of the Pierce Commission which was set up by Sir Alex Douglas-Home, the foreign secretary, to determine how far a proposed constitutional settlement for Rhodesia devised by Sir Alec and Ian Smith the Rhodesian leader was generally regarded by both blacks and whites in the wake of the Salisbury government's unilateral declaration of independence.

While Lord Pierce was the judicial figurehead, Glyn Jones was the commission's Central Africa expert and, as such, a key figure. It was he who was primarily responsible for ensuring that the commission effectively carried out what became an unprecedented exercise in mass consultation. In eight weeks the commissioners traversed Rhodesia in groups of two and made direct contact with an estimated quarter of a million people. Jones was also centrally involved in assisting Lord Pierce in the drafting of the report which found that the settlement terms were unacceptable and massively rejected by the Africans.

Eight years later Jones was again called into service in Zimbabwe when he acted as an official observer of the general election that heralded the country's legitimate independence.

Glyn Jones, usually known as "Jonas", was an exceptional African adminstrator. He had great empathy with the local communities among whom he worked and never lost sight of the importance of achieving grass roots support for development programmes. His appointment as governor was unexpected. It was unusual for a chief secretary to become governor of the same territory without a period of service elsewhere and the fact that this happened was an indication of the high regard with which he was held in the colonial service.

He was an extrovert by nature with a practical, down-to-earth approach to life. Small in stature, with a tough and rugged appearance, he was inclined, by diplomatic standards, to look slightly scruffy; his shorts, said one contemporary, were usually slightly too long. Much of his early time in the colonial sevice was spent living for months at a time under canvas in the Zambezi valley, one of the remotest and most primitive areas of the African bush, which was later to be flooded by the lake formed by the building of the Kariba Dam.

Jones never lost his enthusiasm or his concern for Africa. At the age of 57, before leaving his post as governor general in 1966, he climbed the 10,000 foot peak of the Mlanje mountain, the setting for scenes in the Laurens Van der Post book *Venture to the Interior*.

He is survived by his wife Nancy, and his daughter Elisabeth. His son, Timothy, died in Nyasaland aged 14.

b 9.1.08   d 10.6.92   aged 84

PETRA KELLY

One of the three founding members of Die Grünen – the German Green Party – and a former member of the Bundestag.

ALONE among the founders and main personalities of the German Green party, Petra Kelly was its big international star, and a woman of immense and charismatic appeal. She first burst on the scene in her early thirties – handsome but frail-looking, vivacious and highly-strung, with an urgent style of oratory and the air of a martyr who bears the whole world's burdens. Many compared her to Joan of Arc and even to dispassionate observers her earnestness and waif-like intensity made the notion seem not totally absurd.

She cut an uneasy figure within the Greens' ranks; she was infuriated by their bickering and poor discipline, while they in turn resented her stardom and tried to elbow her to the sidelines. She fought for ecological causes, but above all against nuclear weapons, tirelessly. She was brought up in the American civil rights movement where her idol was Martin Luther King, with whom she shared a spiritual element: but she added her own touch of emotional German romanticism. She won wide sympathy even from many Germans who found her ideas dotty or dangerous.

The Greens' breakthrough into the Bundestag in 1983 owed much to her charismatic nature and the manner in which she could thrust ecological concerns to the front of people's minds, even in a prosperous society like that of the Bundesrepublik. Today, though the party's parliamentary representation was totally wiped out in the last German elections, she – and it – can claim the major role in creating of a highly industrialised society the most environmentally conscious of the world's developed states. The lasting effect of her efforts is reflected in practical measures which affect German commercial, social and domestic life at all levels and which have thrust *Umweltschutz* (conservation) to the forefront of national consciousness.

She was born Petra Karin Lehmann, the daughter of a left-wing journalist and a country girl. She went to a convent school and had thoughts of becoming a Dominican nun. After her parents' divorce, Petra, then aged 13, moved to America with her mother who had remarried an Irish-American officer named Kelly. In Washington she took a degree in political science, worked for two years in Hubert Humphrey's office and joined political demonstrations – notably against the Vietnam war. Key influences were Joan Baez and Martin Luther King, whose principles of non-violent resistance became her guidelines. Later she worked in Brussels with the EEC Commission, which nurtured her loathing of bureaucracy.

Kelly was attracted into the West German Social Democrat Party by Willy Brandt's idealism, but later left in disgust at the hard pragmatism of his successors. Then in 1979 she founded Die Grünen, which provided the perfect outlet for her passionate, crusading nature. During these years she went on demos and sit-ins everywhere, including Berlin, the Nato HQ, Frankfurt Airport. She was often accompanied by her aged grandmother, and they made an eye-catching pair.

The Greens brought a new dimension into German politics – "We are the anti-party party", said Kelly; "we are opposed to the cold German sense of order." In the 1983 elections the Greens made their first breakthrough into the Bundestag, winning 28 seats: but Kelly took her place there with mixed feelings, for she was not convinced of the value of parliamentary action. But she got sucked into politics and became a media idol, being featured on the covers of both *Stern* and *Der Spiegel*. This angered many other leading Greens, who stressed that the party was a team of equals, utterly opposed to all personality cult.

In 1983–4 they voted her off the party executive and the front bench, and tried to apply against her the Greens' "rotation" system, whereby any elected person must stand down after two years. Kelly argued that this system was wasteful and inefficient, for to gain valid political experience took time. Finally she persuaded the party to let her be an exception; then in the 1987 federal elections she was returned to the Bundestag with a new popular mandate.

Though still dedicated to Green ideals, Kelly grew disillusioned with a rag-bag of a party that she found "chaotic and amateurish". Her feelings were shared by her intimate consort ex-Major-General Gert Bastian, a former tank commander who, under her influence, had joined the Greens after being forcibly retired from the Bundeswehr in 1980 for speaking out against Nato's deployment of a new generation of US nuclear missiles, Pershing II and Cruise, in Europe.

But in 1984 Bastian resigned, partly because he judged that the Green peace campaigners were being far too biased in seeing Reagan alone as the villain and refusing to accept that Moscow was also to blame for the Cold War. Kelly agreed with him. No friend of communism, she was once deported from East Berlin for trying to demonstrate there against the nuclear arms policies of West *and* East.

In a party deeply split between "Realos" and "Fundis" (the former believed that the Greens had no choice but to enter party politics and aim for a share of power; the latter argued that such compromises would be fatally corrupting), Kelly stood in the middle. She shared the Fundis' fears that to work within a "bourgeois" parliamentary system could alienate Greens from their principles, and she opposed the view of the Realo leader Otto Schily that the party, where possible in Bonn or the *Länder*, should try to enter "Red/Green" ruling coalitions with the SPD. In the event, the party's failure to clear the five per cent hurdle for parliamentary representation in the first all-German elections, in 1990, made the question academic and Die Grünen ceased to be a parliamentary force (retaining representation however, in the parliaments of four of the *Länder*, Bremen, Lower Saxony, Hesse and Brandenberg); nevertheless their influence on the wider world stage is incalculable.

Petra Kelly herself always scorned the wilder excesses of some purist Green fanatics, and she hated the materialistic Marxist faction within the Fundis: she was always a spiritual person, a disciple of Gandhi as well as of King, and her childhood vocation for the nunnery never quite left her. She campaigned incessantly for Turkish workers, homosexuals and other minorities, for feminist causes, and against pollution and nuclear energy.

She would sleep only four hours a night, and the intensity of her life took its toll, bringing her often to the edge of nervous collapse. She spoke very fast non-stop with a manic urgency: yet she had a wonderful sweetness and naturalness of manner and was never spoilt by fame. Even those who opposed her views often grew to feel warm affection. One letter from President Reagan's ambassador in Bonn read, "My dear Petra . . . Do take care of your health . . . Your good friend, Arthur Burns."

b 29.11.47   d 12.10.92   aged 44

WILBUR MILLS

Wilbur Daigh Mills, one of the most influential members of the United States Congress for almost two decades.

THERE was a time when the name of Wilbur Mills was synonymous with power in Washington DC. As chairman of the Ways and Means Committee of the House of Representatives, he was the man who held the purse strings of government. Other congressmen, and even presidents, were forced to take Mills and his conservative views very seriously indeed. One House colleague said at the height of his power: "I never vote against God, motherhood or Wilbur Mills."

There was a time, in the early 1970s when Mills's name was being mentioned as a possible nominee for the US Supreme Court, or even for the presidency. But all that came to an end on October 4, 1974, when a Washington policeman stopped a weaving car near the Jefferson Memorial. The car was driven by Mills, who was drunk. He might have survived the incident but for the fact that his passenger, a certain Ms Annabel Battistella, jumped from the vehicle and promptly leaped into the Tidal Basin. Ms Battistella, it transpires, was better known as a striptease dancer who performed under the name of "Fanne Foxe, the Argentine Firecracker".

The press descended on the story in droves, and Mills's political career was finished. Though he did win election to his nineteenth and final House term a month after the incident, he was forced to relinquish the chairmanship of the Ways and Means Committee. "I drank booze, and I mixed the drinks with some highly addictive drugs," he later confessed.

Born in an Arkansas hamlet with 905 inhabitants, Wilbur Mills was the son of the town's grocer and bank president. He gained his law degree from Harvard in 1933, became a county judge at the age of 24, was elected to Congress as its second-youngest member four years later. There, his diligent attention to detail soon brought him into favour with the Speaker of the House, Sam Rayburn, and he was appointed to the Ways and Means Committee where he ultimately wrote most of the Federal tax code and exercised control over practically every aspect of government spending.

His political views were those of the archetypal Southern Democrat, opposing the granting of civil rights to minorities and supporting racial segregation. "I couldn't stay in Congress unless I voted the way I do on these highly emotional issues," he once said. During the 1950s he voted in favour of the legalisation of wire-tapping, and for making Communist party membership a crime.

Mills became chairman of the Ways and Means Committee in 1957 by virtue of the seniority system. Once, when President Kennedy went to Arkansas to dedicate a dam, a White House aide said: "If Wilbur wanted us to go down to Herber Springs and sing 'Down By the Old Mill's Stream', we'd be glad to do it." During the Nixon administration, however, his relations with the White House soured. Mills's last appearance on Capitol Hill was to give evidence before a Senate sub-committee on health as a recovered alcoholic. "I thought it was a failure on my part. It's a disease from which you can recover and gain back your position in life." But he never did.

He is survived by his wife and two daughters.

b 24.5.09   d 2.5.92   aged 82

SIR ROBERT MULDOON

Sir Robert Muldoon, GCMG, CH, PC, prime minster and minister of finance of New Zealand.

ROBERT Muldoon dominated the political scene in New Zealand for more than a decade in the 1970s and 1980s and even after being removed from the centre of power was a figure whose statements always had to be taken account of by those who succeeded him there. He was an accountant by training, and economics were his forte. Yet he became known not so much for his economic policies, controversial though they sometimes were, as for the bellicosity of his personality. In everything he did Muldoon was a slugger, sometimes figuratively, sometimes literally, as when he waded into a street demonstration and punched one of its participants on the jaw. "One at a time and you are welcome", he shouted to those of the demonstrator's friends who showed some inclination to take him on.

Both at home and abroad he showed absolutely no respect for those of his political peers whom he happened to think were barking up the wrong tree. Not for him the oleaginous, circumlocutive language which has in these times progressively sapped the vitality – and a necessary core of truth – from so much of what politicians say. His behaviour might be boorish and his opinions wrong-headed, uncivilised or downright foolish. But he could never be accused of that species of cynicism which has lowered the profession of politician in the public esteem throughout the world. He hated political chit-chat; as such he was not the delight of political journalists who interviewed him. He was not a man to provide reams of undemanding speculative copy or what passes in broadcasting circles as a "good" argumentative interview designed as much to flatter the ego of the interviewer as to inform the listener. When questioned about what he thought, he said his piece and that was that. Thus, when asked on the air whether he felt any resentment against a political opponent who had attacked him, he took the wind out of his interviewer's sails by replying. "Not at all, I'd just like to tear his guts out."

Muldoon's period as prime minister was constantly charged with controversy. He owed his survival for so long at the top to the fact that in political astuteness and performance he was head and shoulders above his challengers, whether they came from Labour on the left or from the right wing of his own National Party.

Throughout his years as prime minister New Zealand experienced bad times economically. But Muldoon argued that the country's difficulties were largely due to factors beyond New Zealand's control, such as the cost of imported oil and the protectionist policies pursued towards their farm products by the industrially advanced countries. And for a time the voters accepted that.

He was also able to excite public interest, in spite of the economic gloom in bold development projects, particularly in the area of energy – such as exploitation of the Maui gas field off the Taranaki coast.

Robert David Muldoon grew up in difficult circumstances. His father was an invalid, the result of first world war injuries. His mother supplemented a meagre pension by working as an upholsterer. The family's condition was close to poverty. Muldoon was educated at Mount Albert primary school from where he won a scholarship to Mount Albert Grammar. He was too young for regular military service when the second world war began in Europe. He joined the territorials and took his accountant's examinations while still in camp. Later he saw service in New Caledonia and then in Italy. After the war he won an armed forces bursary to study cost accounting in Britain.

Returning to New Zealand, he joined an Auckland firm of chartered accountants and at the same time became a member of the National Party. After

two unsuccessful tilts at parliament, in 1954 and 1957, he won the Tamaki seat from Labour in 1960. From 1963 to 1966 he served as parliamentary under secretary to the minister of finance and in 1967 became finance minister himself. He held that post until 1972 and made a name for himself by building up New Zealand's foreign exchange reserves.

In 1972 the National Party, now led by Sir John Marshall, was defeated in the polls. Muldoon had served under Marshall as deputy prime minister, and moves were soon set on foot by a group known as the Young Turks within the parliamentary group to replace Marshall with Muldoon; they came to fruition in 1974. They left wounds in the party which never entirely healed.

The belief had been that Muldoon's more aggressive style would be better suited to the business of unseating Norman Kirk, then leading a Labour administration. As it happened Kirk died shortly afterwards and Muldoon led the national party to a decisive victory in 1975. He became prime minister and minister of finance at the same time.

The power of his personality apart, Muldoon had been promoted by his backers as something of an economic miracle-worker. He himself proclaimed monetarist principles and the virtues of restraining intervention by the government, but as the economy ran into trouble he moved quite sharply to sustain demand. During his time in office he introduced controls on wages, prices and interest rates, and they were much criticised within his own party. He himself countered with characteristic robustness, maintaining that he continued to believe in free enterprise and dismissing advocates of a completely free market as economic troglodytes with no concern for the social consequences.

On international platforms, such as those offered by various Commonwealth forums, the Asian Development Bank, the World Bank and the International Monetary Fund (of which he served as chairman in 1978), Muldoon generally took the side of the developing world in the North-South debate. He called for a reform of the international monetary system and urged the richer industrialised countries to improve the trading opportunities of the poorer countries, or risk a dangerous disintegration worldwide.

In 1981 at the Commonwealth Prime Ministers' conference he came under criticism from Mr Robert Mugabe, prime minister of Zimbabwe, over the South African rugby tour of New Zealand that year. He replied in characteristically robust style and later told reporters: "I suppose when you have been in the jungle for a few years shooting people, you can't understand."

Muldoon showed a similar robustness in backing Britain in the Falklands crisis in 1982. A New Zealand frigate was dispatched to the Caribbean to take the place of a British frigate patrolling off Belize, so freeing the British ship for service elsewhere.

At home Muldoon was respected across the political spectrum, but he was not particularly liked. His talents, built round a sound grasp of his subject and the quick riposte, often left his critics bruised. His abrasiveness, for which he made no apology, was new to the electorate, and many remained wary.

He was nevertheless re-elected in 1978 and again, though with a wafer-thin majority, in 1981. By 1984, however, when he called a snap election in July, he had come under widespread criticism, not least from within his own party, where his market interventions were blamed for spawning the right-wing New Zealand Party. This siphoned support from his own National Party, which was defeated in the election in a Labour landslide. Nevertheless, even in these circumstances Muldoon was reluctant to relinquish control of the country's affairs and he almost brought on a financial and constitutional crisis when he refused to devalue the New Zealand dollar during the transition to the Labour government of Mr David Lange.

Within a few months the critics within the National Party succeeded in dislodging him from the leadership, and he retired to the back benches. However, even there he continued to goad those in power as well as to criticise his own party and its new leader, his former deputy, Mr Jim McLay. His aggressive style often hit the headlines, as on the occasion in December 1984 when he was ordered from the parliamentary chamber for calling the former All Black Chris Laidlaw (who was at that time an adviser on African affairs to Mr Lange's government) a "traitor to New Zealand".

When the National Party returned to government under Mr Jim Bolger in 1990 Muldoon was not offered a cabinet post and refused a junior ministerial post outside the cabinet. He remained cantankerous to the last, announcing his intention of being, if not a thorn, then "a little prick" in the side of government. Eventually he resigned his parliamentary seat of Tamaki and forced a by-election early this year in protest at the government's economic policies. He claimed that the National government, in its aim to "redesign" New Zealand's welfare state with its generous pensions and other benefits, had become "a prisoner of the extreme right and has stopped caring about people".

In spite of his aggressive public image, Muldoon was shy and almost insecure in private. He generally shunned the social scene. He was a prolific journalist, and published several books about his political life, but his chief recreational interest was horticulture, in particular the raising of various types of lily. In his later life his health was not good and he underwent surgery for cancer of the bowel as well as major heart surgery in recent years. Astonishingly, none of these periods in hospital were able to subdue his ferocious energies and it was ideology and not ill-health which, in the upshot, prompted his withdrawal from parliamentary life.

He married in 1951 Thea Dale Flyger. They had a son and two daughters. His wife and children survive him.

b 25.9.21   d 5.8.92   aged 70

VISCOUNT MUIRSHIEL

Viscount Muirshiel, KT, CH, CMG, PC, Secretary of State for Scotland from 1957 to 1962.

FEW members of Harold Macmillan's original Cabinet shared John Maclay's record of continuous service. He had been in Parliament since 1940 and, before becoming Secretary of State for Scotland, had held office also as parliamentary secretary to the Ministry of Production, minister of Transport and Civil Aviation and minister of state for the Colonies. His term at the Ministry of Transport was short but arduous, and the strain of re-forming the nationalised system of road transport plus coping with a crisis over London fares proved too much for his never robust health. As a National Liberal he represented Montrose Burghs until its disappearance as a separate constituency in 1950, when he was elected as Liberal Conservative MP for West Renfrewshire. For some years he was chairman of the Liberal National Parliamentary Group.

The Scottish Office was a testing department for any minister, involving as it did a medley of responsibilities. To a man of Maclay's conscientious and self-critical temperament it presented a particularly formidable challenge which he faced with steady courage. Apart from a complexity of legislative and administrative cares he carried the constant, nagging burden of an unemployment figure well above the average for the United Kingdom. The decline of the traditional industries of coalmining and shipbuilding brought constant anxiety. He set himself, from the first, the task of evolving a new industrial structure for the country. He was tireless in striving to attract fresh enterprises and he had much success in seeking to change the basis of the economy so as to make it less dependent on the older industries. But it was a slow process, beset by many frustrations, and Maclay's efforts were not always recognised.

He was essentially a patient and modest man, but he was not adept at concealing his sensitivity to criticism. He had weathered many stormy passages over such issues as housing, teachers' pay, pit closures and, of course, unemployment. Maclay could, however, be surprisingly tough when necessary. Everyone recognised his inflexible integrity and his transparent sincerity and fair mindedness.

John Scott Maclay was the younger son of the first Baron Maclay, who was minister of shipping and a member of the Cabinet in the first world war. Maclay was educated at Winchester and Trinity College, Cambridge, where he rowed in the winning university crew of 1927. He went into the family shipping business until the oubreak of the second world war when he joined the Royal Artillery, but he was seconded in 1940 for duties at the Ministry of War Transport. He went to Washington to assist Sir Arthur Salter (later Lord Salter) whom he succeeded as head of the British Merchant Shipping Mission. He was made CMG for his services.

Meanwhile, in 1940 he had been returned unopposed as National Liberal member for Montrose Burghs. Five years later Winston Churchill appointed him parliamentary secretary to the Ministry of Production in the Caretaker Government. From 1947 to 1951 he was chairman of the British committee of the International Chamber of Commerce. Maclay fought hard to prevent the abolition, under the labour governement's Representation of the People Act, of his historic constituency, but he failed, and for personal reasons decided not to stand for the new constituency of South Angus of which Montrose Burghs formed a part. He was returned as a Liberal and Conservative for his home division of West Renfrewshire in October 1951.

In the new Conservative government Maclay became minister of Transport and Civil Aviation. Early in 1952 a crisis arose over increased fares in the London area and this, with the strain of devising constantly changing policies for the denationalisation of road transport, so seriously undermined his health that he had to resign. He spent two months in Scotland recuperating. He was sworn a member of the Privy Council, but it was not until October 1956 that he returned to office as minister of state for the Colonies in the Eden government. When Harold Macmillan formed his administration in January 1957 he chose Maclay to be Secretary of State for Scotland and he held the post for longer than any other minister had previously in its modern form.

It was a formidable assignment. He worked quietly away at measures to revive Scottish industry according to the new structural pattern which he knew was necessary. His method was patient persuasion and encouragement to make the fullest use of the Local Employment Act. He deserves much credit for the number of new factories built in Scotland during his term of office and for the new towns which came into being. He also had the satisfaction of seeing construction undertaken of the Forth and Tay road bridges, the inauguration of the first nuclear power station and of the Glasgow redevelopment plan, the modernisation of the fishing fleet and important measures of rating reform, hospital building and

the liberalisation of the licensing laws.

He was less successful in solving the perennial problem of the Highlands and in making a lasting impression on the hard core of unemployment. He got more blame for his failures than praise for his achievements. He ran into stormy trouble over his refusal in May 1961 to be stampeded into hasty action by a strike of teachers, but he inaugurated a useful review of conditions in the profession.

In the same year his housing bill came under heavy Opposition attack. But he endured one of the most uncomfortable half-hours of his political career one afternoon in July 1962 when he had to face the fury of Scottish Labour members over a decision, not of his making, to close more than a score of Scottish coal mines in the ensuing four years. It was Maclay's task to justify the government's plans to alleviate the effects of the closures. It was not the first time he had had to bear the brunt of Opposition clamour, but it was to prove the last. A few days later it was learnt that he had surrendered his office to the prime minister who was engaged in a major reconstruction of his government. It emerged from the exchange of letters that many months earlier Maclay had told Harold Macmillan that for private and family reasons he was beginning to feel the burden of office too heavy. "You have given absolutely of your best," the prime minister wrote, and it was a tribute to which all who knew Maclay would concur. Maclay became a Viscount in the birthday honours list of 1964.

He remained active in business and public affairs. He was chairman of the Joint Exchequer Board for Northern Ireland from 1965 to 1973 and held several directorships of leading companies. He was Lord Lieutenant of Renfrewshire from 1967 to 1980 and chairman of the Scottish Civic Trust from 1967 to 1989.

Maclay maried in 1930 Betty L'Estrange Astley, daughter of the late Major Delaval Astley. She died in 1974.

b 26.10.05   d 17.8.92   aged 86

MAHMOUD RIAD

Mahmoud Riad, for ten years Egypt's foreign minister and secretary-general of the Arab League from 1972 to 1979.

MAHMOUD Riad was one of the Arab world's most prominent statesmen over several decades and lived to be, in his retirement, one of its more influential elder commentators on international affairs. Serving Egypt's last three, dissimilar regimes under presidents Nasser, Sadat and Mubarak, he was primarily a diplomat, an organisation man whose own position on issues was not always apparent. In his last years, he found greater freedom of expression, revealing that he still harboured some nostalgia for Arab nationalism and the Nasser era. He was also strongly sympathetic to the Palestinian cause and disagreed with the peace settlement President Sadat made with Israel.

Born into a middle-class family, Riad enrolled at the military and staff college in Cairo after completing high school and obtained a doctorate in engineering in 1940, when Egyptian public opinion under King Farouk tended strongly towards Nazi Germany. He saw service in the fighting between Arabs and Jews in 1948-49 and, after the defeat of the Arab armies in the Israeli war of independence, he was chosen to lead the Arab military delegation in the mixed armistice committee, in which capacity he negotiated with the new state of Israel until 1952. He then left the army as a lieutenant-colonel to head the Palestine desk of the foreign ministry.

That was the year of the military coup that toppled the monarchy and replaced it with the regime of Colonel Gamal Abdel Nasser. Riad was sympathetic to the new rulers and his diplomatic career made rapid progress. He was promoted to lead the foreign ministry's Arab affairs department until, in 1955, he was sent to Damascus as ambassador. During the crisis over the invasion of the Suez Canal zone by Israel, Britain and France in 1956 Riad solicited public and diplomatic backing for Egypt among the Syrians and helped to prepare the two countries for their ill-fated amalgamation in the United Arab Republic in 1958.

From 1958 to 1962 Riad served as foreign affairs adviser to the president before being sent to New York for a two-year spell as Egypt's permanent representative at the United Nations. In 1964 he was appointed minister of foreign affairs. Two years later he had a brief spell in the office of the Arab League but he was reinstated as foreign minister in 1967 and shortly afterwards was promoted to deputy prime minister.

In the wake of the Arab defeat in the Six-Day War of June 1967 Riad played an active part in the diplomatic activity that led to the drafting by Lord Caradon, then Britain's permanent representative at the UN, of the security council resolution 242. This urged the Arab states to recognise Israel and guarantee its security within the pre-1967 borders in return for Israel vacating all the land it occupied during the war. He was also instrumental in persuading all but three African states (South Africa, Malawi and Lesotho) to sever diplomatic relations with Israel because of its refusal to withdraw from the Sinai peninsula. At that time Egypt – together with India and Yugoslavia – was one of the leaders of the new non-aligned bloc of nations and Riad succeeded in persuading many countries in the communist and developing worlds to boycott Israel.

Anwar Sadat, who succeeded Nasser as president in 1970, did not have the same regard for Riad. However, he nominated him in 1972 for the secretary-generalship of the League of Arab States. Riad's long experience of inter-Arab rivalry was found useful there. He was able to prevent a number of crises from getting out of hand but he was unable to avert the great division of 1979, when Egypt was expelled from the league for its separate Camp David peace agreements with Israel.

Although Riad had opposed President Sadat's policy, he resigned from his post as secretary-general when the headquarters of the league were transferred to Tunis. During his retirement Riad was often consulted by President Mubarak and other Arab leaders for advice on their foreign relations. In addition he wrote a number of books, principal among them being his memoirs, *The Struggle for Peace in the Middle East*. Prior to the invasion of Kuwait by President Saddam Hussein's forces, Riad warned against the Iraqi leader's ambitions and urged Arab states to join hands with the West to re-enforce the status of Kuwait. But he later criticised the United States for inflicting too much civilian destruction on Iraq.

Mahmoud Riad's style of living was comparatively modest. In addition to their home in Cairo, he and his wife maintained an apartment in London where they spent about two months of each year.

Riad is survived by his wife and their three sons.

b 8.1.17   d 25.1.92   aged 75

SYD VINCENT

Sydney George Vincent, Lancashire miners' leader.

SYD Vincent succeeded Joe Gormley as leader of the Lancashire miners and when Gormley resigned the presidency of the National Union of Mineworkers there were those who believed he might succeed him once again. But a newly-introduced union rule excluding the candidacy of anybody over 55 was successful in ruling out Vincent and allowing Arthur Scargill a comfortable victory. If Vincent had become president, events might have been somewhat different. But in the long run he would have been no more successful than Scargill in arresting the decline of the industry and the palpable impotence of a once-great union. The fact remains, too, that he was no Gormley. They were both moderates, both slow-talking Lancastrians, but Gormley had considerable political skills which he demonstrated at the highest level while Vincent was obviously happier in local negotiations at the pits than in Whitehall or Congress House.

Vincent was born in Leigh, Lancashire, and began work as soon as he was 14. He became first a checkweighman, assessing the weight of coal produced by miners who were paid according to its weight, and then became a pit secretary for the union. He was elected a full-time NUM agent in 1965 and in 1971, when Gormley was elected president of the NUM, his chosen candidate, Vincent, was elected to follow him as Lancashire area secretary. Vincent was therefore on the union's national executive during the three great post-war strikes – in 1972 and 1974, when the miners were able to claim victory against the Heath government, and in 1984-85, from which the NUM emerged split, bitter, and weak.

The last strike was the worst time in Vincent's union life. The majority of his Lancashire miners opposed industrial action. His attempt to force a national ballot, which would have either called off the strike or given it legitimacy, failed disastrously. When the strike began, however, Vincent typically put union loyalty before everything. He backed Scargill and after some of his members went back to the pits he unhesitatingly suspended them. The strike also produced a particularly personal disaster when he was discovered enjoying a holiday with his girl friend in the Tenerife sunshine while his members were facing their worst winter since 1926.

But he was forgiven. He was regarded with affection even by most of his union opponents. His dyed black hair, his splendid voice, renowned for his Sinatra songs at countless conferences, his outrageously coloured ties, and his natural gregariousness made him noticeably more popular than Gormley. Vincent was also interested particularly in his members' industrial welfare. He represented the NUM on the National Safety and Health Executive.

His wife predeceased him, as did one son, and he is survived by a son and a daughter.

b 13.5.21   d 1992   aged 70

LI XIANNIAN

Li Xiannian, president of China from 1983 to 1988 and head of the Chinese People's Political Consultative Conference from then until his death.

LI XIANNIAN's career in the service of China's revolution was longer and more continuous than that of any other member of the first generation of Chinese Communist Party leaders. He once had the temerity to criticise Mao Tse-tung when Mao was still party chairman, and he was strongly opposed to the pace and scope of economic reform promoted by Deng Xiaoping. Unlike Deng, who was twice discarded and narrowly escaped ruin if not worse, Li saw unbroken service in Peking in the upper ranks of government and party from the time of his appointment as finance minister in 1954 until his death.

His elevation to the presidency in 1983 was partly a tactical move by Deng Xiaoping to remove from the centre of power a man who retained some sympathy with Maoism. But it was also a fitting culmination of a long career which had begun in the days when the communists were struggling to overthrow the Kuomintang and had continued through the vicissitudes of post-1949 China. Afterwards, although his post as chairman of the Chinese People's Political Consultative Conference (CPPCC) was largely powerless, he remained until his death one of eight aged leaders – informally called "the immortals" – credited with exerting a powerful influence on Chinese politics from behind the scenes.

Li Xiannian was the son of a poor peasant, and apprenticed at an early age to a carpenter. He joined the army in its northern expedition in 1926 but when the Kuomintang broke with the Communists in the following year Li joined the Communist Party. He spent five years, not in the liberated area in Jiangsi province where Mao's career took shape, but in a similar area, known as Oyuwan, which straddled the provinces of Hubei, Henan and Anhui.

The political leader there was Zhang Guotao who later quarrelled with Mao and left the party. As in Jiangsi, the guerrillas were under constant attack and in 1933 they moved into northern Sichuan; there they were joined by the Jiangsi contingent which was by then some months into the journey since known as the Long March.

At this juncture, and more than once afterwards, disagreements led to the party's military units following different routes under different commanders. Li's odyssey lasted the longest. The force under his command had only reached the fringes of Gansu and Qinghai province by the time that the various tributary streams of the original marchers were gathering round Yanan. His battered and tiny contingent, much reduced by desertion, was the last to arrive at the Communist headquarters at the end of 1937.

During the wartime truce between the Communists and the Kuomintang Li was briefly associated with a second army, known as the New Fourth, which was set up in central China. But he then returned to Hubei, where he took part in the formation of what became the Second Field Army, commanded by the popular General Liu Bocheng, which shared in the final Communist victory in 1949. Li was Liu's deputy and Deng his political commissar.

After 1949 Li served in his home province of Hubei as party secretary, military commander and governor before being transferred, rather surprisingly, to the finance ministry in Peking in 1954. He became a vice-premier in the same year and at the eighth party congress in 1956 he was promoted to the politburo.

He contrived to keep on good terms with most of his colleagues most of the time, and held posts as an economic planner continuously through the trials of the Great Leap Forward (1958–61), the reversion to incentives that followed (1962–65), outright attack on the party in the Cultural Revolution (1966–68) and the continuing struggle within the party until Mao's death (1969–76).

As finance minister in 1958 Li criticised Mao's attempt to bring about instant growth as unattainable. Li was dubious about communes but unwilling to oppose Mao outright. His anxieties over the balance between central control and local initiative reflected an issue which bothers China to this day.

During the Cultural Revolution Li suggested that the "Little Red Book" – the sacrosanct collection of Mao's sayings – should not be taken too literally. He was attacked in Red Guard posters, was briefly sacked as minister and once had to face severe heckling from three thousand teenage Maoists. But he survived, as many of his colleagues did not, and later in the 1970s, when the Cultural Revolution was under attack, he no doubt gained from the criticism he had suffered.

After Mao's death he emerged as the third member of the trio led by Hua Guofeng – the other was Ye Jianying – and at the 11th party congress, controlled by Hua, he was made a party vice-chairman and a member of the standing committee of the politburo.

Only when Hua's over-ambitious economic plans were put into effect in 1977 and 1978 did Li run into trouble. The sober, hard-headed realist had joined in too sanguine a view of the Chinese economy, especially the ill-founded prospect of vast oil production. With the cutbacks of the early 1980s, when Deng took charge, Chen Yun was given authority over Li as supervisor of the Chinese economy.

He differed with Deng on the speed and extent of economic reform, continuing to place his faith in centralised control. He was at odds, too, over the party's image and while other senior party leaders began wearing Western-style suits in the mid-1980s, he remained a dour figure in Mao suits and cloth shoes.

After five years as president he was forced out to make way for Yang Shangkun, the present head of state but he continued to play a political role, replacing Deng Yingchao, the widow of Chou En-lai, as the chairman of the Chinese People's Politcal Consultative Conference. His influence was noted when the consultative conference delayed circulation of Deng's speeches when Deng launched a programme of economic reforms in an attempt to out manouevre government hardliners. Li was also believed to have criticised Zhao Ziyang, the liberally inclined party leader in the run up to the pro-democracy campaign in 1989 and when the pro-democracy activists occupied Tiananmen Square Li was among the senior leaders who urged the government to bring the situation under control.

Li was last seen in public in February 1991 and had not attended meetings of the CPPCC for more than a year but he was believed still to be a significant political figure. Li's official obituary issued jointly by the Communist Party, the parliament, the cabinet and the military lauded him as "a great proletarian revolutionary, statesman and strategist, a firm Marxist and an outstanding party and state leader".

Li was probably not simply a factional leader. Caution, skill in political manoeuvres, adaptability and, not least, an ability to avoid provoking enmity must all have contributed to his remarkable survival.

b 1905   d 22.6.92   aged 87

THE RIGHT REV GERALD ELLISON

The Right Rev Gerald Alexander Ellison, KCVO, PC, Bishop of London from 1973 to 1981.

GERALD Ellison was the son and grandson of distinguished clergymen and was perhaps one of the last great statesman bishops who have given much to the Church of England and the nation in the last 150 years.

Although easy to caricature as a pompous and conservative churchman, he was in fact very far from that as a close look at his life makes clear. Could a conservative, for instance, have voted as early as 1966 for the ordination of women to the priesthood or appointed two Suffragan Bishoprics to firmly convinced socialists?

Ellison was the son of J. H. J. Ellison who at that time was the vicar of Windsor, as his father had been before

him. Gerald was in every sense born to the ecclesiastical purple; his father's first wife, who had died tragically young, was the daughter of Randall Devidson who had been Dean of Windsor before eventually becoming one of the best known Archbishops of Canterbury of this century. Gerald was thus brought up in the shadow of the throne and of Lambeth where he remembered dining with Davidson in the days when there were 30 domestics in the palace.

He began his education as a chorister at St George's, Windsor, where the foundations were laid of his lifelong love of music and his very considerable expertise, and he always retained his affection for the Chapel. From Windsor he went to Westminster where he was a fine oar and, going up to New College, he was soon in the Oxford boat. He rowed in the races of 1932 and 1933, and in 1934 was president but stood down from the race through lack of form. He retained his lifelong association with rowing and often umpired the boat race and judged at Henley.

From New College he went to Westcott House, Cambridge. He later became chaplain to Cyril Garbett who was then Bishop of Winchester and began an association which was to be the foundation of his subsequent ministry. In 1939 he immediately volunteered and joined the Navy where he became Chaplain of the battleship HMS *Barham*. After a disagreement with the captain over the arrangements for divine service he was transferred to the *Orion* and was mentioned in dispatches for his part in the Battle of Cape Matapan. His firmness over the incident on the *Barham* saved his life for she was subsequently sunk with great loss, including that of his successor.

In 1943 Garbett, who had by then become Archbishop of York, obtained Ellison's release from the Navy and he again became Garbett's chaplain. He spent only three years at York, but they were seminal ones; Garbett's methods were very different from those of his predecessor William Temple, and Ellison had to use all his tact in interpreting the new archbishop to a sometimes bewildered and unhappy diocese. It required, too, not a little courage to stand up to the archbishop who could at time be somewhat overbearing, but at the same time he learned an immense amount about the job.

From Bishopthorpe he went to be Vicar of St Mark's, Portsea, where in 1947 he married Jane Gibbon, daughter of Brigadier John Gibbon. After only four years there he was offered the Suffragan See of Willesden by Bishop Wand and thus began his association with London. From Willesden he went in 1955 to be Bishop of Chester where he was to remain for 18 years. He was a member of the Archbishop's commission on Women in Holy Orders and came down firmly on the side of the ordination of women to the priesthood.

From Chester he came to London in 1973. There he soon saw that the diocese was too large and unwieldy and before he had been a year in office he had started on the task of setting up the area system under which the Suffragan bishops were given a very large degree of autonomy.

In London Ellison usually chaired the Church commissioners' committees when the archbishop was not able to be present. He also became the spokesman for all Church legislative matters in the House of Lords where his meticulous preparation and grasp of detail made a great contribution.

In the Synod he became a more and more important figure and his magisterial speeches delivered in his strong, firm voice, and not without humour, carried great weight in that assembly. Such was the public man, a bishop of imposing presence, wise in judgment and in his public utterances, who understood Parliament and Whitehall, a splendid chairman, a person greatly trusted and respected, but perhaps a trifle forbidding and aloof. The private man known to his friends and to so many of his clergy was different. Deeply pastoral, his care for his clergy was very real though he could not abide humbug and false pretentions which may perhaps have alienated him from some. Intensely musical, he had a lifelong affection for Gilbert & Sullivan and was a frequent attender at the concerts in the Albert Hall.

When he left London he spent a year setting up a new constitution for the diocese of Bermuda before retiring finally to Cerne Abbas. There he was in great demand and preached at many functions.

He is survived by his wife, a son and two daughters.

b 19.8.10   d 18.10.92   aged 82

GRAND AYATOLLAH
KHOEI

*Ayatollah Seyed Abul-Qasim al-Khoei,
the spiritual leader of a majority of Shia
Muslims.*

GRAND Ayatollah Khoei was the most
prominent Object of Emulation in the
world of Shia Islam for the past three
decades. As such, his writings and
conduct were the standard on which Shias
were supposed to model their own lives.
He was, however, a traditional figure,
firmly believing in the need for the clergy
not to become preoccupied with temoral
matters. Though activists inclined
towards his activist rival, the late
Ayatollah Khomeini of Iran, a majority
of Shias are believed to have preferred his
"quietist" ways. At the end of his life,
such was his importance that the leaders
of both Iran and Iraq deemed it politically

necessary to declare three days of national
mourning to mark his death.

He was born into a family of provincial
clerics in Khoi, in Iranian Azerbaijan near
the old Russian border. At the age of 13,
after a traditional education in Persian
poetry and Arabic religious texts, he was
sent to the holy city of Najaf in Iraq,
where he spent the rest of his life. His
subsequent education consisted of
attending the lectures of prominent Shia
clerics associated with the shrine of Ali,
the first imam of Shiism, until such time
as he was himself prominent enough to
earn his livelihood from donations
contributed by his personal followers.

In the 1960s his fame as a teacher and
sage spread outside Iraq and he was able
to set up theological colleges and
charitable foundations in a number of

countries which, in return, attracted more followers and students to his door. In 1971, when the Absolute Object of Emulation of the time, Grand Ayatollah Mohsen al-Halim, died after some persecution at the hand of Saddam Hussein, the rising strongman of Iraq, Khoei was acclaimed his successor by a majority of the Shias.

The acclamation, however, was not universal and Khoei found a rival in Khomeini. The latter was, altogether, of another type of Muslim cleric. Unlike traditional, quietist Shias, who believed that the Saviour, the absent twelfth Imam, would only save the world if corruption became widespread, Khomeini believed in political activism to achieve justice. Thus Khoei never became an "absolute object of emulation", but the majority spiritual leader, while the young tended to graduate towards Khomeini.

During the latter's exile in Najaf from 1965 to 1978, the two men hardly met and were believed to have little warm feeling for one another. However, the traditional code of conduct between Shia clerics prevented them from criticising each other in public.

In November 1978 Iran's Queen Farah, travelled to Najaf to ask Khoei to make a gesture of support towards her husband's tottering regime. But, though Khoei did receive her he refused to intervene.

His policy of non-intervention continued with regard to the government of Saddam Hussein also, which was, in itself, regarded as a sign of disapproval. This was at a time when Saddam spent large amounts of money on Shia shrines and institutions to woo the majority faith of his country. However, the policy was accompanied by brutality towards dissident clerics, as exemplified by the executions of the ayatollahs Mohammad Baqer al-Sadr and Mehdi al-Hakim in 1980 and 1983 respectively.

Khoei was subsequently placed under close police surveillance until at the height of Shia uprising in central and southern Iraq in the spring of 1991 after the last Gulf War, he appealed to the world to aid the Shias. The government ordered the arrest of over one hundred members of his family and staff and took him to a Baghdad television studio, where he was seen to be receiving and praising the ruler. His spokesmen said that his relatives would have otherwise died. His eldest son and many members of his staff are still missing.

The Ayatollah does not leave an obvious successor among the Shia clerics of Iraq, whose numbers are thought to have been reduced by the government from some 8,000 in 1970 to about 50 today. His charitable foundations are now likely to be wooed by the rulers of Iran while the foundations will search for another grand cleric in Khoei's quietist mould. The bulk of supporters live in Iraq, Pakistan, India, Afghanistan, Lebanon and east Africa.

b 1899   d 8.8.92   aged 93

PASTOR EILIF KROGAGER

Danish Lutheran priest who pioneered cheap holidays and founded the Tjaereborg travel agency.

KNOWN as Denmark's "flying vicar", Pastor Eilif Krogager, a fiery Lutheran priest in the tiny west Jutland hamlet of Tjaereborg, near Esbjerg, pioneered overseas travel for Danes, who had been starved of sun and foreign travel during the Nazi occupation in the second world war. In 1950 Krogager took a flock of 70 parisioners with him on a now historic bus tour to Spain, thus starting Tjaereborg travel agency, with the local bishop's approval. This was to lead to a business with a £450 million turnover and offices abroad, including London, challenging many local charter operators.

From modest beginnings, using the vicarage as its headquarters, Tjaereborg Travel was soon operating a fleet of 80 buses to holiday destinations in the Mediterranean area, notably Spain. In 1962, Krogager moved into the air charter package holiday market, purchasing two second hand DC6 airliners from Swissair and setting up his own Sterling Airways which was later to become Western Europe's largest privately-owned charter airline with a fleet of 40 aircraft, dispatching over a million Scandinavians on cheap charter tours to sunny holiday resorts in the south every year.

Although Tjaereborg specialised in charter holidays at exceptionally low rates to the Mediterranean, it also offered an extensive programme of tours to not-so-sunny capital cities such as London and Paris, to ski-centres in the Alps, Austria and Norway and to more exotic destinations in Africa, the Far East and the United States.

In the 1970s, under Krogager's direction, Tjaereborg opened in Germany and the British travel trade was taken by surprise when it started operations in London offering holiday packages on a cut-price, direct-sales basis. As well as straight travel operations, Krogager launched Tjaereborg into the hotel business, buying or buying shares in hotels in Austria, Italy and Spain as well as operating a major airline catering service based at Copenhagen International Airport.

Krogager was an ardent champion of cheaper air travel. Under his leadership, Sterling Airways engaged in protracted struggles against the scheduled airline SAS (Scandinavian Airlines Systems) on the lucrative Copenhagen-London run, offering fares at only a quarter of those charged by SAS.

Krogager resigned from his priesthood in 1972 to devote himself solely to the travel industry. "I am only a mediocre priest," he once said. "I have preached the same sermon for close on 40 years." Indeed, to many Krogager was regarded as more of an astute businessman than a man of the cloth.

Krogager disposed of Tjaereborg to its main rival in Denmark's charter holiday market, the Copenhagen-based Spies Travel Agency. His charter airline Sterling Airways was sold to a Danish-Swedish consortium in 1987.

He is survived by his actress wife, Gorma, and their daughter.

b 5.2.10   d 7.1.92   aged 81

DAVINDER SINGH PARMAR

Sardar Davinder Singh Parmar, president of the British Sikhs Association.

SARDAR Davinder Singh Parmar was a descendant of the Kanhya confederacy, which was the most important of the twelve Royal Houses of the Sikh-led Punjab in the last century.

His great-grandfather was General Arjun Singh who served in the Anglo-Sikh wars and on December 16, 1846, signed the Treaty of Bharowal with the British after the Sikh defeat at Sobraon. This resulted in the annexation of the Punjab.

Davinder Singh continued his family's tradition both of gallantry and of service. He took an active part in the defence of the Golden Temple at Amritsar during the fierce fighting which followed the partition of India in 1947. He continued fighting even though he was slightly injured in his heel from machine-gun fire. He was renowned throughout Indian royal circles for his skill and daring while pursuing tiger, bear and leopard. Villagers would call on his services to track down big game that was a danger to human life. Later in life he became more conservation-minded, preferring to use a camera instead of a gun.

Singh moved to England in 1954 with his English wife at a time when there were few Sikhs in this country, but remained keenly concerned with the events in the Punjab. He soon became a focal point for Sikhs in Briatin, and was the founder in England of the Akali Dal, which is one of the most prominent and powerful Sikh political parties in India. He was one of the first Sikhs in Britain to press for an independent Sikh state in the Punjab. He became president of the British Sikhs Association, which embodied his interest in human rights.

He was distinguished in Sikh circles as the founder of the Khalistan movement in Britain and as a staunch advocate of an independent Sikh state. In 1984, following Operation Blue Star, in which thousands of Sikhs perished in conflict over the Golden Temple, he was elected minister of defence of the Khalistan government in exile.

Outside Sikh circles his is probably best known for his successful campaign of the 1970s to change the law which required Sikhs to wear crash helmets on motor cycles. Singh's photograph is in a standard textbook on Sikhism depicted riding a light motorcycle outside No 10 Downing Street wearing a turban to challenge the law. This law had necessitated the removal of the turban, which is contrary to Sikh belief and practice. He argued that under Queen's regulations in the British Raj, Sikhs were expected to adhere strictly to the religious rules concerning appearance; they could be court-martialled if they failed to do so. So why could they not be allowed to observe these practices when using motor cycles in Britain?

Outside the political sphere, as well as inside it, to Sikhs internationally and to all those who knew him, he was regarded as a man of unwavering integrity and great generosity of spirit; a popular man, concerned not just with national but also individual problems. He had written his memoirs which are awaiting publication.

Sardar Davinder Singh leaves a widow, two sons and two daughters.

b 31.12.26   d 27.8.92   aged 65

RICHARD BROOKS

Richard Brooks, American screenwriter and film director, and author of The Producer, *one of the most incisive novels about Hollywood.*

WITH his crew cut grey hair, craggy features and a pipe generally in the corner of the mouth Richard Brooks fitted very well the popular image of an old style Hollywood film director. The gruff manner, supplemented by the occasional verbal explosion, helped too. And Brooks was a Hollywood man through and through, establishing his career at a time when the studio system still ruled. He understood how the place worked and made sure that it allowed him to direct films which included *The Blackboard Jungle, Lord Jim, Elmer Gantry* and *Looking for Mr Goodbar.*

In common with many other film directors Richard Brooks began his Hollywood career as a script writer. He arrived with a reasonable track record as a journalist, specialising in sports reporting, after graduation from the Temple University School of Journalism in Piladelphia. He had also published a novel, *The Brick Foxhole*, written while he was serving in the US Marines. This was later bought by RKO and under the title *Crossfire*, atmospherically directed by Edward Dmytryk, became one of the best of the postwar American thrillers as well as being a sharp indictment of anti-semitism.

Brooks's own scripts, which started after he had left the marines, were rather less distinguished at the beginning, *Cobra Woman* (1944), a farrago with Maria Montez, Jon Hall and Sabu, had some fairly risible lines, which might not have been of Brooks's making. Happily he moved on to classier material, co-writing Robert Siodmak's *The Killers* and doing the same with the director John Huston for *Key Largo*. Both films won acclaim for their ecomony and tension.

The first film he directed himself was *Crisis* (1950), based on a George Tabori story, for MGM with Cary Grant, a sombre thriller carrying much of the mood of those earlier films. *Deadline USA* (1952) reunited him with Humphrey Bogart, who had starred in *Key Largo*, this time playing a crusading newspaperman. But it was *The Blackboard Jungle* (1955) which really brought Brooks to the attention of the cinema going public. The story of a teacher (Glenn Ford) who gradually garners the respect of a classroom of slum kids made its mark as a piece of Fifties social realism, although it looks fairly sentimental today. But it also had, as the credits unrolled, a number called "Rock Around the Clock" played by a group named Bill Haley and the Comets.

Brooks later confessed himself surprised by the success of *Jungle*, which had begun as a tale of idealism based on the Egan Hunter novel. The reviews were not all that favourable, but the public queued at the box-office. And no-one could deny that Brooks helped spawn the whole rock'n roll movement.

Thereafter he turned to more literary subjects, regularly leaving the present. *The Brothers Karamazov* (1958) was long and star-studded, with Yul Brynner, Maria Schell and Richard Basehart. No-one could complain about lack of fidelity to Dostoevsky in the script, which Brooks provided himself. But it did not spark the imagination. By the time of *Lord Jim* (1964) he was in a sufficiently powerful position to act as his own producer. It, too, was long but attracted a lot of publicity because of its cost and its far eastern location scenes. *Jim* was chosen for the Royal Film performance of 1965. Despite the presence of Peter O'Toole and James Mason in the cast it was also reckoned a rather heavy affair. The cynics began to say that Richard Brooks himself

had become the victim of the Hollywood which he had analysed so probingly in his novel, *The Producer*, published in 1952.

This ignores his success in transferring two Tennessee Williams plays to the screen: *Cat on a Hot Tin Roof* and *Sweet Bird of Youth*. He sanitised the scripts a little, judging that what was acceptable in the theatre might not be so on the screen – scarcely a concern which applies nowadays. But under his direction Elizabeth Taylor and Paul Newman gave powerful performances in *Cat* as did Newman in *Bird*. The screenplay of *Elmer Gantry* (1960), based on the Sinclair Lewis novel of a small-town evangelist, won Richard Brooks an Oscar. In it he directed Jean Simmons whom he married shortly after filming had finished, when her divorce from Stewart Granger came through. The marriage was dissolved 17 years later.

Gantry, with strong performances from Burt Lancaster and Shirley Jones and a score by André Previn, still stands up well and could be considered Brooks's best film. Its shortcoming, in common with *Lord Jim* and *Karamazov*, is excessive in length. *In Cold Blood* (1967), based on Truman Capote's piece of reportage of a family murdered by itinerant gunmen, brought him notoriety for the brutality of both the subject and its treatment: no qualms now, as there had been with Tennesse Williams, in spelling everything out.

Nor did Brooks feel many constraints in *Looking for Mr Goodbar* (1977), with Diane Keaton as a teacher of deaf children who turns into a less saintly person when she cruises the Manhattan singles bars by night. When it was unwisely scheduled for BBC TV in the Christmas of 1984 it was hastily dropped even after cuts had been made.

Richard Brooks regularly worked with Hollywood's biggest stars and quite often he got the best out of them. His cinematic principle was that if you can write it then you can direct it. That was what he put into practice.

b 18.5.12   d 11.3.92   aged 79

SIR KENNETH MacMILLAN

Sir Kenneth MacMillan, principal choreographer to the Royal Ballet, died during the last act of his own ballet Mayerling at Covent Garden.

WITH the death of Sir Kenneth MacMillan, British ballet has lost one of its most distinguished and distinctive creators. Dame Ninette de Valois, who accepted the 15-year-old MacMillan as a student at the Sadler's Wells Ballet School in January 1945, once wrote that "his work is as varied as it is fearless". It was the adventurous aspect of MacMillan's creativity, his willingness to risk everything in pursuit of a theatrically brave form of dance, that brought him his greatest triumphs as well as some of his deepest concern about the misunderstanding of his choreography.

Kenneth MacMillan was born in Scotland where his father ran a chicken farm — unsuccessfully. Bad debts forced the family to move abruptly to Great Yarmouth when Kenneth was six. In the aspirant dancer accepted by de Valois in 1945 there were already present emotional strands which would influence the creativity of the mature artist. His mother, to whom he was particularly close and who took him to variety and pantomime, died when he was 11. His father, often out of work in the 1930s, was a remote figure, and of his siblings it was a deaf sister with whom he found the closest relationship. In these facts we can trace evidence of that feeling for the "outsider", the character at odds with family or society, which was to become a recurrent theme of his ballets.

He was early fascinated by the cinema, where be became aware of the possibilities of dancing in the Astaire-Rogers musicals. Emulation of tap-dancing led on to lessons, appearance in concert parties, and even impromptu performances in Great Yarmouth pubs to earn pennies from summer visitors. His subsequent decision to learn classical dancing came from reading *The Dancing Times,* and the announcement of an audition for the Sadler's Wells School inspired him to write a letter, purporting to be from his father, declaring: "My son, who is nearly 15, wants to be a ballet dancer and many people think he is very talented."

The "many people" may have been an exaggeration, but Ninette de Valois was in no doubt about the abilities of the boy whom she accepted for her school. Within 15 months he had made sufficient progress to merit inclusion in the Sadler's Wells Opera Ballet (soon to become the Sadler's Wells Theatre Ballet) which had been initiated to maintain ballet at its home theatre and to nurture young talent for the larger Sadler's Wells company. With that company he made his debut as a dancer, then transferred to the Covent Garden troupe where his elegant classical style was to be admired as Florestan in *The Sleeping Beauty* and in the trio of Balanchine's *Ballet Imperial.*

His dancing career, however, gave place to choreography, a change hastened by a developing distaste for performance. Encouraged by friends in the Theatre Ballet, MacMillan made a workshop piece, *Somnambulism,* in 1953, and followed it with *Laiderette,* whose success indicated the sureness of the young choreographer's gift. Ninette de Valois commissioned his first professional ballet, *Danses Concertantes,* for the Theatre Ballet, and with its premiere on January 18, 1955, it was clear that a powerful choreographic talent had arrived.

During the next decade Macmillan was recognised as a markedly original creator. His ballets for both sections of what was now the Royal Ballet told of an exceptional skill in reworking the academic vocabulary of steps, and of a developing concern with the way that dramas of the psyche could be told in dance. In *Noctambules* of 1956, characters revealed their inner selves under hypnosis; in 1958 *The Burrow* — the ballet in which he discovered Lynn Seymour as his Muse — showed people under extreme mental pressure. In *The Invitation* of 1961 sexual tensions found vivid realisation in movement, and in Lynn Seymour and Christopher Gable, Kenneth MacMillan revealed a pair of dancers of extreme beauty and expressiveness.

The importance of MacMillan's gifts, and his identity as the leader of a second wave of British choreography in succession to Sir Frederick Ashton, were confirmed when, in 1965, he produced his full-length *Romeo and Juliet* at Covent Garden. A sensational success, it prefaced a major change in his career.

He had for some time considered setting Mahler's *Das Lied von der Erde.* The Covent Garden board felt that the score was sacrosanct. But MacMillan's contemporary and friend, John Cranko, director of the Stuttgart Ballet since 1961, welcomed the opportunity to stage it. *Lied* was produced for the Stuttgart Ballet at the end of 1965 and was quickly recognised as one of MacMillan's most intense and beautiful ballets.

In the following year he was invited to move to Berlin to direct the ballet company at the Staatsoper, and he accepted, taking with him Lynn Seymour as his principal ballerina. For the next three years MacMillan laboured tirelessly to shape the company as a worthy classic

ensemble, staging new ballets — notably the one-act *Anastasia* for Seymour — and producing handsome versions of *The Sleeping Beauty* and *Swan Lake.*

The onerous double task of directing and administering the Berlin troupe took temporary toll of MacMillan's health. His inadequacy in the German language did not help either. By 1970 he had returned to London and to Covent Garden. Sir David Webster, general administrator of the Royal Opera House, had advised MacMillan when he left for Berlin that he was to be director of the Royal Ballet when Sir Frederick Ashton relinquished the post. Thus it was that MacMillan took up his appointment in the autumn of 1970, with John Field as co-director. The joint directorship had been mishandled by the Opera House, and within three months Field resigned and MacMillan became sole artistic director at a time when the two sections of the Royal Ballet were undergoing considerable reorganisation.

His seven years as head of the company were marked by exceptional success and by troughs of public and press dislike — or, as he preferred to say, incomprehension. Both the full-length works he made during this time — *Anastasia* and *Manon* — were attacked by certain critics, and as strongly supported by others. His shorter ballets also divided opinion, yet the enduring popularity of such pieces as *Elite Syncopations* and *Requiem* suggest how their merits were finally understood. Overriding all else was MacMillan's concern to display and develop the classic and expressive gifts of a real ballet company that remained on peak form during the years of his directorate. On a personal note, his marriage in 1974 to the Australian artist Deborah Williams was to give him enduring happiness and new confidence to a man who was naturally shy and uncertain in the presence of those whom he did not know well.

It would be wrong to pretend that administration had not affected MacMillan's creative energies. At the end of the 1977 season he resigned as director of the Royal Ballet, and as if to prove that his gifts were thereby liberated, he produced two of his finest works in the following year, the full-length *Mayerling* for the Royal Ballet, and *My Brother, My Sisters* for Stuttgart. Both confirmed the choreographer's mastery at analysing character and emotion through tellingly expressive movement.

MacMillan's concern about the sometimes enclosed and self-absorbed nature of ballet was manifest in several works that followed. With the full-length *Isadora* for Covent Garden, he sought to break from the dance-studio into the theatre; with *Playground* for the Sadler's Wells Royal Ballet, he made what was almost a ''play for dancers'' that examined the nature of mental instability. In *Valley of Shadows* and *Different Drummer* his desire to show ballet as an art of the late-twentieth century, a means of expressing contemporary concerns rather than fairytale fantasy, was again a guiding creative ideal.

Ventures into directing plays, and to working in television, were further evidence of his concern for the larger theatrical implications of his art. In 1984, while remaining chief choreographer of the Royal Ballet, he became associate director of the American Ballet Theatre for some five years. For ABT he staged new works as well as producing *The Sleeping Beauty*; a *Manon* was planned but cancelled for economy reasons. Ill-health became a problem in 1988, when he suffered a heart attack, but his creativity continued unabated.

The Prince of the Pagodas, to Benjamin Britten's score, was staged at Covent Garden to coincide with MacMillan's sixtieth birthday. He turned again to his *Romeo* designer, Nicholas Georgiadis, but the evening was not the triumph it should have been and a planned revival has been postponed. Sadler's Wells revived his shorter works earlier this year, including *The Burrow*. His last major ballet, again for Covent Garden, *The Judas Tree,* returned to a favourite theme of sexual violence in its sombre docklands setting.

At the time of his death Kenneth MacMillan was working on the choreography for Nicholas Hytner's staging of the musical *Carousel,* which opens at the National Theatre on December 10. His contribution was about 80 per cent complete and the remaining movements will be based on what has already been established.

The basis of Kenneth MacMillan's creativity was the classic dance which he learned from his student days. His love and understanding of it were a constant of his career; his talent and his cast of mind impelled him to see how he might develop it in the quest for expressive truth. He saw ballet as an art that, like the cinema or the theatre, must deal with the human condition as found in our time. In his full-length ballets he made a vital extension to the range of an 19th century form, giving it new horizons, new impetus. In his shorter works he could make plotless academic dance and thereby extend the movement language; more significantly, he sought to show the springs of human feeling, and the complexities of the psyche, through movement both revelatory and beautiful. He was a poet of the heart's anguish, and a creator of unforgettable dance imagery.

b 11.12.29   d 30.10.92   aged 62

SATYAJIT RAY

On location 1964

Satyajit Ray, Bengali film director who turned out 35 films from his native Bengal

A MONTH ago Satyajit Ray was awarded an honorary Oscar for a lifetime's achievement in the cinema, the only Indian to receive such a prize. He was too ill to receive it and three members of the Adademy of Motion Picture Arts and Sciences flew to Calcutta to present him with the award in the hospital where he had been since the beginning of the year.

That Oscar was fully deserved. Ray was one of the great humanists of world cinema, a man who towered above other Indian directors. He chose to work totally apart from India's vast, brash commercial film industry centred on Bombay, staying quietly in his native Bengal where, starting in 1954, he turned out a stream of more than 35 films, mostly low-budget, which encompassed the full range of local society from the rich to the achingly poor.

His warm compassion for people of all kinds, together with his rich sense of their comic and pathetic sides, led him to be compared to Jean Renoir; his wistful, poetic nostalgia, and his awareness of life's wasted opportunities, brought echoes of Chekhov; and his feeling for the social nuances and hidden tensions of a still puritanical and repressed society led to comparisons with Henry James.

Though deeply sensitive to Bengali culture and spirituality, Ray was a cosmopolitan, much more at ease with Western culture than, say, the great Japanese directors. He was thus able to interpret Indian life and values to Western audiences as vividly and sympathetically as any other artist has ever done. This did not stop local critics being censorious about Ray's more recent films which, they claimed, were insufficiently critical of the society around him. Non-Bengalis were ready to attack him for being too rarified and for presenting an India for overseas consumption.

Ray was fond of describing himself as middle class. He was born into an artistic family – his father was a writer and painter, his grandfather a friend of Rabindranath Tagore. He studied for three years in Tagore's shadow, in the college that the great man had founded at Santinekatan. Tagore was to be a life-long influence. Another early mentor was Renoir who encouraged Ray to start making films when he himself was in Bengal, shooting *The River*.

While earning his living as an illustrator in an advertising agency, Ray spent his Sundays over three years filming *Pather Panchali*, the first part of his celebrated *Apu Trilogy* about Bengal peasant life. The film's gentle simplicity and lyric vision excited the 1956 Cannes Festival where it came as a new voice from a little-known world. Around the globe it won ten prizes. The two later films followed the boy Apu into manhood and the inevitable Indian struggle for survival.

Another early film, *The Music Room* (1958), was the elegiac portrait of a decaying landowner, neglecting his business and burying himself in music and art: it showed that Ray, despite his Leftish views, could be as sensitive to the dying world of patrician grace as he was to the plight of the peasantry. In his middle period, two poetic masterpieces were *Charulata* (1963) and *Days and Nights in the Forest* (1970). The first, from a story by Tagore set in the 1880s, was a delicate study of an educated woman torn between her neglectful husband and a literary cousin. The languor of Indian upper-class life, the sounds and shadows of the household, the gentle regret of desire unfulfilled – all were beautifully conveyed. In *Days and Nights*, Ray took a seemingly trivial tale of four young men from Calcutta, fooling about on a holiday jaunt in the hills, and made of it a serene and perceptive study, both comic and tender, of the transience of happiness and the search for love. The delightful pastoral setting was counterpointed by the theme of the tensions of Indian city life.

Ray was by now being accused by some Indians of neglecting political and urban realities and escaping into rural and historical idylls. Partly in answer to this he next made a number of films about urban life in Calcutta. *Company Limited* (1970) was a study of India's new managerial ruling class – of an ambitious young man who sells his integrity to advance his career as a factory executive. *The Middleman* (1975), equally acute and ironical, was about a young upper-caste graduate who – like so many – fails to find a proper job and is reduced to the ignominy of touting and pimping for businessmen.

Other notable films of this period looked at some of the social and political problems of India's past. *Distant Thunder* charted the impact on a Bengal village of the great famine of 1943, and also examined the cruelties of the caste system. *The Chess Players* (1977) was Ray's only film to be made not in Bengali but in Hindi and English, and with a relatively large budget: starring Richard Attenborough, it was about the British annexation of Oudh in 1856. Ray carefully avoided passing judgment on the cultured but effete local rulers whose corruption had made the take-over inevitable. But his clear implication was that Indians had only themselves to blame for British colonisations – and this did not endear him to his fellow countrymen. In 1982 came *Ghare Baire* ("Home and the World"), based on a Tagore novel about the Bengal bourgeoisie.

He was certainly more highly regarded in the West than in his own country. The Indian film industry resented his refusal to compromise with it. Repeatedly, he refused offers to work in Bombay or Hollywood, believing that his strength lay in staying close to his Bengali roots, where in his early work he was a true neo-realist, much influenced by de Sica and, like him, often using non-professional actors.

His essential quality was his feeling for character, its quirks and oddities as well as its deeper emotions, and his subtle portrayal of loyalty, humiliation, love and yearning. His constant theme was the tension between change and tradition in modern India, and his method was a gently contemplative style of film-making.

One token of his culture-bridging, and of his skill, is that he succeeded in translating Edward Lear and Lewis Carroll into Bengali. He had, after all, in true middle class fashion been brought up on *The Boy's Own Paper* and Wodehouse.

Satyajit Ray is survived by his wife, Bijoya and his son, Sandip.

b 22.5.21   d 23.4.92   aged 70

EUGENE BLACK

Eugene Robert Black, president of the World Bank from 1949 to 1962.

THROUGHOUT most of his presidency of the World Bank, Eugene Black was probably the best-known financial figure in the world, both as head of an independent agency providing aid for development projects in some 60 countries, and as a vigorous advocate of development assistance and critic of policies that he believed hampered economic progress. Although he himself had played no part in the founding of the World Bank and had only a small share in establishing its fundamental policies, it was under his leadership that it emerged as perhaps the most successful of the international organisations set up in the wake of the second world war. Few men have done more than this apparently conventional American banker to raise the living standards of the poorer peoples of the world.

Eugene Robert Black came of a prominent Southern family: his father, Eugene R. Black, Snr, was governor of the Federal Reserve Bank of Atlanta and served as governor of the Federal Reserve Board; his maternal grandfather, Henry Grady, was a famous Southern editor in the Reconstruction period. Black was educated at the University of Georgia, and later served in the US Navy during the first world war.

After the war he pursued for a quarter of a century a successful but entirely conventional banking career. For some years he was Atlanta representative for a New York investment bank; later he assumed responsibility for the Southern offices of its successor company, the Chase-Harris, Forbes Corporation. In 1933 he moved to New York, joining the Chase National Bank, of which he became a vice-president in 1937. He was primarily concerned there with the New York bond market and he acquired a reputation as an extraordinarily skilful salesman of bond issues.

Black's association with the World Bank began in 1947. The Bank, a child of the Bretton Woods conference, had begun operations the previous year. It had been slow to find its feet, partly because of disagreement over the respective roles of its management and nationally-appointed board of directors, partly because its available resources, consisting of little more than the United States subscription, were clearly inadequate for the task of financing post-war reconstruction and economic development.

When John J. McCloy was appointed president of the Bank, Black was brought in to support him as executive director representing the United States. It was hoped that Black's influence in Wall Street, then the only possible source of further funds for the Bank, would prove sufficient to overcome the bond market's deep suspicions of the unproved and unusual new organisation.

Black succeeded brilliantly. Mainly through his efforts, a large issue of Bank bonds was successfully floated on the New York market in May 1947 and further issues followed. Simultaneously, Black led a campaign of persuasion across the United States that resulted in removal of most of the legislative obstacles that in many states had prevented institutional investors from buying the Bank's securities. Early in 1949, Black was appointed senior vice-president of the Chase Manhatten Bank and prepared to return to private banking. Shortly afterwards, however, McCloy became High Commissioner in Germany, and Black was chosen to succeed him as president of the World Bank.

There followed 13 years of unbroken success for Black and the Bank. The Bank's borrowing operations were widened to include most of the world's capital markets. Its lending rate increased gradually from about £50 million to £250 million a year, and it accompanied its loans with a steadily broadening range of technical assistance services. Black jealously maintained the Bank's independence and professional standards. He displayed a conservatism (particularly on the subject of the role of private enterprise in development) that sometimes provoked irritated criticism but which was largely responsible for the high standing of the Bank in circles that looked with little enthusiasm on other international organisations. This high standing ensured that the Bank was always able to raise as much money as it needed for its lending; it also gave great influence to Black's calls for increased support for the international aid effort.

Black's genuine and deeply-felt concern for the needs and aspirations of the developing countries, his personal friendship with many of their leaders and his obvious independence, led to his mediation of several disputes between member countries of the Bank. Together with his deputy, Sir William Iliff, he reconciled the financial claims of Britain, Egypt and the Suez Canal Company after the crisis of 1956 and in 1960 brought about a settlement of the Indus waters dispute between India and Pakistan. It was on his initiative also that consortia of lending countries were formed under the Bank's leadership to coordinate efforts to finance the development plans of India and Pakistan.

Black was troubled by ill health in his final years at the Bank and he resigned in December 1962 some months before expiry of his term of office. Subsequently he renewed his connection with the Chase Manhatten Bank but he did not lose his interest in the problems of economic development: he served in 1963 on the Clay Committee that examined US aid policies.

At the same time he was made chairman of the Brookings Institution – one of the foremost Washington "think-tanks" – and became a director of *The New York Times*, the Chase Manhattan Bank, the Equitable Life Assurance Company, the International Telephone and Telegraph Company, the Royal Dutch Petroleum Company, American Express and several other companies and financial institutions. He also served as financial adviser to the ruler of Kuwait in the 1960s and was chairman of the John F. Kennedy library.

Tall, sparely built, with a relaxed air and a voice that proclaimed his Georgian origins, Black was a man of great personal charm. His interests were not limited to banking; he was an enthusiast for both baseball and Shakespeare and he gave much of his time to service on the boards of many educational and charitable foundations.

Black's trusteeships included Johns Hopkins University, the Institute for International Education, the National Trust for Historic Preservation and the Ford Foundation. In his seventies, however, he began to give up most of his business activities and he and his wife, who at one time had four homes, finally retired to their house on Long Island.

Eugene Black's first wife, Dolly, died in 1928. He remarried in 1930 and is survived by his second wife, Susette, two sons and one daughter.

b 1.5.98   d 20.2.92   aged 93

KEITH FUNSTON

George Keith Funston, a former college president who switched careers to lead the New York Stock Exchange through an era of great expansion in the 1950s and 1960s.

KEITH Funston could justifiably claim to be the father of popular capitalism in the United States. When he became president of the New York Stock Exchange in 1951, just over six million Americans were investors in corporate stocks. By the time he retired, in 1967, that figure had tripled and the volume of trading had soared.

When he took over the Wall Street job. Funston knew next to nothing about the workings of the Stock Exchange. For the previous six years he had been president of Trinity College, Connecticut. He came, however, with two great advantages: a talent for public relations and a host of contacts in the corporate world, gathered during his service on the War Production Board during the second world war.

He also possessed a keen sense of the national mood in the 1950s and set about promoting investment in American companies as a means of combating communism. To this end Funston set up a scheme that allowed small investors to buy stock by putting up as little as $40 every three months. He called it "people's capitalism," and it worked. Soon, however, the increasing volume of trade had led to a greater element of gambling on the stock exchange.

In 1961 Funston warned the public of the dangers of excessive speculation; a warning nobody heeded. In the following year the price of stocks duly crashed, and Funston was forced to play a leading role in restoring confidence to the market.

His support of measures to discipline those who failed to follow trading rules after the panic caused by the assassination of President Kennedy in 1963 also won him wide praise, and he was credited with staving off the threat of much stricter regulation by the Securities and Exchange Commission.

After leaving the Stock Exchange in 1967 Funston became part-time chairman of the Olin Mathieson Chemical Corporation.

He is survived by his wife, Elizabeth, one son and two daughters.

b 12.10.10   d 15.5.92   aged 81

THE EARL OF IVEAGH

The third Earl of Iveagh, head of the Guinness brewing family and chairman of the company from 1962 to 1986.

LORD Iveagh was responsible for the Guinness brewing company's evolution from a family company to a major international business concern. In the process of this he presided over the decline of the Guinness family's influence and the recruitment of Ernest Saunders, the man who became the company chairman, instigated the take-over bid for Distillers and was eventually jailed for organising an illegal share support scheme.

The actions of Arthur Francis Benjamin Guinness, known to his friends as Ben, were clearly guided by the dictum laid down by the first Lord Iveagh who in the 1920s declared: "I believe that a business either goes forward or goes back – it seldom remains stationary and when it arrives at that point something ought to be done to get it moving again."

When Lord Elveden – as the third earl then was – became chairman of the Guinness brewing company, worth an estimated £85 million, in 1962 he was just 24 and only three years out of university. He was the fifth descendant to head the firm founded by Arthur Guinness in

1759, the year Captain Cook, the explorer, was given his first command. Arthur Guinness's son, also named Arthur, made the brewery the biggest in Ireland while under his son, Sir Benjamin Lee Guiness, the brewery became the largest in the world. It was his son, Edward Cecil Guinness (the first Arthur Guinness's great-grandson) who was created the first Earl of Iveagh and when he died he had seen the company through an unparalleled increase in sales right up until the Depression. Under the direction of the second earl Guinness embarked on its world famous advertising campaign (which introduced such slogans as "Guinness is Good For You"), expanded still further and began a process of diversification.

The third earl grew up in Suffolk on the family estate at Elveden and went to the local school with the village boys before proceeding to Eton and Trinity College, Cambridge, where he read history. He became heir when his father was killed in 1945 at the end of the war. In spite of the early enforced preoccupation with the family business he had a taste for study and collected antique silver, 18th century French drawings and Irish books and bindings.

He was appointed to the Guinness board in 1958, becoming an assistant managing director of the Park Royal Company in 1959 and of the parent and Dublin companies in 1960. Two years later he became chairman. The Guinness board of directors at that time consisted of nine members of the Guinness family and nine outsiders.

In 1963 he married Miranda Smiley, daughter of a Scottish land-owner and a cousin of Lord Cowdray, at a comparatively modest London wedding. Three years later he became an Irish citizen by adoption when he and his wife decided to live mainly at the Guinness family home of Farmleigh, Castleknock, Co. Dublin. He succeeded to the earldom in 1967. Meanwhile under his chairmanship the process of diversification at Guinness continued apace. From being primarily a brewery

the company became a mini conglomerate embracing five sectors other than brewing. Management attention was spread from the beer business to orchid growing in Madeira, film finance, boats on French canals, snake venom production and black plastic bumpers for cars. The company owned an advertising agency. It was in lighting. It even made toilet bags for the Department of Health and Social Security and it owned Callard and Bowser, the confectionery firm.

By 1980 Iveagh recognised that the parent board lacked the management expertise to cope with all these different types of businesses with which it was saddled. City advisers told him the company needed a manager, not a brewer, who could develop the Guinness core product internationally. The man he picked for this task was Ernest Saunders. Within two years, under Saunders's guidance, Guinness had sold off 140 of its subsidiaries and doubled its profits. Then came expansion through a series of increasingly hostile take-overs with Guinness gaining control of Arthur Bell & Son and then of Distillers.

Meanwhile the strain of running the company had taken its toll on Iveagh. Always a plump man he had put on more weight and spoke hesitantly and nervously. Shy and reticent, he was no match for the forceful figure who was transforming the Guinness company's fortunes. During the trial of Saunders and his associates, Iveagh disclosed that during the 1970s he had spent two and a half years in hospital with intestinal disorders and that this had been followed by a nervous breakdown in 1976. Saunders, he told the court, had kept him in the dark, during the take-over activities.

Although he played no direct part in the take-over battles Iveagh supported Saunders in his refusal to agree to Thomas Risk, the governor of the Bank of Scotland, taking on the chairmanship of the merged boards of Guinness and Distillers and carried out Saunders's wishes in making this clear to the nominee. Four days later he stepped down as chairman in favour of Saunders taking the nominal title of company president.

According to Saunders Iveagh promised that the Guinness family would never renege on undertakings to safeguard Saunders's financial interests. Iveagh was, however, a party to the board decision in January 1987 to sack Saunders without compensation. Appearing on television afterwards, he observed of Saunders: "Once a friend, always a friend, but I do feel let down." Nevertheless Iveagh benefited hugely from Saunders's efforts. In 1981 when Saunders joined the Guinness board, the company share price stood at 50 pence. At that time Iveagh owned ten million shares worth £5 million, and the Iveagh Trust 11 million shares. By the time Saunders was sacked in 1987, the share price had risen to around £3.20 and Iveagh's personal wealth had increased to more than £30 million.

From 1975 to 1978 Iveagh lived in the Irish Republic, rather than pay income tax in both countries. Later he made £5.7 million when he sold the contents of the 105-room Elvedon Hall in Suffolk in what Christie's called the "sale of the century".

Iveagh was a member of the Irish senate from 1973 to 1977 and was a member of the board of the Bank of Nova Scotia and a director of several Irish and Canadian companies. He was chairman of the Iveagh Trust, a housing charity established by his great-grandfather at the end of the last century. He was at one time chairman of Wright Farming Institute of Microbiology at St Mary's Hospital, Paddington, president of the Multiple Sclerosis Society of Ireland and honorary treasurer of the Irish Heart Foundation.

Iveagh's marriage was dissolved in 1984. His death came three weeks after he left the Guinness board, leaving it, for the first time, without a descendant of the company founder.

He is survived by two sons, Edward Guinness, Viscount Elveden, aged 22, who succeeds to the earldom, Rory and two daughters, Lady Emma and Lady Louisa.

b 20.5.37   d 18.6.92   aged 55

Lord Iveagh arrives at Southwark Crown Court (1990)

LORD KEARTON

Lord Kearton, OBE, FRS, chairman of Courtaulds (1964–75), chairman and chief executive of the British National Oil Corporation (1976–79).

OF THE score or so businessmen who played an influential role in reshaping British economic and indeed social life, during the 1960s and 1970s, Lord Kearton was among the most distinguished and individualistic. He was one of the very few men to have taken hold of a substantial and largely decaying chunk of British industry and transformed it into an international leader in its field.

First coming into the public eye at the time of the unsuccessful Imperial Chemicals Industries bid for Courtaulds in 1961, he was the natural choice to become chairman after the dust of the take-over battle had settled. He had seen the merit of an ICI-Courtaulds alliance but had objected strongly to the way the negotiations were handled and the terms

that were being offered. His role in fighting off the bid was decisive, enabling him to emerge as the dominant personality in Courtaulds.

He was equally dynamic leading the British National Oil Corporation, the body set up in 1975 to handle the country's stake in North Sea oil. He built up the corporation rapidly so that in less than three years it was involved in every type of North Sea oil industry activity, controlling the sale of 175,000 barrels a day, spending £50 million a year on exploration and infuriating the private sector oilmen who accused it of delaying exploration by holding up the licensing process by protracted negotiations over the terms.

Kearton's forcefully applied industrial strategy won him both supporters and opponents; no one in the business world could be indifferent to what he did and the manner in which he did it.

(Christopher) Frank Kearton, the son

of Christopher John Kearton and Lilian Hancock, was educated at Hanley High School and St John's College, Oxford, where he gained a first class honours degree in national science (chemistry). In 1933, he joined the Billingham division of Imperial Chemical Industries. For five years from 1940 he worked in Britain and the United States on the Atomic Energy Project. In 1946, he joined the fibres and textiles company Courtaulds, where he was in charge of chemical engineering research at Coventry. In 1952, he was appointed a director of the company, becoming a deputy chairman in 1964.

During 1966–68 Kearton was also a very active chairman of the newly created Industrial Reorganisation Corporation. His role on this government-sponsored body and later as chairman of the British National Oil Corporation, as well as his position at the head of Courtaulds (during a period of great transformation both in British industry generally and in the textile field) enabled him to influence, powerfully, the direction of British industry.

Fuelled by his own strong and sometimes impulsive temperament, his industrial forays kept him constantly before the eyes of the public, as well as the more intensive gaze of most of the boardrooms in the country.

Kearton was a shrewd and doughty fighter of business battles and preferably in the open rather than behind closed doors. Probably his toughest business battle was fought in 1962, when he was still deputy chairman of Courtaulds, during the weeks that the Courtaulds directors fought, successfully, to defeat a takeover bid from ICI. Behind the attempt by ICI to merge two such substantial enterprises was a contrast between the industrial philosophies of the two boards: ICI – with the advantage of a far more impressive profits record – set on achieving increasing vertical integration in the man-made fibres industry; Courtaulds determined to maintain its independence. Of all those on the Courtaulds board who conducted the defence of the company, it was

Kearton who attracted most public attention with his strongly worded, confident, and often scathing arguments, chiefly against the way in which the negotiations were managed and against the terms proposed.

Courtaulds' defeat of the ICI bid established Kearton's reputation and helped to secure him the chairmanship of the company (which he led with exceptional vigour and success); but it left a few scars in relationships which endured for years afterwards and of which he was highly conscious.

Under Kearton, the £360 million Courtaulds group pushed up its sales and profits substantially during the 1960s and, following a vigorous takeover policy, established itself as the dominant company in British textiles, aiming to become a fully "vertical" concern, strong in all sections of the business from production of fibres to retailing, and expanding ambitiously overseas. It was this programme of growth and diversification which again led to another of the major takeover incidents in Kearton's career, in 1969, when Courtaulds made an offer for the shares of English Calico, the sewing thread and textile printing group, which, although only recently formed, had extensive retail outlets.

This move, seen as the brain-child of Kearton, was both industrially and politically controversial, since it meant a startling change in the pattern of Britain's textile industry and since the monopolies commission had only a year previously ruled that Courtaulds should not make further acquisitions in textiles, clothing or distribution without government permission.

In making the bid, Kearton was undoubtedly encouraged by the government's own support for the creation of larger industrial groups in the United Kingdom to compete more effectively internationally. As chairman of the Industrial Reorganisation Corporation (which started under a cloud of business suspicion but which gradually inspired industrial confidence during

1968–69) it had also been Kearton's role, with government finance, to foster company mergers in key sectors of British industry.

Kearton's public career was punctuated by lively disputes, including the notable occasion when he accused various institutions of the City of London of prejudice and inefficiency, after the City's take-over panel had criticised the conduct of his own company. In business controversy he was both sensitive and vehement, but sometimes rather abashed after he had spoken his mind. Those who had known him in his early years would recall that, like Arnold Bennett, he had after all come to London from the Potteries, with no instinctive respect for the "Establishment" in his soul. He was something of a "card" with a rueful sense of humour. Among his friends and his colleagues, he won respect as well as affection. And he was tireless in working both for the improvement and rationalisation of his own company organisation and the British textile industry, and in public service.

It was characteristic of him – of his sense of duty, contrariness and energy combined – that when a few weeks off the age of 65, after retiring from Courtaulds, he should take on the chairmanship of the newly established British National Oil Corporation and continue to relish active public engagements, including broadcasting.

To start with, he was chief executive as well as chairman of the BNOC, since the government found the latter post difficult to fill, partly because of the hostility felt towards its oil policy by the petroleum industry. Kearton was not deterred by this or by criticism that he was now exemplifying a British tendency to run important industries with old men at the top.

Kearton's energy was, in any case prodigious. His working routine was to rise at 4.30am to keep abreast of his "part-time" activities: Hill Samuel, the merchant bank, the Atomic Energy Authority, the Central Electricity Generating Board and the RSPCA. His vitality was infectious as was his sense of fun.

As well as his two periods of major industrial service for the government, Kearton accepted responsibilities as a part-time member of the Atomic Energy Authority, and with the British Transport Commission, the Electricity Supply Research Council, and Confederation of British Industry, and the National Economic Development Council. He was knighted in 1966 for his services to exports and made a life peer in 1970, sitting in the Lords as an independent. In 1980 he became Chancellor of Bath University.

Kearton married Agnes Kathleen Brander in 1936, and there are two sons and two daughters of the marriage.

b 17.2.11   d 2.7.92   aged 81

GEOFFREY KENT

Geoffrey Charles Kent, chairman of Mansfield Brewery and former chairman and chief executive of Imperial Group.

GEOFFREY Kent did much to make smoking cigarettes fashionable in the 1950s and 1960s and later brought about radical changes in brewery advertising. Essentially an advertising man, he rose to be head of Imperial Group in the 1980s, when it owned the Player, Embassy and Wills cigarette brands as well as the Courage brewery. Sadly, he also inherited a disastrous acquisition of Howard Johnson, the chain of American roadside restaurants and an unsuccessful poultry operation. Those problems led to Imperial being taken over by Hanson in 1986. But three years later Kent became chairman of Mansfield Brewery and there reproduced his marketing talents on a regional stage.

Kent, an only child, was brought up in Lancashire and attended Blackpool Grammar School. Any thoughts of further education were stifled by the second world war, during which he served in the RAF and became a flight lieutenant in Coastal Command. His wartime experience, gave him his lifelong love of flying, culminating in a solo crossing of the Atlantic.

After the war he joined Coleman Prentice and Varley, then one of London's foremost advertising agencies. He later moved on to another agency, Johnson & Johnson, before being headhunted to be the marketing manager for Player in 1958, after restrictions on cigarette importation and promotion were lifted. That development heralded an explosion of competition among cigarette manufacturers, who lost no time in taking advantage of the relatively new medium of television advertising.

Kent was responsible for the long-running slogan, "People Love Players". One was Player's No 6, a small tipped cigarette which women smokers liked. It became the biggest-selling brand, with over 25 per cent of the market at one time. But Kent may be better remembered for creating the John Player Special brand of cigarettes, with its distinctive black pack and equally distinctive motor racing sponsorship.

JPS sponsored Lotus in the Formula One championship from 1968 to 1985, winning the World Constructors' Championship on five occasions and the World Drivers' Championship four times with such drivers as Jim Clark, Emerson Fittipaldi and Mario Andretti. Kent was a passionate follower of the sport, and could often be found in the pits, stopwatch in hand.

Beer marketing had been as stilted and male-orientated as cigarette advertising until Kent took charge at Courage. Again he revolutionised attitudes with his "Cockney Pub" campaign, using grainy black and white film and the catchphrase "gerrtcha".

From 1981 to 1986 Kent was chairman and chief executive of Imperial Group. But he did not readily adapt to the financial and entrepreneurial skills required at that level. His career was prematurely interrupted in 1986 when Imperial was taken over by Hanson after a bitter struggle which overturned plans for Imperial to merge with United Biscuits.

Disillusioned, he spent two years unattached to a company before Mansfield Brewery asked him to join the board. The following year he became chairman, and applied his marketing talents to developing two new brands, Cask Riding and Cask Old Baily.

However, Kent also handed down the lesson he learned at Imperial. Mansfield's many diversifications, extending to soft drinks, fast food and carpet cleaning, were sold in a strategy based on a return to the company's beer roots.

As well as flying and motor racing, Kent was a keen skier. But it was no coincidence that these are all individual rather than team sports. He was regarded as a loner who could be rather distant. He did not build personal relationships easily, retreating at Imperial into what he called strategic management. This involved laying down guidelines and letting executives implement them with little further day-to-day involvement.

Kent kept his business and private lives separate. He lived quietly for 30 years in Gonalston, near Player's Nottingham headquarters, where he is survived by his widow, Brenda. They had no children.

b 2.2.22   d 23.9.92   aged 70

Diamonds by Garrard

Cigarettes by John Player

John Player Special
FILTER 20

John Player Special

LORD McFADZEAN OF KELVINSIDE

Lord McFadzean of Kelvinside, former civil servant and arch-monetarist who became successively chairman of Shell Transport and Trading, British Airways and Rolls-Royce.

FRANK McFadzean, a short and stocky Scot with an impish sense of humour, was one of an aggressive breed of businessmen who came to the fore as Margaret Thatcher rose to power, displaying adherence to monetarist economics and strict financial discipline. These views brought him into frequent conflict with business colleagues, government ministers and trade union leaders, but nevertheless set in train an approach to management which has survived to the present day.

The son of a solicitor, McFadzean was born in the golfing town of Troon on the Ayrshire coast. He left school at 14 and, apparently bored by his comfortable middle-class existence, ran off to join the Merchant Navy. But he fell ill in New Orleans and decided to return home and complete his education. This he did in determined style by teaching himself in Glasgow's Mitchell Library to the point where he was able to pass the entrance examination for Glasgow University.

It is believed that he was accepted to read philosophy and law, but he added economics after stumbling by accident into an economics lecture. He took a degree in business adminstration at the London School of Economics and followed the Indian Civil Service course at Cambridge. He became an honorary fellow of the LSE in 1974.

McFadzean began his career in the civil service. He joined the Board of Trade in 1938, moving to the Treasury a year later. He served with the army in Egypt during the war, reaching the rank of colonel. After the war McFadzean worked for the Malaysian government until 1949, when he was employed by the Colonial Development Corporation to help run three of the 100 projects in the ill-fated ground nuts scheme. Two of his projects were profitable. But McFadzean fell out with Lord Reith, who had been made chairman of the Colonial Development Corporation. McFadzean's letter of resignation crossed in the post with Reith's letter firing him.

McFadzean went to Shell, which historically has long-standing connections with south-east Asia. He started in finance administration, then went to Egypt as treasurer of Anglo-Egyptian Oilfields and the Shell Company of Egypt. In 1962 he was made a director of Shell International Petroleum Company. Two years later he became managing director of the Royal Dutch/Shell Group of Companies. In 1971 he was appointed managing director of Shell Transport and Trading, the British end of the Anglo-Dutch combine, taking the chairmanship the following year.

The major development of his four years as chairman was the decision by the Arab oil-producing states to cut production in order to raise prices and strengthen their economic and political bargaining position. The major oil companies were forced to act as a buffer between the producing and consuming countries. The companies endeavoured to apply a policy of equal suffering, whereby the production cuts would be applied in equal proportion to the importing countries.

This provoked a fierce reaction in Britain from Edward Heath, the then prime minister. He summoned McFadzean and Sir Eric Drake, the chairman of British Petroleum, to Chequers, where he tried to twist their arms not to cut supplies to the UK. McFadzean had little sympathy for Heath, because of what he saw as government failure to plan for such a shortage. But he was able to point out that Royal Dutch/Shell was 60 per cent conrolled by the Dutch, so his hands were tied.

Harold Wilson knighted McFadzean in 1975 and appointed him chairman of British Airways the following year, after McFadzean retired from Shell at the mandatory age of 60. McFadzean brought his customary vigour to his new job. BA had been formed from the merger of the British Overseas Airways Corporation and British European Airways, but the two airlines had continued to run independently. McFadzean brought them together and imposed considerable staff cuts, to the fury of the trade unions. He also took on the government, challenging its "buy British" policy on the grounds that it conflicted with the requirement that BA should be profitable. He won the right to buy Boeing aircraft, hastening the decline of large-scale civil aircraft manufacture in the United Kingdom.

But these confrontations took a toll: in 1978 he suffered a heart attack, which played a role in his decision to leave BA in 1979. However, by now Margaret Thatcher was prime minister. Impressed by his achievements at BA, she recommended him for a life peerage in 1980 and made him chairman of Rolls-Royce, the aero engine company which had to be rescued from bankruptcy in 1971 after the costs in a contract to supply the RB 211 engine for the Lockheed TriStar had soared disastrously beyond estimate. In three years there, he started preparing it for its eventual privatisation and put it in a better position to compete successfully with its big American rivals. He returned the business to profitability in 1982.

Meanwhile Lord McFadzean had been developing his academic credentials. He was elected visiting professor of economics at Strathclyde University in 1967, three years later becoming chairman of the steering board for the development of business education there. In 1971 he became chairman of the Trade Policy Research Centre.

In 1968 he wrote the first of three books expressing his austere monetarist view of economics and business. This was *Galbraith and the Planners*, an attack on the liberal economist, J. K. Galbraith. In 1977 he wrote *The Economics of John Kenneth Galbraith, a Study in Fantasy.* In between these he wrote *The Operation of a Multi-National Enterprise.*

In 1938 McFadzean married Isabel Beattie, who died in 1987. They had one daughter, Felicity, who is married to Lord Marsh, the former Labour Cabinet minister. In 1988 McFadzean married Sonja Khung, who survives him.

b 26.11.15   d 23.5.92   aged 76

LORD ROOTES

Former chairman of the Rootes car company.

LORD Rootes had the unenviable task of presiding over the decline and eventual take-over of Rootes Motors, the Coventry-based company which was responsible for many of the best-known names in the post-war British car industry, including Humber, Hillman, Singer and Sunbeam Talbot.

He devoted most of his working life to the company, which was founded by his father, the first Lord Rootes. But in the 1960s the company became plagued by strikes and found it harder and harder to match the investment in low cost and high volume which the big American manufacturers were achieving. In successive stages

he agreed to sell first a part then finally the whole of the equity to the Chrysler Corporation which later sold its British activities to Peugeot of France.

But when William Geoffrey Rootes was born in Loose, Kent, in 1917 his father's business was thriving. It was one of a number of British car manufacturers who were competing with one another in what was becoming a fast-growing industry. The first Lord Rootes, Sir William, emerged as one of the survivors in what became a series of corporate dogfights between the wars.

Geoffrey Rootes was educated at Harrow and spent fascinated holidays touring the family's factories with his father. He went on to Christ Church, Oxford, and read modern languages. When he graduated in 1937 he was keen to start work as an apprentice at the Humber works in Coventry. But two years later he was claimed by the war, which he spent with the RASC in the British Expeditionary Force to France, in the Western Desert and in Italy. He rose to the rank of major.

On demobilisation he went straight back to Coventry, working with his uncle, Sir Reginald Rootes, to re-equip and re-organise the factory. He inherited the family's flair for production engineering, travelling extensively to learn foreign manufacturing techniques. He also helped to direct the development of the group's distributing and servicing arms. But the emphasis on production rather than marketing may have proved a fatal flaw in the commercial battles to come.

In 1950, at the age of 32, Geoffrey became managing director of the group's manufacturing division, going beyond Coventry to embrace the commercial vehicle factories at Luton, Dunstable and Maidstone, and the coach-building works at Acton, Cricklewood and Dartford as well as assembly plants abroad. By 1961 he was involved in a £23 million project to build new factories in Scotland for production of the Hillman Minx. Geoffrey was continually travelling between the group's plants at this time, usually trying

out new models on the road. In 1962 he took over from Sir Reginald as group managing director, and two years later succeeded to his father's barony.

But that marked the high point of his career. Since the late 1950s the company had been losing money and in 1965 he had to sell a majority of the shares in Rootes to Chrysler for a much-needed cash injection of £27 million. But the Rootes family retained 51 per cent of the voting rights. In 1967 Lord Rootes became chairman of the company. But soon afterwards the financial position had so deteriorated that he had to go to Tony Benn, then minister of technology, to ask for further support to save the company from having to sell control to Chrysler. Benn tried to persuade Leyland and British Motor Corporation to put money in as part of a call to rally round the flag. However, after those companies had examined Rootes' finances, they insisted that the government would have to put in the bulk of the necessary cash and guarantee bank loans. Harold Wilson, then prime minister, was reluctant to do so for fear of antagonising Washington. Chrysler took control in return for another £20 million.

In 1972 Edward Heath's government sold Chrysler the Industrial Reorgani-

Hillman Minx

sation Corporation's interest in what by then had been renamed Chrysler UK. Later that year the Americans bought the remaining shares for £6 million, of which the Rootes family collected approximately £1 million. No dividend had been paid on the shares since 1965.

Lord Rootes continued as chairman until 1973 when he finally severed the family's connection with the business his father had founded. He had, meanwhile, taken up other interests. he had already headed the trade body, the Society of Motor Manufacturers and Traders. In 1969 he became chairman of the American wing of the Export Council, and joined the councils of the Confederation of British Industry and Warwick University. In 1973 he was appointed to the boards of Rank Hovis McDougall, the food group, and the engineers Lucas Industries.

Lord Rootes also extended his interests in sports and charities. He was an enthusiastic participant in shooting, fishing, ornithology, tennis and skiing, and owned his own grouse moor in Perthshire. He took up leading positions in the Game Conservancy Council, the British Field Sports Society and the World Wildlife Fund.

From 1983 to 1988 Lord Rootes was Berkshire president of the St John Ambulance, becoming a knight of St John on his retirement from that post. He was a Fellow of the Royal Society of Arts. His philosophy was to enjoy each day as it came, and he was a devoted family man.

He leaves his widow, Marian, a daughter and his son, Nicholas, who succeeds to the title.

b 14.6.17   d 16.1.92   aged 74

Humber Pullman

SIR BASIL SMALLPEICE

Sir Basil Smallpeice, KCVO, who was at the head of both BOAC and the Cunard shipping company in a long career.

IN a distinguished career of more than 50 years in industry and commerce, Basil Smallpeice will be especially remembered for three attainments. He was the first man with no professional aviation or shipping background to become the executive head of a major British airline (BOAC) and of a major British shipping company (Cunard). He was closely involved in the bringing into service of commercial jet aircraft (the Comet and the 707) and in launching a "New Look" on to the seas – the QE2 and containerised cargo. Moreover – having been (as many would judge) unjustly sacked from BOAC by a ministerial intervention, he went on to become a respected administrative adviser to the Royal Household. To all these tasks he brought quiet determination, management skill and personal integrity together with much hard work in the face of, often, frail health.

Basil Smallpeice – a scion of an ancient Guildford family which – way back – came to spell its name with an "e" before "i" – was born in Brazil the son of a senior clerk in the London and River Plate Bank. After a serious bout of malaria, he was brought back to England and went as a boarder to Hurstpierpoint Prep School and then to Mydnehe House near Eastbourne. And that was, but for two brief periods of leave, the last he saw of his parents for the next eleven years, during which he went on to Shrewsbury School. Those years of family deprivation between the ages of eight and nineteen – so typical of the "Empire building" expatriates of those days – left a profound psychological effect on young Smallpeice. The result was a sensitive diffidence, an introspection and a certain intellectual arrogance.

After qualifying as a chartered accountant he joined the new Hoover company at £300 a year and, on the strength of that, got married to a schoolfriend of his sister, Kay Brame – thereby repairing some of his earlier loss of home life. Seven years later, diligently self-educated in management, he moved from Hoover to Doulton, the family china and porcelain business, as chief accountant. While there, he was elected to the council of the Institute of Chartered Accountants and, still looking for solace from his early tribulations, became an earnest member of the Christian Frontier Council in the Church of England.

In 1948 Smallpeice first found himself at the centre of transport affairs, 55 Broadway, when Sir Reginald Wilson persuaded him to join the newly formed British Transport Commission, that vast overlord of the various British railway companies set up under Lord Hurcomb. As director of costs and statistics, Smallpeice found himself faced with an impossible task. The work brought him in contact, however, with Sir Miles Thomas, the newly appointed chairman of BOAC, the nationalised British Overseas Airways Corporation. At 43, Smallpeice was offered the post of BOAC's "financial comptroller" (to "count and compare").

He brought to BOAC a conscientious

determination to get its financial affairs under control – for the first time. He had no technical, no trade union and no aviation experience but he learned quickly. He went steadily up the BOAC ladder. He was appointed to the board in 1953 and to be deputy chief executive under Whitney Straight in 1954. When, in 1955, Straight went to Rolls-Royce and, in 1956, Miles Thomas to Montsanto Smallpeice was appointed BOAC's managing director at a time of wide management unsettlement there. BOAC had just been through the Comet tragedies, was faced with delays in aircraft deliveries and suffered a further aircraft disaster. Thus, the new managing director was faced with a daunting task right at the start.

Faced with problems outside his previous experience, Smallpeice wisely decided to tackle the situation with a new top management team of experienced professionals who had cut their teeth with Imperial Airways before the war – Keith Granville, Ross Stainton, Gilbert Lee, Charles Abel, Winston Bray and Basil Bamfylde. It was a good team. Two of them became future chairmen.

In the fast developing civil airline business, the next few years were beset with problems of new aircraft types, problems of over-manning, and problems concerning the government financing of nationalised industries. In July 1960 Duncan Sandys, the minister of aviation, appointed Sir Matthew Slattery to succeed Sir Gerard as chairman of BOAC, Slattery and Smallpeice worked well together.

During 1962 differences arose between the board of BOAC and the ministry of aviation, now under Julian Amery. The fact that BOAC had to show both operating and capital losses resulted in a crisis of confidence between the ministry and the corporation at a time when, thanks to vigorous action, the tide was beginning to turn. In the political climate of distrust between the ministry and the board, Julian Amery invited a leading accountant – John Corbett – to report to him on BOAC's finances and management. The Corbett report was not shown to either the chairman or the chief executive of BOAC. What is clear, however, is that it was highly critical of Basil Smallpeice's direction of BOAC's affairs – made, however, without any detailed consultation with him or his senior colleagues.

By the time that report was in the hands of the minister the airline had returned to profitability, albeit (at £8.7 million) on a relatively small scale. In the event, in November 1963, Sir Matthew Slattery and Sir Basil Smallpeice were asked to resign. To their credit, they did so with a good grace which could not conceal their sense of injustice.

After 14 years with BOAC, at the age of 57 Smallpeice was out of a job. But not for long. In April 1964 he was appointed to the board on Cunard. And in November 1965 he was elected chairman.

Smallpeice presided over the final eight years out of Cunard's 93 years of transatlantic services. He saw the QE2 into operation and was a major influence in bringing about the new era of containerised cargo before yielding to a takeover bid from Trafalgar House in August 1971.

Meanwhile, from October 1964, Smallpeice had been appointed a part-time administration adviser to Her Majesty's Household, especially to introduce modern budgetary control methods. He continued in that post for 16 years to 1980.

Earnest, sincere – always anxious to achieve good personal relations – but constrained by his rudimentary technological knowledge and experience, and always suspicious of political motivation, he was held in respect by all his colleagues while he greatly valued the regard in which he was held by a legion of friends.

Kay Brame died in February 1973 and he married, secondly, in November that year, Rita Burns who survives him. There were no children.

b 18.9.06   d 12.7.92   aged 85

SIR REGINALD VERDON-SMITH

Sir Reginald Verdon-Smith was chairman of the Bristol Aeroplane Company and of the British Aircraft Corporation (BAC), among the many influential positions he held in British industrial, commercial, public and academic life. He was Pro-Chancellor of Bristol University, 1965–86.

REGINALD Verdon-Smith spent many years in the centre of the maelstrom which surrounded the British aircraft industry during the war, through the early days of readjustments to peacetime conditions and through the mergers which brought about the British Aircraft Corporation and led to the foundation of British Aerospace on January 1, 1978. With his passing there departs from the aviation scene, as from academic life and the world of business generally, one of its most enterprising and wide-ranging personalities of high integrity. In particular, he was the last patrician example of the generation of founding fathers who launched the British aircraft industry in 1910. He was in a direct line

of descent from the far-sighted Sir George White, pioneer of electric tramways in Britain and of the manufacture of aircraft at Bristol.

William Reginald Verdon-Smith was the son of Sir William Verdon-Smith, whose mother was a sister of the first Sir George White. Reginald Verdon-Smith (the name Verdon came from that of their family doctor) was educated at Repton School from where he won a scholarship to Brasenose College, Oxford. There as a Vinerian law scholar in 1936 he gained a first in jurisprudence. He also acquired an abiding delight in the academic scene which, with close-knit Oxford friendships, remained with him for the rest of his life.

After a brief experience as a barrister at the Inner Temple (he was called to the Bar in 1938) he returned gratefully to the relaxed, but purposeful, atmosphere of the west country at Bristol. He joined the 28-year-old family business – the Bristol Aeroplane Company – in what was, still, the peacetime rosy glow of the RAF expansion scheme. In this atmosphere the priorities were firmly set on aircraft development and production rather than on economy. In 1947 he was appointed assistant managing director and in 1955 he succeeded his father as chairman.

By that time what had been the long and profitable military production of Blenheim and Beaufighters, and the favourable contracts from the Ministry of Supply for the Bristol Brabazon airliner and its associated assembly hall and runway at Filton, had come to an end. The new, 43-year-old chairman was thus faced with the difficult task of converting a company which was still a family one into a much leaner commercial enterprise.

Although the Bristol Aeroplane Company had gone public in 1935 with capital of £1.5 million, the transformation of Bristol aero engine production to cope with the new generation of gas turbine power-plants was problematical. There were severe icing problems with the early Proteus turboprop which led to delays in bringing the Proteus-powered Britannia into

Beaufighter being assembled (1941)

airline service. This imposed serious financial strains upon the company. In consequence Verdon-Smith was in no position to resist – as he undoubtedly wished to – political pressures brought in 1959 to merge Bristol Aero Engines with Armstrong-Siddeley Motors and, in 1966, to follow this with a takeover from its former rival, Rolls-Royce, of which he became vice-chairman.

Meanwhile the new British Aircraft Corporation (BAC) had been formed on July 1, 1960, as a holding company for the aircraft and guided weapons interests of the Bristol Aeroplane Company, the English Electric Company, Hunting Aircraft and Vickers Limited. Marshal of the Royal Air Force Viscount Portal of Hungerford, the RAF's wartime chief of staff, was chosen as its chairman and Verdon-Smith became one of three deputy chairmen.

During this time he was also chairman of Bristol Siddeley Engines (BSE) and in connection with the company's engine repair and overhaul operations he came suddenly before the public eye in 1968.

In what became known as the "double-charging" affair, BSE was ordered by the government in 1967 to repay nearly £4 million excess profits for the overhaul of aero engines. Verdon-Smith and Mr Brian Davidson, BSE's business director, were summoned before the all-party House of Commons Public Accounts Committee to explain this overcharging. Although the committee exonerated Verdon-Smith of any intention of misleading it over quotations for government contracts in previous years it felt that the company's response had been ambiguous. Verdon-Smith and Davidson were dismissed from the public positions they held at that time. In Verdon-Smith's case this meant his membership of the standing advisory committee on the pay of senior civil servants, of the review body on the remuneration of doctors and dentists and of the advisory council of the Overseas Service Resettlement Bureau. A principled man, Verdon-Smith found this extremely hurtful and he also resigned from the board of BSE.

The industry – indeed industry at large

– felt, too, that he had been harshly dealt with by the then minister of technology, Mr Benn. Fourteen leaders of industry, including the president and director of the CBI wrote to *The Times* to deplore the aspertions cast on Verdon-Smith's integrity. Certainly the affair did his career no harm. When the question of the succession at BAC came up in 1969, with the strong support of Sir George Edwards, BAC's managing director, Verdon-Smith succeeded Lord Portal as chairman.

Those were difficult days for the aircraft industry while major aircraft projects, such as Concorde and the Tornado, were being designed, developed and built as multinational projects. In all of this Verdon-Smith provided a wise, sensitive and unflappable presence in close accord with Sir George Edwards. When he eventually retired in 1972 he was succeeded by Sir George.

For one who was so much in the public eye, Verdon-Smith vigorously eschewed personal publicity, even to the extent that, in a definitive book about the 200 types of Bristol aircraft since 1910, his name was not even mentioned. By contrast he enjoyed the company of family and long-time friends and the confidence of all his contacts with the City of London.

His life went far beyond the bounds of the aircraft industry. He was an eminent Bristolian in both business and academic life and was Pro-Chancellor of Bristol University from 1965 to 1986 and chairman of its council, as well as being chairman of Lloyd's Bank International, vice-chairman of Rolls-Royce, president of the Society of British Aircraft Constructors and master of the Worshipful Company of Coachmakers and Coach Harness Makers and of the Society of Merchant Venturers. A keen and expert golfer and small boat sailor, he prized greatly his membership of the Royal Yacht squadron and the Royal Lymington.

In 1946, Sir Reginald married Jane Margaret, daughter of V. W. J. Hobbs. They had a son, William, and a daughter, Elizabeth, who married Sir George White, great-grandson of the first Sir George White and fourth baronet. They thus continued the White-Smith dynasty.

b 5.11.12   d 21.6.92   aged 79

Beaufighter 1841P nightfighter (1941)

SIR CHARLES VILLIERS

A City merchant banker who was recruited to be managing director of the Industrial Reorganisation Corporation and later appointed chairman of British Steel during a most difficult period in the Corporation's history.

AN ARCHETYPAL City figure, Charles Villiers had spent most of his business career in the higher echelons of the City establishment before he accepted the chairmanship of one of the most difficult state industries; and that was at a time of life when most of his contemporaries would have contemplated a quiet and comfortable retirement. It was characteristic of a man whose strong sense of duty, patriotism and willingness to accept a challenge impelled him to embark on perhaps the toughest assignment in a long and distinguished military and professional career.

For him it was to be the crowning achievement of a colourful life. But the transition from the tightly-knit world of the City and its banking parlours to the high profile exposure of a problem-laden nationalised industry destined to be at the centre of political and economic debate was one which even Villiers, blessed as he was with charm, confidence and urbanity, found difficult to achieve.

His tenure at BSC proved to be as controversial as that of his immediate predecesor, Sir Montague Finniston – albeit in a rather different way – and culminated in 1980 in the first national strike in the steel industry since 1926. But Villiers's spirit remained undiminished although his *amour-propre* had been bruised.

Although the achievement of the objectives he had set were not to be realised in his time at British Steel (the principal cutbacks were to be implemented by his successor) Villiers laid down the strategy for the corporation's survival. It involved painful works closures and thousands of job losses and a complete abandonment of the expansionist policies which had been promoted in the late 1960s and early 1970s.

The son of Algernon Hyde-Villiers,

who was killed in action during the first world war, and the late Lady Aldenham, Charles Hyde Villiers was the offspring of a very old family which had enjoyed strong ties with both the monarchy and political life for generations. After Eton and New College, Oxford, he spent the first few months after coming down working as assistant to the Rev P.B. "Tubby" Clayton of Toc H before taking a post with the merchant bank Glyn Mills in 1932.

He joined the Grenadier Guards in 1936 where his qualities of leadership, courage and organisational skills were quickly recognised. He served at Dunkirk, received a wound to his neck (about which he remained self-conscious) and was then drafted to the Special Operations Executive. He spent the rest of the war with the SOE and parachuted into Austria and Yugoslavia where he helped to organise partisan resistance fighters. His contribution to the efforts of the Yugoslav resistance movement was to be later recognised in the Award of the People which Yugoslavia conferred upon him in 1970. Villiers emerged from the war with the rank of lieutenant-colonel and a Military Cross.

Soon after his second marriage to the daughter of the Belgian Count Henri de la Barre d'Erquelinnes, he picked up the threads of the merchant banking career he had left, initially with Herbert Wagg, and subsequently with the merged company of J. Henry Schroder Wagg.

Throughout the 1950s and 1960s Charles Villiers deployed his considerable banking expertise and charm and was closely involved in some of the more significant transactions of those years. He played a key role in the negotiations which led to the creation of the vast brewing combine of Bass Charrington, to whose board he was subsequently appointed. A personal friend of the Kemsley family, he acted as their adviser in the negotiations which led to the acquisition of *The Sunday Times* and other titles by Lord Thomson of Fleet.

He liked to describe himself as a Tory radical and it was that streak of radicalism combined with his knowledge of corporate finance which was brought to the attention of Peter Shore, in 1968 minister at the Department of Economic Affairs. Villiers was plucked from the cosy and relative obscurity of the City to take over as managing director of the Industrial Reorganisation Corporation. The IRC was conceived by the Labour government to be a force for long overdue change in the structure of British industry by encouraging and assisting mergers in key sectors of manufacturing deemed to require the IRC treatment in the national strategic interest.

It was a hectic three years. The IRC under Villiers attracted a team of talented young Turks (several of whom subsequently emerged as the heads of major public companies) to expedite the IRC's brief.

Apart from a short spell between 1972 and 1973 with the Northern Ireland Finance Corporation, where he was known to his colleagues as Le Grand Charles, Villiers returned to merchant banking and remained as vigorous as ever. The patrician self-confidence he exuded went virtually unnoticed in the banking parlours. At Guinness Mahon and subsequently Guinness Peat, he was respectively chairman and executive deputy chairman.

He was knighted in 1975 for services to industry. But a year later when another Labour government recruited him to take over the reins at the BSC, many of his new colleagues found his style irksome, discomforting and, at times, more than a trifle embarrassing.

He was cast in the mould of the late Lord Melchett, the first BSC chairman, and proved a sharp contrast to his immediate predecessor, Finniston whose public squabbles with the BSC's political masters appeared unseemly to a man of Villiers's background.

With characteristic reforming zeal, Villiers sought to restore morale, customer confidence and pride in the corporation, to reverse the growing financial haemorrhage and to chart a course to survival amid a deepening recession. He persuaded his political masters that only severe surgery could provide any realistic prospect of returning the effectively bankrupt organisation to viability.

Capacity had to be brought into line with the best estimates of future demand. It would mean works closures, shedding of thousands of jobs and the ditching of ambitious expansion plans. The contraction began – and continued long after he left the BSC.

Not everyone was impressed. In 1978 he fell foul of the Select Committee of Nationalised Industries which accused him of failing to inform ministers of the increasingly parlous financial state of BSC.

The steel industry unions found in his style of management too many echoes of the squirearchy into which Villiers had been born. His background and manner engendered suspicion, mistrust and, worst of all cynicism among the workforce.

Yet ironically, Villiers held firm and progressive ideas on industrial democracy and worked energetically as chairman of the corporation's job creation subsidiary to encourage new industries to move into those areas blighted by the closure of iron and steel works which he had deemed necessary.

On his retirement from the BSC, he continued with that work and sought tirelessly to use his banking skills and contacts to stimulate the growth of small new businesses.

Outside his extensive and busy professional life he maintained a keen interest in the arts and was a trustee of the Royal Opera House and chairman of the Theatre Royal, Windsor.

He is survived by his widow, a son and two daughters.

b 14.8.12   d 22.1.92   aged 79

APPRECIATION

YOUR otherwise full and sensitive obituary of Sir Charles Villiers erred on one point. He was, in my experience anything but "and archetypal City figure."

In 1980 I was working on inner City regeneration problems. He had become chairman of British Steel (Industrial) Ltd., having just retired from the British Steel Corporation. As such he was encouraging, as your obituary recorded, new industries to move into those areas blighted by the steel closures, and thus bring hope back to those threatened communities.

I wanted the benefit of his overview, experience and thinking. He generously offered all of that and more. He invited me to his office in Victoria. We first met on December 30, 1980.

The two-week Christmas break was by then becoming regrettably, an established feature of British commerce and industry. The area around his office was deserted; parking was easy.

I was shown up to his office. There was the lone figure of Sir Charles, in his shirt sleeves, pouring over plans, analysing cash flows, wanting to exchange ideas on the urgent, and until then largely neglected, economic and social problems of the inner city and the abandoned industrial wastelands. We discussed (and subsequently visited) the innovative and exemplary St Helen's Trust and worked on schemes for financial help to small business, using the then burgeoning Enterprise Agency network.

These were not the engagements of the archetypal City figure during the Christmas and New Year holiday period, nor at any other time.

Ansel Harris

SAM WALTON

Samuel Moore Walton, reputedly the richest man in America and certainly the most successful merchant of his time.

THE secret of Sam Walton's success was simple: he had a talent for inspiring his employees to serve their customers. A gifted, homespun orator, he made personal visits to dozens of his Wal-Mart stores each week, preaching the same message: help customers, cut costs, and share the profits. The technique built his empire from a single shop in Arkansas in 1962 to a current chain of 1,752 stores in 42 states, with annual sales of $44 billion and profits last year of $1.6 billion.

Walton was named by *Forbes Magazine* as the wealthiest person in America in 1985. He hated the distinction, saying: "All that hullabaloo about somebody's net worth is just stupid, and it's made my life a lot more complex and difficult." But America's worship of the dollar made it impossible for him to escape the awe and adulation, and his wealth was certainly remarkable. Divided among five family trusts, it is currently valued at $23 billion in Wal-Mart stock alone, drawing annual dividends of $93.5 million.

Sam Walton grew up in Missouri, where he was an Eagle Scout, quarterback of the state champion football team and president of the student council at his high school. He worked his way through the University of Missouri, delivering newspapers and waiting at table while earning a degree in economics, then served as an army captain during the second world war.

He opened his first shop in 1945 with the aid of a $25,000 loan from his father-in-law. It was part of a cut-price franchise chain. Walton worked with the chain until 1962, then branched out on his own in the belief that the way ahead lay in under-served rural areas. The idea proved phenomenally successful, largely because of Walton's personal touch and organising ability, and his willingness — rare among American businessmen — to share his success with his employees. He established profit-sharing plans which enabled low-paid workers to retire with comfortable and even lucrative pensions.

Wal-Mart went public in 1970, and the stock soared as Wall Street noted an unbroken pattern of high profits and fast growth. From 1981 to 1991 the shares produced an average annual return of 46.8 per cent, and an investment of $3,000 in 1981 is today worth $170,000. Last year the chain passed Sears Roebuck and Co to become America's largest retailer, serving its stores from 19 cavernous distribution centres, each with six miles of rack space, 2,000 trucks and a fleet of aircraft.

Until recent months, when he finally succumbed to a long-running battle with hairy-cell leukaemia and multiple myeloma, Walton continued to fly his own twin-engined aircraft from town to town, often visiting as many as six of his stores in a single day. He was far from being a remote tycoon. In 1983, after Wal-Mart's profits exceeded expectations, he kept a promise to his employees by putting on a grass skirt and dancing a hula in the middle of Wall Street.

He is survived by his wife, three sons and a daughter.

b 29.3.18   d 5.3.92   aged 74

C. V. WOOD

C. V. Wood Jr, who supervised the transport of London Bridge to its new home in Arizona, and was largely responsible for the creation of the first Disneyland theme park.

NO ONE could accuse C. V. Wood of thinking small. When the first Disneyland opened under his supervision in California, in 1954, the world had seen nothing quite like it. With its huge scale, innovative rides, and almost excessive respectability, it was a far cry from the raucous frenzy of the traditional amusement park.

Disneyland, with its nostalgic population of cartoon characters, fitted the American notion of "family entertainment." Together with its twin in Florida it soon became, and remains a mecca for American families on holiday, while Euro Disney is attempting to create the same ambience in France.

Wood's pioneering work, as vice-president and general manager under the late Walt Disney provided much of the inspiration for the parks. After supervising selection and purchase of the land for the world famous attraction he stayed on as managing director for the first year of operation, establishing many of the policies that have given the Disney theme parks their distinctive qualities.

But his most spectacular achievement was, in 1968, the removal, transportation and reconstruction of London Bridge in Arizona, half-way around the globe. The bridge, built in 1831, had begun to subside under the weight of modern traffic, and the City of London Corporation must have been overjoyed to find a buyer when they decided to replace it with a new one. To sell it to America, where the selling of the Brooklyn Bridge is the archetypal confidence trick, was a delicious twist.

Some said Wood had "bought a bridge he didn't need for a river he didn't have" and there were those at the time who thought that Wood's employers, the

London Bridge being dismantled for transport to America (1968)

McCullough Oil Company, had been conned into believing that they had really bought the more spectacular Tower Bridge. But Wood knew what he was doing. He dug a channel from Lake Havasu, on the California-Arizona border, and there rebuilt the bridge which had been dismantled, stone by numbered stone, and transported overland from Long Beach.

The City of London Corporation was

paid $2,460,000 for the bridge, but it cost several million more to transport and rebuild it. Wood proclaimed that it would become an even greater tourist attraction than the Grand Canyon. This was an exaggeration, but it has certainly attracted remarkable crowds over the years.

Although C. V. Wood was born in Oklahoma he was raised in Texas where he earned a degree in petroleum engineering. Just what the "C. V." stood for, if anything, remained a mystery even among his business colleagues who knew him as "Woody." He retired in 1980 as

chairman and chief executive of McCullough, but he was not yet finished with the entertainment world. In 1987 he joined Lorimar Telepictures, worked on its merger with Time Warner, and then led the latter company's entry into the studio-tour business. That assignment culminated in Warner's opening of Movie World in Australia last year.

He is survived by his wife, the film actress Joanne Dru, one son, C. V. Wood III, one daughter and three stepchildren.

b 1921   d 16.3.92   aged 71

SIR WILLIAM McEWAN YOUNGER

Sir William McEwan Younger, DSO, DL, chairman of Scottish and Newcastle Breweries.

WILLIAM McEwan Younger played a significant role in the commercial and political life of Scotland in the 1960s and 1970s. He was chairman of Scottish and Newcastle Breweries from 1960 to 1969 and managing director for all but the last two of those years and was the dominant force in extending the brewery's interests nationally.

A man of strong and independent views, he had no brief for the received wisdom of the brewing industry of the

day, which relied on expansion by acquisition of tied trade in tenanted houses through the issue of share capital. He was a convinced free trader in every sense of the term and a strong believer in competition. Acquisition was by organic growth and the use of cash, and market share was to be gained by the development of strong brands and the use of clever marketing. His prime strategy in building up the brewery was to seek outlets in free houses, rather than for it to build its own chain of public houses. He was a pioneer in the use of cans, and when he retired in 1969 Scottish and Newcastle had almost ten per cent of the beer trade in the UK while possessing only a few hundred tied or managed houses.

When an opportunity was offered to join with Tennents, and thus make a combine that could totally dominate the brewing industry in Scotland, he refused it, saying it would eliminate competition and thus be bad for both customer and producer.

Though diffident to the point of shyness in personal relationships, his extraordinary business self-confidence and original mind made him an inspiring boss to work for, and he backed his subordinates to the hilt if they used their own initiative.

Born at Melrose, William McEwan Younger was brought up on the banks of the Tweed. He was educated at Winchester and Balliol College, Oxford, where he developed a life-long love of mountaineering. In later life he was elected as honorary fellow of Balliol. On leaving Oxford he succeeded his father in the family firm of William McEwan, the Edinburgh brewers which had been started by his great uncle.

During the second world war he commanded successively the 40th Light AA Regiment RA, taking part in all the North African campaigns, the landing at Salerno and the Italian campaign. He achieved great distinction during the first siege of Tobruk when the battery he commanded successfully beat off repeated Stuka attacks, claiming more than 50 enemy aircraft. For this he was awarded the DSO.

After the war he returned to Edinburgh and set about reviving the brewing industry in Scotland. Under his leadership the integration of McEwan's and William Younger's was completed, followed by the absorptions of Bernard's, Morison's and the Robert Younger's breweries and finally a merger in 1961 to form Scottish and Newcastle Breweries. By nature and upbringing a Conservative of the "one nation" variety, he stood unsuccessfully as a parliamentary candidate for West Lothian. He continued to take an active part in Conservative politics for many years. He was an enthusiastic supporter of Edward Heath's leadership and was chairman of the Conservative party in Scotland from 1971 to 1974, for which he was made a baronet.

Always a radical in political thought, he was a founder member of, and major contributor to, the Institute of Economic Affairs. He was on the board of the British Linen Bank, the Scottish Widows Fund and Life Assurance Society, and Scottish Television and was a particularly successful chairman of the Second Scottish Investment Trust. He was actively involved in assisting his fellow Scots to take advantage of the industrial changes taking place internationally, helping to devise a scheme to enable industrialists, planners and trade unionists to meet their foreign counterparts. He was a founder and chairman of the Highland Tourist (Cairngorm Development) Ltd.

A notable contributor to charity he gave his house at Balerno to be a school for the Save the Children Fund.

He was married first to Nora Balfour from whom he was divorced in 1967, and by whom he had one daughter, Caroline, and then to June Peck, who nursed him with devoted attention through his last illness.

b 6.9.05   d 15.4.92   aged 86

The Abbey Brewery, Edinburgh (1861)

LORD DEVLIN

Lord Devlin, PC, FBA, former law lord and writer.

PATRICK Devlin was an outstanding judge and brilliant jurist. Throughout his life he was a formidable champion of justice, a profound lawyer and a perceptive observer of the acts and omissions of the legal establishment. After a distinguished career he used his searching concern about potential miscarriage of justice as a leading campaigner for the release of the Guildford Four. He was also the first non-journalist chairman of the now defunct Press Council and a notable chairman of public enquiries whose findings were renowned for their clarity of thought and sturdy integrity.

At the age of 42 Devlin was the youngest judge to be appointed this century when he became a Justice of

King's Bench Division in 1948. His most celebrated case was the trial and acquittal in 1957 of John Bodkin Adams, the Eastbourne doctor accused of poisoning a patient.

Devlin was born into a Roman Catholic family. His father was an architect practising in Aberdeen. His two brothers were Christopher Devlin, the Jesuit priest and author, and William Devlin, the actor. Two of his sisters were nuns. He thought of going into the priesthood. Devlin was educated at Stonyhurst and Christ's College, Cambridge, where his academic achievements gave little indication of his subsequent brilliance. At the Cambridge Union, however, he displayed all the charm, logic and eloquence of the consummate advocate. He succeeded Michael Ramsey, the future Archbishop of Canterbury, as president of the union in 1926.

He was called to the Bar in 1929 by Gray's Inn, having been a pupil of Cartwright Sharp. Almost immediately after his call, he became legal secretary to the Attorney-General, Sir William Jowitt, and returned with Jowitt to practise in the Temple in 1931. Although he was prosecuting counsel to the Mint from 1931 to 1939, most of his work lay in the commercial field. During the second world war he helped in the legal deparment of the ministry of supply. He took silk in 1945. In 1947 he was appointed Attorney-General to the Duchy of Cornwall. In 1948 he was made a judge of the King's Bench Division at the age of 42.

For the next 15 years he sat as a judge and there were few better in this century. Although he had virtually no experience of criminal work at the Bar, he soon became a first-class Assize judge. One of his directions to the jury in a murder trial on provocation was described by the Lord Chief Justice as a model for all time. His conduct of the famous trial and acquittal of John Bodkin Adams at the Old Bailey showed a determination to adhere to principles of evidence in the face of great public hostility to the accused.

The trial also produced a clash with the Attorney-General, Sir Reginald Manningham-Buller, made all the more piquant by the fact that both men were at that time considered to be in the running for the succession to Lord Goddard as Lord Chief Justice. Many years later, after the deaths of all the important participants in the trial, Devlin published an account of it in which he criticised the conduct of the attorney-general. This provoked profound indignation in some legal quarters. It was the only time in a long public life in which he was subjected to serious opposition. He took little notice of it.

In all his judgments he showed an exceptional flair for a discussion of the principles governing the case, and for reconciling or explaining previous decisions according to such principles. He thought long and deeply and undertook endless research when engaged in this task. His judgments became particularly brilliant, if sometimes rather long, after he became Lord Justic of Appeal in 1960 and a Lord of Appeal in Ordinary in 1961. Before these rapid promotions he had been for three years the first president of the Restrictive Practices Court.

This was a position of novelty and importance, and one which most of his brethren on the Bench are reputed to have shunned. They thought it wrong for the judiciary to enter the arena of political controversy which they feared might be involved in considerations of economic policy and "the public interest", on which the Restrictive Trade Practices Act of 1956 required the court to pronounce. Devlin had no such inhibitions. He believed that it was perfectly possible and proper for a judge to apply such considerations without jeopardising his political neutrality, provided he scrupulously followed the terms of, and guidance given by, the act. By his conduct of the court he broke down any subsequent judicial distrust of this activity.

In 1963 he was 58 and at the height of his powers. He was the youngest law lord and clearly destined soon to preside over the country's highest court. Suddenly he resigned. The cause of this drastic step was not clear. Some thought that he had found it difficult to work with the Lord Chancellor, Lord Dilhorne, as his old adversary Sir Reginald Manningham-Buller had now become. Others thought he wished to devote himself to his Wiltshire farm. Others attributed it to growing deafness, although at this stage it was an almost conscious defence against the chatter of fools.

The real reason was an increasing impatience with the method and conditions of work which then prevailed in the House of Lords. His visits to America and his friends among American lawyers, among whom Dean Acheson was prominent, had convinced him of the superiority of the procedure of the Supreme Court, with its written briefs and limited time for oral argument. He considered that the practice in the House of Lords, in which counsel read out, often for days on end, the entire record of the proceedings in the lower courts, to be boring, wasteful and extravagant. He canvassed support for a radical reform on the American model but received virtually none. Now most of his suggestions have been adopted.

Coupled with this frustration came irritation at the absence of decent facilities in the House of Lords. In the law courts a judge is accustomed to a large room which can house his library, a clerk and a secretary. When he was promoted to the Lords, Devlin found that he was given a desk and a small share in a typing pool. His efforts to secure better conditions of work produced no greater success than his efforts at modernising procedure.

His resignation coincided with a development in the work and prestige of the Press Council. Cecil King and other newspaper proprietors were anxious to raise the authority of this body by securing as its chairman a figure of national reputation and high judicial qualities. Devlin was the perfect man for the job, which he conducted with great

Lord Devlin as a Lord Justice of Appeal (1960)

diplomacy, always remembering the voluntary nature of the council and never reverting to the more dictatorial manner of the Bench. He regarded the council not as a censorious tribunal, but as a body whose function was to harmonise relations between the press and the public.

Before his resignation, he had acted as chairman of various public enquiries. In 1955, he examined the working of the dock labour scheme, a task he was to revert to ten years later. In 1959 he chaired the commission to enquire into civil disorder in Nyasaland. The report vindicated the governor's resort to emergency powers, but was awkward and unwelcome to the government of the day in some of its phraseology, particularly the statement that Nyasaland was albeit temporarily, ''a police state''.

After his resignation, he became more than ever in demand for public duties. In 1964 he became a member of the *Tribunal Administratif* in Geneva, a body concerned to hear grievances of the employees of international organisations. In 1965 he was appointed chairman of the joint board of the national newspaper industry.

A great deal of his energy was devoted to warding off attempts to lure him back. He preferred to spend his time writing, lecturing and broadcasting. Of all these arts he was a master. He specialised in discussion on the interrelation between law and morality. He did not separate the two as strictly as some other polemicists. He thought that the function of the criminal law was something more than the preservation of public order and that it emodied and nurtured the morality of the community it served. He was challenged in this view by Herbert Hart, professor of jurisprudence at Oxford, and for years these two giants of controversy were locked in intellectual combat by the written or spoken word in Europe, America and Australia. The argument reached the heights of philosophy and at this level it was generally thought that the professor had won.

Devlin was a great expounder of such English problems as the function of the jury, the principles of criminal prosecution, the nature of motoring offences, the rights and duties of doctors to incurable patients, the utility of preliminary proceedings and the desirability of reporting them in the press. He had a unique gift by which he could reason closely and professionally and yet make it all intelligible and interesting to the laity. Although a conservative by temperament, he was a reformer in legal matters. He would have made a great Lord Chancellor.

Academic distinctions crowded upon him. While a puisne judge, he was appointed chairman of the council of Bedford College, University of London. Characteristically he resigned when he became sceptical of the value of higher education for most girls. In 1965 he became a doctor of law of Oxford, and in 1966 of Cambridge, Leicester and Sussex. He was an honorary fellow of Christ's College, Cambridge, and High Steward of the university.

No one meeting Devlin for the first time would have assumed him to be a judge. He did not possess a commanding figure. He did not seem bowed down with learning. He was neither pompous nor reserved. He had enormous charm and a great sense of humour.

He was blessed in his family life. In 1932 he married Madeleine, the younger daughter of Sir Bernard Oppenheimer. They had four sons and two daughters. At university Devlin renounced the Roman Catholic faith. Several years later, his wife and five of his children adopted it. These conversions in no way impaired the idyllic happiness of their life together on his farm in Wiltshire – a county which increasingly absorbed his attention and of which he was chairman of Quarter Sessions for many years – and in their house in the Algarve, where he spent two or three months every year writing his books. The best of these was *Too Proud to Fight*, a brilliant study of the forces operating in the mind of President Woodrow Wilson.

Indeed as he approached the age of 70

he became increasingly active. He was in great demand on television. He served as an arbitrator in a series of heavy commercial disputes in India. Every year he would chair at least one public enquiry, such as that for the Confederation of British Industry on employer organisations or that for his fellow author and friend, Roy Jenkins, on problems of identification in criminal evidence.

Devlin will be remembered as much for what he did in public life outside the court room as for his forensic and judicial achievements, distinguished though he was as an advocate and judge. One of his abiding concerns was for the integrity of the criminal justice system and the maintenance of jury trial.

He had a horror of miscarriages of justice and a keen nose for smelling them out. In 1986 he read Robert Kee's remarkable book, *Trial and Error*, and was persuaded that there had been a gross miscarriage of justice in the case of the Guildford Four who had been convicted in 1975 of murder in terrorist bombing attacks on public houses frequented by soldiers.

He was especially troubled by rejection by the Court of Appeal of new evidence. He believed that by themselves dismissing the appeal the members of the Court of Appeal had assumed the role of a jury. The credibility of the new evidence, he argued, was not for them; the accused had a right to have it considered by a jury before they could be convicted.

He joined with Lord Scarman in the campaign for the review of the Guildford Four – a campaign which, supported by Cardinal Hume, proved successful. The case illustrates his zest for a fight in a cause which he held dear and his tenacity in defence of what he saw as true principle.

Devlin was reconciled with the Catholic Church in his last few days. He leaves his widow, six children and innumerable grandchildren.

b 25.11.05 d 9.8.92 aged 86

GIOVANNI FALCONE

Giovanni Falcone, head of the Italian justice ministry's criminal affairs department and a renowned scourge of the Mafia, was killed in an explosion.

GIOVANNI Falcone was a short, handsome, vain and tough man with a formidable memory and a plump stature resulting from the sedentary life forced upon him by the dangers of his calling. For reasons of security he could not easily play tennis, golf or any other outdoor sport. For 12 years the effectiveness of his anti-Mafia activities meant that he was forced to live the life of a recluse.

As the architect of the Italian authorities' biggest success against the secret crime network he was credited with, and bore the consequences of, the trial in 1986 in which 338 mafiosi were sentenced to 2,665 years, 19 of them for life. As a result, Falcone and his family had to live with a permanent bodyguard of 25 policemen armed with machine guns working six-man seven-hour shifts and with guard dogs and electronic sensors in their garden. Even his bath was protected by bullet proof glass.

His office had sealed doors and he travelled everywhere with a five-car escort. Only once in five years did he visit a cinema and when he did so his bodyguards cleared three rows behind him and three rows in front, searched the ice-cream sales woman and patrolled the aisles. In 1989 his enthusiasm for boating almost led to his death when his enemies tried to blow him up on a boat near his rented seaside house.

Giovanni Falcone grew up in Kalsa, one of the most ancient quarters of Palermo and a working class district notorious for its mafiosi. He was thus well-suited to his anti-Mafia role, once saying: "Whever I have to predict what the Mafia will do next, I say to myself 'If I were a mafiosi, what would I do now?' "

He was educated to be a naval officer but turned to the law and became a public prosecutor at Trapani in the west of the island, then a bankruptcy judge. In 1978, he was assigned to Palermo and soon began handling the island's top Mafia cases, including the 1982 assassination of General Carlo Dalla Chiesa, a veteran of Italy's anti-terrorist struggles.

Falcone soon became prominent in trying Mafia cases.

His big breakthrough came in October 1983 when, during a triple murder investigation, police in Sao Paulo arrested a Sicilian fugitive called Tommaso Buscetta. He was wanted in Italy for breaking parole after serving all but eight months of a nine year sentence for smuggling and conspiracy. When news of his arrest was telexed to Palermo, Antonio de Luca, Sicily's senor detective, took the first plane to Brazil armed with a dossier on Buscetta's suspected drug smuggling activities, a request for his extradition and the hope that he might be persuaded to talk.

Seven months later Falcone himself flew to Brazil and ensured that Buscetta's return to Italy was marked by conspicuous security precautions and that he was taken to a safe and secret location. What he told Falcone eventually filled 700 typed pages and provided a fascinating history of the Mafia in Sicily from the post war days of smuggling contraband cigarettes to its present day control of heroin traffic to America.

He described the Mafia's rigid structure and the strict territorial boundaries and detailed the way in which it was ruled by a 12-man commission or *cupola* which imposed its own law on Sicily. Buscetta's confession was the first precise account by and insider of the workings of the Sicilian Mafia and its relations with the Sicilian "families" operating in America. The confession confirmed Falcone's belief that the Mafia operated like a hidden government without whose approval no crime or murder could be committed on Sicily.

In 1989, he was the victim of a smear campaign when letters were sent to senior state authorities denouncing him. The Italian Supreme Court also delivered what appeared to be a set-back to his anti-Mafia campaign by permitting the early release of several of the Mafia chieftains convicted in the mid-1980s.

In the same year an attempt to blow up Falcone was thwarted when his bodyguards spotted divers swimming along the coast near his seaside villa outside Palermo. After a search they found a large waterproof sack with two briefcases filled with 100lb of plastic explosive.

Earlier this year Falcone left his job in Palermo to take up his new post in Rome.

In Rome, Falcone and his wife – each of whom had been married before and had no children – lived in a cramped three-room flat inside a police barracks. To go to his office at the ministry of justice only 300 yards away the whole machinery of bullet-proof cars and armed escorts were set in motion.

For most Italians, Giovanni Falcone was a champion of justice and a symbol of bravery. In describing the intricacies and ruthlessness of Mafia power to interviewers, there was always extreme clarity in his words, but there was also a dry, often scathing sense of humour and a wry smile which conveyed an air of almost amused detachment from the horrors he was describing and against which he had fought for most of his working life. In a book he wrote on the Mafia, published last year, Falcone said that he was not Robin Hood, nor a kamikaze or a thug. "I am simply a servant of the state."

b 18.5.39　d 23.5.92　aged 53

Aftermath of explosion that killed Falcone

COMMANDER
ROY HABERSHON

Roy Habershon, MBE, first head of Scotland Yard's bomb squad and a former CID commander.

ROY Habershon's greatest moment probably came on a cold Friday evening late in 1975. As he walked away from a police command post set up in Marleybone he could hardly contain his satisfaction that the most effective IRA unit seen on the British mainland had been captured without loss of life after a siege lasting almost a week in nearby Balcombe Street on the edge of the West End.

Always noted as a thorough policeman, his day was not done, despite the celebrations. Climbing into his car he drove off into the night to visit the hideouts used by a gang which had terrorised central London and left a trail of murder and bombings behind it.

Habershon, a familiar face to millions of television viewers at the height of the IRA campaign, might never have been in command of the bomb squad but for the good fortune which put him in the right place at the right time. He began his police career in 1946 after war service with the RAF and rose steadily and undramatically during the 1950s and 1960s working at the Yard or outside on police divisions. He earned a reputation as a good leader, winning the admiration of junior officers and maintained a reputation for integrity and honesty.

In 1971 he was detective chief superintendent covering the Barnet area on the fringes of the Metropolitan police area at the time the Angry Brigade, an alliance of leftwing and anarchic groups, launched a series of bombings aimed at establishment targets. On January 12 two bombs shattered the front door of the Barnet home of Robert Carr, then the secretary for employment, and Habershon, as senior local detective, took command of the investigation with a small squad which was to be the forerunner of the bomb squad and latterly the anti-terrorist squad.

Expanded with officers from Special Branch and the Flying Squad, the squad and Habershon were moved to Scotland Yard and placed under the overall control of Commander Ernest Bond.

The Angry Brigade's operations were over by 1972 but the real work of the new squad was just about to begin. In March 1973 the IRA began their first attempt at a large attack in London with a quartet of car bombs outside Scotland Yard. The Central Criminal Court, a BBC office and an Army recruiting centre off Whitehall. Nine terrorists were later convicted at Winchester crown court which witnessed one of the few times when Habershon's sharp tongue was beaten by an adversary.

Asked by the judge why one of the men had taken part in the bombings Habershon began to reply with the words: "The kindest thing I could say . . ." when Dolores Price, another of the terrorists, shouted back: "We don't need your kindness Mr Habershon."

In 1974 he was appointed MBE and left the squad for a time. But he returned in 1975 as commander. It was a time when the IRA unit later known as the Balcombe Street gang was devastating London streets in a campaign which had undertaken 50 missions over a period of 18 months, including bombings and shootings. A police operation involving hundreds of officers secretly patrolled the streets nightly as Habershon's men tried to plot the unit's next step in London's West End.

On December 6 the IRA unit chanced its arm once too often. Spotted by police heading for Mayfair, some of its members were chased into a block of flats in Balcombe Street where they took an elderly couple hostage and were trapped. The siege provided a dramatic confrontation which was resolved as much by patience as determination. After six days the terrorists gave themselves up, thanks to negotiators who included Peter Imbert, now commissioner of the Metropolitan police.

Habershon moved on to become head of the Yard's serious crimes branch but he did not remain at headquarters. A hard-headed Yorkshireman, always ready to make and defend his case vigorously, he left the senior ranks at Scotland Yard to become a CID commander in north London. He retired in 1980 having earned 23 commendations. He then became a director of the firm Control Risks, advising on security.

He is survived by his wife, Edith, and a son.

b 15.5.25   d 18.3.92   aged 66

LORD HAVERS

Lord Havers, PC, Attorney-General, 1979–87, and Lord Chancellor, June–October 1987.

LORD Havers left the indelible stamp of his personality on that important area of British public life where the law and politics intermingle. He rose to the peak of the legal profession when he became Lord Chancellor, but he filled that office for only 134 days before resigning on health grounds. Before that he had already made his mark in an unusually long and controversial term as Attorney-General. He held that post for eight years, longer than anyone since 1737.

The lot of any Attorney-General, part lawyer, part politician, the government's chief legal adviser and effectively chief public prosecutor, is never an easy one, and Havers's term, from 1979 to 1987, covered a particularly fraught period of political history.

The tensions were not lessened by the fact that he served under a strong-minded prime minister not slow to put a sharp edge to every issue on the politico-legal front: the law on picketing; decisions to prosecute civil sevants for leaking confidential information; the international law aspects of the Falklands dispute; investigation of police irregularities; loss of faith in the impartiality of the jury system; the strange legal status of the secret services – it was a testing list of decisions that landed on his desk. He rose to the challenge robustly and with style – and in his relationship with the prime minister he showed his own strength of mind.

Havers was educated at Westminster. During the second world war, as an RNVR officer, he served in the Mediterranean, Normandy and the Far East but decided against taking a permanent commission in favour of going up to Corpus Christi College, Cambridge. He was called to the Bar by the Inner Temple in 1948 at the age of 25 and joined the chambers of Fred Lawton (later Lord Justice Lawton) and Gerald Howard, MP, his pupil master. He served as recorder of Dover (1962–68) and of Norwich (1968–71) then becoming deputy chairman of West Suffolk Quarter Sessions and chancellor of the dioceses of Edmundsbury and Ipswich, then of Ely. He took silk in 1964 and became master of the bench in 1971.

He entered politics relatively late – which perhaps explained why his instinct when the political side came into conflict with the legal was to give his first loyalty to what he saw as the impartiality of the law. He was first elected as a Conservative MP for Wimbledon in 1970 when he was 47. He succeeded to the safe seat long occupied by Sir Cyril Black, a politician with strong views on moral issues, who may have had a hand in the succession: Havers had written a report (subsequently acted upon) to strengthen the law on pornography, and he acted as counsel for Black when the latter brought a private prosecution against the book *Last Exit for Brooklyn.*

Havers's court appearances were not always, however, in defence of conventional values: another brief was on behalf of the Rolling Stones Mick Jagger and Keith Richard when, in 1967, both were tried for alleged drug offences at West Sussex Quarter Sessions. As defence counsel Havers confessed to the court: "Sometimes I wonder if all of us in this court are not too old to try this case." That observation did not, in the first instance, help Mr Jagger who was convicted of being in possession of prohibited drugs when the judge ruled that the jury *must* return a guilty verdict, notwithstanding that the drugs were described as being merely travel sickness

remedies which Mr Jagger was taking in the full cognisance of his doctor. On that celebrated occasion the effective defence of Mick Jagger was left to *The Times* whose leader "Who Breaks A Butterfly On A Wheel?" was probably instrumental in leading to the eventual acquittal of both men on appeal.

Havers was also part-author of a number of books designed for a popular market on sensational cases, including the notorious "Bacarat" case involving alleged cheating at cards in the presence of King Edward VII. In 1987 he was a judge for the Whitbread literary awards.

Two years after entering the Commons Havers was appointed Solicitor-General by Edward Heath, succeeding Sir Geoffrey Howe, with Sir Peter Rawlinson (later Lord Rawlinson of Ewell) as Attorney-General.

An early source of controversy was a decision not to pursue firms accused of breaking sanctions against Rhodesia. On the legislative side, a major responsibility was the Contempt of Court Bill which, among other things, regularised the position of journalists seeking to protect their sources. He was also centrally involved in Mrs Thatcher's decision to expose, in the Commons, the government's knowledge of Anthony Blunt's traitorous links with the Soviet Union, and in the prosecution of two other traitors, Geoffrey Prime and Michael Bettaney. His most dramatic courtroom success came in 1982 when his cross examination of Professor Hugh Hambleton, a Canadian economist, culminated in Hambleton confessing in court to passing Nato secrets to the Soviet Union.

Earlier Havers had led for the Crown in the trials of the Birmingham Six and the Guildford Four. In November 1981, despite the security precautions that surrounded him, his home in Wimbledon was bombed by the IRA while he and his family were on holiday in Spain. He reacted with aplomb, saying to his wife: "Darling, we seem to have had a slight accident at home."

Meanwhile, wearing his prosecutor's

hat, Havers hit the headlines when the "Yorkshire Ripper" came to trial. He accepted a plea of diminished responsibility, but the judge, probably reflecting public opinion, refused to accept it and insisted on a full-blown trial for murder. It was an embarrassment for the Attorney-General, senior member for the Bar – but there were greater embarrassments to come.

Many of them were concerned with official secrets. He prosecuted Sarah Tisdall, the Foreign Office clerk who leaked details of cruise missiles. He was responsible for the unsuccessful case against Clive Ponting, who leaked documents about the sinking of the Belgrano during the Falklands war.

During the Falklands conflict Havers proved a loyal and sympathetic colleague to the prime minister, not least because he was one of the few ministers who had seen naval service. Her appreciation of him survived even during the most remarkable adventure of his political career, the Westland crisis early in 1986.

He had just undergone a heart bypass operation, and was absent while conflict developed between the two most interested ministers, Leon Brittan (backed by the prime minister) and Michael Heseltine, over the future of the Westland helicopter company. It fell to his deputy, the Solicitor-General, to write to Mr Heseltine with advice on legal aspects of the problem, and passages from this confidential letter, harmful to Heseltine's political case, were published in the media. There was no doubt that the leak, by a civil servant to the Press Association, had been authorised at a high level and had taken place after exchanges between Brittan's department and Downing Street.

Havers returned from his sick-bed to this storm. He was clear in his mind, first, that the breach of confidentiality of a government law officer's letter was a gross impropriety; and secondly that the leak had to be treated as an offence under the Official Secrets Act as much as the one which had sent Sarah Tisdall to prison. When it was hinted to him that he was being unduly legalistic about a piece of government Real-politik, he retorted that unless the leak was taken seriously he would order Scotland Yard into Downing Street next morning to conduct a criminal investigation.

After that, at least one head had to fall: Leon Brittan accepted ministerial responsibility and resigned. Before that, Mr Heseltine had walked out of the cabinet in protest against the prime minister's handling of the dispute. It was widely thought that the whole episode brought the prime minister herself closer to resignation than she ever had been.

Then there was *Spycatcher*. Havers attracted criticism for the determined way that the government pursued the book's author, Peter Wright, in courts around the world, to condemn him for revealing details of his work for the security services. Havers accepted his responsibility, but there was one point in this episode, too, when he found himself in confrontation with Downing Street. When the cabinet secretary, Sir Robert Armstrong, was giving evidence in the Australian court, he indicated that Havers had been party to an earlier decision not to prosecute the author of another book on the security services: Havers forced Armstrong to retract. There was also criticism that no action had been taken against individuals who had leaked information to other authors, seemingly with the tacit approval of the authorities.

In 1987 the prime minister showed her loyalty to him by promoting him to be Lord Chancellor, but his health was not good enough for him to continue for long. Retiring from the Woolsack he became chairman of R.J.M. Outhwaite, the Lloyd's underwriters, the Solicitors Law Stationery Society and the Playhouse Theatre.

Lord Havers married in 1949, Carol Elizabeth Lay. He was knighted in 1972 and created a life peer as Lord Havers in 1987. He is survived by his wife and two sons, one of whom is Nigel Havers the actor. The other, Philip, followed his father to the Bar.

b 10.3.23   d 1.4.92   aged 69

ALBERT PIERREPOINT

Albert Pierrepoint, Britain's chief hangman from 1946 to 1956.

FOR a period of ten years after the war Albert Pierrepoint was the dispassionate occupant of the ghoulish office of chief executioner. He came from a line of hangmen and took a quiet pride in the effectiveness with which he discharged his duties. For the first 56 years of this century three members of the Pierrepoint family, Albert's father Henry, his uncle Thomas and finally Albert himself, were, in succession, the official chief executioners of Great Britain. It was not,

to be sure, a succession as lengthy as that of the Sansons of France, who held the post for seven generations and at one time had six brothers operating simultaneously, but it gave Pierrepoint a sense of belonging to a profession which had its own niche — indeed a certain status — in society.

In his 25-year career as, first, assistant and then chief hangman, he executed 433 men and 17 women, more than any other hangman this century. Among these were Haigh the acid bath murderer, Ruth Ellis, the last woman to be executed in Britain, and Derek Bentley, whose conviction of the murder of a policeman in 1953 is still among the contentious verdicts of the post-war era. His reputation as a hangman was an international one and he was often invited to instruct the prison services of other countries on executions.

As a boy Albert Pierrepoint was never in any doubt about what he wanted to be. When asked as a 12-year-old to write a school essay about his ambitions, he committed his credo to paper with the assured candour of youth: "I would like to be public executioner as my dad is, because it needs a steady man with good hands like my Dad and my Uncle Tom and I shall be the same." Paradoxically, after hanging was abolished in 1969 he came to take a less enthusiastic view of his life's work and was ever afterwards in the forefront of the campaign against the return of capital punishment.

As a child Pierrepoint's inclination to become a hangman had received early impetus from the serialisation of his father's memoirs in a local newpaper. As he recalled in his memoirs the job appealed to him because it gave an opportunity for travel, something not among the luxuries that could be afforded by people of his family's humble station in the inter-war years. Nevertheless he was thought to be "too young" by the Home Office official who interviewed him when he applied for the job at the age of 27. As in France, the job was not salaried, the hangman receiving a fee for each execution. Nevertheless the lineage told and Pierrepoint was accepted into his family's profession, serving as an assistant hangman until he succeeded his uncle as chief executioner in 1946.

In the course of his duties, Ireland, the United States and Germany were among the countries in which he was asked to officiate. He took a sober view of his task as being to assist his clients out of this life in the most humane way possible. The standards set by his father were always paramount in his mind: "My father could dispatch a man in the time it took the prison clock to strike eight − leading him from his cell on the first stroke and having his suspended, dead on the rope, by the last stroke. That seemed a very worthy ambition to me."

As a result he became an assiduous student of the technical aspects of his work and kept careful notes of weight, height and length of drop after each execution he performed. He deplored the levity and jocularity which he found attending the business of executions in some other countries. In Dublin he was shocked to be offered a whiskey on the scaffold almost before the thump of the trap had ceased reverberating around the execution shed. He found it distasteful to be offered a cold buffet and drinks by the American army before an execution which was scheduled for midnight. He was also scathing about technical inefficiency, dismissing the old-fashioned American cowboy knot and the standard five-foot drop which, he claimed, had prolonged the agonies of the German Field Marshal Keitel for 24 minutes after his conviction of war crimes at Nuremberg. Pierrepoint did not execute any of the major Nazi criminals at Nuremberg but he was heavily employed among the smaller fry, including Josef Kramer, the "Beast of Belsen", and his three most sadistic women guards,

Elizabeth Volkenrath, Irma Grese and Joana Bormann. On one occasion he executed 27 individuals in a day.

As time went on he also deprecated the low quality of entrants to the profession and was particularly severe on the dependence on alcohol prevalent among some of the younger men to help them do their job. If it was suggested to him that reliance on a drink to assist the discharge of such a repugnant task might be a sign of a humane and sensitive nature he would reply that a hanging botched through shaking hands or slapdash calculations offered no humanity to the wretch who had to endure it.

Pierrepoint resigned his post in 1956 not on account of any moral repugnance but over a dispute about his remuneration. Thereafter he kept a pub in Oldham which rejoiced in the name "Help the Poor Struggler". With time, perhaps, to reflect on his experiences he fairly soon came to revise his opinion on the profession to which he had previously seemed to ascribe a well-nigh metaphysical status. The faces of the many he looked into during their last moments on earth did, in retrospect, convince him of the futility of the apparatus of condemnation and execution of which he had been such an enthusiastic cog. In his autobiography, *Executioner: Pierrepoint*, which was published in 1974, he was to write: "The fruit of my experience has this bitter after-taste: that I do not now believe that any one of the hundreds of executions I carried out has in any way acted as a deterrent against future murder. Capital punishment, in my view, achieved nothing except revenge."

He is survived by his wife, Anne.

b 1905   d 10.7.92   aged 87

ISAAC ASIMOV

Isaac Asimov, prolific Russian-born American science fiction writer and populariser of scientific ideas in his many non-fiction works.

ALTHOUGH his latter work had been predominantly non-fictional, perhaps no contemporary science fiction writer had more influence on the genre as it is today than Isaac Asimov. He was, among other things, awesomely prolific. His admonition in *Who's Who* under the heading, Recreation, to those of frailer constitution, contains his uncompromising credo: "a man's work is his play: my recreation is writing." A punishing writing schedule which, until comparatively recently involved eight hours a day, seven days a week at the keyboard of his word processor in his 33rd floor Manhattan apartment, had produced almost five hundred titles at the time of his death.

But sheer weight of production would never have achieved the impact Asimov made if it had not been for the persuasive quality of his scientific ideas. He had been precociously creative as a child, and this precocity was only underpinned and given greater authority by the formal qualifications he gained in chemistry, which culminated in a doctorate in 1948. Thereafter he embarked on a successful career as a university teacher. But by that time he had already made his mark with the science-fiction reading public with his celebrated story "Nightfall". This reputation was extended with the appearance of *I Robot* (1950), with its development of the "Laws of Robotics" first posited in "Nightfall", an ethical system for the actions of artificial intelligences which elevated robots from the mindless monsters of pre-Asimov sci-fi and influenced almost every writer who subsequently touched the subject. This and the philosophically ambitious *Foundation Trilogy* have remained among his most enduringly popular fictional works.

It has to be conceded that much of Asimov's original inspiration for his most effective ideas came from that influential science fiction magazine editor John W. Campbell – but it was, nevertheless, Asimov who gave them shape and, through his scientific knowledge, their convincing quality. Indeed, among his myriad of books are many which are lengthy presentations of complex scientific concepts. These concepts are always present, too, in his mammoth space romances. Few of his works are short, though, at the same time, among his short stories are some of the finest in the genre. When he worked on the small canvas Asimov could be at once witty and poignant.

Isaac Asimov was the son of Judah and Anne (née Bermant) Asimov. His parents emigrated in 1923, to New York City, where they opened a candy store. Isaac went to Broolyn Boys High School where, Sam Moskowitz wrote in his *Seekers of Tomorrow* (1966), he was a nasty boy: "egocentric, introverted and sarcastic". But that was by way of being a little joke.

Judah Asimov always sternly told his boy that the pulp magazines he sold from his store were degenerate; but he relented when he saw an educational value in *Amazing Stories*, edited by Hugo Gernsback, to which Isaac became devoted: "It received," recalled Asimov, "the august paternal nod. Science fiction, he decided, might improve my mind by interesting me in science . . . From then on I was hooked."

The gifted boy went on to Columbia University, where he studied chemistry. He graduated at 19. During the second world war he worked at the Naval Air Experimental Station at Philadelphia; later (1945–46) he served as a corporal in the army. He gained his PhD from Columbia in 1948, and in the next year joined the Boston School of Medicine, where he eventually became a professor.

He had started to write at 12. Six years later he took his first science fiction tale to the great John Campbell, editor of *Analog*. Later, in 1938, he sold the magazine another story. Thereafter his name figured in all the periodicals dedicated to science fiction, and in 1950 he published his first book.

The story with which Asimov excited his readers – and it still excites novice devotees – was "Nightfall", which he sold to Campbell in 1941. Campbell invented the idea around which it revolves: what if the stars should appear for only one night in a thousand years? Here first appear the famous "three laws of robotics," (true for such robots as have been or may be invented), again formulated by Campbell, extended in the collection *I Robot* and used by countless science fiction writers since. Asimov's full-scale novels sold by the million. Chief among them, perhaps, was the *Foundation Trilogy* (1952–53), which was, characteristically, conceived by its author after he had read Gibbon – only Asimov's Empire is a galactic civilisation of the future which collapsed and is then re-born.

Thereafter he did not write much more fiction of this type (his readers yearned for it), and *The Gods Themselves* (1972) was reckoned, as a disappointed fan wrote, "to lack vision". But Asimov never even touched the trashier end of the science-fiction mode – and he was much imitated.

He wrote lucidly and well (rather than gracefully) and was a superb plotter. To these qualities he added scientific integrity of a high order. He could have been a writer of the calibre of his great predecessor H. G. Wells, but he lacked the poetry, the imagination and the interest in character. Indeed, character-isation in his novels was more or less lacking. *Fantastic Voyage* (1966) was a "novelisation" of a screeplay by Harry Kleiner for a film about a surgical team that is miniaturised and sent into the bloodstream of a wonded scientist. It happened to be typical of the sort of efficient fantasy which Asimov produced, even though the original idea was not his own.

From the 1960s onwards, by far the

largest proportion of Asimov's immense output was non-fictional. His interests shifted from science to history, to religion, and even to literature.

He wrote a two-volumed guide to Shakespeare, *Asimov's Guide to Shakespeare* (1970). He had done exactly the same for the Bible, *Asimov's Guide to the Bible* (1969–70). But his books of scientific poplularisation were better – and one can believe that he typed at a speed of 90 words per minute. He wrote, as was once said of the Dutch author Vestdijk, "faster than God can read". Among books which touched upon most subjects known to man were: *Building Blocks of the Universe* (1957 revised 1961); *The Intelligent Man's Guide to Science* (1960) – this became, of course, when revised, *Asimov's Guide to Science* (1972); *Realm of Algebra* (1961); *The Roman Republic* (1966); *Asimov's Annotated "Paradise Lost"* (1974) – which was not used in many schools or universities; and *In Memory Yet Green: The Autobiography of Isaac Asimov 1920–1954* (1979).

In addition he wrote a dozen books for the young, on subjects ranging from mythology and history to the organisation of the solar system, edited *The Isaac Asimov Treasury of Humour* (1971) and (under the authorial guise of "Dr A.") wrote *The Sensuous Dirty Old Man* (1971).

He wrote five books of limericks, one of them in collaboration with a noted American poet, John Ciardi. But he continued, in his own words, to "steer clear of the mysteries of the human personality and human relationships". "I'm on fire to explain," he commented, "I don't indulge in scholarly depth." He was, undoubtedly, an amazingly industrious man, as well as a born entertainer and populariser.

Asimov continued to be prolific in spite of the fact that he had not been in good health for the last ten years and more. A heart attack in 1977 hardly slowed him down, nor did triple bypass surgery in 1983. Only quite recently had he announced that a prostate operation had finally slowed him down and that he would be taking life more easily in the future. A few weeks ago he had finished a sequel volume to his *Foundation Trilogy*. It is scheduled for publication next year under the title *Forward, the Foundation*. He won many prizes, including the Hugo (1963) and the Nebula (1972) – both for science fiction.

Asimov, who became an American citizen in 1928, was twice married. First in 1942, to the former Gertrude Blugerman, by whom he had a son and a daughter. This marriage ended in divorce. In 1972 he married Janet Opal Jeppson.

b 2.1.20   d 6.4.92   aged 72

ELIZABETH DAVID

Elizabeth David, CBE, cookery writer and expert on the cuisine of the Mediterranean.

ELIZABETH David was the doyenne of English cookery writers. She influenced the generations who came after her, whether they, too, were intending to be culinary experts or merely taking a well-thumbed Elizabeth David Penguin from the kitchen shelf for the next day's dinner party. "Elizabeth David says . . ." was the regular way of resolving how much spice – and which spices – should be added to a stew and how much garlic should be put in a dressing.

At its best, her prose was as precise as her instructions, unlike that of some of her predecessors who sometimes wrapped up advice on what to do in the kitchen with impenetrable sentences. She was a pleasure to read, a stylist of true distinction. Perhaps only in Britain would she have been classified as a "food writer", too often rather a damning phrase. Elizabeth David combined a scholar's feeling for history with the traveller-aesthete's gift of conveying a sense of place.

Elizabeth David's father was the Conservative Member of Parliament for Eastbourne; her mother the daughter of the 1st Viscount Ridley. At the impressionable age of 16 she was sent from her English boarding school to study French literature and history at the Sorbonne, living for 18 months with a family in Passy. It was then that she first became aware of food, the daily fare of the French bourgeoisie coming as a startling contrast to the bland food to which she had been accustomed.

On her return to London she worked briefly as an actress, then as a vendeuse for Worth, where her striking looks stood her in good stead. She was living in Greece at the outbreak of war and was evacuated to Egypt, where she lived first in Alexandria and later in Cairo. There she worked as a librarian for the ministry of information. In 1944 she married an English officer, Anthony David, and went to live in India, where he was stationed. The marriage was not a success, and she rarely referred to it. There were no children.

In the winter of 1946 she returned to England alone and went live in a small hotel in Ross-on-Wye. Here, amid the gloom and deprivation of postwar England, she began to write about the food of the Eastern Mediterranean. In 1950 *A Book of Mediterranean Food* was published by John Lehmann, with drawings by John Minton, another expert on the eastern reaches of that sea. Its impact was colossal, both on those who were too young to remember the prewar years, and on an older generation. Other books followed in rapid succession. *French Country Cooking* (1951), *Italian Food* (1954) and *Summer Cooking* (1955). The following year she started writing regularly for *The Sunday Times, Vogue* and *House & Garden*. in 1960 *French Provincial Cooking* was published, based on a series commissioned by *Vogue*. The next year she gave up working for Condé Nast and *The Sunday Times*, and began writing for *The Spectator*, which freed her from the chore of writing recipes.

In 1965 she opened her kichenware shop in Elizabeth Street in Belgravia. This involved her in annual trips to France searching for merchandise, a distinct pleasure and rarely a chore. Over the next years she published a series of pamphlets for sale in the shop, one of which was the basis for her next book: *Spices, Salt and Aromatics in the English Kitchen*, which came out in 1970. Three years later she fell out with her partners and severed all connection with the shop, although it continued to trade under her name. In 1976 she was appointed OBE, in 1986 CBE, and in 1977 *English Bread and Yeast Cookery* had been published, destined to be her last original work.

The same year she was made Chevalier du Mérite Agricole, and two years later she received an honorary degree from Essex University. In 1982 she was made a fellow of the Royal Society of Literature, but despite repeated efforts on the part of her friends and colleagues she was never given the accolade she merited. Her last published work, *An Omelette and a Glass of Wine*, came out in 1984.

As the years passed she became more and more obsessed with research, and the *joie de vivre*, which had filled so much of her earlier writing, became muted. Her very first books shared an infectious enthusiasm for the joys of eating and living well, while the recipes were often sketchy, probably written from memory. With *Italian Food*, however, the first book written *in situ*, her tone became more scholarly, the recipes more precise. After a return to her former style in a short book, *Summer Cooking*, she resumed her research with *French Provincial Cooking*, probably her greatest book and the one no amateur − or professional − chef is likely to be without. Ten years passed before her next book, originally intended as the first in a series on English food. The title alone of *Spices, Salt and Aromatics in the English Kitchen* shows the change in attitude, as it defines with typical accuracy its range of contents. This interesting book proved a watershed in her career, for after it her passion for research seemed to get out of control.

Seven years later her long-awaited *English Bread and Yeast Cookery* finally appeared, a disappointment to many of her admirers. A heavy tome, over-filled with intricate variations on the same theme, this was a work of reference rather than a pleasure to read. The following years were spent researching a book on sorbets and ices which was never completed. But the academic period towards the end of her life was balanced by the publication of *An Omelette and a Glass of Wine*, a collection of pieces written mostly between 1955 and 1965. These provided a timely reminder of her powers to amuse and entertain, as well as to instruct. Her wit was devastating, often caustic, usually at someone's expense.

She was highly critical, but fair, giving praise rarely, for her standards were very high. She did not suffer incompetents and the dim-witted gladly, if at all, as customers in her Elizabeth Street shop often found, to their discomfiture. This may have been a family trait, for her sister Felicité could be equally crushing with foolish enquiries in Sandoe Books, just off the King's Road, where she worked. Many people found Elizabeth David intimidating, yet she could be friendly and encouraging to younger writers. She had beautiful manners and was an accomplished letter writer. She was shy, unwilling to talk in public, or even to give interviews. In latter years she refused to be photographed, preferring to re-use earlier pictures by Cecil Beaton or the painter Derek Hill on her dust jackets.

She became more and more reclusive and rarely went out except to see close friends. These had always been important to her, and included such figures as Norman Douglas, almost 50 years her senior, Derek Hill, and her publisher and editor, Jill Norman.

But even friends were kept at a distance. One, returning from abroad, tried to get her telephone number from directory enquiries, only to be told they were under strict orders not to divulge it under any circumstances, even in the case of death.

For more than 34 years she shared a house in Chelsea with her younger unmarried sister Felicité, who died in 1986. Despite mutual regard and affection they lived quite separately. Elizabeth David was a solitary figure in old age, living alone with her books, and memories of a warmer, more enchanting past, as in 1939, when she "fell under the spell of the Levant — the warm flat bread, the freshly pressed tomato juice, the charcoal-grilled lamb, the oniony salads, the mint and yoghurt sauces, the sesame seed paste, the pistachios and the pomegranates and the apricots, the rosewater and the scented sweetmeats, and everywhere the warm spicy smell of cumin".

b 26.12.13   d 22.5.92   aged 78

APPRECIATION

I READ your obituary of Elizabeth David (obituary, May 23) with interest having met her some years before she became a cookery writer. When she received her honorary degree at Essex University she told her audience that it was I who had nagged, cajoled, "indeed bullied" her into becoming a writer. This generous tribute somewhat overstretched the facts. I was simply instrumental in persuading my editor, Anne Scott-James, to publish her first pieces in what was then *Harper's Bazaar*.

Besides being an artist struggling to find a medium to express her gifts, she had already attempted painting and acting. Elizabeth was a conversationalist with the compelling powers of the Ancient Mariner and talk begun over her kitchen table in Chelsea at lunch time might well be prolonged into dinner. Given a more strictly academic education she might have entertained the high table at some Oxford college and written books on recondite subjects for scholars. Happily for most of her life the artist and essayist prevailed over the scholar. In this mood she wrote as one of her editors commented, "like an angel".

Veronica Nicholson

ROBERT GITTINGS

Robert Gittings, CBE, literary critic, poet and biographer of Keats and Thomas Hardy.

ROBERT Gittings was best known for his contributions to Keats scholarship. His biography of the poet is currently the definitive one. But he wrote many other books, especially a pioneering biography (in the sense, at least, that it offered us a more unsparing scrutiny of its subject's personal life than had to that point appeared) of Thomas Hardy. And he was a distinguished minor poet.

His father was a naval surgeon whose life at that time consisted of two-year spells of duty, so the young Gittings saw the life of many ports, Plymouth and Rosyth among them.

Gittings began his literary life as a poet, much encouraged by the staff of his school, St Edward's, Oxford; it was through schoolboy poems published at that time that he began his lifelong friendship with Arthur Harris, better known later as the verse playwright Christopher Fry, towards whom he acknowledged a profound debt.

Gittings went up to Jesus College, Cambridge, on a scholarship.

In 1932 he had published his first book, a collection of verse called *The Roman Road*. In 1937 he followed this with *The Story of Psyche*, a blank-verse re-telling of the myth. This was praised for its careful craftsmanship, but it was suggested that "the deeper tones of imaginative experience" were beyond the author's capacity. This remained the standard judgment on his verse, which was none the less always conscientiously exact. He was in this sphere a graceful continuer of the Georgian tradition.

Gittings had been writing radio scripts throughout the 1930s and in 1940 he joined the staff of the BBC to do the same job. He remained there until 1963. He was the producer of the highly regarded series called *Famous Meetings*, as well as many other programmes. He found well deserved literary fame in 1954 with the publication of *John Keats: The Living Year*, which remains his best, most original, most memorable and most directly-felt book. Dealing with the most productive year of Keats's life, September

1818 to September 1819, it shone new and imaginative light on the poet's development. In it Gittings discovered a new and undoubted importance in Keats's hitherto scarcely noticed liaison with Mrs Isabella Jones.

After two more books on aspects of Keats and an abortive foray into the field of Shakespearian studies (*Shakespeare's Rival*, 1960) Gittings produced in 1968 his magisterial biography *John Keats*. This was the fullest account of the poet's life ever to appear and although some readers preferred the critical approach taken in the biographies by Aileen Ward and Jackson Bate (both of which owed more than a little to *The Living Year*), this was certainly ahead in facts and new discoveries. Gittings's method was to make the fullest use of what he described as "non-academic sources". He became known as the most assiduous detective among British biographers and thus greatly compensated for his failure ever again quite to capture the sense of excitement that he had conveyed in *The Living Year*.

John Keats, which won the W. H. Smith Award of 1969, carried considerable authority. Even those who could not agree with all of Gittings's interpretations or felt he had not succeeded in capturing quite the psychological penetration of *The Living Year* had to concede that the book allowed them, as no other had before it, to live with the poet "almost from hour to hour". It was a major achievement.

Gittings's next project was a life of Thomas Hardy, of whom no biography had by then appeared that could be described as even adequate. His edition of Emma Hardy's *Some Recollections* (1961), done in collaboration with another writer, had received very rough handling from the late Henry Reed and was subsequently revised. Reed, who had known the second Mrs Hardy well, had for long been expected to write the definitive biography. But illness prevented that happening. Gittings failed to obtain Reed's co-operation in his work. This was a loss, as Michael Millgate's later biography, written with the benefit of Reed's expertise, showed.

Gittings accomplished his task in two volumes: *Young Thomas Hardy* (1975) and *The Older Hardy* (1978). These were received with respect and (especially the first volume) with gratitude for bringing hitherto unknown facts to light. But the biography did not excite the kind of attention that the work on Keats had done.

Earlier complaints about Gittings's lack of verbal – and critical – flair were revived. This was probably because he too evidently disliked Hardy as a man while grudgingly acknowledging his greatness as a writer. Curiously, he found little beauty or generosity of spirit in Hardy; yet readers had always discerned it from his books. The biography was for a time influential on a generation new to Hardy's writings, although Millgate's slightly later, more scholarly one, initiated independently, appeared in the general estimation to correct Gittings's moralising account. But the work did and does stand out as a conscientious record of the facts, and must serve any future biographer.

Gittings edited several books, including a notable annotated selection of Keats's letters, as well as an extended essay, *The Nature of Biography* (1970). His *Collected Poems* appeared in 1976. He also wrote a number of plays and a *son et lumière* entertainment entitled *Conflict at Canterbury* (1970).

In 1934 he married Katherine Edith Campbell, by whom he had two sons. This marriage ended in divorce and in 1949 he married the writer Jo Manton, by whom he had a daughter. He was visiting professor at Vanderbilt University in 1966, at Boston University in 1970 and at the University of Washington on two occasions (1972 and 1974). Cambridge University awarded him an honorary doctorate in 1970 and in the same year he was appointed CBE.

Together with Jo Manton he wrote several books, including an admirable biography, *The Second Mrs Hardy* (1979).

b 1.2.11   d 18.2.92   aged 81

ALEX HALEY

Alex Palmer Haley, the black American author of Roots, *which became a world-acclaimed television production.*

FAME came late to Alex Haley. He was 55 years old when *Roots: The Saga of an American Family* was published in 1976 and he became, overnight, the literary champion of his race. No other African-American had ever attempted to trace back his family history from its tribal origins, through the horrors of the slave trade, and on to achieving something approaching equality in the world of the white man. Though some contemporary critics condemned it as a mere novel, and Haley himself admitted that many episodes were fictionalised for dramatic effect, the impact of *Roots* was tremendous. It won the 1977 Pulitzer prize and an estimated 130 million people saw the initial showing of the 12-hour television version in 1977. Many millions more have seen it since.

The origins of the book were almost accidental. Haley, who left school at the age of 15, had begun writing while serving as a cook in the US Coast Guard during the second world war. At first his literary efforts were confined to writing love letters on behalf of his illiterate messmates but he soon turned to whiling away the months at sea by writing short stories. It took eight years and several hundred rejection slips before his first story was published. The coast guard, seemingly impressed, created a new post especially for him: Haley, became the service's chief (and only) journalist.

In 1959 Haley retired from the coast guard to become a full-time writer. It was a skimpy existence until, in 1962, he recorded a conversation with the jazz trumpeter Miles Davis and turned it into the first of the *Playboy* interviews. Regular commissions followed and an interview with Malcolm X, radical spokesman of "the Nation of Islam", so impressed a publisher that Haley was asked to turn it into a book. As a literary "ghost," Haley was an instant success. The *Autobiography of Malcolm X*, published in 1965, sold six million copies in eight languages. Malcolm X was assassinated two weeks after the manuscript was finished.

But Haley was on his way. He signed a contract with Doubleday & Co to write a book about the American South before the 1954 supreme court decision declaring school segregation unconstitutional. It was never written, because while in London on another writing assignment Haley visited the British Museum and saw the Rosetta Stone. It was the beginning of his long journey to *Roots*. As a child Haley had heard strange words of an African language passed down through his family from their slave forebears. Now he mused that if, like the strange hieroglyphics on the Rosetta Stone, those sounds could be properly deciphered, they, too, might unlock a buried past. On impulse, when he returned to the US he went to the National Archives in Washington and asked to see the census records of Alamance County, North Carolina, for the years following the Civil War. In these he found the names of several ancestors and the hunt was on.

For twelve years, supported by piecemeal advances from his long-suffering publishers and *Readers Digest* Haley became obsessed with tracing his maternal bloodline back through seven generations in the United States and several more in a village on the banks of the Gambia River in West Africa.

With the help of a linguist at the University of Wisconsin Haley succeeded in identifying the African words he had heard used by his family as being in the Manding dialect of Gambia. He spent $80,000 and travelled half a million miles in his quest, eventually tracking down the key figure of "Kunta Kinte", who had been kidnapped in Gambia and sold into slavery in 1767.

Haley had been lucky. In the Gambian village of Juffure he found a tribal historian who chanted for him the history of the Kinte tribe from its earliest origins in old Mali, and told of the kidnapping "when the King's soldiers came." Kunta Kinte, Haley was convinced, was the same man as his ancestor, known as "Kin-tay," who was brought as a slave to Annapolis, Maryland.

Through Lloyds of London he set out to identify the actual event, and discovered that the slave ship *Lord Ligonier*, captained by Thomas E. Davies, had sailed with captives from The Gambia on July 5, 1767. Documents in the Library of Congress confirmed that the *Lord Ligonier* had discharged her cargo of slaves in Annapolis on September 29 of that year. On September 29, 1967, exactly 200 years later, Alex Haley stood on an Annapolis pier and wept. It took another seven years to put the book together. Haley was nothing if not scrupulous in his research. He visited more than 50 libraries and archives on three continents before settling down to the formidable task of converting his vast trove of material into a readable narrative. At one point, to gain authenticity, he booked passage on a freighter sailing from West Africa to the US and spent each night down in the hold. There, stripped to his underwear on a rough board between bales of raw rubber, he tried to imagine what it was like "to lie there in chains, in filth, hearing the cries of 139 other men screaming, babbling, praying and dying around you."

Some critics were dismissive of the "factional" style of *Roots* and others disputed its factual accuracy. After an article in *the Sunday Times* questioned the work's fundamental findings, Haley came to London to defend what he described as his "symbolic history." He admitted that when dealing with oral evidence lacking any written records as in Gambia, he could not be positive about every detail. But, he said, he had spent years researching the book and everything in it stood up to scrutiny. *Roots*, he said, should be contrasted with the "Tarzan and Jane" image of Africa that he claimed had been the American cultural approach for generations.

Roots proved to be Haley's last work of significance. After it he wrote a novella, *A Different Kind of Christmas*, which told the story of Fletcher Randall, a wealthy Southern plantation owner who undergoes a moral conversion and joins the underground railroad network that helped free slaves. This work made little impact, however, and with 500 American colleges building courses around the *Roots* book, Haley discovered a talent as a public speaker and found himself in huge demand on campuses across the country.

He became a familiar figure on the US speaking circuit, and was fulfilling an engagement on the West Coast when he was suddenly taken to hospital.

b 11.8.21   d 10.2.92   aged 70

WILLIAM DOUGLAS HOME

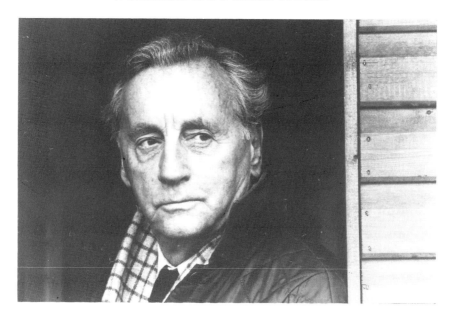

William Douglas Home, playwright and author.

WHEN in April 1951 William Douglas Home went to see Tommy Brand, later Lord Hampden, to ask for his daughter's hand in marriage there seemed a high possibility of refusal. Douglas Home, on his own reckoning was a "cashiered officer, and an ex-convict, what's more. Not to mention a dramatic author, so-called, with a new play on in London that won't last a month." But he got his wife, Rachel, in a marriage which lasted until his death and he went on writing plays, more than 40 of them. There were flops, usually when he turned to historical subjects: no-one now much remembers *Betzi* or *The Douglas Cause*. But William Douglas Home at his most urbane could command the theatre's top stars and at one point had four plays running simultaneously in the West End.

The Douglas Homes were a large, comfortably rich and tightly-knit family. William's elder brothers were Alec, who was to become Conservative prime minister, and the ornithologist Henry,

whose son Charlie was to edit *The Times*. He followed both to Eton, where he overcame his prep school nickname of "Codfish" and where Alec described him as "rather good-looking, in an Asiatic kind of way". His father, the thirteenth Earl of Home, attained theatrical immortality when William used him as the model for the eccentric peer, the Earl of Lister, in his early success *The Chiltern Hundreds*, who is in the habit of potting rabbits from his dining room window.

William Douglas Home's Oxford career was erratic. He was rusticated for attending smart London dinner parties, when he should have been behind New College's gates, and made the national press – "PEER'S SON SENT DOWN". He drove to his finals in a phaeton drawn by a large horse irreverently named Lily after Oxford's lady mayoress. And eventually he picked up a fourth for answering a lot of questions, but not necessarily those set by the examiners. More importantly he formed a lifelong friendship with the future cricket commentator, Brian Johnston.

His taste for the theatre was sparked

by a performance from John Gielgud in *Richard of Bordeaux*. While at Oxford he wrote a play called *Great Possessions*, about Buchmanism, which was staged at the "Q" Theatre and moved to the Duke of York's. He applied for RADA, was accepted without huge enthusiasm, and eventually made his stage debut with the Brighton repertory company in 1937. The immediate pre-war years, partly spent in an Eaton Square flat shared with Johnston, were distinctly Wodehousian. Douglas Home took his tails to the theatre, sometimes to wear as one of the butlers he was required to play on stage but more likely to don after the curtain had come down for a post-theatre dinner party.

The outbreak of war brought out Douglas Home's first major *crise de conscience*. He was a conscientious objector in the sense that he always believed there was room for negotiation with Germany because of the number of citizens there unsympathetic to the Nazi cause. However, he did join up and became an officer. This did not prevent him, though, fighting three by-elections while in the army (always unsuccessfully) as an Independent standing against Churchill's demand for "Unconditional Surrender".

Douglas Home's strongly held beliefs were put to their severest test when he was part of the force ordered to take Le Havre. He insisted that the civilians should be evacuated before the bombardment, a request which was refused on the grounds of lack of time, although the German commander was agreeable. Captain Douglas Home spent the battle, during which there was considerable loss of life, on the sidelines. He drew attention to his action in a newspaper letter and, mainly because of this, was court martialled, stripped of his rank and sentenced to a year's imprisonment.

He paid deeply for his actions and the scar remained. As late as 1991 he applied

At Oxford University with Brian Johnston (1934)

for a rescinding of the court martial order and the Queen's pardon, but the appeal was turned down. In 1944 he was sent first to Wormwood Scrubs and then to Wakefield Prison. These experiences formed his first great theatrical success, *Now Barabbas*, written in 1946 after his release. This wholly realistic play of prison life began at the Boltons Theatre Club in Chelsea, before moving to the Vaudeville. It was later filmed with Richard Greene and Cedric Hardwicke.

The Vaudeville was also the theatre for his next play, *The Chiltern Hundreds*, which ran for two years. It, too, was filmed, with the title changed to *The Amazing Mr Beecham* for the American market. In it William Douglas Home used both his family and his knowledge of politics. He touched a chord in what seemed to many to be a topsy-turvy post-war world and he provided a plum part for the veteran actor A. E. Matthews as the Earl of Lister. Matthews, in his mid eighties, was asked how he managed to keep acting and replied "I read *The Times* obituary column and if I'm not there I go on stage." Douglas Home could have written that line, which was later recycled by many actors.

Plays followed in a steady flow, some well received and some not. When the audience — and especially the gallery — showed disapproval Douglas Home was quite ready to show his own distaste for them in a curtain speech. His light boulevard comedy style was generally preferred to his historical pieces. In the latter, such as *The Thistle and the Rose*, he was apt to raid his own family history. There was trouble, too, when he attempted a subject considered risqué. *Aunt Edwina* concerned a sex change, which some of Home's regular admirers considered rather disgusting, and not even a series of impassioned stage speeches could keep it going.

Probably his biggest popular success came in 1955 with *The Reluctant Debutante*. The cast was much to Home's liking. He shared a passion for horse racing with Wilfrid Hyde-White; Celia Johnson was a friend and a favourite actress, who was to appear in several more of his plays; the girl of the title who rebels against the London "season" marked the debut of Anna Massey. All brought exactly the polish to proceedings, required by "The Deb". It had a long run at the Cambridge before going to Broadway and onto the screen. For the film William Douglas Home had to do a little hasty rewriting when MGM insisted on casting Sandra Dee in the title role.

Douglas Home became an international name and for a moment it looked as though Hollywood might gobble him up. Dino de Laurentis signed him to script a picture called *The Best of Enemies*, starring David Niven and Alberto Sordi, but there were few of his words left in the final version, as he described ruefully in his second volume of autobiography, *Mr Home, pronounced Hume*.

Back in London there was a revolution in theatrical taste to contend with. John Osborne's *Look Back in Anger* had set the Royal Court Theatre alight and a great gap was opening between Sloane Square and Shaftesbury Avenue. Douglas Home remained firmly anchored at the latter address and had no truck whatsoever with the so-called kitchen sink movement. He preferred to stay with white tie and tails, so much so that his children once saucily suggested that his next play should be called *Butlers in Space*. But he did begin to have the first of many brushes with theatre critics, especially those of a leftish dispostion, which continued over the years.

The output remained unabated, with the previous mixture of hits and flops. Among the former was *The Secretary Bird*, which recovered from an obscure opening in Swanage to provide a juicy part for Kenneth More. It came to the Savoy, was a success in Australia and sufaced in Paris under the title of *Canard à l'orange*. *Lady Boothroyd of the Byepass* was written for the Cassons, but eventually ended as *Lloyd George Knew My Father*, with Ralph Richardson in the lead. Douglas Home was fluent, too fluent his detractors claimed. *The Dame*

Canvassing in Edinburgh (1957)

of Sark was written in five days, he recalled, just in time to catch the Saturday racing on television, an important hour in the family home as far as its head was concerned.

William Douglas Home was very much part of the commercial theatre establishment but he remained unperformed by the subsidised sector. The nearest he came to it was in 1975 with *The Kingfisher*, which Ralph Richardson wanted to do at the National. Peter Hall was in agreement and Lindsay Anderson was set to direct. But the National suddenly came under attack for putting on too many "lightweight" comedies and then transferring them to the West End. So the project was abandoned and *The Kingfisher* became another Shaftesbury Avenue play, with Richardson, Celia Johnson and Alan Webb, running for six months at the Lyric.

This and a lesser piece, *Rolls Hyphen Royce*, were his last successes, with *The Kingfisher* going to Broadway and Australia (with Googie Withers and John McCallum). Douglas Home went on writing during the Eighties but often the plays did not get beyond a regional run. He was openly disappointed that his attempt to have his army cashiering revoked by the Ministry of Defence was unsuccessful — a television programme was made about the episode after a collection of the letters he wrote home from the front had been published in 1985 under the title *Sins of Commission*. In 1991 his third volume of autobiography came out, *Old Men Remember*. That was to be the final reminiscence of a man who had been an entertainer from his schooldays on.

He leaves his widow, Rachel (Baroness Dacre), a son and three daughters.

b 3.6.12   d 28.9.92   aged 80

BILL NAUGHTON

Irish born novelist and playwright whose most notable success was "Alfie".

BILL Naughton, son of Irish parents who left for Lancashire in search of a better life soon after he was born, was most famous for his novel *Alfie* (1966). This was a reworking of a tale of a sexy opportunist. *Alfie* first saw life as the radio play *Alfie Elkin and his Little Life* (1962), and then in the London stage production at the Mermaid in 1963, with John Neville in the title role and Gemma Jones as one of the women he wronged. It was filmed soon after, rather slackly directed by Lewis Gilbert but with Michael Caine as a memorable Alfie and Vivien Merchant playing the put-upon female.

The film, helped by Caine and a title song, spurred sales of the book and turned Naughton into one of the most successful of the "North Country" writers. But Alfie, although an example of well-executed popular writing and

important in its own right, was by no means his best work.

Naughton grew up in Lancashire, as he vividly related in the semi-fictional sketches of his first (and best) book, *A Roof Over Your Head* (1945). He was educated at St Peter & St Paul School, Bolton, and thereafter, during the late 1920s and 1930s, worked as a weaver, coal-bagger, long distance lorry driver and, finally, before taking to writing, as a civil defence driver during the war.

A Roof Over Your Head, published by Pilot Press, was commissioned by Charles Madge who was at one time, like Naughton, a member of the Mass Observation team. It remains one of the most moving accounts of what life was like under the shadow of the dole queue in the north of England. It was described by John Betjeman as a "work of genius", although Naughton himself could never see why. His later writing became sentimental, if only in the best possible manner; but these early sketches (which end with fragments from a wartime diary) are all the more effective for being entirely unsentimental. Not a few readers have been reminded by it of the relentless accuracy of L. S. Lowry.

Pony Boy (1946), a story for boys, which followed it, is almost as good, as are the majority of the stories finally collected as *Late Night on Watling Street* (1959). These first appeared in magazines in the 1940s and 1950s and helped to make Naughton's name. By the time he came to write the novel *One Small Boy* (1957), the story of how a west Irish family just like his own came to the Lancashire mill towns, he had lost the touch of genius, although even this is a charming and enlightening book.

Much of Bill Naughton's early dramatic work was for radio and he wrote for all levels of brow. He was just as likely to be heard on the Light as on the Third Programme. He began writing stage plays in the late 1950s. The first, produced as *My Flesh, My Blood* (1957), eventually became *Spring And Port Wine*; it was produced at the Mermaid, the London theatre with which Naughton will always be associated, in 1965 with Alfred Marks in the lead. It then became a film in 1970, directed by Peter Hammond and starring James Mason as a stern father who has a not-too-convincing change of heart. With *All in Good Time* (another Mermaid play) and *Alfie* it forms the dramatic trio by which Naughton will be remembered.

The sometimes brutal realism of *Alfie* was just enough to keep its sentimentality in check, and Naughton deserved its immense success. Alas, his attempt to capitalise on it, *Alfie Darling* (1970), his feeblest effort, was of no consequence, although he had nothing to do with the abject script for the filmed version of 1975. *The Family Way* (1966), for which he wrote the script with Ray Boulting and the experienced Jeffrey Dell, about a bridegroom who cannot consummate his marriage, was sharper in its shorter television version, *Honeymoon Deferred*, but nevertheless had its undeniably comic moments in the British good-clean dirty-joke farcical tradition.

Probably the best of Naughton's later work is to be found in his many radio and television plays, which included on television the *Nathaniel Titlark* and *Yorky* series (the latter written in collaboration with Allan Prior).

Radio drama is still an unduly neglected form in Great Britain, but there is no doubt that such plays as *Timothy* (1956), *Seeing a Beauty Queen Home* (1960) and *The Mystery* (1973), which won the Prix Italia in 1974, would sound just as well today as they did when they were first performed. There were other writings, including three more sets of stories, two more children's books, and several stage plays, including some for his adopted town of Bolton.

But most notable were the two books of autobiography, again going back to his childhood, *On The Pig's Back* (1987) and *Saintly Billy* (1988). Both of these were published by the Oxford University Press, and a third, *Neither Use Nor Ornament*, awaits publication elsewhere.

Bill Naughton was fundamentally a very serious man as well as a master of the playwriting craft and a superb humorist. Like many another in his position, he received the attentions of the media, but hardly approved of them. In his days as a long-distance lorry driver (upon which he drew for that best of all his stories, *Late Night on Watling Street*) he had haunted second hand book shops and discovered the *Meditations of Marcus Aurelius*. This is time led to a devotion to *The Cloud of Unknowing* and the works of Meister Eckhart. When (only partly for tax purposes) some 20 years ago he retired to Ballasalla in the Isle of Man, he did so in order to grow roses and to contemplate. In this he probably found what he had missed in commercial success, for he was in no sense vulgarly "occult".

He had two children by his first marriage, which ended in divorce. His second wife, the former Ernestine Pirolt, survives him.

b 12.6.10   d 8.1.92   aged 81

RAYMOND
BROOKS-WARD

Raymond Brooks-Ward, equestrian commentator and horse show director.

RAYMOND Brooks-Ward, known as the voice of show-jumping, had been a television commentator for over 30 years, but behind the scenes he had also been a great promoter of, and fund-raiser for, equestrian sports and a highly successful show director. His advice and business expertise, as well as his public profile, were highly valued in the equestrian world.

Brooks-Ward grew up in Hertfordshire and developed his interest in horses through the Enfield Chase branch of the Pony Club. Fox-hunting became his great passion in life. From 1958 to 1971 he was master of the West Lodge Basset Hounds, and in 1972 he became a joint master of the Enfield Chase, remaining with it until he moved to Cornwall, where he became master of the North Cornwall Hunt.

His love of hunting had first taken root in 1951, when he joined the Royal Corps of Transport. He was with the army for

three years, but, by his own admission, spent much of that time hunting with the Aldershot Beagles.

A brief spell in the hotel industry, following in his father's footsteps, was given up in favour of running a dairy farm in Hertfordshire, but his involvement as a commentator at local shows gradually developed and it was not long before he was supplementing his farmwork with commentating at big shows all over the country.

In 1956 he gained his first experience in television when asked to stand in for the racing commentator Peter O'Sullivan. He joined ITV in 1960 as a show jumping commentator and ten years later moved to the BBC with which he began covering eventing and dressage, as well as show jumping. His most recent commentaries were heard from Barcelona, where he covered all the Olympic equestrian events, and he was due to be commentating again for the BBC at the British Open Championship at Gatcombe Park.

As well as his work for television, Brooks-Ward was involved in public relations and sponsorship for the sport. In 1974 he set up British Equestrian promotions (BEP) with his friend Bob Dean with the aim of running horse shows and finding sponsors. Among the shows he directed were the Royal International and the Horse of the Year Show at Wembley. He was also the driving force behind the Christmas show at Olympia, which was established in 1972 and has become the most popular indoor horse show in the country.

Brooks-Ward left BEP to set up the British branch of Best Communications Management with his eldest son, Simon, and his most recent project was the Pavarotti International Show in Italy. He had been working with great enthusiasm on this before his sudden death at his home near Truro. A great family man, he was particularly fond of his Cornish farmhouse, from where, in addition to his riding interests, he loved going out to mess about in boats.

His influence in the horse world was far-reaching and his enthusiasm never diminished. Captain Mark Phillips, director of the horse trials at Gatcombe Park, described him as "the public face, image and voice of all equestrian sports". Hugh Thomas, who worked with Brooks-Ward at BEP for seven years and is now the director of Badminton Horse Trials, said: "We have lost a good friend as well as one of the greatest equestrian personalities. He was a warm, generous and kind-hearted man who has helped a great many of us in the equestrian world."

Brooks-Ward once said of his work: "I never tire of it. It's like theatre. An actor puts as much into the 300th performance of a play as he puts into the first."

Speaking to *Radio Times* in 1986, he said that he saw his role as commentator as being to "fill in the background without being too obtrusive", adding: "People like to know little tit-bits, like what events a certain horse and rider have won before, where they've had clear rounds, how high they've jumped and bits of family history. Richard Dimbleby used to say that if you were doing half-an-hour's commentary, you should do one-and-a-half-hour's homework. I've never forgotten that, as he was the best commentator ever."

Brooks-Ward leaves a widow, Dinny, and three sons, Simon, James and Nicholas.

b 9.4.30   d 22.8.92   aged 62

Raymond Brooks-Ward hunting, Hertfordshire (1980)

SIR RICHARD FRANCIS

Sir Richard Francis, director general of the British Council from July 1987 and former director of news and current affairs for the BBC.

DICK Frances will justly be given much credit for the way he remodelled the British Council over the past five years, improving its work, its status and its budget. But he will probably be best remembered by the public for his time at the BBC, where he was in charge of news and current affairs and then managing director of radio for four years before his resignation in 1986.

Francis was a classic example of the BBC high flyer whose career was suddenly grounded for good in one of the numerous blood-lettings which characterised life in the Corporation in the 1970s and 1980s. When Alasdair Milne was forced by the BBC governors to resign as director general in 1986, Francis, who had had many a tussle with Milne, thought that he was a leading candidate for the job. A considerable number of Francis's supporters and

admirers believed likewise. Instead, he was told by the governors that not only would he not be considered, but that he could expect no further preferment. Shocked and incredulous, Francis resigned on the spot.

Dick Francis was a true Yorkshireman, with a strain of Yorkshire pugnacity. He was born in Harrogate and went to Uppingham, where he showed plenty of self-confidence and was a good actor, specialising in comedy roles. He managed only a third at University College, Oxford, but continued to act with OUDS. Called up for National Service in the Royal Artillery, he was immediately identified as officer material and commissioned in 1957.

After the Army he entered the BBC as a general trainee (Corporation code in those days for a "flyer"). Following the expected pattern of such privileged entrants, he distinguished himself first as a radio features producer. He was switched to television, where he was seconded to light entertainment, which he did not enjoy. He was shunted off to drama, then to afternoon programmes and finally current affairs, which proved to be his forte.

As a producer on *Panorama*, Dick Francis was soon entrusted with many major assignments, especially wars, which he covered in every continent. His productions of programmes on the Congo and Vietnam were particularly admired. By 1965 he was assistant editor of *Panorama* from which me moved on to head *Twenty Four Hours* and to become projects editor, current affairs. In 1968 and 1969 he was in charge of the European Broadcasting Union coverage of the American elections and of the first Apollo launch.

In 1972, when he was assistant head of current affairs, he surprised many of his colleagues by accepting what was then considered the backwater appointment of controller BBC Northern Ireland. When he assumed charge of the BBC's operations in the Province the following year, the "Troubles" were at their height. He established the principle, jealously preserved by his successors in Belfast, that no programme concerning Northern Ireland should get beyond the planning stage at the BBC without full consultation with the controller there.

Because of his successful incumbency in what had become an internationally-known notorious trouble spot for broadcasters, Dick Francis now came to be regarded as the leading expert on such situations, and was much in demand as a speaker at conferences. His lecture "Broadcasting to a Community in Conflict", delivered at Chatham House in February 1977, is still thought of as a classic of its kind. In Northern Ireland itself, he is best remembered for having launched BBC Radio Ulster.

After Northern Ireland he became a member of the BBC board of management, as director of news and current affairs. His skill as a lecturer made him even more in demand in this new role. Two of his most memorable orations were "Television – The Evil Eye?" at the Royal Television Society in 1981 and "What Price Free Speech", delivered to The Law Society the following year.

Although he was a friendly and amiable man, with a considerable sense of humour, Dick Francis stood out as a conspicuously sober-sided, conservative and restrained figure among a BBC board of management dominated at that time by the bagpipe-playing Alasdair Milne, the perennially jocose Bill Cotton, and the rumbustious Aubrey Singer. "Plodding" was a description often unfairly applied to him by his critics, although one of his BBC colleagues took a different view and referred to him as "the last of the cigar-chomping Concorde travellers". Francis was used to criticism, and he also enjoyed the privileges of management.

His appointment in 1982 as managing director of BBC Radio was received with equal measure of rejoicing and dismay by the radio staff, some of whom saw him as unadventurous, while others thought that his was exactly the steady hand at the helm needed at that moment. The latter description, when he heard of it, gave him

particular pleasure, because his abiding passion was ocean racing at which he scored many successes. Also, the achievement of managing director status put him firmly in line for the highest BBC office, though this was not to be.

On the day in 1986 when he left Broadcasting House for the last time, deeply distressed after his resignation, a colleague said to him prophetically: "Never mind, Dick. If you can't be DG of this lot, there are other things to be DG of." Within a year he was director general of the British Council. It was a surprise appointment in many ways: the council had tended to draw either from academia or from areas of sevice less public than the BBC.

His first task was to restore reasonable relations with the Foreign Office, which had become decidedly sour by the time of Francis's arrival, one of the reasons why the council was distinctly short of cash. Francis made the peace and he got the money. During his period with the council its budget increased by 20%. His colleagues were at first taken aback by his sometimes abrasive manner and the way he treated those with whom he did not agree. Initially it was put down to the BBC years but later understood as being the carapace of a basically shy man.

Francis was determined to preserve and even extend the Council's overseas network and to fight for the role of English as a world language. He was early to spot the opportunities presented by the changes in Eastern Europe and to make sure his team was suitably strong there.

At home he supervised the move of half of his staff to Manchester, which was much resented in some quarters, and it is a sadness that he did not live to see the opening of the new offices there next month.

Last year he was appointed one of the 16 members of the newspaper watchdog committee, the Press Complaints Commission.

Dick Francis was married twice and had two sons from each marriage.

b 10.3.34   d 26.6.92   aged 58

DESMOND HACKETT

Desmond Hackett, sports writer of the Daily Express.

IN THE days when the *Daily Express* sold more than 4 million copies a day and had no reticence in proclaiming itself the world's greatest newspaper, Desmond Hackett was its greatest sports writer. He was primarily a football correspondent but he also reported athletics and golf and was willing to cover any other type of sport if required. There was little football on television when he came to Fleet Street and what there was appeared only in black and white.

He was born at Morecambe and began his career covering speedway. He was soon reporting football and moved to the *Daily Express* in London where its editor, Arthur Christiansen, had been looking for somebody to succeed Trevor Wignall as the paper's star sports writer. Christiansen first brought Henry Rose from Manchester to London as a possible replacement but this was not a success. Rose was known in sporting circles as the King of the North. He was more famous than many players in the 1950s but he failed to transplant well to London. He was sent back to Manchester, where he wrote as successfully as ever, and when he died in the 1958 Munich air crash it was Hackett, his successor, who was sent to report his funeral and began typically: "Even the skies wept for Henry Rose yesterday."

Hackett wrote for the man on the terrace – and the men and women who did not go to matches – and was a master of the gimmick. His trademark was his brown bowler which caused cheers of recognition from the crowds when he entered a press box. He offered to eat his bowler if Colchester United beat Leeds United in one cup-tie. Colchester won and he duly ate it in front of the photographers – though there was a suspicion that what he ate was designed by a confectioner rather than a hatter. He also offered to clean Jack Bodell's windows if the British heavyweight won a certain fight. Bodell did win and the windows were cleaned by Hackett – wearing his brown bowler of course.

His reporting of the 1964 Olympics in Tokyo is still remembered by many as Hackett at his best. He is also remembered for his coverage of the 1954 World Cup in Berne when a match between Hungary and Brazil ended in a riot.

Hackett in action, coat off, scarlet braces displayed, words tumbling on to his typewriter, face sweating, was a fearsome sight to his usually slower opponents. He was a consistent drinker like many of his colleagues, but his consumption of black velvet never affected his work. A fortnight after the anniversary of Henry Rose's death, which Hackett always observed, he went to a public house for a casual drink with a friend. He came back to his Wimbledon home, sat with a glass of Guinness in one hand and a glass of port in another, dozed off and never recovered consciousness. It would have been a typical last sentence in a Hackett article.

b 14.3.12   d 20.2.92   aged 79

SIR HAROLD HOBSON

Sir Harold Hobson, CBE, drama critic of The Sunday Times *from 1947 to 1976.*

FOR almost thirty years Harold Hobson was essential reading every Sunday morning for anyone with any concern for the theatre. He was there during the right decades when British theatre was going through its great resurgence. And Hobson was ever a champion of new drama, whether it came from Brenton or Beckett, Pinter or Billetdoux. He was there, too, at a period when the influence of the Sunday newspaper critics was at its peak. Hobson and Tynan could turn a box-office round after the dailies had had their say. They did so in the case of John Osborne's *Look Back in Anger*. But more often Hobson and Tynan, the two weekly colossi, would disagree. And that added spice to the Sunday breakfast table, as well as probably giving them both pleasure.

Harold Hobson will be remembered as an endearingly contentious writer in a form of criticism always notable for its individualists. Penelope Gilliatt coined the phrase about the characteristic sound of the English Sunday being that of Harold Hobson barking up the wrong tree. But very frequently he barked up the right one. Few other writers on the theatre in Hobson's period aroused more argument. Certainly no one responded to it with a more appealing good nature.

He was primarily an essayist at a day when the essay was beginning to fall from grace. Hobson was lucky to have the theatre as a theme. Though by no means so discursive as James Agate, his predecessor, he would write expertly round a play without hiding his firmly indepedent views under too complex a web of illustrative allusion. He was apt, as a Christian Scientist, to put a religious gloss on plays where none was visible to non-Christians.

His opinions could be surprising; sometimes they sounded almost deliberately perverse. But in his work, as in his friendships, he liked to tease; it delighted him when someone would tread furiously on his trailing coat. It was impossible to be at odds with him for long, though one might wish sometimes that a man of his talent, in so influential a post, could be more selective in his enthusiasms. Still, the stage of his day owed much to his championship of Harold Pinter, whose quality he discerned in *The Birthday Party* when other critics had rejected it. He applauded the work of John Osborne and Samuel Beckett; he was rarely out of touch with new movements in the drama; and as an ardent supporter of the French theatre in many moods, he carried on where Agate left off.

But after that championsip of *Look Back* he was less supportive of the work of the Royal Court, where George Devine and his team of young turks were trying to break loose from the straitjacket of boulevard comedy, than he might have been. Hobson's favoured playwrights were more likely to be Fry and Whiting.

He was rarely in tune with the American theatre and found little inspiration in the sheer Broadway professionalism which totally revolutionised the musical in the postwar years. Nor was Shakespearian criticism among his strengths: he could be an idiosyncratic judge of acting.

But Hobson was unconcerned that his views might be idiosyncratic at times or untrendy. He had no intention of being a "safe" critic. He loved the theatre, he enjoyed talking about it. He wrote about it with passion and when he was strongly moved, as in his notices of Pinter or Claudel, and his appreciations of Ralph Richardson (on whom he wrote a monograph) and Edwige Feuillère, he could reach genuine eloquence.

Few London critics covered so long a span. Sunday by Sunday Hobson's choice was observed with amusement at his foibles, respect for his sincerity, and affection for the man himself, a "character" in a role where it is not enough to be gently effacing. He tried, he explained once, to say what the average play-goer would be saying in ten years' time; on those terms he probably had as many hits as misses.

Born at Thorpe Hesley, near Rotherham in Yorkshire, he was the son of Jacob Hobson and Minnie McKegg.

Through all difficulties he entered Oriel College, Oxford, by way of Sheffield Grammar School, and graduated in 1928. In 1931 he began to write drama criticism in London for the *Christian Science Monitor* (he was an ardent Christian Scientist), and in 1946 he became the paper's London literary editor, a post he combined with his work for the theatre and (from 1947 to 1951) as television critic for *The Listener*.

He first became familiar in London drama criticism when he acted as James Agate's understudy towards the end of that powerful figure's reign at *The Sunday Times*. Hobson was appointed assistant literary editor of the paper in 1944; from the following year he was also a second string critic whose reviews, in Agate's increasing absence, appeared frequently in the theatre column. It caused no surprise in his office when he succeeded Agate in 1947; thereafter he went steadily forward.

At first he was anxious to write books. He had already pbulished a novel, *The Evil in Woodford Wells*, a graceful fantasy inspired by his pleasure in cricket and his admiration of Max Beerbohm. He went on, perhaps injudiciously, to follow Agate's *Ego* series by two volumes, *Theatre* and *Theatre 2* (1948 and 1950) that mingled a daily journal with passages from his reviews. He was more at home in the anthology with comments, *Verdict at Midnight* (1952); but his best work is found in *The French Theatre of Today* (1953) where he could express his excitement in the Paris stage, its dramatists (Genêt for one), and its players. In 1960 he was created a Chevalier of the Legion of Honour, but he returned the decoration eight years later in a typically chivalrous protest at the treatment of Jean-Louis Barrault.

In 1971 he was created CBE for his services to the theatre and knighted in 1977.

He married, secondly in 1981, Nancy Penhale.

b 4.8.04   d 12.3.92   aged 87

PETER JENKINS

Peter Jenkins, journalist. Since 1987 he had been associate editor and political columnist of The Independent; *he had previously made his reputation as one of the most original columnists of his generation, on* The Guardian *over a period of 25 years from 1960; from 1985 to 1987 he was political columnist on* The Sunday Times.

PETER Jenkins was one of the outstanding analysts of British politics of the past quarter century. At a time when most Fleet Street columnists took a parochial view of political life, as if all that mattered did so in Westminster or Whitehall, he lifted his sights and made the world his horizon. He consciously took as his models such American columnists as Walter Lippmann and the Allsop Brothers, who did not limit their political vision to Washington.

Jenkins was a prolific writer, at one time producing four columns a week for *The Guardian* and almost as many for

The Independent. He used to carry a portable filing system wherever he went, so that if the events of the day did not give him the right material he could always dig in his files to find something else to write about. Having adjusted his vision to the world, the world duly became his oyster. Jenkins was constantly on the move with contacts in high places from Washington to Bonn and beyond. Any rival eagerly anticipating an exclusive interview in any corner of the globe always feared the sight of him waiting on the seat outside to trump his or her ace.

Unlike his American counterparts, Jenkins was no jingoist or drum-beater for his country. Although by instinct and belief a writer of the left, he was first and foremost a reporter, interested in discovering the facts, then trying to decipher in which direction the chaos of daily events seemed to point. He was profoundly attached to his country but he knew in his bones that this was not the British century.

He would describe himself as "a poet of decline", by which he meant that it had fallen to him to chronicle Britain's descent from world power to a place firmly set in the second rank. But always there was a tinge of regret that his country's greatest days were irrevocably past. This often lent his judgment a maudlin quality, well suited to the newspapers for which he mostly wrote.

Jenkins grew up in Suffolk, the son of a pharmaceutical chemist, and read history at Trinity Hall, Cambridge. He saw National Service as a young officer and took part in some of the last manoeuvres of Britain's Mediterranean fleet. He had been on board ship when the fleet sailed in full ceremonial rig into Malta's Valetta harbour.

He joined *The Financial Times* in 1958 and moved two years later to *The Guardian* where he became the paper's labour reporter under John Cole, who was the labour correspondent and is now the BBC's political editor. For a brief spell he covered Britain's first attempt to join the European Community, before returning to London to take over Cole's job. As labour correspondent he had Bernard Ingham, later Mrs Thatcher's press secretary, as his deputy.

Soon he shifted to become a columnist with a wide ranging brief and he remained that for the rest of his life, apart from a brief spell during the Watergate years as *The Guardian*'s Washington correspondent. He developed an authority among the paper's readers that was unequalled by any other writer. He was the leading chronicler of the Labour governments of the 1960s and 1970s, notably of their internecine warfare.

In the mid-1980s he switched to *The Sunday Times*. At first he was reluctant to leave *The Guardian*, arguing that having been there for a quarter of a century he should not then quit. But he finally felt that being at one newspaper for so long was actually a very good reason for quitting. Jenkins did not settle happily into the mould of weekly journalism or take to the right-wing character *The Sunday Times* had by then acquired. His last years were spent with *The Independent*, where he felt entirely at home as columnist and policy adviser.

Jenkins was no narrow-minded political guru. He enjoyed a much broader range of interests than Westminster or Washington, Nato or the EC. He was fond of describing politics as the best of all spectator sports but, unlike some of his professional colleagues, never entertained the slightest desire to enter the fray himself. Perhaps the nearest he came to strong commitment was his flirtation with the Social Democrat party, led by his great friend David Owen in the mid-1980s. That and his passionate devotion to European unity were perhaps his only lapses from journalistic objectivity, but were none the less engaging for that.

Jenkins's 1970 book *The Battle of Downing Street* was a lively insider's account of how the unions had destroyed Harold Wilson's government by their intransigent refusal to accept any reform

whatever. His 1987 book *Mrs Thatcher's Revolution* described how the unions duly got their comeuppance. Its sub-title *The Ending of the Socialist Era*, perceptively embraced much more that was in the wind than most other commentators had by then realised. When John Major was Chancellor of the Exchequer, Jenkins invited him to dinner at the Garrick Club. They had never met before and Jenkins greeted him mockingly with the words: "I hear you are going to be the next prime minister." Mr Major modestly demurred. Clearly Jenkins thought the possibility a huge joke. But nobody laughed louder than he when it came true.

When not observing the game of politics, Jenkins was in recent years more often to be seen at the theatre or art galleries than on the race courses he had so much enjoyed in his youth. He was briefly *The Spectator*'s theatre critic and himself wrote a political play, *Illuminations*, which failed to move from the Hammersmith Lyric in spite of having Paul Eddington as its star. He also wrote a television series, *Struggle*, about Looney Left Town Hall politics.

This did well enough to be repeated but Jenkins did not return to the stage. He took to denouncing the theatre as a much rougher old world even than Fleet Street or Westminster.

Occasionally aloof to colleagues he did not regard as his equals, he was a loyal admirer of those whom he felt were as serious in their vocation as he was. He was a jovial host in his Victorian Clapham home and in his last years he began to write enthusiastically about art.

Jenkins was devoted to his first wife, Charlotte Strachey, who died young, and no less devoted to his second wife, Polly Toynbee, the BBC's social affairs editor.

There was a daughter of his first marriage and a son and two daughters of his second.

b 11.5.34   d 27.5.92   aged 58

RIXI MARKUS

Rixi Markus, MBE, who fled to Britain from Hitler and became a leading international bridge player.

WITH the death of Rixi Markus, one of the last links with the origins of contract bridge has been severed. She was a member of the Austrian team which won the first two European Women's Championships (in 1935 and 1936) and the first Women's World Championship (1937). Hers was the only team in the history of bridge which was never defeated.

Her personal record is unlikely ever to be equalled. She won 12 international championships (more than any other woman) and was the first woman to become an international grand master. Only Helen Sobell, who played with Ely Cuthbertson and became the legendary Charles Goren's partner, can challenge her as the strongest woman player to date. Her partnership with Fritzi Gordon, who died on February 8, was famous and stormy. They won the world women's pairs in 1962 and, by a record margin, in 1974. Their supremacy was also marked by winning the world mixed teams' event in 1962 and the Women's World Team Olympiad in 1964 – the only two bridge olympiad events Britain has ever won.

In speed of analysis Markus was in a class of her own. Problems about which good, or even very good, players agonised for several minutes would be solved by Markus in an intimidatingly small number of seconds. She did not apply her formidable mental powers to the minute dissection of bridge *arithmetica*, but she did write several books, of which *Bid Boldly, Play Safe* and *Common Sense Bridge* rank with the best.

Markus was born Erika Scharfstein in Gura Humora, a small town of the Austro-Hungarian empire which is now in Romania. Her family was Jewish, clever, iron-willed and prosperous. By the time he was 20 years old her father owned forests, sawmills, a small brewery, vineyards in Hungary, and much else.

Adolph Hitler's activities made life inconvenient for Viennese coffee-house bridge players, especially Jewish ones, and in 1938 Markus escaped to England with her young daughter Margo, though not without once being deported, straight back from Dover to Ostend. She persevered on that occasion – determination was not a quality she was ever short of – and made the rest of her life in England. She was always fiercely proud of her adopted country, and it is possible that nothing gave her greater pleasure than being appointed MBE in 1975 for services to bridge.

She always turned up for the summer festival in Deauville and always went to St Moritz for the month of January. She broke a leg ski-ing there in her seventies, and an arm shortly before her eightieth birthday, but the doughty spirit of the Scharfsteins kept her travelling the world and arguing the toss till her last days.

Her only child Margo – who lived an equally glamorous, helter-skelter, doughty life in New York and Hollywood – died of cancer in 1976, aged 46, and Rixi never remarried, despite many romances. Her last book. *A Vulnerable Game* (1938), contains not a single bridge hand. It is the story of a twentieth-century life, and a minor classic of its kind.

b 27.6.10   d 4.4.92   aged 81

DR MAGNUS PYKE

Dr Magnus Pyke, scientist and televison communicator.

FEW people who ever saw Magnus Pyke performing on television will forget his gift for vivid expression, his utter lack of self-consciousness and his ability to play the mad scientist, apparently with great fervour and enjoyment. But some viewers may have been misled by his gimickry into failing to notice that he had a serious purpose, great integrity and much humanity.

Although he was wont to use such a broad brush in speech and writing that he could sometimes err in points of detail, his main themes were sound and the scientific views he expounded with such apparent ease and with such consummate skill were essentially correct.

Pyke was born in London and educated at St Paul's School. He found that his good memory helped him to do well at examinations, win prizes and sufficient scholarships to pay his school fees.

His father died when he was 15 and still at school. Four years later he sailed for Montreal where he studied agriculture at Macdonald College, McGill University. He obtained his BSc in agriculture in 1933. He became chief chemist in the research laboratories of Bemax in Hammersmith, London, in 1934, a job he held until 1941, though during those years he was able to do research on vitamins with Professor (later Sir) J. C. Drummond at University College, London, and to obtain his PhD in biochemistry in 1936.

In 1941 he joined Drummond who was by that time scientific adviser at the wartime Ministry of Food. In the ministry Pyke was very active, particularly in studying the nutritional effects of wartime food restrictions. He became involved in a practical way in wartime industrial and hospital feeding and surveyed the nutritional value of meals served in such establishments. This work led him to prepare a series of simple lectures on nutrition for practical caterers, and these lectures were later published as the Ministry of Food's *Manual of Nutrition*, which proved an instant success as an educational tool. Indeed, it became a Whitehall best-seller. The first editon of the *Manual* was published in 1945, the second in 1947 and so on to the eighth edition in 1970, the later editions being prepared by Pyke's successors at the Ministry.

He left the Ministry temporarily in 1945 to become nutritional adviser to the Allied Commission for Austria (British element) in Vienna. He returned in 1946 for two years, during which he concerned himself particularly with the nutritional value of diets available at that time for prisoners, invalids, the aged and infirm, and students. He also took an active interest in nutrition education.

Early in 1949 Pyke joined the Distillers Company and six years later became manager of the company's Glenochil Research Station at Menstrie, Clackmannanshire, a position he held until he retired at the age of 65 in 1973. He was secretary and chairman of council of the British Association for the Advancement of Science from 1973 to 1977.

Pyke's first broadcast was made while he was at the Ministry of Food, and it was about the nutritional excellence of cabbage. From there he progressed by way of an attack on chlorophyll, which was being promoted at the time as a desirable ingredient of toothpaste and other toilet preparations, in which he poured scorn on the notion that the natural constituent of all green plants could have anything like the magic qualities claimed. He was applauded for quoting the couplet:

The goat that reeks on yonder hill.
Has browsed all day on chlorophyll.

Much later he achieved popular acclaim through his regular appearances for seven years in the mid-1970s on the TV science series *Don't Ask Me* and *Don't Just Sit There*. Fame brought its rewards: an appearance as the subject of *This is Your Life*, invitations to participate on radio in *Any Questions* and *Desert Island Discs* and in many other radio and television programmes and to lecture throughout the world.

He was awarded the Pye Colour Television Award as the most promising newcomer to television in 1975 and was also selected by the young people watching the BBC television programme *Multi-Coloured Swap Shop* for the star award for 1977–78 in the category of expert.

His prowess on television and radio was not understood by some of his scientific friends and the manner of his performances always placed him at risk of not being taken seriously. Pyke himself, however, was very serious indeed about the need for scientific communication and the responsibility that experienced scientists have of learning how to communicate their knowledge to non-scientists. Early in his career at the British Association he arranged for the preparation by a small committee of a useful and penetrating study on *Science and the Media.*

Pyke not only broadcast and lectured prolifically; he also wrote. He started with a novel *Go West, Young Man, Go West*, written while he was a student in Canada, and he proceeded after the *Manual of Nutrition* to write popular scientific books, mainly about food and nutrition, at the rate of nearly one a year from 1950 onwards.

In 1937 he married Dorothea Mina Vaughan, an accountant whom he had met through an early common interest in sailing on the Thames at Hammersmith and through a joint friendship with A. P. Herbert.

She predeceased him and he is survived by one son and one daughter.

b 29.12.08   d 19.10.92   aged 83

ERIC SEVAREID

Eric Arnold Sevareid, reporter, war correspondent, author, and doyen of American telvision journalism.

THE job of a journalist, as Eric Sevareid saw it, was simple enough: the raising, rather than the asking, of questions. And in a career that lasted almost half a century, he raised quite a few. He was dismissive of his own talent. "A general journalist," he once said, "is jack-of-all-trades and master of none, save the trade of being jack-of-all. He knows just about enough about almost everything to know when something hitherto unknown comes along."

The son of second-generation immigrants from Norway, Sevareid always had a taste for adventure. At the age of 18, after graduating from high school "pale, skinny, and having learned nothing except how to put the school paper to press," he joined a friend in canoeing 2,200 miles from Minneapolis to Canada's Hudson Bay. The exploit helped land him a job as a copy boy on the *Minneapolis Journal*, and six weeks later he had become a reporter.

At first, it seemed that the profession might not stick. Sevareid left to try his hand at gold-mining, went broke, then decided to take a degree in political science at the University of Minnesota. He travelled to Europe in 1937, studying at the London School of Economics and the Alliance Francaise in Paris, before landing a job as reporter with the Paris edition of the *New York Herald Tribune*.

And then, in August 1939, Sevareid received a telephone call that changed his life. It was from Edward R. Murrow in London, who was then assembling a team of reporters to cover the threatening world war. "I don't know very much about your experience," Murrow said, "but I like the way you write and I like your ideas." He offered him a job with the Columbia Broadcasting System.

Sevareid began travelling with the French army and air force in France, Belgium, Holland and Luxembourg, broadcasting war news back to the United States. He was the last American to broadcast from Paris, fleeing with his wife and newly-born twin sons just before it was taken over by the Germans. Soon afterwards he scored a gigantic scoop when he was the first to report that France was about to capitulate.

After the fall of France, Sevareid joined Murrow in London to cover the Blitz and the Battle of Britain. Returning to America, homesick and ill, he told an audience still hesitant about getting into the war: "When you've seen the homes of civilians destroyed, hospitals bombed, and helpless women and children killed in the streets and in air raid shelters, you have a new idea of what's important."

As a war correspondent in 1943, on assignment to China, Sevareid was forced to bail out of a crippled aircraft and spent a month living with head-hunters in the Assam jungle before reaching safety. Undeterred by the experience, he returned to Europe, joining Tito's partisans in Yugoslavia and landing with the first wave of American troops in southern France and crossed the Rhine into Germany.

Sevareid's war reporting had been spiced with the sort of articulate philosophy that was to become his hallmark. Towards the end of the conflict he said in a broadcast from London: "Only the soldier really lives the war. The journalist does not. He may share the soldier's outward life and dangers, but he cannot share his inner life because the same moral compulsion does not bear on him. War happens inside a man. It can never by communicated. A million martyred lives leave an empty place at only one family table. That is why, at bottom, people can let wars happen. And that is why nations survive them and carry on."

With the war ended, Sevareid became a mainstay of the CBS political team, especially in the Presidential elections of 1948, 1952 and 1956. Though he always considered himself a writer rather than a performer, his witty and forthright style of presentation made him a natural for the television era, and in 1964 he became a regular participant with Walter Cronkite on the CBS Evening News. Sevareid specialised in spirited and incisive two-minute editorials, which won him a wide following. Yet he never lost his nervousness before the camera. "A lot of people start blooming when that little light goes on," he once told an interviewer. "I start to die."

In addition to his television work Sevareid wrote a weekly column syndicated in 100 newspapers, and published several books, mostly autobiographical. He retired from CBS in 1977 but continued to work as a consultant. He is survived by his wife and three children from a previous marriage.

b 26.11.12   d 9.7.92   aged 79

ANTONY TERRY

Antony Terry, MC, former investigative journalist on The Sunday Times.

AT THE height of his distinguished career, Antony Frédéric Aimé Imbert Terry was a unique investigator of many chilling aspects of the Cold War in Europe, among them espionage and clandestine smuggling of East Germans to the West. He was well equipped for the task: ice-blue eyes, capable of making others flinch; impeccable German and French; a memory retentive of minutiae; tenacity in pursuit of scoundrels, and an interrogatory style – brusque, incisive, relentless – that could make conspirators, conmen and commissars jump through his hoops. Yet neither his friends nor his colleagues ever found flint in his heart.

One of his most outstanding traits was in regarding himself (despite his remarkable specialisms) as a journalistic *garde mobile*, willing to undertake any

assignment beyond his European "patch". He was often called upon to do so. His reports from Biafra graphically described the suffering there in 1970. At other times he was hunting down Nazi war criminals in the jungles of South America or probing suspicious circumstances of a colleague's murder in the Middle East.

Antony Terry was born in North London but spent much of his childhood and early youth in Berlin, where his father was attached to the British embassy between the wars. Ferociously strong for one so slightly built, he was, until the final decade of his life, intensely self-reliant; a rather solitary, bespectacled figure who seldom spoke of his youthful years, preferred working alone (although he actually excelled at "team journalism" on those occasions demanding his participation), and quietly cultivated sources of information which constantly gave this unassuming, invariably dark-suited newspaperman a distinct edge over professional rivals. He had an awesomely comprehensive filing system, at first in Bonn and later in Paris, and he would often point out to younger colleagues that "reconnaissance is never wasted."

In his typically modest way he rarely talked of the Military Cross he was awarded for leading a diversionary commando raid against an Axis port in the second world war. Major Terry and his men drew German fire as they crossed an iron bridge, bullets ricochetting against its girders, and were captured. His team was actually being lined up against a wall by German soldiers to be shot when saved by the distraction of another British team's limpet-mines going off under the battleship *Tirpitz* a short distance away. (The ship survived and was moved to Norway but was finally sunk by the Lancaster bombers of 617 "dambusters" squadron in Tromsö Fjord in 1944). Major Terry was sent to a prisoner-of-war camp where he immediately organised a clandestine news-sheet.

At the conclusion of the war his fluency in German dialects and familiarity with the German psyche made him a formidable allied interrogator of suspected war criminals. Sometimes in jest, post-war journalist colleagues surmised that his expertise in obtaining answers to difficult questions from resistant subjects might be attributed to the skills he acquired from those official interrogations.

On joining *The Sunday Times* after the war, at the invitation of Ian Fleming, Terry became a tireless foreign correspondent. In 1956, though trapped for more than a week in the British legation in Budapest following the crushing of the Hungarian uprising, he was able to send dispatches of horror "almost too terrible to describe". His intimate knowledge of German affairs

and political movements was at least as great as the most sophisticated native commentators. He appeared regularly in televised discussions in Bonn long after being posted to Paris in 1972 as European editor of his newspaper.

But his professional zeal and frequent travelling took their toll on his home life, and his marriage to Sarah Gainham the novelist foundered in the sixties. Later, in Paris, he formed a warm relationship with Edith Lenart, a journalist working for the Economist Intelligence Unit. More than anyone else, she was responsible for demolishing the stern reserve that some associates used to find so deflective. Infused by her warmth, elegance and gaiety, he became an outgoing companion. They married in London in 1984.

Though formally retired as a staff correspondent, he continued to be retained by *The Sunday Times*. From the villa he rented in the south of France he filed regular despatches, responding with typical alacrity and thoroughness to the many demands editors made on his time. He also frequently entertained his old London-based colleagues at the villa which was situated in the hills above Nice.

Even when he moved to Wellington, New Zealand, five years ago, to be near his wife's daughter (by Mrs Terry's previous marriage), his newspaper still made grateful use of his extraordinary judgment, investigative skills, breadth of experience and unmatched contacts.

Antony Terry was among the last of a peculiarly gallant and fastidious breed of reporter; self-disciplined, self-motivated and, in a sense, creatively remote from head office. Former colleagues held him in awed esteem; many of them in deep affection.

b 18.5.13   d 1992   aged 79

JOHN CAGE

John Cage at Pamplona

John Cage, American composer, philosopher and writer.

JOHN Cage was far more than a composer. His detractors, of whom there are many, would also say he was far less than one. He challenged every assumption about the roles of musicians, composers, listeners, even of the instruments themselves. He wrote a piece consisting literally of nothing – or rather, of whatever extraneous noise happened to be occurring. His brainwave of placing miscellaneous rattling and distorting objects inside a grand piano opened up a world of experimentation for those who chose to follow that path – and was at the same time regarded by many music-lovers as an act of monumental stupidity. He entrusted the format of other compostions entirely to chance.

Such achievements seem stale today, so often and so extremely have they been followed up. But forty years ago Cage was a giant among rebels, shaking up an American musical establishment that was dominated and awed by elderly European émigrés. And not only the musical establishment: few composers have caused as many ripples as Cage – with his theory of art as a random event depending on chance – in the philosophies of other avant-garde artforms: of dance, particularly, and of visual art, rock music and theatre.

Cage was a figure who raised the strongest passion, for and against. "If my work is accepted," he once said, "I must move on to the point where it isn't." He was, particularly in the Sixties and Seventies, not one to miss out on a fashionable social or political bandwagon, and the list of commentators who denounced him as a poseur or, worse, a con-man is formidable.

Nevertheless, he was a powerful enough thinker about music, and music's place in our lives, never to be a mere follower after fashion. He was one of the first to state explicitly the *credo* of mid-20th century avant-garde art: that art is whatever an artist says it is. "I have nothing to say, I am saying it, and that is poetry," he claimed.

Although his reputation was as an *avant-gardiste*, even an anti-musician, whose influence was felt in both music and the other arts, his early training was fairly conventional. He left college at 18 to go to Europe, where he studied the music, arts and architecture of Paris, Berlin and Madrid over a period of some 18 months. After his return and a time of writing poetry and music, as well as painting, he went on to New York, where he studied theory and composition with Adolf Weiss. At the same time he also came under the influence of Henry Cowell at the New School for Social Research.

Cowell's open mind and radical musical thinking, charcterised above all by his refusal to admit the self-containment of modern Western musical cultures, affected Cage deeply, but his outlook was further broadened and disciplined by a course of counterpoint he undertook with Anrold Schoenberg in California in 1934.

Thus was formed the artistic mind of a revolutionary whose work was to cause controversy throughout his life, but whose very notoriety bred demand for him as a cult figure to the extent that, in the United States at least, he ultimately became accepted as a member of an artistic establishment populated by such figures as Morton Feldman, David Tudor, Earle Brown, and the artists Robert Motherwell, Jasper Johns and Robert Rauschenberg.

But the road to achieving that status was long. His earliest compositions are striking for their close relationship to Schoenberg's 12-note techniques, with works like the *Six Short Inventions* (1933) and the *Composition for Three Voices* (1934) addressing the problem of keeping repetitions of notes as far apart as possible. A step towards a more complex

serialism is indicated in *Music for Wind Instruments* and *Metamorphosis*, both of 1938, which each use sections of note rows transposed to pitches determined by the interval structure of the series itself.

This direction, however, was not to be pursued for long. In Los Angeles in the 1930s Cage had become involved with a ballet group for the first time and in 1937 he became composer-accompanist for Bonnie Bird's dance classes in Seattle. In 1938 he formed a percussion orchestra in that city, and the following year, now back in California, he gave a concert of percussion music with the composer Lou Harrison.

Percussion instruments, redolent of Far Eastern cultures, remained a focus for his activities, as did ballet. Shortly after travelling again to New York in 1942, this time to settle there, he gave a concert which included three of his own percussion works. This event established his name, and before long he formed what proved to be an enduring and mutually beneficial liaison with Merce Cunningham's innovative dance company. He had already "invented" the prepared piano, the instruments that caused many to raise a doubting eyebrow, in 1938. Since the preparation consisted of inserting nuts, bolts, pieces of paper and similar paraphernalia between the strings and under the dampers, the reaction was unsurprising.

Yet his intentions were less anarchic than they seem. Cage had wanted to turn the piano into a one-man percussion orchestra for a ballet commission, *Bacchanale*, simply for economic reasons. Later, in 1949, that innocent and sensible solution to a practical problem produced the major cycle *Sonatas and Interludes*, a work of immensely varied colour and great meditative beauty. Meanwhile he had by no means neglected the world of slightly more conventional percussion: *First Construction (in Metal)* (1939) demands a vast array of metallic instruments, including brake drum, water gongs and Japanese temple bells. And he opened up to himself the infinitely flexible sound-world of electronics in *Imaginery*

Landscape – 3 (1942), scored for audio-frequency oscillators, variable-speed turntables for playing recordings of certain frequencies and electric buzzer, an amplified wire coil and an amplified marimba.

Because such works rely on complex or indeterminate pitches, it was natural that Cage should turn to rhythm as an organisational force, a development which gave rise to even more of an oriental flavour, and increasingly an oriental philosophy, in his work. In the late 1940s he began studying Eastern philosophy and then Buddhism. In 1950 he was reading the *I Ching*, the Chinese book of Changes, and thereafter began using elements of chance in his work. *Imaginary Landscape 4* (1951) demands 24 players on 12 radios, each player tuning according to strict directions. Of course the results are entirely unpredictable. In 1952 came what is still perhaps his most notorious piece, *4mins 33secs*, for any instrument or instruments. The players sit silently. The "piece" is only the ambient noise. Such music inevitably caused derision among many who were unable or unwilling to see what Cage was trying to achieve. Together with the pianist-composer David Tudor he toured Europe in 1954, playing his music and expounding his philosophy to what were usually hostile audiences.

He returned in 1958, travelling to Darmstadt; at Berio's request he went to Milan, where he spent four months working in the radio station's electronic studio. This was shortly after the premiere of his *Concert for Piano and Orchestra* in New York, a work whose deliberately anarchic music – there is no score, only a set of chance derived parts which may in any case be interpreted liberally – caused a hostile reaction comparable, according to many reports, with that which greeted the premiere of *The Rite of Spring* in Paris in 1913.

In the Sixties he became aware that people were actually beginning to listen, that his music had a role to play in forming attitudes in society. His explanation for his art was simple. As he wrote in 1961 in *Silence*, one of several volumes of essays and lectures, his intention was "to affirm this life, not to bring order out of chaos or to suggest improvements in creation, but simply to wake up to the very life we're living, which is so excellent once one gets one's mind and one's desires out of the way, and let it act of its own accord".

Between 1961 and 1969 he produced only a dozen or so projects, among them *Atlas eclipticalis*, whose notes are based on constellation patterns, and the cycle of variations. Then came, in the late Sixties, a series of extravagant electronic pieces, works like *HPSCHD, Musicircus and Variations VI*, but in 1969 *Cheap Imitation* signalled another new path emphasised in 1972 when he orchestrated the piece, providing an absurdly demanding rehearsal schedule and stipulating that any inadequate player should be asked to leave.

No longer was he dealing in anarchy, in refusing to tell someone else exactly what to do; this was a musical manifestation of his dalliance with Maoism. Also important at this time were the writings of the 19th century anarchist Henry Thoreau, which harmonised both with Cage's political thinking and with his intention of "imitating nature in her manner of operation". *Branches and Child of Tree* take that premise to the extent of being composed for vegetable-derived instruments, though amplified through industrial electronics. Further ecological pieces were *Telephones and Birds* (1977), *Lecture on the Weather* (1975) and the beautiful *Litany for the Whales* (1980), for two voices.

In may ways Cage's attitude to art and life can perhaps be best summed up in his reaction to witnessing the Opera House in Frankfurt go up in flames in 1987, with all the props for a new work of his inside. The story is that he turned to the choreographer Merce Cunningham, his life-long friend and collaborator, and said, simply, "Isn't that beautiful?" "Not now, John," came the reply.

b 5.9.12   d 12.8.92   aged 79

SIR GERAINT EVANS

Sir Geraint Evans, CBE, Welsh operatic baritone.

HUMANITY characterised every operatic role Sir Geraint Evans played on stage. And he sang a great number, well over 70 in a career that lasted from his first appearance at Covent Garden in January 1948 to his farewell at the same house in June 1984. At the start there was Mozart: Papageno touching and naive, Leporello seedy and knowing, and above all Figaro, the part which he sang more often than any other. These were the interpretations that led to invitations to Europe and America at a time when few overseas managements considered British singers. Later came the reprobates and curmudgeons: Wagner's Beckmesser, Donizetti's Don Pasquale and Dr. Dulcamara, the creation with which he chose to take his leave. And, larger than all, there was Verdi's Falstaff, which he first sang at Glyndebourne and which inspired Vittorio Gui to say that here was the best resident of the Garter Inn since Stabile. Into these and many more Geraint Evans breathed life, and more than that, a joy of life. He once confessed that he built his performances from the feet up, using shoes that were a little too tight, to help with Beckmesser's crabbed comments, or boots a little too large, for a Wozzeck who had to trudge around the stage. Detail was something to which he paid great attention.

Geraint Evans was never a lyric baritone. Not for him the grand villains of Verdi, or even Rigoletto, a role he tried briefly and quickly dropped as lying too high for him. The voice was in essence a bass-baritone and he was careful to discard anything for which he was not naturally suited in range or appearance – an attempt at Don Giovanni was discarded as fast as Rigoletto. He generally relied on charm, Welsh *hwyl*, superb diction and, above all, a natural sense of theatre. He was not one for the lieder recital or even oratorio, he was happiest applying the greasepaint and treading the boards.

Geraint Llwellyn Evans grew up in the mining village of Cilfynydd in a terraced house a few doors down from Merlyn Rees, who became Labour's home secretary. His father worked in the pits, but had no desire for his son to do the same. The young Geraint left school at 14 and eventually found employment as a window dresser in Pontypridd for Mr. Theophilus, whose shop retailed "High class ladies' fashions". His mother had died when he was a baby, but at least his father liked music: he was a choirmaster and organised local expeditions to hear the leading singers of the day in oratorio. Young Geraint tried his hand at numbers such as "The Road to Mandalay" and, still in his teens, won a solo spot in a radio programme from Cardiff called *Welsh Rarebit*. He was a late student at the Guildhall School of Music, spent the war as a radar operator, and eventually got into the British Forces Network in

Hamburg as a singer and producer. After further studies in that city, and in Geneva, Geraint Evans was taken on by the embryo company struggling to stage opera at Covent Garden.

When he was assigned his first role, the Nightwatchman in *Meistersinger*, he went out and bought a vocal score for ten shillings and recalled having to go through quite a number of pages before discovering his single – and brief – appearance. His potential was spotted by the autocratic music director of the time, Karl Rankl, who took the risk of giving him the title role in a new production (by Peter Brook) of *Le nozze di Figaro*. It was a part he was to repeat season after season at the Garden and to sing all over the world, notably at Salzburg with Fischer-Dieskau as the Count. Evans's retainer was not the pugnacious revolutionary now fashionable, but rather a nimble-witted, quick-footed servant jealously guarding his independence. Another regular Evans part of the period was Schaunard in *Boheme*, with which he made his Vienna State Opera debut as a last-minute replacement. Karajan thought well enough of the performance to offer him a contract with the company, but Evans declined believing that his career should still be in London.

Benjamin Britten considered him for the title role of *Billy Budd* and even offered to alter some of the higher lying passages. But Evans contented himself by playing Mr. Flint before, in later years, becoming a notable Captain Claggart, an interpretation which he modelled on Charles Laughton in *Mutiny on the Bounty*. The association with Britten became close: it was difficult to surpass Evans as Balstrode in *Peter Grimes* or Bottom in *A Midsummer Night's Dream*.

Glyndebourne was not going to allow Geraint Evans to be the exclusive property of Covent Garden. He arrived at Sussex in 1950 to take over Guglielmo in *Cosi fan tutte* from Erich Kunz. There were vocal similarities with the great Viennese baritone and a good deal of overlap of repertory. Eventually Evans was to sing Papageno, very much Kunz's private property, in Vienna itself.

The house was to hear him in his favourite Mozart roles: Leporello, Papageno and finally in 1958, Figaro. Surprisingly he did not sing Don Alfonso (*Cosi Fan tutte*) there. This, again, was an Evans speciality and, again, he made that "philosopher" a more benign and genial a man than is now the custom. But the role for which he will be longest remembered at Glyndebourne is Verdi's Falstaff. He grew into it, quite literally with a bit of extra padding here and there, after first singing it in 1957. A year later, when the company went to The Theatre des Nations season in Paris. Evans had perfected his interpretation. There was a gasp of delight as Falstaff emerged in Act II in full courting fig for his dalliance with the merry wives of Windsor. And with a femal cast led by Ilva Ligabue and Grazialle Sciutti they were worth a dalliance.

Evans had also become the master of the single telling phrase. His delivery of the words "Sono stanco" (I'm weary) at the end of *Falstaff* was a humble admission of defeat that said everything. It stayed in the mind just as did his expression of admiring awe when Leporallo tells Donna Elvira the exact number of Giovanni's Spanish conquests: "Mille e tre".

Back at Covent Garden it was realised that the success of Geraint Evans abroad helped win his colleagues – and especially the Welsh ones – overseas engagements. There were jokes about the "Messiah Express", the train which took singers back to Cardiff on Friday nights when there was no Saturday opera performance. Gwyneth Jones, Margaret Price and Stuart Burrows were among those winning European and American reputations and in several cases Evans had put in a good word for them.

The house with which he became most associated outside London was San Francisco, making his debut there as Beckmesser, whom he turned into a fussy, twitchy pedant with (for Evans) a rare streak of malevolence. He returned there season after season for the next two decades and was awarded the house's opera medal when he sang Don Pasquale there in 1980.

As Geraint Evans's mane of wavy dark hair began to acquire silver streaks he realised the rewards available in Donizetti's comedies. He kept Mozart in his repertory – and Berg's Wozzek – but he was more likely to be heard as Pasquale or the itinerant quack, Dulcamara, in *L'elisir*. Both men were filled out with eccentricities, often of Evans's own devising. He could be a scourge of directors, especially junior ones entrusted with reviving the productions of others. But Evans was ever expert at winning the audience's affection: he made sure that a tear was shed for his pouter pigeon of a Pasquale and that everyone left *Elisir* hoping that Dulcamara would go on making a living from his cheap elixir. It was no surprise

that he chose the latter role for his 1984 farewell to the house at which he had already sung 1185 performances; although at one time he had considered making it Beckmesser to bring his career full Wagnerian circle.

That final evening was attended by the Prince of Wales – Evans had been knighted at the time of the prince's investiture in 1969. Simultaneously the singer published his memoirs, *A Knight at the Opera*. He had suffered from bouts of ill-health and retired to Aberaeron and the seaside. He had his family around him and his boat. He was content to sally forth from time to time to support music and especially Welsh music.

He is survived by his wife, Brenda, whom he married in 1948, and by their two sons.

b 16.2.22   d 19.9.92   aged 70

Geraint Evans in Don Giovanni *(1973)*

SIR CHARLES GROVES

Sir Charles Groves, conductor.

CHARLES Groves was one of the most dedicated, hardest working conductors of his generation. Noted for his championing of British music, he was also a sensible, often inspired interpreter of the classics. His most notable posts were as conductor of the Bournemouth Symphony Orchestra from 1951 until 1961 when he became director of the newly formed Welsh National Opera. He remained there until 1963 when he was appointed musical director of the Royal Liverpool Philharmonic until 1977. In these posts he conducted a vast repertory, never with anything but the utmost understanding. This can be confirmed on his numerous recordings with the RLPO and other orchestras.

A Falstaffian figure who, in later life, sported a white beard and flowing white hair, Groves displayed little of a maestro's flamboyance, expressing the view that fire and warmth should come from within the orchestra.

Groves was a boy chorister at St Paul's Cathedral. Music was already important to him as a solace as he was an only child who was orphaned at the age of ten. His father had been invalided out of the trenches and died when he was six; his mother died four years later. He went on to study piano and organ at the Royal College of Music. He had ambitions to become a pianist but they never materialised. He was naturally gifted with great fluency and the ability to sight read almost any music, but confessed years later, to having been lazy about fingering and memorising. While at the college he played bass drum in the orchestra of Delius's *A Village Romeo and Juliet*, when Beecham was conducting. While he was a student he accompanied chorus rehearsals for the Brahms Requiem in

1937 conducted by Toscanini who exerted a strong influence on Groves, as did Beecham and Furtwängler.

In 1938 he joined the BBC as chorus master again preparing the choirs for Toscanini's performances, accounts of the Missa Solemnis and Verdi's Requiem. He was also in charge of the chorus for the famous 1938 broadcast of *Manon* with Maggie Teyte and Heddle Nash, later recalling the excitement of the occasion. Stanford Robinson was the conductor of those performances, so successful that they had to be repeated in 1939. During the first part of the war Groves worked with the BBC Theatre Chorus in Bedford, where the BBC had been evacuated. In 1943 he was promoted to principal conductor, first of the BBC Revue Orchestra (and conducted, among other things, Weill's *Lady in the Dark*). In 1944 he became principal conductor of what then was the BBC Northern Orchestra, a good post in which to learn a large repertory out of the limelight. Indeed, before long he conducted each and every concert. He remained in that job until 1951, when he moved to Bournemouth. Three years later he played a leading role, including selling raffle tickets in the streets, in the fight to save the orchestra — then called the Bournemouth Municipal Orchestra — when it was threatened with disbandment by the corporation's withdrawal of its grant.

When he moved to the Welsh National Opera, he took the Bournemouth Symphony with him and did much to establish the company's choral and orchestral traditions, and conducted many performances of works then considered rarities, such as Verdi's *I Lombardi* and *The Sicilian Vespers*, productions brought to London when they won critical acclaim.

During his highly successful reign at Liverpool, he greatly improved standards of playing. From 1967 he managed to combine that post with being associate conductor of the Royal Philharmonic under Kempe's aegis.

In 1978 he succeeded Mackerras as music director of the English National Opera, but — in spite of a well-received and rare revival of Weber's *Euryanthe* — the appointment did not prove a success and he relinquished the post the following year, then dedicating himself to work as a freelance. In the 1980s he made some notable appearances in the United States, in particular conducting the Los Angeles Philharmonic in the Hollywood Bowl. He also worked with several orchestras in Europe, most notably the Munich Philharmonic.

In 1974 he was entrusted with the last night of the Proms. Four years later he held up the performance for 15 minutes, ignoring the chanting of some of the promenaders and amusing the others with an impromptu and witty speech while awaiting the arrival of two trumpeters. The orchestra was performing Beethoven's Seventh Symphony, which without sufficient trumpeters, Groves said, would be like falling flat on one's face when competing in the Olympic long jump.

He was always ready with good advice to conductors trying to make their way in the profession. He did an enormous amount behind the scenes to encourage the young and, indeed, to foster the progress of music generally in this country.

Off the podium Groves showed the same good sense as he demonstrated on it, and was equally down to earth, as ready to enjoy a rugby match as a symphony (he once played "in the Wasps F team", as he self-depreciatingly put it). He was an enthusiastic cricketer — a wily slow bowler in his day — and a lover of the novels of Dickens and Jane Austen. He was also a calm, thoughtful spirit, as far away as can be imagined from the customary view of the maestro, a term that did not suit him at all.

He was created a CBE in 1968 and knighted in 1973. He is survived by his wife, Hilary, two daughters and a son.

b 10.3.15   d 20.6.92   aged 77

DON LANG

Don Lang, trombonist, rock and roll vocalist and band leader.

DON Lang's musical career began in the dying years of the big band swing era, but he was to achieve his greatest fame during the emergence of rock and roll in the Fifties when his Frantic Five ensemble dominated the popular television show *Six Five Special*, forerunner of *Top of the Pops*. Although the aptly named Frantic Five – they were an exceedingly energetic group on stage – accompanied many rock and roll stars of the day, such as Tommy Steele and Cliff Richard, when they appeared on the programme, they notched up some impressive rock and roll successes of their own with Lang himself doing the vocals.

In May 1958 his recording of "Witch Doctor" reached No 5 in the British pop music charts and remained there for 11 weeks. A year earlier the success of his rendering of Chuck Berry's "anti-classroom" hit "Schoolday" prevented the composer's version from climbing any higher than No 16 for his debut in what was then called the British Hit Parade.

"Schoolday" was to cause mildly nervous tremors among educationists both sides of the Atlantic because its rallying cry "Hail, Hail, Rock and Roll" echoed down many a college corridor; the gentle protest lyrics suggesting that pupils preferred playing the juke-box to dipping pens in inkwells.

Lang, whose original name was Gordon Langhorn, grew up in his native Halifax; his musical career began with the double bass but he changed to the trombone, moving to London where, in 1949, he was to join the well-known swing band of the day led by Vic Lewis. Lewis freely based his style on his big band idol Stan Kenton who favoured massive brass emphasis in his "progressive jazz" arrangements. Langhorn was a featured soloist, first in Lewis's expanded orchestra for his ambitious "music for modern" tour, and also for the reduced dance band format that was to follow. Langhorn was one of a distinguished list of ex-Lewis players who were to succeed in fronting their own bands; others on the list were Ken Thorne, Johnny Keating, Stan Reynolds, Ronnie Scott and Tubby Hayes. Langhorn left Lewis for a spell with the equally popular Ken Macintosh Orchestra during which he co-wrote one of the band's biggest swing hits "The Creep". By the mid-fifties big bands were becoming not only less popular but prohibitively costly to maintain; seeing the light, Langhorn became a highly successful "session" musician, meanwhile launching what was to become his parallel career of vocalist, with his singing version of Woody Herman's instrumental "Four Brothers". He was also one of the musicians who anticipated the rise of rock and roll; he truncated his name to Don Lang and formed the Frantic Five.

Don Lang remained an enthusiastic and dedicated professional even in his declining years, during which he courageously fought his illness; he continued playing sessions wherever and whenever he was able.

He is survived by his wife May and their son and daughter.

b 19.1.25   d 1992   aged 67

OLIVIER MESSIAEN

Olivier Messiaen, the French composer who changed the nature of European music more than anyone else in the last half century.

ALTHOUGH his art at first evoked fierce controversy – largely on account of its unashamed mixture of Catholic piety with lush eroticism, of rich western harmony with the sounds and rhythms of Asia, of abstract speculation with vulgarity – Olivier Messiaen lived long enough to hear his works performed and applauded throughout the world, to find his music as omnipresent as that of the birds he so much admired and imitated, and to find himself perhaps the most revered of living composers.

What had once shocked by its lack of taste came to be appreciated as the expression of a man whose openness, humility and candour made taste an irrelevance. What had seemed naive came to be cherished rather as simplicity, the blessed simplicity of one whose faith gave him the confidence to make his music open to a bewildering variety of materials, without discrimination: plainsong,

artificial modes, rhythmic patterns from Hindu and Greek culture, the percussion of Africa and the Far East, luscious harmonies redolent of cheap music, as well as complex chords suggested by the cries of birds, by mountains and canyons, by colours and by the word of God.

If, nevertheless, his influence in his own age and continent was immense, that was because his religious intuitions coincided with a musical insight central to the art in the twentieth century, the insight that music need not proceed smoothly forwards towards resolution and cadence, but can instead extend endlessly; or keep repeating itself, or leap suddenly from one thing to another.

Born in Avignon, Olivier Eugène Prosper Charles Messiaen was the elder of two sons born to the poet Cécil Sauvage and her husband Pierre Messiaen, a distinguished lycée teacher of English who had translated the complete works of Shakespeare. In 1917 Messiaen began to learn the piano and compose, and two years later he entered the Paris Conservatoire, where he remained until 1930. His teachers included Maurice Emmanuel, who stimulated his interest in modes and exotic rhythms. Marcel Dupré, who encouraged him toward the organ, and Paul Dukas, a model of creative ethics.

In 1931 he was appointed organist of La Trinité in Paris, where he played regularly until his death. At first it seemed that he would have the typical career of a French organist-composer, his output consisting of organ works (*La Nativité du Seigneur*, 1935; *Les corps glorieux* 1939), interspersed with religious meditations for orchestra (*L'Ascension* 1933) and songs. These last were religious too, written to celebrate the experience of divine love granted in sexual and parental love (he had married the violinist Claire Delbos in 1932; their son Pascal, the composer's only child, was born in 1937).

The pattern altered when, as a soldier, he was taken prisoner-of-war in 1940. In captivity he wrote the *Quatuor pour la fin du temps*, a crystallisation of his early style, and when he returned to Paris in 1942, a place was found, despite opposition, for him to teach at the Conservatoire. There his early pupils included Boulez and also the pianist Yvonne Loriod, whose virtuosity encouraged him to make the piano, not the organ, the centre of his composing life: for her he wrote the *Vingt regards sur l'Enfant-Jésus* (1944) and the solo parts in the *Trois petites liturgies* (1945) and the *Turangalila-symphonie* (1946–48).

This last work – like the songs of the 1930s, though on the vaster scale of ten movements for large orchestra – is a celebration of love in both cosmic and human aspects. It represents the emergence of the composer as a public figure (there has been no other symphonic work since *L'Ascension*, and during the 1950s and 1960s it gradually entered the international repertory and helped to establish its composer's reputation.

He, though, was going in other directions. Faced with the evidence of a rigorous rethinking of Schoenbergian serialism in the early works of Boulez, the erstwhile teacher became again a student, and from the delirious abundance of the

Turangalila turned to the deliberate constraints of the *Mode dè valeurs et d'intensités* for piano (1949) where system threatens to take control and the effect is seemingly as random as the pattern of stars in the night sky.

This was only a passing phase, but it refreshed his approach to the minutiae of his art and also made him suspicious of musical invention: henceforth, for more that a decade, he found his material by listening to birds in the wild, jotting down their song using conventional notation and without the aid of a tape recorder. This he did at his summer home in the Alps where he did most of his composing, elsewhere in France, and in other parts of the world which his growing reputation enabled him to visit (he had been passionately fond of birdsong since his childhood and was a member of several ornithological societies). Works of this period include the *Catalogue d'oiseaux* for piano and *Chronochromie* for orchestra.

In 1962, following the death of his first wife in 1959, he married Yvonne Loriod, whose musical and personal support was crucial to him for the rest of his life. During the same decade he began to gather together all the various strands in his composing life, at first in smaller works and then in the monumental, concert-long *La Transfiguration* for chorus and orchestra (1965–9). This was followed by three others: *Des canyons auz étoiles* . . . for piano and orchestra (1971–4), the opera *Saint François d'Assise* (1975–83) and *Le Livre du Saint Sacrement* for organ (1944).

After this came a sequence of smaller pieces, composed in the intervals between international tours when he and his music were celebrated. A further large-scale work for an immense orchestra, *Eclairs sur l'Au-Detlà* is apparently complete and due for its first performance in New York in November. Among his many honours were membership of the Institut de France (1967) and the Erasmus Prize (1971).

b 10.12.08   d 28.4.92   aged 83

DAVID BELL

David Bell, MBE, who was able to use his own experience of severe wartime injuries to benefit the disabled.

DAVID Bell practised courage and persistence in the face of misfortune which left him doubly disabled – both blind and handless. His father was "an old contemptible" and had been taken prisoner in the Battle of the Somme. David Bell was educated at Leith Academy and before the war was an apprentice draughtsman although he was a St Andrew's ambulance volunteer and after the war intended to study medicine. After Munich, he tried to join 603 Squadron RAAF but being in a reserve profession was rejected. He then wangled his way into the Royal Engineers and was in the First Field Squadron Royal Engineers from Tobruk to Benghazi. At the Battle of Knightsbridge he was clearing mines in outer defences to let guards and tanks out when a mine blew up in his face. He lost his sight, part of one arm from above the elbow, the other from above the wrist and was unconscious for two months.

Evacuated to South Africa he recovered and surgeons rebuilt his limbs to give him a residual grip in his left arm. But he had no sense of touch. General Smuts who visited the hospital was so impressed by David Bell's spirit that he presented him with his own Victory Pin.

Bell returned to England in 1943, to the St Dunstan's rehabilitation centre where he was taught how to type and took up the trombone. He intended to study languages and become an interpreter but his marriage to Miss Sibyl Page, who was a volunteer with St Dunstan's, changed that plan and he decided to go into business. He returned to Edinburgh in 1946 to start a small shop. In this he was aided by St Dunstan's and King Farouk of Egypt. King Farouk had read Bell's story in a British newspaper and sent a gift of 25,000 monogrammed Egyptian cigarettes to help start the business. Bell was able to run the small tobacco and confectionery shop with the aid of special equipment from St Dunstan's allowing him to take money and give change – he manipulated this with startling speed and precision.

The business prospered and expanded but he decided to resume his education by going to Edinburgh University. Being handless he was unable to use braille but was helped by many student friends who read to him and composed lecture notes with him. He graduated with an MA in 1952 and a BComm in 1955. He was the subject of Eamonn Andrews's *This Is Your Life*.

He campaigned actively for European reconciliation and in 1972 was appointed MBE for his work for the disabled.

In the 1970s he continued to campaign but suffered increasingly poor health and for this reason moved in the mid-1980s to Haywards Heath to be near the St Dunstan's Blind Ex-Servicemen's Association. A bon viveur, he was an inspiration to many sighted as well as disabled people.

b 6.2.21   d 2.3.92   aged 71

ELIZABETH DUCKWORTH

Elizabeth Duckworth, London society cook.

TO MANY who lived and moved in London society from the 1930s, the death of Elizabeth Duckworth will seem like the end of an era. A resident of Mayfair for 56 years, she was one of the great characters of its *Upstairs, Downstairs* world. Officially, she belonged downstairs, but she was never a respecter of persons. Her grandeur of spirit, and sometimes manner, made her as much at home upstairs – in the drawing-room with royalty, the rich, famous and occasionally infamous – as she was in the kitchens she ruled so regally.

Elizabeth Irene Green was born at Peterstow, Ross-on-Wye, and the Herefordshire accent she retained all her life gave an emphasis and authority to her pronouncements. And pronouncements they were: she demanded a healthy respect on the part of the listener.

In 1932 Elizabeth Green married the Whighams' butler, Leslie Duckworth, and in 1935 the Duckworths took over the running of the Whighams' Mayfair house, 48 Upper Grosvenor Street. On their death this passed into the ownership of Margaret Sweeny, who in 1951 became the third wife of the 11th Duke of Argyll. The Duckworths stayed with the family.

Mrs Duckworth was far more than merely the duchess's cook and housekeeper. She was a friend and confidante, and during her employer's extensive foreign travels, became a mother-figure to the duchess's two children by her first marriage, Brian Sweeny, and Frances, now the Duchess of Rutland.

In her 40-year reign at Upper Grosvenor Street, Mrs Duckworth cooked for royalty, for many members of the cabinet, for Hollywood film stars, and for a procession of appreciative tycoons. The society photographer Brodrick Haldane, a frequent guest, said, "She was an artist with food. It was not merely a question of taste but of presentation. The appearance of every dish, both in arrangement and colour, was exquisite."

In 1956, when Leslie Duckworth collapsed and died from a sudden heart attack at nine o'clock in the morning, she continued her cooking of the ducal breakfast, observing sadly: "Life has to go on and people have to eat."

In 1963 the Duke of Argyll's divorce action against his wife developed into a major society scandal. Mrs Duckworth immediately sided with the duchess and was unswerving in her support, yet she never entirely lost her affection for the duke and regularly paid tribute to his charm.

In 1974, she retired to her own apartment in Balderton Street, Mayfair.

Elizabeth Duckworth was one of the few people who never appeared to be in awe of the duchess. She frequently corrected her or told her she was ill-advised, yet behind this severity lay a deep devotion and affection. When, in 1990, financial problems forced the duchess to exchange the splendour of Grosvenor House for the refuge of a nursing home in Pimlico, much of Mrs Duckworth's *raison d'être* seemed to depart as well. The Northern Ireland secretary, Peter Brooke, her Member of Parliament, stepped in to replace the modest pension the duchess could no longer pay her. But after 62 years contact with her employer had been severed and the last two years of her life were overshadowed by loneliness. She had no children.

b 1.1.07 d 6.12.91 aged 84

THE DOWAGER DUCHESS OF LEINSTER

Formerly Mrs Conner, wife of an apartment block caretaker until a tenant, the bankrupt Duke of Leinster attracted her to become his fourth wife. She then led an erratic and unorthodox life.

THE upbringing of the Dowager Duchess of Leinster had not prepared her for exalted rank. Vivien Irene Felton was born in a Battersea council house, the third daughter of an impoverished accounts clerk, Thomas Albert Felton, and his wife, Lilian Adshead.

In 1937, at the age of 17, she married a battersea businessman, George William Conner, and gave birth to a son, Anthony Raymond. The Conners were a happy and united family until 1956, at which time they were caretakers at a block of service flats in Kensington.

Among the tenants was a tall and charming man who called himself "Mr FitzGerald" and conveyed the impression to Vivien Conner of "an absentminded professor". He was, in fact, Edward FitzGerald, 7th Duke of Leinster, the premier duke, marquess and earl of Ireland, who was described by his second wife as "fey, wistful, vulnerable — in this world but not of it".

Originally the heir to a considerable fortune, he had signed away the ducal income of over £1,000 a week to the baronet, Sir Harry Mallaby-Deeley, founder of the Fifty Shilling Tailors, in return for a capital sum to pay his youthful debts. He did this as a gamble, never expecting to inherit, but his elder brother Maurice, the 6th Duke, died in 1922 at the age of only 34 in an Edinburgh mental asylum and Edward succeeded to the dukedom without residences or heirlooms and with only £1,000 a year as income.

By the time of his meeting with Vivien Conner he had been made bankrupt three times and had married three times: first, the stage soubrette, May Etheridge, who committed suicide soon after their divorce; second, Rafaelle Kennedy, an American beauty from Brooklyn; and third, the musical comedy star, Denise Orme, formerly Lady Churston, who in 1956 was living apart from the Duke at Woburn Abbey, the home of her son-in-law, the Duke of Bedford.

The third Duchess died in 1960. After obtaining a divorce from her husband Vivien Conner became the Duke's fourth wife at a secret, early morning ceremony at Brighton Register office on May 12, 1965.

Soon afterwards, they opened a fashion boutique, called La Duchesse in the Brighton Lanes but this, like so many of the Duke's business ventures over the years, proved a commercial failure. Vivien Leinster showed great resourcefulness, however, in unscrambling the Duke's 28-year-old third bankruptcy. The registrar who heard the case commented that "most of the creditors must be with the angels", but with great determination the Duchess obtained her husband's discharge, enabling him to take his seat belatedly in the House of Lords in 1975 after 53 years as a duke.

In November of that year the Leinsters attended their first and last state opening of Parliament and on the following day sailed to New York on the liner *Queen Elizabeth 2* to raise money for a new charity, the All Ireland Distress Fund, for victims of terrorism. Predictably, however, they encountered hostility from American groups in sympathy with the IRA and the tour was abruptly curtailed.

Back in Britain bitter family divisions arose over a Leinster trust fund of which the Duke and Duchess were beneficiaries, but from which neither was receiving an income. The dispute escalated and on march 8, 1976, amidst considerable publicity, the 83-year-old Duke killed himself in a Pimlico bedsitter with a massive overdose of nembutal sleeping tablets.

His distraught widow gave evidence at the inquest, after which her stepson Gerald, the 8th Duke, provided her with a small apartment in Sloane Avenue Mansions, Chelsea. The Dowager Duchess went to work for Help the Aged, opening several of their charity shops, and in 1978 took a post at the Royal Marsden Hospital, Chelsea, dropping her title and calling herself simply Mrs Vivien FitzGerald.

She took up painting with impressive results and in 1987 moved to a seafront flat in Brighton to rejoin her first husband, George Conner. But Brighton was also the town where she had married the Duke, to whose memory her devotion never faltered. She is survived by her only son, Tony Conner.

b 19.2.20   d 1992   aged 71

VICTORIA LIDIARD

Victoria Lidiard, who was imprisoned in 1912 for her activities as a member of the women's suffragette movement.

ON VICTORIA Lidiard's sideboard at her flat in Hove, East Sussex, stood a large, framed picture of her at 10, Downing Street a few years ago. Mrs Lidiard was justly proud of it: one of Britain's last remaining members of the women's suffrage movement, photographed alongside the country's first woman prime minister. It typifies her character that it is she, a woman who went to prison for the right to vote, and not the then prime minister, who is doing the smiling.

Victoria Lidiard's father, an antiques dealer in Bristol, did not consider the education of women important. However, her mother thought differently and sent all her daughters to book-keeping classes. Mrs Simmons felt that women should be more than wives and mothers; for when Christabel Pankhurst and Annie Kenny, both key figures in the Votes For Women campaign, came to the Victoria Rooms in Clifton to speak, she marched her eldest three daughters along to hear them. And so the young Victoria and her sisters, by now all elegant Edwardian women with carefully rolled hair and high-necked blouses, joined the Women's Social and Political Union in Bristol and campaigned for the right to vote.

Their activities included disrupting political meetings and selling the magazine *Votes For Women* on street corners. To behave with such licence in days when women were not even expected to drive a car, was fairly radical; then to board a train to London, and participate in a window-smashing protest down the length of Oxford Street, as Victoria Lidiard did in 1912, shows the depth of her commitment to the movement.

However, her stay in London was to last more that the planned weekend. After the march, she walked from Tottenham Court Road to Whitehall and deliberately threw a stone through a window in the War Office. Apparently, the policeman could hardly believe she had committed such a crime, because she "looked so innocent". She was conducted to Bow Street Magistrates Court by four police officers, one on horseback. When they found more than eight stones in her pockets ("In case the first one wasn't sufficient") Victoria Lidiard, then aged 23, was sentenced to two months' hard labour in Holloway jail.

She was imprisoned on March 5, 1912, and put in solitary confinement in a cell containing merely a straw mattress on a board. Along with the hundreds of her fellow protestors in Holloway, Lidiard refused to repent, or to wash; "we were political prisoners". Every night, one of her sisters used to come and shout messages of support from across the road.

She met her husband, Major Alexander Lidiard, while he was on holiday in Herne Bay, Kent. Suitably enough, she was at the resort in order to sell *Votes For Women*. They were ideally matched; he "thoroughly approved" of her political activities, and was in fact a member of a male suffragette support group. Married in 1918, the year women finally won the vote, they were together for 54 years.

After the war Victoria Lidiard and her husband trained as ophthalmic optomatists.

She was a member of the National Council of Women for most of her working life, an organisation she always said revealed how capable women were at running things; "women never depart from the question," she would say. "You never heard National Council women rant and rave off the point."

One of her prize possessions was a large book on the suffragette movement. In the frontispiece is a certificate from the Bristol Women's Social and Political Union, which reads: "To Victoria Simmons, in recognition for the Cause of Women's Enfranchisement." Beneath it is written a Walt Whitman quotation: "How beggarly appear arguments before a defiant deed."

Victoria Lidiard's defiance and passion lasted with her for over a hundred years; as she saw it, there were some injustices which required more than mere arguments. Fighting for the right to vote was one such injustice; according to Lidiard, it seemed to be "simply the right thing to do".

b 23.12.89   d 3.10.92   aged 102

SIR RALPH MILLAIS

Sir Ralph Millais, 5th Bt, former businessman and vintage motoring enthusiast.

THROUGHOUT a long life which saw him as, variously, stockbroker, tour promoter, RAF officer and tulip grower, the steadfast passion of Ralph Millais was the maintaining and racing of vintage motorcars. He was especially drawn to the cars of the 1920s and 1930s and owned many famous historic examples in the years following his first acquisition, a Talbot, as a Cambridge undergraduate. But perhaps the two motor cars dearest to his heart were a Type 59 Bugatti and the magnificent 300 bhp 4-litre Sunbeam Tiger which he raced with considerable success at Silverstone and other tracks in the 1950s and 1960s. In his most successful year, 1965, three of the four trophies which were won by his cars were captured by the Sunbeam.

Ralph Regnault Millais was born in Pitlochry in Scotland, the son of Sir Geoffroy William Millais, 4th Bt. The family, Norman in origin, had moved to Jersey at the time of the Conquest and the first Millais came to live in England in the 1820s.

Ralph Millais was a grandson of the pre-Raphaelite painter John Everett Millais and, though not a practising artist himself, he grew up in a household much influenced by artistic associations that were to become part of his life. He was educated at Marlborough, where at 14 he acquired his first motorcycle, a Levis two-stroke (later exchanged for the more potent 16H Norton).

From Marlborough he went to Trinity College, Cambridge, where his passion for motor sports was really kindled. His first car was an 8/18 Talbot with which he competed in the MCC London-Exeter trial of 1923 — only to be disqualified for getting ahead of the sedate 20mph schedule which governed the event. Later at Cambridge he acquired his first really "hairy" car, a racing bodied AC, which was used on the road without mudguards or silencer, and was capable of 96mph. Millais entered it in the Inter-Varsity speed trials of 1926 but burst a tyre and ran off the course.

On leaving Cambridge in 1926 Millais worked for a year as (unpaid) assistant private secretary to the Home Secretary, William Joynson Hicks. It was the year of the General Strike and an eventful one for Hicks whose department came in for daily criticism. Millais had a close-up view of the situation.

At this period Millais lived with his aunt, Lady Alice Sophia Caroline Stuart Wortley, third daughter of John Everett Millais, at her home in Cheyne Walk, Chelsea. Through his aunt he met the composer Elgar and often listened to them playing the piano together in the drawing room. Elgar's friendship with Lady Alice is said to have inspired the composer's Violin Concerto.

Millais then joined the stockbroking firm of Vivian and Gray, but the crash of 1929 curtailed this career and he had to look for work elsewhere. Among his jobs over the next few years were promoting tours in Europe and the Soviet Union for that pioneer of cheap travel, Sir Henry Lunn, and selling Daimler cars. During the second world war he served in the RAFVR with the rank of wing commander in a special camouflage unit whose function was to create dummy landing strips up and down the country to confuse enemy intelligence. During this time he succeeded his father who died in 1941.

After the war he turned market gardener, growing apples and tulips in Kent. But the racing of vintage cars was always paramount. His knowledge of cars and his memory for detailed specifications was quite extraordinary. He had owned a string of cars before the war: a 3-litre Sunbeam tourer; a Type 38 Bugatti saloon (always stigmatised by Millais as a "bad car" for its propensity to break its crankshaft); a 4-litre Le Mans type Peugeot; and a Type 44 Bugatti, to name but a few. Now, in the post-war years, there followed a Packard, a Lancia, a Lagonda and a monster 7-litre Duesenberg.

But his most coveted possessions were the Sunbeam Tiger and the Type 59 Bugatti, together with what was probably his favourite road car, the 1932 2.3-litre Alfa Romeo which had done the fastest lap at Le Mans in 1935. These cars were much seen at Silverstone and other tracks in the 1950s and 1960s. Often Millais raced them himself, though as the years went by such a formidable machine as the Sunbeam Tiger would generally be taken by a younger driver; in 1965 Millais's cars won three Vintage Sports Car Club trophies: the Boulogne, the Itala and the Seaman were won by the Sunbeam Tiger, and the Pomeroy by the Alfa Romeo.

Millais kept up his interest in cars well into his eighties, acquiring Ferraris, a Mercedes and another Alfa. He parted with his last car, a beautiful Aston Martin V8 sports saloon, just a few weeks before his death. In Winchelsea, where he lived for the last 21 years of his life (and where his grandfather had painted *The Blind Girl*) he was known for his love of art and music; besides cars his other enthusiasm was salmon fishing in Scotland.

Millais was three times married and leaves his widow, Babette, and the son and daugher of his first marriage. His son, Geoffroy Richard Everett Millais, succeeds to the baronetcy.

b 4.3.05   d 11.5.92   aged 87

TEASY WEASY RAYMOND

"Teasy Weasy" Raymond, OBE, flamboyant hairdresser and race-horse owner.

BEFORE the swinging sixties had even begun "Teasy Weasy" Raymond had created himself, with the greatful assistance of the tabloid newspapers and television, as a larger than life celebrity, shining out in the grey days of post-war Britain. Television was bringing a more sophisticated lifestyle into the nation's homes and having their hair styled was an instant and economical way for women of all classes to add a touch of glamour to their lives. Raymond was one of the first to combine the two to exploit the nationwide desire for a brighter more sophisticated existence.

With his neatly razored, pencil-line moustache, his bouffant hair-style, daringly exotic style of dressing, his Rolls-Royces and racehorses, he set a slightly shocking standard which had the public agog. As well as being a good hair-stylist he was a master of self promotion, becoming known as Teasy Weasy after a kiss-curl style he created which he said was named after one of his cats. In bringing celebrity status to hair-styling he set the standards. Vidal Sassoon, the celebrity hair-stylist of a slightly later period, called him "The Gov'nor".

Raymond was christened Raymondo Pietro Carlo and first worked in his father's barber's shop, making moustaches from clippings left on the floor. But he always yearned for stardom. He played the violin, but not as well as a fellow musician named Mantovani, and longed to become an actor but failed to be discovered. He also tried wrestling at £5 a bout but then took a more genteel path, opening his first hairdressing salon in Mayfair at the age of 26, just prior to the second world war.

His customers soon included the Duchess of Windsor, Gertrude Lawrence, Googie Withers and Valerie Hobson. His innovations included introducing a champagne rinse and coloured wigs. When Vivian Leigh went to Hollywood to star in *Gone With the Wind* Raymond joined her to style her hair.

Pursuing his love of horseracing he wore a pastel coloured morning suit to Ascot and when, thus attired, he was refused entry to the royal enclosure he designed himself a Georgian style morning suit in silver grey and black. As an owner he won the Grand National twice with Ayala in 1963 and Rag Trade in 1976.

At the height of his success when he had a chain of 34 hairdressing salons, he suffered a collapse of his health and a series of personal misfortunes. First came a heart attack in 1962, followed nine years later by cancer of the mouth, necessitating surgery which left him with severely impaired speech. Then in 1979 his pregnant daughter Amber, her husband Stephen Chase Gardner and their two sons were killed in a motorway crash after attending a family wedding.

Raymond is survived by his second wife, Rosalie, whom he married in 1965, and two daughters, Cherry and Scarlett.

d 1992   aged 80

ADEL ROOTSTEIN

Adel Rootstein, who created the modern shop window mannequin.

THE hand of Adel Rootstein can be seen in department store windows everywhere. Her achievement was to create a new generation of lifelike display mannequins, an important development for the fashion business and for the popular street-theatre of the shop window display.

Adel Rootstein used to say she came from a long line of Jewish refugees. She was born in the small South African spa town of Warmbaths, where her Russian parents had a small hotel, and came to London at 21. She got a job as a window-dresser in Aquascutum. Two years later she married her boss, Rick Hopkins, and started a small business in a basement in Earls Court making display department props.

It was the early 1960s and the haughty waxwork display mannequins of the day were out of step with the lively new fashions. So Adel Rootstein produced a new one, a mannequin modelled on Twiggy, skinny, coltish and flat chested. At last the fashion trade had a display mannequin that could wear a miniskirt with conviction. The Twiggy mannequin was a huge success and the reigning mannequins were doomed. They had broken the one rule that mattered in their world. They had become out of date. Adel Rootstein's path was now clearly marked. She would make realistic mannequins modelled from life.

So the beautiful people of the day started peopling the shop windows – Sandy Shaw, Joanna Lumley, Janet Suzman, Joan Collins, Patti Harrison and Susan Hampshire, as well as modish young women from London society, Lady Caroline Percy, Lady Mary-Gaye Curzon, Lady Jacqueline Rufus Isaacs. The Duke of Northumberland did not object to his daughter Lady Caroline, taking up this unexpected line of work but asked her not to use her title.

New male mannequins were needed, too, so Patrick Lichfield, Simon Ward and Jeremy Brett found their replicas glowering at them through the plate-glass, too. Adel Rootstein, diffident but persuasive, broke new ground in other directions. She claimed to have made the first high fashion black mannequin and, a little later, the first oriental mannequin.

The figures were modelled from life and then cast in fibreglass. Wig-makers and make-up artists added the finishing touches and the final effect was eerily realistic. Rootstein's mannequins had navels and nipples and she paid particular attention to body language. The figures stood, sat and lounged about as if leading an intense life of their own.

Her husband joined her at an early stage and before long they had factories, offices and showrooms in London and New York and agents all over the world. Adel Rootstein claimed to have 20 per cent of the world market.

She and her husband owned the business entirely until this year when they sold it to Yoshichu Mannequins of Japan, a company that had been making Rootstein mannequins under licence for some years. Part of the contract was that the business should continue as before. The new owners accepted that Rootstein was no longer playing an active role.

What she was doing, instead, was fulfilling a lifelong ambition. She had left school at 14 and had always regretted her lack of a formal education. At 40, a successful businesswoman, she had gone to night school to take O and A levels. Then, four years ago at 58, a petite, shy woman in a 1960s bob, she enrolled at the Slade School of Fine Art.

She took her final degree in June.

b 1930   d 20.9.92   aged 62

Joanna Lumley being modelled for mannequins

VISCOUNTESS ROTHERMERE

Viscountess Rothermere, wife of the third Viscount Rothermere, chairman of Daily Mail and General Trust. She was born Patricia Matthews.

AMONG socialites Viscountess Rothermere was one of the great creative spenders of wealth in modern times and her nickname "Bubbles" (though she loathed it as suggesting something superficial in her makeup) felicitously described a character bursting with energy and vivacity and possessed of an unquenchable love of champagne.

As a young woman she had been an actess who attracted notice for a role she had in the film about Douglas Bader, *Reach for the Sky*. On another occasion she was voted one of the ten most beautiful women in London. But it was as a party giver that she stamped her image on the society around her. A veritable female Lucullus in the gastronomic sumptuousness of their organisation, she also had the knack of being principal actor at her own social occasions.

Whatever the temperature of the occasion it was sure to rise steeply when the hostess made her entrance. This capacity owed much to her thespian training and dominating character. But it extended also to her spectacular dress sense. In matters of fashion she had an eclectic style which might throw together a blouse by Yves St Laurent, a stole by Zandra Rhodes and a skirt by Gina Fratini — then set them off with a shrieking satin hair ribbon.

Ribbons and bows were favourites with

her and she carried them off in situations fraught with peril and envy, in which others would surely have fallen. True, she often provoked charges of vulgarity — "festooned in acres of chiffon........Hog-tied with bows", snarled one newspaper columnist of an appearance on a televison chat show. But her charisma as a hostess was independent of physical trimmings and she stole the show at gatherings through sheer force of personality.

Lady Rothermere was born Patricia Evelyn Beverley Matthews, the daughter of a Hertfordshire architect. After drama school she began a career as an actress under the name of Beverley Brooks, taking the name of her first husband, Captain Christopher Brooks, an ex-guardsman. It was while she was playing a junior lead in a play at the Edinburgh festival that she was spotted by a talent scout from the Rank Organisation.

A promising film career now beckoned. In addition, in 1955, the photographer Baron voted her one of the ten most beautiful women in London.

Among the films in which she appeared was *Reach for the Sky*, Rank's screen version of Paul Brickhill's book of the same title about the legless wartime fighter ace, Group Captain Douglas Bader. In it Mrs Brooks played Sally, a girlfriend of Bader who leaves him after he loses his legs in an air crash.

At this point Darryl Zanuck wanted to buy her contract and take her to America. But developments in her personal life intervened. In 1956, too, her marriage to Christopher Brooks had been dissolved after the birth of their daughter. She was by now an object of interest to the Hon Vere Harmsworth, son the proprietor of the *Daily Mail*. The choice facing her was to continue her acting career or to marry into the Harmsworth dynasty. In the event, she chose the latter course, marrying the Hon Vere Harmsworth in 1957. "I think I wasn't confident enough to go that other way", she subsequently recalled. "I loved my husband and I wanted a family". She was to make of her new role a perhaps more spectacular success than she might have been in Hollywood (though Lewis Gilbert, who directed her in *Reach for the Sky* is on record as saying that she could have become a star).

With an energy that seemed undiminished she now created for herself a life of skiing, dancing and walking, entertaining international statesmen, businessmen, show-business personalities and aristocrats and dividing her time between homes in London, Sussex, California, Jamaica, Paris and New York. "I didn't just marry a man" she once said of her marriage. "As my father-in-law pointed out to me, I married an empire."

When her husband inherited the title on the death of his father in 1978 Mrs Vere Harmsworth (or Pat Harmsworth, as she was more generally known) became Viscountess Rothermere.

Her lavish entertaining and exuberant high spirits had their critics, notably among gossip columnists on newspapers which were rivals to the *Mail*, who liked to portray her as a pneumatically-constucted scatterbrain. But she shrugged off criticism, throwing herself into her business interests and charity work — an aspect of life that complemented the party-going and party-giving. Nevertheless she did once confess that vicious talk hurt her and that she hated denigratory conversations

The other side of her exuberant generosity was a character of some thoughtfulness. In spite of her vast circle of friendships, which included Princess Margaret and Princess Michael of Kent, and a sense that she was always giddily at the turbulent centre of the social universe, she once confessed of herself: "I'm quite a private person. I don't let too many people get close to me. Maybe that's a mistake — but I don't know."

There is a son, Jonathan, and two daughters, Geraldine and Camilla, of her marriage to Viscount Rothermere, as well as the daughter, Sara-Jane, of her first marriage.

d 12.8.92   aged 63

PAMELA SCOTT

Kenyan farmer who was chatelaine of the historic house "Deloraine". She was brought up in the heart of the imperial British tradition but her greatest love was for Africa.

PAMELA Scott was a remarkable link between Kenya's patrician colonial past and the succeeding era of populist black nationalism. For half a century she was the formidable chatelaine of Deloraine, one of the historic houses of the former White Highlands, where she was known as one of the most public-spirited and resilient of the settlers determined to "stay on" enthusiastically after independence in 1963. While retaining her links with many of the grandest families of Britain, she formed strong and influential bonds with many emerging figures in post-colonial Kenya, including Jomo Kenyatta and the present president, Daniel Arap Moi. Her commitment to an independent Africa, often bluntly and

sometimes humorously expressed, was exemplified by her generosity as a hostess and educator and by long service to the causes of agriculture, wildlife, history and anthropology.

Pam Scott was the daughter of Lord Francis Scott, youngest son of the 6th Duke of Buccleuch and 8th Duke of Queensberry, descendant of Charles II through the unfortunate Duke of Monmouth. Her father was the elected leader of the European settlers during the decade following the pioneer Lord Delamere's death in 1931.

In childhood and youth, the Duke and Duchess of York (later King George VI and the present Queen Mother), the Prince of Wales (later King Edward VIII) and the Gloucesters all stayed at Deloraine, where Pam Scott helped entertain them. Deloraine was one of the first two-storey country houses in Kenya, with wide verandahs on both floors, huge cedar beams supporting the ceilings, and a fine garden vivid with bougainvillea, poinsettia and an array of tropical plants and trees.

During the Mau Mau rebellion in the 1950s the colony's embattled governor, Sir Evelyn Baring (later Lord Howick) and his wife Molly, spent many weekends at Deloraine, planning stategy and relaxing in the beauty of the Rift Valley. Malcolm MacDonald, Ramsay's son, the first British High Commissioner during the transition to independence, was another friend who sought her counsel.

She was thus brought up in the heart of the imperial British tradition, but her greatest love was for Africa and Kenya, no matter who was in charge.

Arriving by ship at Mombasa in 1920, when she was not quite four, she soon forged a lasting rapport with the country's indigenous inhabitants. Her first childhood dwelling was a straw-thatched mud hut, which served as home for a year until Deloraine was built in the foothills of the Great Rift Valley escarpment, north-west of Nakuru. Lions roared at night. Buffalo, rhinoceros, leopard and bongo roamed the forest fringing the farm. Many of the local tribesmen went almost naked, carrying spear and shield. It was a life of adventure and fun.

She hated boarding school in England, where she was sent aged 15, and hated "coming out" in the London season even more. But when she was 18, her father, immersed in politics, made her manager of Deloraine's undeveloped 3,500 acres, which had been marginal grazing land for the Masai. She only occasionally left the farm or the country for the next 50 years, building dams and schools, laying scores of miles of pipelines and fencing, expanding her core herd of 17 cows to 1,700 mostly Ayrshire crossed with the sturdier though less productive humped Sahiwal cattle indigenous to Gujarat.

When she sold the farm in 1979 to a company backed by President Moi, she had widened her acreage to 5,000-plus and was one of the largest milk producers in the region. The few score of "squatters" hired in the 1920s from at least a dozen tribes from all parts of the country had become a fixed community of more than 1,000 souls. Her entire management and workforce was black. After the sale she continued to live on the farm at Deloraine until she died.

She provided education loans and scholarships to more than a hundred village children. Those who benefited now include a bank manager, a doctor, senior civil servants and one of the country's leading architects.

During the Mau Mau rebellion, she lived alone at Deloraine, guarded at night by a couple of spear-carrying Masai. She was never troubled. But it was after independence that she came into her own, becoming one of the first whites to take Kenyan citizenship and expanding her circle of friends to embrace all colours and walks of life.

Ducal "seasonal migrants" from the British shires, as she called them, would find themselves sipping tea – or gin and tonic – on her verandah with local politicians, priests, zoologists, writers, the village witch-doctor or the local Ndorobo hunter from the forest, clad in a skin of hyrax fur.

The warmth with which she was accepted by the new black establishment flowed largely from her goodwill to the new country and the total, sometimes breathtaking, honesty with which she spoke her mind. She never truckled to the new leaders, as many self-consciously progressive Europeans did, or pretended that cultural differences or corruption did not exist. She was loyal to her past as well as to the new order, insisting that the colonists had done more good than harm but that Africans had a right to run their own country as they saw fit.

She was particularly irritated by *White Mischief*, James Fox's racy account of the murder of Lord Erroll, because she feared its portrait of a small group of decadent, upper-class layabouts would be recorded in history as an accurate picture of settlers as a whole, who, in her view, had struggled courageously to build the backbone of a modern country out of nothing. On one occasion, while touring the harsh Barningo area, an accompanying British general's wife objected to the smell of a sick Tugen tribeswoman whom Miss Scott had picked up from the roadside to drive to hospital. "If you don't like it, get out and walk yourself," she snapped. The complaint ceased.

For many years she was the sole white governor of Egerton College, the largest agricultural training institute in black Africa, now a full-fledged university. During one fund-raising event for her local school, President Moi summoned her to the podium and announced: "This one looks white. But she is black at heart."

Small, rotund and fair-haired, with sharp features and piercing blue eyes, Pam Scott could disarm strangers with her sharp tongue and brusque manner born largely of shyness. But those who knew her will mark her down as one of Kenya's great white Africans.

Her memoirs, *A Nice Place to Live*, were published last year. She never married.

b 7.7.16   d 5.2.92   aged 75

AMHERST VILLIERS

Amherst Villiers and Judge Prosser at high court (1991)

Charles Amherst Villiers, engineer, inventor, wartime ferry pilot, whose skills ranged widely over a spread of interests from advanced technology to fine arts.

A BRILLIANT innovator, whose restlessly questing mind ranged widely and skilfully over a catholic spread of interests – from advanced technology to fine arts – Charles Amherst Villiers brought infectious enthusiasm, much charm and boundless energy to everything he did during a long and adventurous life. Tall, slim, elegant and of immaculate manners but – by nature a "loner" – Villiers eschewed working for long as a member of any close-knit team. In consequence he never achieved the rewards and the recognition which his talents would otherwise have brought him. In the 1980s he was involved in a long drawn-out legal battle with Rolls-Royce whom he was suing for an alleged breach of a joint development agreement of 1983, concerning work carried out on a 1937 Phantom III. The action was suspended last year when Villiers fell and fractured his hip.

Born at Gloucester Place in London, the son of Ernest Amherst Villiers (from 1905 to 1910 Liberal MP for Brighton and the nephew of the first Lord Amherst of Hackney) Charles Villiers went first to Oundle School in 1913, then as an apprentice to the Royal Aircraft Factory at Farnborough and, from 1919 to read physics at Cambridge University.

While at Oundle he had first encountered what was to become his lifetime obsession of "messing about with internal-combustion engines". At Farnborough in 1917 he met W. O. Bentley and at Cambridge, in 1919, Raymond Mays. Both Bentley and Mays were to become close associates of Villiers during the next 20 years.

From Cambridge Villiers joined the Coventry-based Armstrong-Whitworth

Development Company, headed by Major F. M. Green, late of Farnborough. That took Villiers to Sweden to work with the Ljungstrom Turbine company on hydraulic and steam turbines. On his return to England in 1922 he left Armstrong-Whitworth to join Raymond Mays who had acquired two of the one-and-a-half litre Brescia Bugatti cars – "Cordon Rouge" and "Cordon Bleu". Thanks to new camshafts, designed by Villiers, Mays set up hill-climbing records at Shelsley Wash in 1923, exceeding in performance much larger cars of greater nominal power. As a result, Ettoire Bugatti – "Le Patron" – invited the 23-year-old Villiers to come to his works at Molsheim for a six-month working stint.

When Villiers returned to England and the Brooklands Motor Course he launched out on a long and successful career of boosting racing car performance largely through superchargers of which he became a leading exponent. In 1925 Villiers was commissioned successively by S. F. Edge (of AC Motors), by J. F. C. Kruse and by Raymond Mays to super-charge some of the more advanced cars of those days – from the one-and-a-half litre AC to a 7.7 litre Rolls Royce. The success with them led to an invitation from Sir Malcolm Campbell to replace the 18 litre Sunbeam aero engine in his Bluebird car by a 24 litre Napier Lion aero engine for an attempt on the world's land speed record. With that, in due course, Campbell achieved 206mph at Daytona Beach.

By then Villiers had established himself as a consulting engineer in Sackville Street, London, whence flowed the famous era of the "Blown Bentleys" for the well-heeled "Bentley Boys" – Woolf Barnato, J. D. Benjafield, Sir Henry "Tim" Birkin, Frank Clement, Sammy Davis, the Dunfee brothers Jack and Clive, Glen Kidson and Bernard Rubin all supported in their endeavours by the Hon Dorothy Paget.

The four-and-a-half litre "Blower Bentley" of 1929 and 1930 became a legend for its performance at Brooklands and Le Mans, while in 1932, driven by Sir Henry Birkin, it set up a new Brooklands lap record of 138mph only to be broken, in 1935 by another car which owed much to Amherst Villiers – John Cobb's Napier-Railton.

When war came Villiers set all of this on one side to join Air Transport Auxiliary at White Waltham, ferrying military aircraft from factories to RAF squadrons. He was recruited from this, in 1943, by the Canadian Car and Foundry Company, building Hurricanes in Montreal, to lead their research division and to design a six-engine long-range military transport aeroplane. Villiers was to spend the next 20 years in North America covering an extraordinary range of projects – all the way from his presidency of the American Rocket Society in 1948 to the design of anti-ship missiles at the Grumman Corporation and to work on the 100-ton Arcturus satellite for the United Aircraft Corporation of Hertford, Connecticut. That was followed by a year at Boeing in Seattle on lunar systems, by two years with Douglas Aircraft at Santa Monica on an ambitious plan to put men on Mars and, then, by six years of research with bendix-Aviation-Eclipse and at the University of California.

Villiers returned to England in 1965 to the motor-car industry and to collaborate with Peter Berthon on the one-and-a-half-litre BRM engine and with Graham Hill on the Cosworth.

At the age of 66 Villiers decided completely to change course. He turned from technology to religion and portrait painting – in London, in New York and in Florence. Over the next few years his work included portraits of Cardinal Spellman, Ian Fleming, Graham Hill, Pope John Paul II and a large wall painting, "The Miracle of Santa Clara". Villiers was a remarkable man. If he had accorded the same priorities to his business relationships as he did to his inanimate achievements there were few heights which he might not have scaled.

b 9.12.00   d 12.12.91   aged 91

FRANCIS BACON

Francis Bacon, the British painter.

NO other post-war painter tranformed British art with as much energy, flair and obsessive conviction as Francis Bacon. After a surprisingly tentative beginning, when he wavered between painting and designing furniture and rugs, the self-taught Bacon vision arrived fully-formed in 1944. And it already had the ability to unnerve. In a searing orange triptych, he painted three alarmingly distorted figures at the base of a cucifix. Half-human and half-animal, they writhe, push their distended necks forward and open their mouths in desolate howls.

When this excoriating triptych was exhibitied at the Lefevre Gallery, it announced a new post-war mood of uncompromising anxiety. The advent of the cold war, combined with the horror of Hiroshima, confirmed Bacon's preoccupations. He returned, time and again, to the image of a solitary male figure enclosed in a bare interior.

During the 1950s this anguished presence often gave vent to his disquiet with a scream, nowhere more vehemently than in an extended series of paintings based on Velasquez's celebrated portrait of Pope Innocent X. In the original canvas, which Bacon never went to inspect in Rome, the Pope looks masterful and shrewd. But Bacon transforms him into a screaming grotesque, trapped like a prisoner in an electric chair, rather than on a Pontiff's throne.

In later life, Bacon himself came to regret spending so much time on the Pope images. He thought they were too sensational, and went on too long. But they were certainly instrumental in establishing him with a formidable international reputation.

On the whole, though, Bacon's figures remain indoors rather than out in the open. Landscapes were rare in his work, and the paintings of recent decades concentrate, with remarkable consistency on clothed or naked figures in the archetypal Bacon room. As if to stress how little his art had changed, he embarked in 1988 on a second, larger version of his 1944 triptych. The lacerating orange became a more sumptuous red, and the three figures are surrounded by more space than in the earlier version. But they twist and yell as hideously as before, and Bacon demonstrated his regard for the new triptych by presenting it to the Tate Gallery.

Francis Bacon was born of English parents. His father trained horses in Ireland. Bacon had little formal education except for a brief period at a boarding school in Cheltenham. He left home early and spent some years in Paris and Berlin. By 1930 he was in London earning a precarious living as a designer of furniture and rugs.

He had already begun to paint, but of his first experiments very little remains. There were some abstract paintings — they are seen in a picture of the corner of his studio painted by a great friend of that time, Roy de Maistre. There are one or two pictures which found their way into private collections — the best known is a *Crucifixion* which was reproduced in Herbert Read's *Art Now* (1933) — but everything else Bacon destroyed. After 1936 he abandoned painting completely for eight years.

There was nothing tentative about his re-appearance in the closing years of the war. From 1945 onwards he began to show pictures of great technical assurance and startling originality. The crucial moment was his first one-man exhibition at the Hanover Gallery in 1949 which thrust him to the forefront of contemporary painting.

Just as the name Kafka has passed into the language as evocative of a certain kind of anxiety-ridden *impasse*, so Bacon's name now began to be used descriptively. This is an indication of the way in which these pictures reflected a recognisable range of feelings. They were of men's heads set against thick curtains or enclosed in glass boxes, their eyes often obliterated and their mouths stretched open as if to scream. Melodramatic, they were also contemplative and the mood of extreme, yet stoical, despair seemed of a piece with the mood of Sartre's *Huis Clos* and the early Beckett novels.

It was perhaps this literary side to them which first captured the imagination of the public. Not since Fuseli had the horrific been the overt subject-matter of painting, and the novelty was both shocking and absorbing. There were other equally disturbing features. His painting was, for instance, the very antithesis of abstract at a moment when the general drift of painting seemed to be inexorably in an abstract direction. It was illusionistic, although in a novel and non-academic way; it drew upon the Old Masters, on Velasquez in particular, and equally on photography, not only for its imagery but for its surface appearance too.

It was impossible to place him comfortably within any existing framework. Certain critics, notably Robert Melville and David Sylvester, wrote about him brilliantly and with deep partisanship. Others tended to dismiss him as a morbid sensationalist and a light-weight, a view in which they were strengthened when in 1953, on the occasion of a retrospective exhibition of Matthew Smith at the Tate, Bacon contributed a short tribute to the catalogue in which he said: "I think that painting today is pure intuition and luck and taking advantage of what happens when you splash the stuff down . . ." However, within a year or two London was to become familiar with the achievements of the American painters of Bacon's generation. Chance and intuition with paint had begun to take on wider meanings and Bacon looked less isolated, more profound and even more original than before.

His painting was shown in the British Pavilion at the Venice Biennale in 1954, and from now onwards his reputation rose steadily in Europe and America; indeed it could be said that as far as the international standing of British art went, Bacon did for painting what Henry Moore had done for sculpture a few years earlier. There was a major retrospective exhibition at the Tate Gallery in 1962, which later toured Europe, and from this point onwards hardly a year passed without some important showing somewhere in the world. He was the first English painter of this century to be taken seriously in Paris, where queues formed to see his retrospective at the Grand Palais in 1971–2. He was shown at the Metropolitan in New York in 1975.

In one of his first statements about his work Bacon had said: "Painting is the pattern of one's nervous system being projected on the canvas." It was always to have for him this quality of naked attack. It was able, as nothing else, to convey feeling directly, to "come immediately on to the nervous system". Above all it was able to do so through the mysterious equivalence of paint and flesh. He saw this power as an unbroken inheritance from the past, continually to be revivified by the risks and intuitions of the present. He had little regard for abstract art, which in his view avoided the challenge that made painting worthwhile.

For him the proper subject for art was the human figure, and specifically the portrait. As his work matured he dropped much of the menacing *mise en scène* of the earlier pictures, and his figures became more particular portraits. He painted the same close friends over and over, working from photographs and memory, placing them in simple modern interiors, naked or clothed and concentrating on their faces with what to many observers seemed to be sadistic violence. Bacon would always deny this reading.

Neither his international reputation nor the success that went with it made Bacon a conformist figure. He sat on no committees and accepted no honours. He was indifferent to officialdom. Robert Melville once wrote of him: "He is at home in the complicated night life of big cities, interested in the exhibitionism and instability of the people he chooses to mix with and absorbed by extreme situations." His art was very close indeed to his life, and his life was lived on the very fringes of normality.

He was a man of infinite charm and generosity with a great gift for friendship. A prodigious host, his life was uncluttered by possessions. His appearance was ageless. His influence on younger artists during the 1950s and 1960s was very considerable – not stylistically, for he had few imitators – but through his attitude to his work and the sense he gave of the ultimate seriousness of art.

Bacon's outstanding reputation was recognised, in 1985, by a second retrospective exhibition at the Tate Gallery. Until then, no living British artist had been granted such an honour.

b 28.10.09   d 28.4.92   aged 82

DAVID BATHURST

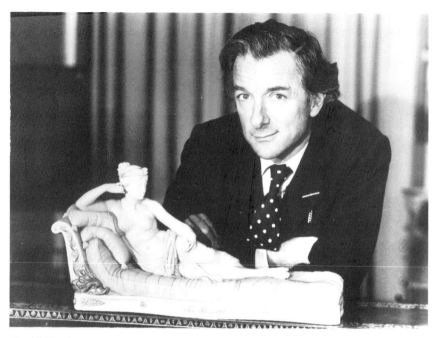

David Charles Lopes Bathurst, auctioneer and art dealer, and former chairman of Christie's.

DAVID Bathurst was one of the brightest young stars at Christie's for more than 20 years and seemed poised to shake off the firm's stodgy image when he took over as chairman in January 1985. Witty, amusing and gifted with a sharp business brain, his effervescent touch suited the optimism of the times. He seemed set for great things but his career at the auction house was highlighted by what became known in the art world as "The Cristallina Affair", in which he falsely announced the sale of two French Impressionist pictures at a New York auction.

He became caught up in a tortuous court case in which an art investment group called Cristallina SA sued Christie's and Bathurst for alleged negligence, breach of contract and fraud. The action was later settled out-of-court but the New York Department of Consumer Affairs fined the firm $80,000.

Bathurst voluntarily surrendered his licence to sell in the city and, after the firm made an out of court agreement for the payment of an undisclosed sum to the group, he resigned in 1987.

He went on to set up a dealing group and never displayed any bitterness over the effect of the Cristallina affair, tackling his new career with drive and enthusiasm.

Bathurst, the second son of the second Viscount Bledisloe, was educated at Eton and Magdalen College, Oxford. He did National Service with the 12th Royal Lancers and studied at the Carnegie Institute, part of the Carnegie Museum of Art in Pittsburgh.

His introduction to the art world came through his time at the New London Gallery, part of Marlborough Fine Art, and he joined Christie's to start its Impressionist and modern picture department in 1963. He became a director at the age of only 29 in 1966. Early success led to him being posted to New

York with young colleagues in 1978, only a year after Christie's had set up in the United States.

French Impressionist pictures then, as now, symbolised money and prestige, and competition for blue chip collections among the auction houses was intense. Business and social life became one. The breakthrough for Bathurst came in 1980.

He spent a weekend with Mr and Mrs Henry Ford II who had an astonishing Impressionist collection. The weekend was a great social success. There was no suggestion of a sale but when Ford later decided to dispose of ten paintings they went straight to Christie's. News of the sale was a sensation and the pictures were estimated to make $10 million. But in an electric 30 minutes they reached $18.30 million. It was a landmark for its time and noted back in London.

Bathurst's team worked hard but also knew how to play. Office parties were famous. He also had the ability to inspire great loyalty and, in his five years in New York, the saleroom he started virtually from scratch briefly outperformed Christie's in London.

Bathurst's career culminated in his appointment as chairman of Christie Manson & Woods in succession to Jo Floyd in 1984. He embarked on a series of one-to-one conversations with all the directors on future strategy. Bathurst was trying to develop a management structure for the Eighties.

Changes were beginning to take place when the Cristallina affair, which dated from his days in New York in 1981, became public in 1985. More that £14 million was wiped off the market value of Christie's International after Bathurst admitted issuing false information on the sale of two paintings. Cristallina, a Panamanian registered company, had asked Christie's to sell eight paintings. Only a Degas sold but, as Bathurst later admitted to a court, Christie's lied by announcing to the press that another two, a Gaugin and a Van Gogh, had also been sold for £2.5 million. This, he later explained, was to prevent disruption in the art market, though many said it was to protect his own firm's reputation. He resigned as chairman of the English board, as he had by then become.

After his departure from Christie's with two colleagues Bathurst started the St James's Art Group, a dealing partnership in Jermyn Street.

Friends felt the Cristallina affair overshadowed his career, to the point where it obscured his real achievements at Christie's, and that it was for these that he should be remembered rather than for a momentary lapse. Bathurst remained successful and had recently been invited by the Chinese government to hold the first official selling of Chinese contemporary art in London. This exhibition was due to have been held in November but with his death has now been cancelled.

He enjoyed cricket and while still a schoolboy continued the family tradition of bobsleighing on the Cresta Run. His broad interests included opera and the poems of Dylan Thomas. He loved Scotland especially and spent a great deal of time at his house at Biggar in Lanarkshire. It was there, surrounded by friends, that he had a sudden heart attack while out shooting grouse on the hill.

Bathurst married Cornelia McCosh in 1967. They had three daughters.

b 15.12.37   d 19.9.92   aged 54

JOHN BRATBY

John Bratby with his picture of The Queen Mother (1978)

John Bratby, RA, painter and author.

DURING the middle and late 1950s John Bratby was the most public of British artists. His first one-man show of paintings – featuring all the intimacies of family living, from cornflakes and chaos on the kitchen table through every room in the house including the smallest – won high praise from the critics. The blazing colour and sculptural quality of his oils were his trade-mark and his belligerent individuality – which included letters fired off to the press – associated him with the Angry Young Men of the John Osborne generation. He was one of the first media stars of the art world and his work soon hung in the Tate, the Victoria and Albert and the Museum of Modern Art in New York.

In 1967 he began painting portraits of the famous. More than a thousand sitters, ranging from the Queen Mother to Sir Alex Guinness and Paul McCartney, subjected themselves to his highly individual portrait technique – which the journalist Jean Rook said was like being hit by a truck.

But Bratby paintings which were hailed in the 1950s as brilliant examples of a new genre were by this time being ignored, derided or dismissed as crude and uninteresting by the arts establishment. Only in the last few years has his star again been in the ascendant. Last year a retrospective of his work was staged at the National Portrait Gallery, only the second held there of a living artist, and there were shows of his work at the Albemarle and Mayor galleries. Bratby's paintings for the film of Joyce Cary's novel *The Horse's Mouth* in 1958, painted ostensibly by its Bohemian tramp-artist, Gulley Jimson, added its fictional confusions to Bratby's persona. With his bushy white beard he sometimes appeared to be acting out Jimson in real life, to the delight of journalists. This obscured his acutely sensitive and intelligent nature.

John Randall Bratby's grandfather had been artistically inclined, and John was much stimulated by his art teacher at Tiffin Boys' School in Kingston, Harold Watts. He studied at Kingston School of Art from 1949 to 1950 and – having applied to enter the Slade but changing his mind — at the Royal College of Art from 1951 to 1954, where he won the Abbey Minor Scholarship, an Italian government scholarship, and a Royal College minor travelling scholarship. A sensitive student hiding behind a combative smokescreen, he subsequently claimed that he ignored his teachers at the RCA; however, he was remembered by them as the most outstanding draughtsman among the students for many years and as an explosive painter. On his last day at college he knocked on the door of a surprised department head to ask how to make money out of painting to pay for the necessities of life — wife and children, house and car.

At this time, when Expressionism was still far from general British taste, even in the art world, Bratby was interested in the art of Van Gogh, Munch, Kokoschka and the German Expressionists. Yet in the same year, 1954, that he left college he had his first one-man show, of 26 paintings, at Helen Lessore's Beaux Arts gallery. This created a major impression on the critics of the day. *The Times* critic assessed Bratby's impact by saying that, standing in front of his work, one could imagine "what it would have been like to be confronted with a Van Gogh for the first time, in the early years of this century". David Sylvester linked him with the other young painters shown at the Beaux Arts — Jack Smith, Derrick Greaves and Edward Middleditch — and coined the term, to be much used in the future, "The Kitchen-Sink School". John Russell recalled Sickert's decree, "plain living and thick painting", and saw it as modified Expressionism. Another critic said that Bratby painted as if he wanted to imprint every scene on his consciousness.

John Berger, the most influential left-wing critic of the time, who believed in art as a tool of social progress, was initially impressed, whilst observing that such painting would lead either to "blind incoherence or profound discoveries". Bratby's apparent lack of visual discrimination disturbed some critics; and Basil Taylor said that he "treated paint

and colour like a carpet-bedding gardener". Another followed this up by calling it "a rush across a garden in hobnail boots".

Bratby's output of paintings — in oil on hardboard and mostly large — was phenomenal and remained so. He soon left the critics visually exhausted. "As monotonously stunning as fireworks explosions on Bastille Day", was a typical verdict of the time. John Berger, who had probably hoped for a social realist painter to match Guttuso or Peter de Francia, wrote off Bratby in his book of memoirs, *Permanent Red*, as having ruined himself, producing uninspired work.

However, Bratby was accepted for exhibition in the Royal Academy Summer Show from 1955, and in 1956 was exhibited at the British Pavilion at the Venice Biennale in company with other Kitchen-Sink painters and alongside the main exhibits of Lynn Chadwick and Ivon Hitchens. The Beaux Arts painters were seen as related internationally to the Italian social realists and to the French realists as shown by Quentin Bell at the Tate Gallery in 1955 — Buffet, Minaux, Rapp and Rebeyrolle.

Bratby himself, whilst rejecting the Kitchen-Sink appellation, considered himself a new realist who "painted the environment, with no social criticism". He reckoned that the Beaux Arts painters (who also included Bacon, Freud, and Bomberg's pupils, Auerbach and Kossoff, at the time) caught the mood of the decade 1950—60, with its threat of nuclear holocaust.

But Bratby found the Beaux Arts "a dry and unhappy place". After winning the Guggenheim Award for painting in Britain in 1956 and again, with Ben Nicholson, in 1958, and also the John Moores Junior Painting Prize in 1957, he moved his one-man shows to the Zwemmer Gallery for a number of years. Later he went to the Thackeray and Furneaux galleries.

Bratby's fame spread — if in rather distorted fashion — when in 1957—8, Knightsbridge Films embarked on an adaptation of the novel *The Horse's*

Mouth, with its anti-hero (played by Alec Guinness), Gulley Jimson, a Bohemian tramp-artist loosely based on the characters of Gerald Wilde and Stanley Spencer, John Bratby was finally chosen to provide the paintings.

Bratby's brilliant draughtmanship enabled him to present anything in front of him — from cornflake packets, beer bottles, and all the flotsam and jetsam of the kitchen, to perspective views all around the studio, including windows, mirrors and even the painter himself. Then he embarked on series. There were sunflowers, "for their generosity, regality, strength and vigour"; his new snooker table; stuffed animal heads; obsessive portraits of Brigitte Bardot; and, constantly, his family and friends in groups. Less brilliant was the painting: if the drawing was realist, the paint — sometimes applied direct from the tube like toothpaste and giving rise to the jibe "Tubism" — often simply followed the lines of the drawing, or made tessellated infills of such details as window-panes. There was seldom tonal painting to match the realism, and it was nearer to Fauvist colour than to Expressionist. This set up a visual and mental disturbance for the viewer, acting against the bracing joys of reality rather than enhancing them.

Bratby's critics decried his work as superficial, losely put together in improvisational style and garishly coloured. To those who know only his paintings the drawings come as a revelation: and there are some sensitive watercolours also.

However, with Bratby's move to outdoor paintings of boats from 1964, and his love affair with Venice, which took him back there more and more frequently and for longer periods, his touch with oils refined. Indeed, in later years he was able to complete more than 1,000 portraits (mostly at his own invitation) in four-hour sittings apiece in his house at Hastings, with its 20 rooms stacked with paintings.

In 1960 when American Abstract Expressionism eclipsed the unique vigour of Bratby's paintings he took to novel-writing — with considerable intelligence, sensitivity and autobiographical recall (though curiously few mentions of colour). However, the narrator figure tended to intrude too much. The first, *Breakdown* (1960), forecast Bratby's own breakdown of 1972, he claimed. The same could be said of *Break-Pedal Down* (1962): he later smashed his car into a wall. *Breakfast and Elevenses* (1961), with its vividly-recalled stuffy family life and agonies of adolescence around 1939, was dedicated to the theme that "The best Englishmen are twisted, for psychiatric cases are", and suggested boldly in its jacket blurb that Freud would have benefited by reading it. These were followed in 1963 by *Break 50 Kill*.

His writing ability was channelled from 1988 into the revival of the magazine *Art Quarterly*; the first issue was devoted to Venice, the second in 1989 to Paris, with contributions from a wide range of painters and others — John Ward, Bernard Dunstan, Michael Foot, Lord Longford, Michael Winner. Bratby had provided paintings for the film *Mistral's Daughter* in 1984.

John Bratby was elected Associate of the Royal Academy in 1959 but refused full Academician status when offered in 1968; however, he accepted it in 1971.

In 1953 he married Jean Cooke, the painter; they had three sons and one daughter. In 1977, after a divorce, he married the actress Patti Prime, whom he had met in 1974 through the Lonely Hearts column in *Time Out* magazine — as he, typically, made public.

b 19.7.28   d 20.7.92   aged 64

JOHN SPENCER CHURCHILL

John Spencer Churchill, painter, sculptor, author and exuberant exhibitionist.

THE Winstonian bow-tie and king-sized cigar were ever-present and the bald, bull-dog brow and powerful shoulders increasingly resembled the silhouette of his famous uncle. John Spencer Churchill was not one to distance himself from this likeness. Few artists can have received more attention in the press, particularly in the gossip columns, than he did during the 1950s and 1960s, mostly on the strength of his familial connection. But Spencer Churchill had a more genuine talent for painting, especially mural decoration, than the nature of the allusions to him might have suggested and he certainly shared the Churchillian traits of enterprise and unconventionality. Married four times, he was a painter of and for celebrities, a man about town with an eye for a lovely lady; a talented musician, a gymnast of redoubtability in his youth and, for most of his life, a prodigious drinker who, in his autobiography listed his daily intake as follows: 11am: Port, beer or stout; 12noon: Pink gin. Lunch: claret. Post-lunch: Kummel or brandy. Tea: whisky and soda. Cocktail hour: gin and something; Pre-dinner: claret followed by port and brandy. 10pm until 3am: whisky and soda. He claimed this intake was on medical advice, "To keep the arteries open."

His gymnastic ability was attested to by his contemporary, the Earl of Birkenhead, who said that as an Oxford undergraduate Spencer Churchill had won a bet from him by diving over the head of 21 friends kneeling in a row in Peckwater Quad. He once hired the Albert Hall for an hour in order to play *The Mastersingers* overture on the gigantic organ and in *Crowded Canvas*, his autobiography published in 1961, he shocked his friends with the frankness — at least for that time — with which he wrote about the intimate details of his family life.

John George Spencer Churchill was the elder son of Major John Churchill, grandson of Lord Randolph Churchill and nephew of Sir Winston. Like his famous uncle he was educated at Harrow School but went on to Pembroke College, Oxford, and then studied at a series of art colleges including the Royal College of Art, the Central School of Art and Ruskin School of Art. He also received private tutelage from Meninksy, Hubbard, Nicholson and Lutyens. He started his adult life on the Stock Exchange, but stayed there only eight months finding it "too awful for words". So at the age of 20 he gave up the city to devote himself to painting.

His first commission was a mural decoration for Lady Islington and this was followed by one to decorate the Renaissance palace in India of the Maharanee of Cooch Behar with a series of ten-foot-high wall paintings of Italian scenes for which he made preliminary studies in Italy.

Churchill's decorations were often, and conveniently, spoken of as "frescoes" but they were not frescoes in the strict sense of the word because, although painted directly on to walls, they were executed in an oil and wax medium and not with lime wash on the wet plaster. His most talked about early work was a large mural decoration which he painted in the dining room of the flat of Henry Channon, an American living in London. The general subject was a Florentine garden party of The Renaissance, including portraits of 80 of Churchill's friends, among them Prince and Princess Paul of Yugoslavia, Lady Cunard, Lady Diana Cooper and Lord Birkenhead, in sixteenth century costume but with modern hair-dressing and make-up. In general treatment it recalled Rex Whistler's *Pursuit of Rare Meats* in the refreshment room of the Tate Gallery and, in spite of some immaturity in the figure drawing and painting, it showed real imagination and a remarkable power of reconciling portraiture with decorative effect.

Other decorative schemes carried out were a series of wall paintings illustrating the life and adventure of St George in the hall of Aubery Herbert's villa at Portofino; paintings of Marlborough's battles on the walls of the summer-house in Sir Winston's garden at Chartwell

Manor; and a large circular panorama of Rapallo for Lloyd George at one end of the sitting room at Churt, as a reminder of the conference which the former Liberal prime minister regarded as a turning point in history.

Spencer Churchill also tried his hand at sculpture and a figure which he shaped of his uncle was most remarkable for the strong family resemblance between the artist and the sitter.

In 1936 Spencer Churchill, who had married two years earlier, went to Spain where he had a villa at Torremolinos, which at that time was a popular resort of foreign artists and writers and a centre of the Spanish Anarchist Party. Here he became caught up in the Spanish Civil War and with his wife and infant daughter had to be evacuated in a British warship.

In 1939 he opened a shop in front of his studio in Ebury Street, Chelsea, with a permanent exhibition of his works and a monkey eating an orange painted on the window. One wall of the shop was covered with a mural decoration of a scene in Andalusia. To his friends Churchill sent out a circular with a scale of charges, ranging from £10 for a small portrait to £200 for a large mural decoration. On the outbreak of the second world war he was appointed to the corps of camouflage artists, with the rank of captain, and went to France. He was the only artist present to produce sketches of the Dunkirk evacuation.

After the war his artistic work ranged from painted murals on the yacht of President Tubman of Liberia to capturing the likenessess of Sir Bernard and Lady Docker and Miss Israel in the Miss World competition. It was a bohemian existence. He lived in Adam and Eve Mews, Kensington, where in 1955 he and his second wife were arrested for being drunk and disorderly. During the extensively reported trial the prosecution said that after the couple were arrested Spencer Churchill howled like a dog and his wife mewed like a cat. Not so, said Spencer Churchill. He had simply been singing Florestan's aria from Act II of *Fidelio*, having found himself in solitary confinement in a cell, in circumstances similar to those of the opera character. They were each fined five shillings and ordered to pay ten guineas costs.

In 1957 Spencer Churchill painted a mural of the view of London from the South Bank in Simpson's, the Piccadilly store. From 1963 he lived mostly in the south of France and in addition to his paintings also occasionally lectured. Engaged to speak in America his planned subject was "English Mural Painters." But this proposal was not received favourably by his American agent who replied: "Mr Churchill, your name is Churchill. We want to hear about Churchills. The more the better. Also especially if they are Sir Winston Churchill." So the Churchills were what he lectured about.

Spencer Churchill was well regarded by his friends and associates. He had penetrating blue eyes, a deep chuckle and will be remembered as a warm personality who made the best of life. He was married first in 1934 to Angela Clume Seymour, by whom he had a daughter, secondly in 1941 to Mary Cookson, thirdly in 1953 to Kathlyn Tandy who died in 1957, and fourthly in 1958 to Lullan Boston from whom he was divorced in 1972.

b 31.5.09 d 23.6.92 aged 83

JOHN PIPER

John Piper, CH, painter, stage designer and author.

JOHN Piper believed in things English and in many ways he was summed up by the house in which he lived for more than fifty years shrouded by the woods close to the Thames near Henley. His garden, which provided much of the produce cooked by his wife Myfanwy and was celebrated in some of his later work, was very English, in parts gloomily so. His immense kitchen with quantities of china mugs suspended from hooks could only have been found in rural England. The only thing he did not much care for about Henley was the annual regatta and the arrival of what Myfanwy called "Leanderthal Man".

The churches he sketched tended to be English, although there was an early series devoted to Welsh non-conformist chapels. For some of them he designed stained glass windows. Much of his best stage work came in his sets for the operas of his friend, Benjamin Britten. Inevitably, he was accused of being too insular, to which he was apt to reply that

Constable went no further than the Lake District.

John Piper was enormously hardworking and versatile, making a vast contribution to British sensibility and vision over many decades and in many media. His painting went through both representational and abstract periods. Beyond that he devoted himself to printmaking, collage, illustration, stage design, stained glass, tapestry, fabric design, ceramics, poetry, art and theatre criticism, topography and the visual guidebook. He was an artist who persuaded more people to use their own eyes.

John Piper went to Epsom College as a day boy. He had already in his teens begun to make topographical notebooks of architecture around the southeast of England illustrated with drawings and photographs; it is said that he had visited every church in Surrey by the age of 12. From 1921 to 1926 he was an articled clerk in the solicitor's office of his father. On the latter's death in 1926, Piper abandoned the law and attended Richmond School of Art under Raymond

Coxon. In 1927, the year he met Braque at the house of Jim Ede in Hampstead, he transferred to the Royal College of Art, where he was taught painting by Morris Kestelman, and lithography and stained glass by Francis Spear. He married a fellow student, Eileen Holding, in 1929.

During the 1930s Piper contributed art and theatre criticism to *The Listener* and the *New Statesman* and exhibited with the London Group. His paintings were linked by commentators with such other young artists as Ivon Hitchens, Winifred and Ben Nicholson, Frances Hodgkins and Victor Pasmore; some of his early paintings recall those of Christopher Wood. In 1934 Piper was elected a member of the *7 & 5 Society*, which was dedicated initially to "non-representational" art; at this time Piper was interested in a cubistic form of abstraction.

It was in 1934 that Piper met Myfanwy Evans, writer, art magazine editor and, later, opera librettist, whom he was to marry as his second wife in 1937. So close was their working partnership during the rest of their lives together that their individual achievements cannot be precisely separated, least of all by the art historian. Piper used to claim she was his first and last critic and regularly paid tribute to her acute intelligence.

Piper's contributions to pure abstract paintings in the early 1930s were − and remain − visually strong; but he rejected abstraction by 1937 because it lost the lively nourishment of subject. In 1936 Piper had met John Betjeman − another collaborator whose vision was to be ultimately difficult to distinguish from Piper's own, and whose Anglicanism converted Piper. The gathering clouds of war and their travels together in the preparation of the *Shell Guides* to individual counties of England combined to develop an appreciation of the visual heritage of Britain which the war served to intensify and deepen and make more immediate, more vital and more national. It began to transcend the conventional labels of "romantic nostalgia" and "neo-

romanticism". "Visionary topography" might be a better description of Piper's work of this period.

The essential components of his art had come together by the time that he was sent as a war artist to record in November 1940 the bomb devastation of Coventry Cathedral. They include a strong abstract underpinning in the design of a painting and a sense of visual drama, continuously developing from 1937 when he joined Group Theatre as designer along with Robert Medley (working with Britten as composer, Isherwood as dramatist, and Rupert Doone as dancer-choreographer).

He shared with Betjeman an appreciation of the appeal of details of architecture or townscape dismissed by others as too ordinary or too debased. Piper's own eye was acute for the exact representation of architecture, a skill fostered by stage design, by scratching and scumbling the surface of his paintings so that there is a feeling of time and the elements at work on both architecture and landscape. His flirtation with Cubism gave him the freedom to make passing allusions to many facets of a scene, both visual and emotional, within one work. Piper himself summed it up simply as "a feeling for places ... trying to see what hasn't been seen before".

But what deepens all this and makes, for instance, the 26 watercolours of Windsor commissioned by Queen Elizabeth the Queen Mother (then Queen consort) in 1941−42, at the instigation of Sir Kenneth Clark, and which now hang in a single room at Clarence House, into something approaching a national monument in themselves, is a further artistry. There is an intense and dramatic visual presentation of the poignancy of the transient set against the timeless: part of the impulse for the commission was the fear in 1941 that Windsor Castle could be bombed into obliteration at any time. And there is another poignant ambivalence movingly transcended in the paintings of wartime devastation: the 1930s' sense of indulgent pleasure in ruins and their surrounding emotional atmosphere, strangely redeems and transmutes 1940s' destruction and points gloriously, not to the tragedy of war but to the vision of that which is beyond destruction.

For many, it is Piper's paintings of the 1940s which call most deeply to the spirit; even such a peaceful subject as Gordale Scar, painted in 1943, is a masterpiece with all the resonance of a major work by Henry Moore. This sombre mood was to be unexpectedly prolonged into the neo-romanticism of the early 1950s: the gloom of the wartime 1940s gave way only briefly to a few years of exhausted post-war euphoria before the nuclear clouds of the Cold War returned in the 1950s.

After the intensities of war, which called work of similar quality out of several other war artists, some art critics complained that Piper spread himself too thinly. If there was truth in that then enthusiasts for theatre, opera, ballet, stained glass, book illustration, architecture, gardening and other arts can only have felt grateful for the proliferation of Piper's interests.

He had already appeared regularly on television from 1936; and in 1938 his *Shell Guide to Oxfordshire* had been published, as well as his set design for Stephen Spender's *Trial of a Judge* at the Unity Theatre. From 1945 he illustrated all five volumes of Sir Osbert Sitwell's autobiography. In 1946 Piper designed the scenery and costumes for the première of Benjamin Britten's *Rape of Lucretia* at Glyndebourne, to be followed by *Albert Herring* in 1947 and a further close involvement with the English Opera Group at Aldeburgh.

For the Festival of Britain in 1951 Piper designed the mural for the exterior of the Homes and Gardens pavilion and also, with Osbert Lancaster, was responsible for the decoration of the Main Vista. Piper fitted in as well that year four major theatrical productions, for the English Opera Group, Sadler's Wells Ballet, Glyndebourne, and most famously, Britten's *Billy Budd* at Covent Garden; also two exhibitions in Philadelphia and London. Closer to home he took on the

lease of the Kenton Theatre at Henley-on-Thames. That work programme was not untypical of any year of Piper's life.

In 1953 came sets and constumes for Britten's *Gloriana*; while in 1954, Myfanwy Piper's libretto for Britten's *Turn of the Screw* brought Piper even closer to the Red House and the Aldeburgh group. The year 1957 brought the commission for the vast stained glass wall of the Baptistry at Coventry Cathedral, in collaboration with Patrick Reyntiens; this was finished and consecrated in 1962.

The 1960s began for Piper with Britten's *Midsummer Night's Dream*; in 1964–65, he worked on the tapestry for a screen behind the high altar at Chichester Cathedral; in 1967 he completed the stained glass for St Margaret's, Westminster, and also for Liverpool Cathedral.

The designs for the television production of Britten's *Owen Wingrave* in 1971, subsequently performed at the Royal Opera House in 1973, were perhaps less successful. Myfanwy Piper provided the libretto for this, based on Henry James, as she did for Britten's final opera, *Death in Venice*, for the 1973 Aldeburgh Festival. For that the Piper sets in Colin Graham's production remained unchallenged until the revival earlier this year at Covent Garden.

Piper had his first public exhibition of ceramics in 1972; and he broke further new ground when in 1979 – the year of the stained glass for the Robinson College Chapel in Cambridge, and the Benjamin Britten Memorial Window at Aldeburgh – he designed the firework display at the opening of the extension to the Tate Gallery.

And in between all these major commissions Piper fulfilled hundreds of other commissions – all given highly professional attention and preparation. He found time, not for holidays, which he never took, he said, but for working trips abroad, bringing back memorable imagery from the great churches of France and from the architectural theatricality of Venice; and he even managed to carry out official duties: as a member of the Fine Art Commission from 1960; of the Oxford Diocesan Advisory Committee from 1950; and as a trustee of the Tate Gallery from 1946 to 1960, a triple stint, where he was praised for his "enthusiasm, his openmindedness, his good sense, his natural modesty and his excellent taste". He was appointed a Companion of Honour in 1972.

John Piper's retrospective at the Tate Gallery in 1983–4 revealed the rich achievement of an artist who had for some years been neglected or dismissed by certain critics as a lightweight too prone in his painting to the facile, the theatrical and the repetitious. Those critics were apt to ignore that in each separate decade he scaled a separate height: in the 1930s the illustrated guides, in the 1940s the paintings, in the 1950s the theatre designs, and in the 1960s the stained glass, which may well become his most lasting monument. All these achievements are commanding. As a "topographical visionary" Piper stands in a very special relationship to Turner, whose increased popularity may well owe something to his Henley advocate.

A born collaborator, who leaves a huge wake of friends from his multitude of enterprises (for he treated all around as equals), Piper's most elusive achievement is that he was one of a group of mid-twentieth century men – Niklaus Pevsner, J. M. Richards, John Betjeman, Osbert Lancaster, Gordon Cullen among them – who have taught us to look at Britain's visual heritage and see it, not in vain nostalgia, but with enjoyment and for what it is. He is an artist whose stature is to be measured by the sum total of moments of individual human awareness, exhilaration and vision. These he brought to those who look at pictures, to theatre audiences, to readers of books and to church congregations alike.

His friend John Russell once described him thus: "Tall, trim, spare and erect, with the features of an accessible Montezuma, and the gait of one limbering up for the hop, step and jump."

He is survived by his second wife Myfanwy.

b 13.12.03   d 28.6.92   aged 88

SIR JOHN ROTHENSTEIN

Sir John Rothenstein, CBE, director of the Tate Gallery from 1938 to 1964.

JOHN Rothenstein is remembered for his years at the Tate — years marked by a remarkable series of acquisitions for the gallery and for the often tempestuous circumstances in which his stewardship was conducted — and for his writings on art, notably his three-volume *Modern English Painters*, a labour of twenty years which took the story of British art from Sickert to Hockney. When read in conjunction with his autobiography, also an affair of three volumes, it provided not only an illuminating guide to modern English painting but a commentary on the English definition of art itself. His own life, as purchaser at the Tate had been so inextricably involved with modern art history and the British approach to it, that his insights were always close to the pulse of criticism and evaluation as it was happening.

By any standards the furore which attended Rothenstein's period at the helm of the Tate was an extraordinary one. Hounded for the decided nature of his views and for his buying policy, it seemed, often, that he could not survive as

director. But he knew how to fight back (on one occasion he threw a punch at an art critic whom he thought was deriding him at a reception). And in the end his enemies became the victims of their over-violent antipathy to him. And when he left Rothenstein was acknowledged to have given the Tate a new freshness and vitality.

John Knewstub Maurice Rothenstein was the son of the painter Sir William Rothenstein; his mother was Alice Mary Knewstub, whose father was also a painter. When Rothenstein was two the family moved to Hampstead, where the greater part of his childhood was spent. His education was liberal rather than conventional, starting at two day-schools in London, and continuing at Bedales till he went to Worcester College, Oxford, in 1920.

A much stronger formative influence in his childhood and early youth was the circle of people whom he met at his parents' house, which included writers like Conrad and Hudson and artists like Augustus John and Eric Gill; most influential, perhaps, was Max Beerbohm.

By the time he came down from Oxford his father had been appointed principal of the Royal College of Art and here Rothenstein met a remarkable circle of young artists, including Henry Moore, John Piper and Barbara Hepworth.

In 1927, despairing of making a career in this country, he accepted an invitation to go as a lecturer to the University of Kentucky. There he met Elizabeth Smith, whom he married in 1929. After a year he moved to Pittsburgh and in 1930 returned to London.

In June 1938 Rothenstein was appointed director of the Tate Gallery. The assignment was not an easy one. Under previous regimes the administration of the gallery had become chaotic, a situation which was made worse by the ill-defined and often unfriendly relationship between the Tate and the National Gallery, of which it was still technically a part.

War broke out before Rothenstein had been able to make any serious attack on the problems involved in the reorganisation of the Tate.

By April 1946 the Tate Gallery had been sufficiently restored for part of it to be opened and in the following years it gradually came to life again, largely owing to the efforts of Rothenstein. Perhaps the greatest successes of this time were the series of exhibitions held in the Tate but mainly organised by the Arts Council, in which the London public, starved of art for six years, was able once more to see the great masterpieces of French and English art of the last 100 years, and in some cases — as with the pictures from the Kunsthistorisches Museum, Vienna — by old masters. On the whole these were years of pace and achievement, only interrupted by skirmishes with the Royal Academy over the Chantrey Bequest.

In 1950, however, this happy state of affairs changed and the great "Tate Row" began, primarily started by the efforts of Leroux Smith Leroux, the Tate's deputy keeper, who seems to have aimed at dislodging Rothenstein in order to succeed him as director. Even many years on, it was difficult to view the battle objectively. Passions ran so high, so many personal vendettas were involved, so much false information was spread about. The problem was further confused by the fact that for long the only account of the affair was that of Rothenstein himself in the second volume of his autobiography, *Brave Day, Hideous Night.*

What is clear is that Rothenstein was saved by the intemperance of his opponents, who overplayed their hand in such a way as to rally the trustees behind the director. That there had been great carelessness in the administration of trust funds is certain, and that there was much unease in staff relations is also demonstrable; but it must be said on the other hand that these errors could not justify the malice with which Rothenstein was dogged by his opponents.

In the end Leroux's appointment was terminated and he left the Tate. An uneasy peace was re-established, and Rothenstein remained director until his retirement in 1964.

Both by his acquisitions for the Tate and by his writings — notably in the three volumes of his *Modern English Painters* — Rothenstein did much to spread the appreciation of a generation of English artists whose work he had known as he grew up, but his taste was limited. He never sympathised with what were the more advanced movements at the time of his directorship, and he had what can only be called a prejudice against the art of the European continent.

True, under pressure from the trustees he acquired a certain number of important works by contemporary French artists, but he never really supported these purchases with enthusiasm. His attitude towards the Ecole de Paris, which comes out very clearly in his writings, may have been in part a reflection of his dislike of Bloomsbury, which in its turn was probably due to the fact that Rothenstein's father had quarrelled bitterly with Roger Fry.

Rothenstein is survived by his wife, Elizabeth and his daughter, Lucy.

b 11.7.01   d 17.2.92   aged 90

SIR JAMES STIRLING

Sir James Stirling, architect and RIBA gold medallist, exponent of modernism.

JAMES Stirling was that rare creation, a British architect of world renown. Like many men of genius he was for much of his life a prophet with little honour in his own land. An impassioned exponent of Modernism whose later works showed intriguing glimpses of classical revivalism, his buildings managed to attract admiration and hostility in equal measure.

Abroad, both architects and the lay public found it difficult to comprehend the often fierce antagonism towards his buildings in Britain. His work for the city of Stuttgart was received not only with critical acclaim but with public adulation (apart from the great German engineer Frei Otto, who likened his designs for the city's gallery to those for Auschwitz). His reputation was equally high on the other side of the Atlantic. The *Washington Star* devoted a leading article in praise of his output when he received the 1981 Pritzker prize.

Although Stirling's completed *oeuvre* is small, his projects were legion. In recent years he was on the shortlist of numerous national and international competitions, in England notably for the National Gallery extension, Paternoster Square, Bracken House, Glyndebourne and the new Channel 4 building; abroad for the Los Angeles Philharmonic Hall, the Bibliothèque de France in Paris and the Kyoto concert hall in Japan.

Stirling's international reputation rests above all on two works, the engineering faculty at Leicester University and the Stuttgart Staatsgalerie. He was an influential teacher, as lecturer and professor at the Architectural Association in London and also at Yale and at Düsseldorf. His intellect, as much as his large frame and girth, earned him the nickname of Big Jim Stirling. He was typical of a certain type of Briton, querulous, individual, idiosyncratic, unwilling to be pinned to any group, his own man.

Though knighted only 12 days before his death, Stirling steadily collected the world's major architectural awards, the Alvar Aalto medal in 1977, the RIBA gold medal in 1980, the American Pritzker prize in 1981, the Chicago Architecture award in 1985, the Thomas Jefferson medal in 1986, the Hugo Haring prize in 1988 and the Praemium

Imperiale award from Japan in 1990. He was an honorary member of academies in Berlin and Florence as well as of the American Academy and Institute of Arts and Letters.

Born in Glasgow, Stirling was essentially a Liverpudlian. His father was a Scottish marine engineer and the family moved to Liverpool when Stirling was a year old. Thus the visual backdrop to his childhood was Liverpool Docks, where he used to visit his father, then a dramatic vista of masts ("fourteen miles of forest" as Herman Melville once wrote). His visual taste was formed by his perusal of his father's meticulous coloured drawings of ships' machinery.

He was educated at Quarry Bank High School, where he failed his school certificate and then went briefly, to Liverpool College of Art. When war came he was, by virtue of his Scottish connection, commissioned in the Black Watch. But the inanities of regimental life appalled his sensitive (and at the same time volcanic) nature. Dining-in nights, with their indigestible mix of deafening band music and good food, wine and conversation, he found particularly intolerable. Another hate was the twice weekly inspections by the colonel who walked down the line of his subalterns, lifting their kilts with his crummack to make sure that no one was "cheating" and wearing underpants.

When he could stand no more Stirling volunteered for the Parachute Regiment and took part in the Sixth Airborne Division's drop behind German coastal defences on the night before D-Day. His war was not to be a long one. Among the first to engage the enemy, he was also among the first casualties, wounded by a blast of a tank shell 36 hours after landing. He was evacuated to Britain, but as his injury was mainly concussion he was soon back in Normandy. He was then injured again, hit in the shoulder by a burst of machine gun fire during the break-out from Caen. His war was now definitely over and he continued to suffer from some paralysis in his left arm for the rest of his life.

In 1945 he began at Liverpool, then Britain's largest university school of architecture. "There was furious debate as to the validity of the modern movement," he later recalled, adding that the book which most influenced him after Colin Rowe's *Towards A New Architecture* was Saxl and Wittkower's inspiring pictorial survey *British Art and the Mediterranean*.

After a spell as an assistant with Lyons, Israel and Ellis, he set up in practice in partnership with the Glaswegian James Gowan in 1956. It was to a fertile association, "Big Jim" and "Wee Willie" striking the creative sparks from each other that ensured whatever they did was an assault on stock notions of architectural propriety.

Following the acrimonious breakup of his partnership with Gowan, Stirling was awarded the commission for a new history faculty library in Cambridge. Built on an L-shaped plan, enclosing a fan-shaped cascade of glass, it was strongly attacked by teachers and students alike for leaking in winter and overheating in summer, criticism that dogged Stirling's buildings all his career. Demolition was seriously considered but eventually rejected by the university senate in the 1980s.

His other university commission at this time was the Florey building for Queen's college, Oxford, again demonstrating a hard northern industrial aesthetic and attracting criticism for its fierce dominance over a virgin riverside site. Some detected in it, however, a more delicate texture of tiles and glass rather than harsh concrete: perhaps the beginning of a less ideological, more mature Stirling.

In 1971 Stirling was joined in partnership by Michael Wilford at a time when, save for a few exceptional buildings such as his Olivetti Training School at Haslemere, clients seemed to have deserted him. His individuality now asserted itself in a new way. He was the first notable Modernist to attack modern architecture for being boring, servile, arrogant and banal. He claimed it subverted the richness of life. The great exhibition on neo-classical art held at the Royal Academy in 1972 was an intense influence and he moved towards a more classical style of bold and simple geometric volumes.

Stirling had immense talent and fertility as a draughtsman, producing drawings that were works of art in themselves. In a few carefully chosen elevations and perspectives he could convey every aspect of a design and its setting. Not since the end of beaux-arts classicism had any architect shown such a sophisticated ability to handle complicated axes and interweave geometric shapes.

His unquestioned masterpiece in this vein is the Stuttgart Staatsgalerie. In making the public route through the building into a processional way, Stirling awakened a sense of ritual in architecture that harked back to ancient Greek temple sites. Here was a building of elemental simplicity, carefully chosen materials making powerful use of colour.

The gallery did not merely appeal to his peers in the profession, but was a resounding success with the public. Attracting well over a million visitors in its first year, it pushed Stuttgart from 50th to first place in the West German gallery visitor ratings. Stirling further developed the colour elements of Stuttgart in the startling livery of the Braun headquarters in Berlin.

His best-known recent building in Britain is the Clore gallery, added to the Tate to house the Turner collection, again using colour and geometry to express the building's relationship to its setting. This time Stirling had to suffer the criticism of the profession but the accolade of the public. He was perhaps unfortunate as a result not to win the competition for the National Gallery extension, which went to Robert Venturi.

The accolades Stirling received abroad were a stark contrast with the brickbats at home. The Prince of Wales likened his design for Number One Poultry (on the Mappin and Webb site) to a "Thirties wireless set". At one point Stirling even spoke of breaking with Britain altogether, despite his place in the new trinity of British architecture (with Sir Richard Rogers and Sir Norman Foster).

Fond of food and drink and always struggling with his weight, Stirling was warned that a hernia operation could prove dangerous. It proved fatal. He was still at the height of his powers, with years of active designing potentially ahead of him. His most recent completed building was an elegant bookshop to complement the numerous temples of architecture, ancient and modern, at the Venice Biennale. Current projects include a masterplan for the Temasek polytechnic in Singapore and the revival of a 1985 project for a passenger interchanger at Bilbao in northern Spain.

He married in 1966 Mary, one of the two daughters of the modernist architectural and wine writer P. Morton Shand, thus becoming the brother-in-law of Sir Geoffrey Howe. She survives him with their son and two daughters.

b 1926   d 25.6.92   aged 66

Number One Poultry

SALLY MUGABE

Sally Mugabe, the wife of President Mugabe of Zimbabwe and a member of the politburo of the ruling Zanu(PF) party.

UNTIL laid low by illness, Sally Mugabe played an active political and charitable role in Zimbabwe. She earned the honorific title "Comrade Sally" for her visits to the guerrillas in the camps in Mozambique and Tanzania.

By 1962 Mr Mugabe had fallen foul of the authorities himself and was detained for his political activity. She, too, while pregnant, was put under house arrest but she slipped away. The child was later stillborn.

In 1963 she went to Tanzania and gave birth to a son, Nhamodzenyika ("the country's suffering"), who lived for only three years before dying of cerebral malaria in Ghana. Robert Mugabe was by then in his third year of a ten-year detention period and was refused permission to attend the funeral.

"I am a mother," she wrote in her autobiography. "I could have gone out and grabbed Ian Smith by the throat when I had to write and tell my husband that our child had died . . . But he taught me to realise that if you spend all your time wanting revenge you stay always in the position that you were before you gained your freedom." She moved to London, studying and working in a variety of jobs – including a spell as a teacher at the Africa Centre – and spending hours copying in longhand from texts borrowed from the local library to provide her husband with material for his studies in Wha Wha prison.

Independence in 1980 brought the couple to a stable home for the first time, having spent only six years of marriage out of 19 together. From then she acted as Zimbabwe's first lady, bringing a natural grace and West African spontaneity to official functions.

She maintained a relatively low political profile as deputy secretary in the Women's League of the ruling Zimbabwe African National Union (Patriotic Front). Although also a member of the party's politburo she was not easily accepted by most of her colleagues because of her Ghanaian nationality, her inability to speak the Shona vernacular fluently and the fact that she was in her position by virtue of her husband's authority.

This distrust deepened in 1989 when President Mugabe made the error of annulling Women's League elections and putting his wife in charge. He was accused of being manipulated by her. In any event the appointment meant little, as her illness confined her more and more to her bed.

During the last two years she was involved in establishing a campaign to raise money to assist poor and disabled children in Zimbabwe but as her illness worsened she appeared in public only infrequently. Her last public engagement was as hostess to the Commonwealth leaders in Harare in October 1991.

b 1933   d 27.1.92   aged 59

ANNE, COUNTESS OF ROSSE

Anne, Countess of Rosse, mother of the Earl of Snowdon.

GRAND-DAUGHTER of the *Punch* cartoonist and early photographer, Edward Linley Sambourne, Anne Messel married first Ronald Armstrong-Jones and then the 6th Earl of Rosse. In her own right she was one of Britain's most distinguished gardeners and a keen conservationist. In London her great achievement was the preservation of the intensely Victorian 18 Stafford Terrace.

Anne Messel descended from a German family, her grandfather Ludwig coming to England and setting up as a successful stockbroker. Others were architects and her great-uncle Rudolph was a distinguished scientist, who bequeathed a million pounds to the Royal Society. They married into a literary family which included Sheridan and Thomas Linley, composers.

Nymans, the house in Sussex, was bought by Ludwig Messel in 1890. Thus the family had been there for more than a century and house and garden have been nurtured by grandfather, father and latterly Lady Rosse herself. She was raised there and thoroughly trained by the Nymans plantsman, James Coomber, whom she described as "a terrifying Mr Macgregor". He once kept her hard at work for a whole day tying up wall-plants with reef knots. When her father cleared the gorse coverts for the latest batch of rhododendra from Tasmania and Chile, an act that greatly irritated the local hunt, the inferno raged so hard that the three Messel children were almost burned in the fray.

There was Linley, Anne, and her younger brother, Oliver, who raised the art of stage design to match the performance being given on stage and sometimes surpassed it. Anne was born at 27 Gloucester Terrace, London. Soon afterwards the family moved to 104 Lancaster Gate. As a child she gazed at the passing carriages in the Bayswater Road and apparently could see the cupolas and chimneys of Kensington Palace, without knowing the significance it would play in her family's later life.

The Messels also had a country home, Balcombe House, near St Leonard's Forest, but Nymans was always their favourite. Lady Rosse wrote of it: "Little else than farm carts, dog carts, and the carriages of the local gentry disturbed the quiet lane. . . . The Weald and woodlands belonged to themselves and to the neighbourhood, to live in peacefully, to farm in and to enjoy. Sundays were kept as Sundays should be, then, and farmers tossed their hay on summer evenings in linen smocks."

She was educated at home by a governess and in June 1922 was presented at court, already very pretty with her dark brown eyes. Anne met her first husband, Ronald Armstrong-Jones, through her brother Linley. They had been at Eton together and Linley invited him to Nymans in 1924 to ask his advice about the estate. Anne and Ronald were married in St Margaret's, Westminster, in July

1925, the occasion made memorable by the imaginative artistic touches of her brother, Oliver.

Her father, Colonel Messel, gave the young couple the lease of 25 Eaton Terrace, with a suitable endowment. It was soon adorned under Oliver Messel's baroque influence, tempered with the white of Syrie Maugham. They had two children, Susan (the late Viscountess de Vesci) born in 1927, and Antony (the present Lord Snowdon) in 1930.

During these years Anne took a prominent part in English social life. She was photographed by many of the great photographers of the day, often in an arcadian setting. As she veered more to the aesthetic tastes of her younger brother and his friends, so Ronald Armstrong-Jones became more serious and disapproving. His love for fishing and wild-fowling were not hers. Neither did his precision and desire for punctuality trim well with her heady social life. In 1933 they agreed to separate and in due course divorce followed.

Anne found long and lasting happiness with the Earl of Rosse, a man four years her junior. He had worshipped her since he was 18 and now he was able to claim her. In *The Letters of Evelyn Waugh* the editor, Mark Amory, revealed that this romance had endured difficult moments in Venice: "The Countess of Rosse stepped innocently on to a balcony with another man. Though they were not yet married, the jealous Earl of Rosse boxed her ears with some violence. When he sent long-stemmed tuberoses in apology, they were returned." Anne married Rosse in September 1935 and they had two sons, the elder of whom is the present Earl of Rosse.

Lord Rosse gave her the possibility of leading a yet more romantic life in his Gothic Irish castle, Birr, and at Womersley Park in Yorkshire, homes to which she had access for the rest of her life. Birr she adored, particularly the ancient staircase made of yew. Here young Tony Armstrong-Jones played and rowed on the lake and here too, later, he recovered from the polio which threatened his walking. It was Lady Rosse who gave her son his first camera, though she preferred the idea of his being an architect. Nevertheless she delighted in his success in his chosen profession.

During these years her parents lived on at Nymans, which was bequeathed to the National Trust in 1953. However, it remained her home and she and Lord Rosse not only preserved but nurtured it. Rosse continued the tradition of financing Far Eastern expeditions to bring experimental cuttings back to this country. As a gardener and householder, Lady Rosse believed that both house and garden should reflect "the personalities and whims of those who have trod its paths and the aspirations of its makers and improvers; mirroring a glimpse from each generation, that time and growth have moulded into a harmonious whole."

Lady Rosse was fortunate to possess a happy combination of Messel money and Sambourne taste to aid her in her work in the garden. Her husband shared her love of it and they relished their own expeditions to Portugal and the United States in search of plants. In recent years Nymans was run by six National Trust gardeners, overseen by Lady Rosse.

Socially she occupied a rare position. She was grand and very pretty. Society was occasionally disparaging about her. Evelyn Waugh referred to her in his diaries as "Tugboat Annie." And due to an ancient jealousy with Oliver Messel, she became the butt of Cecil Beaton's malice.

In her late eighties she retreated to Nymans, dwelling serenely in a world of her own. Lord Snowdon had a cottage on the land, likewise a welcome retreat from a busy life.

b 8.2.02 d 3.7.92 aged 90

THE MARQUESS OF BATH

Marquess of Bath with Hitler memorabilia

The 6th Marquess of Bath who opened the first of Britian's "safari parks" at Longleat.

ALTHOUGH he was not bright enough to gain admission to Eton and was regarded as "moronic beyond reach" by his headmaster at Harrow, the 6th Marquess of Bath was later to display a remarkable degree of innovative showmanship and entrepreneurial skill. He was the first owner of a stately home in Britain to exploit fully its commercial potential by opening it to fee-paying members of the public when, in 1949, he began charging 2s 6d (12½ pence) to see Longleat House at Warminster, Wiltshire. And in 1966 he opened the first of Britain's "safari parks" having converted 25 acres of Longleat Park into a game reserve featuring 12 lions, later to be joined by rhinos, giraffes, chimpanzees and other assorted wild animals. Both ventures proved immensely popular with the public, due in no small part to Bath's

superficially diffident self-promotion and his flair for publicity. In 1967 he was reported in the tabloid press to have stunned Whitehall by naming five chimpanzees Harold, George, Jim, Barbara and Edward, after the prime minister, three cabinet ministers and the leader of the opposition.

A languid, rangy figure, 6ft 2ins tall, as often as not to be found in frayed corduroys spraying the paths of the Longleat estate from a siphon of weed killer on his back, Bath fitted the mould of an eccentric aristocrat. Although he claimed to hate public speaking and never used his seat in the House of Lords for such activity he was forever being interviewed by the news media and airing, in rapid staccato phrases, provocative views with apparent naivety including the opinion that Hitler was "one helluva man".

If the need to attract visitors led to publicity stunts that compromised his dignity not just as a peer but as a human being, his motive was noble: to keep Longleat House going in the face of death duties and ever increasing maintenance costs.

Henry Frederick Thynne was the second son of the 5th Marquess by Violet, daughter of Sir Charles Mordaunt, Bart. His elder brother was killed in the first world war while serving in the dragoons. Having failed the common entrance examination to get into Eton, he went to Harrow and then to Christ Church, Oxford, where, he later admitted, he was "quite useless". He hated the idea of the two careers his father wanted for him, the army and politics. But after declining to join the army he gave way to politics and reluctantly stood as Conservative candidate for Frome. After defeating the sitting Labour candidate, he served as MP for the constituency from 1931 to 1935. In later life he claimed he was never respected so much as when he bore the letters "MP" after his name but admitted that parliamentary work was "the plague" of his life. He thankfully stood down at the next election to take over the running of his father's estate which included the Cheddar Gorge, a highly profitable trippers' attraction. His only other official positions were as a member of the council of the Duchy of Cornwall from 1933 to 1936 and as a Justice of the Peace for Wiltshire and many years later as chairman of the Football Pools Panel from 1967 to 1987.

During the second world war Bath served with the Royal Wiltshire Yeomanry and, after the commanding officer had been wounded, he led the "Moonrakers" tank charge at Tel El Aqaquoir in the final stage of the El Alamein breakthrough, sustaining a splinter wound in the throat in the process. For this action he was awarded the Bronze Star, conferred by President Roosevelt in recognition of services in the allied cause.

The death in 1946 of his father, the 5th Marquess, resulted in death duties of more that £600,000 having to be paid. Bath was forced to sell much of the family estates and on April 1, 1949, opened

Longleat to the public, acting as chief car park attendant himself and often being mistaken for a gardener because of his informal dress. This hackneyed situation, straight out of a P. G. Wodehouse novel, unceasingly delighted the popular press.

The house, one of the great historic piles of England, had been built between 1568 and 1580 for Sir John Thynne, Bath's direct ancestor, and Elizabeth I had stayed there. It was a mansion of 100 rooms, 60 of which were bedrooms but with only eight bathrooms. Bath's parents had been the last members of the family to live fully in the house, necessitating the employment of 40 servants to run it. Bath and his family lived at a smaller house in the grounds four miles away. The Longleat garden and grounds were remodelled and a chain of lakes made by Capability Brown in the late 18th century. Bath's first idea was to convert the house into a luxury hotel for wealthy Americans and other tourists visiting Britain but this plan fell through because of the lack of bathrooms and the difficulty of providing them. So instead Bath furnished the house as it was before 1914 and opened it to paying visitors. By 1957 the House had clocked up its one millionth visitor.

The 1960s were his best years. Variously described as "Britain's slimmest peer", "the tallest peer" and, because of his calculatedly indiscreet musings on such topics as shop stewards or General Franco, "the Fascist peer", he became a national celebrity. He appeared on television, won a bet against a Forestry Commission official over his method for catching squirrels, donned a wig and sang to 16,000 pop fans at a Longleat Rolling Stones concert and sent a telegram inviting the American boxer Cassius Clay to stay. He also put pedal-boats on the estate's Shearwater Lake.

Longleat possessed one of the world's finest private libraries (although Bath adroitly let it be reported that he had never read any of the contents).

The 1964 season had brought 200,000 visitors but maintaining these numbers called for showmanship and imagination. James Chipperfield of the circus family suggested to Bath that he should set up a safari park on the estate. The idea of having wild animals roaming the English countryside was extremely bizarre at the time. Friends and associates were overwhelmingly against it, saying it would be a commercial failure while the local people were opposed on safety grounds, fearing that the "mad marquess" would let all the lions loose. But Bath revelled in the prospect and the objectors were placated by the recruitment of armed game wardens to control the animals.

In 1966 Bath put his collection of Churchilliana on display, filling three rooms. Together with the lions this boosted attendance by 80,000. Six years earlier uproar had ensued at Sotheby's when Bath purchased two drab watercolour views of Vienna painted by Adolph Hitler for £280. He then got himself into trouble by expressing the view that he admired the Führer's ruthlessness. He could not help but admire someone, he said, who less than ten years after coming to power had almost won a world war, explaining that he was not pro-Nazi, simply fascinated by Hitler as a phenomenon. He had collected the pictures, he explained, the same way as other people collected Napoleana, and he also collected Churchilliana.

Longleat's maintenance costs were continuing to mount. Bath's wealth, though substantial, was tied up in the estate. Besides, visitors came principally for the circus animals and sightings of their owner. Accordingly, from 1967 Lord Bath installed hippos, chimpanzees and giraffes.

Following the successful television series *Upstairs Downstairs*, he exhibited waxworks of servants in Longleat kitchens. In 1972 he displayed costumes worn in a television series about Henry VIII's wives. Revenues fluctuated, however. The rise in oil prices in 1974 reduced his gate by 34 per cent.

He fought on, organising antiques valuations, convening teddy bear rallies, installing fair-ground attractions.

Attendance had dropped since the lions' debut. His bank overdraft mounted, reaching £80,000 by 1979. He had vowed never to part with a single possession from the house, but in 1979 he sold nearly 200 books from the great library, raising £322,865 in all.

By the late 1980s, however, circumstances had changed. Following the real estate boom Bath's wealth was estimated to have increased to around £200 million although it was all tied up in trusts. In any case Bath continued to live frugally, using a battered estate car, lunching either in the staff canteen or having a sandwich in a nearby public house.

Longleat needed constant attention and it was Bath's achievement to have given it. His theatricality was actually in the tradition of the Renaissance noblemen for whom houses like Longleat were built in the first place.

In the last few years of his life he and Lady Bath lived in their private retreat at Job's Mill, close to the main house. His family motto – "J'ay bonne cause" (I have good cause) – was always firmly in mind on his lifetime mission. Some years ago, he declared: "It is my personal creation. I set out to do Longleat up properly and to bring it back to its glory."

He married in 1927 the Hon Daphne Vivian, daughter of the 4th Lord Vivian, by whom he had three sons and a daughter. In 1953 when the marriage was dissolved it became known that the couple had married secretly a year before their public betrothal and it took an Appeal Court ruling in 1955 to establish that their divorce decree should apply to both ceremonies.

Later in 1955 Bath married Virginia, daughter of Alan Parsons and former wife of a country neighbour, the Hon David Tennant. By her he had a second daughter.

He is succeeded by his elder surviving son, Lord Weymouth.

b 26.1.05   d 30.6.92   aged 87

PRINCE GEORGE GALITZINE

Prince George Galitzine, businessman and Russian historian.

GEORGE Galitzine dressed and spoke like an English gentleman. The courtesy with which he invariably behaved was equally English. But his heart belonged to Russia. The Russian blood that ran through his veins could scarcely have been purer. His mother was a direct descendant of Catherine the Great, while on his father's side the Galitzines and the Romanovs could argue with one another over which family had the longer pedigree.

In 1919, when George was three, the Galitzines had to leave Russia swiftly in the wake of the revolution. They went, with little more than the clothes in which they stood, on a British ship first to Odessa, then to Italy and eventually to Paris, which appeared to be the natural place of asylum for Tsarist refugees. The Galitzines decided otherwise and opted for Britain as the country most likely to

give their young family a proper education.

Prince Vladimir Galitzine began by farming, none too successfully, in Surrey. He found much more success with a high class antiques shop specialising in Russian *objêts*, and George's public school fees, first at Lancing and then at St Paul's, were sometimes rendered in paintings. Russian dancers began visiting the Galitzine house and started George Galitzine's love of the ballet. Among the non-Russian dancers Pat (Anton) Dolin became an especial family friend.

A scholarship took Galitzine to Brasenose and while he was at Oxford he was awarded the medal of the Royal Humane Society. In 1936 he was on holiday in Scotland when an aircraft crashed close by at sea. Galitzine, a powerful swimmer, took to the waters and rescued the pilot. A short period of journalism, including a spell on *The Sunday Referee*, was interrupted by the war, when he was commissioned in the Welsh Guards and spent most of his time in intelligence as a "Whitehall warrior". Good use was made of his six European languages.

In 1943 he married Anne-Marie von Slatin, by whom he had two sons and a daughter. The marriage was later dissolved.

After the war George Galitzine had a chance to develop his diplomatic and entrepreneurial skills. He worked for six years in India and Pakistan, part of the time under the aegis of the Conservative government minister Walter Monckton, before joining Plessey in 1953 as sales manager. In the late 1950s his name was linked with the ice-skating star Belita, who was appearing in the musical *Damn Yankees*. But a proposed marriage was suddenly called off.

Instead, in 1963 George Galitzine married in the Russian Orthodox Church in Rome Jean Dawnay, former Dior model and familiar panellist on the television show *What's My Line?*, who was just beginnning to make a name for herself as an actress in plays such as *A Hatful of Rain*. His most successful business venture came with Rank in the early days of the Xerox copying machine. He helped establish offices in France and Italy before in 1961 he made his first return (for Rank) to the Russia he had left so abruptly over forty years before.

Thereafter he missed no opportunity to return to his native land. The best of these came after his retirement from British Steel in 1974. He first took a group of businessmen there but soon realised cultural tours could be rather more interesting. His deep knowledge of Russian history and art suddenly came to the fore and he found himself in great demand as guest lecturer from companies such as Serenissima and Jules Verne. The outcome was *Imperial Splendour: Palaces and Monasteries of Old Russia*, published last year and swiftly translated into French, German and Italian.

In Russia itself, and especially in St Petersburg, George Galitzine became something of a returning hero. He was regularly called "Tovaritch Kniaz" (Comrade Prince), a fairly contradictory form of address which gave him much pleasure.

His daughter, Katya, by his second wife, now lives in St Petersburg and is closely involved in the arts there. Galitzine was in St Petersburg at the time of the coup against Gorbachev and was immediately placed before the TV cameras as a man who had consistently helped reopen those windows on to the west.

b 3.5.16   d 31.3.92   aged 75

THE DUKE OF MONTROSE

The 7th Duke of Montrose, a Southern Rhodesian cabinet minister who was a signatory to the Unilateral Declaration of Independence in 1965.

SOME white Rhodesians who supported Ian Smith's unilateral declaration of independence from Britain favoured the appointment of the Duke of Montrose — or Lord Graham as he was better known in Africa — as "Regent" of an independent Rhodesia. In Britain there were calls for him to be prosecuted for treason and dispossesed of his land in Scotland, if not actually executed as had happened to his illustrious Royalist ancestor, the 1st Marquess of Montrose, in 1650.

As the head of one of Scotland's most ancient families and a member of the Rhodesian Front government, he played a prominent role in the drama of the white rebellion. He flew to London in 1959 to defend the Salisbury government's policies in his maiden speech in the House of Lords and was one of the four Rhodesian Front ministers closest to Ian Smith when the break with Britain was made in 1965. As the senior peer in Rhodesia he had some appeal as a figurehead among those anxious to retain a semblance of British tradition while prolonging for ever white rule in Africa. A large shambling man with an aristocratic eccentricity and a disarming charm, he was an unabashed white supremacist given to warning darkly of the dangers of communist infiltration of western civilisation and sexual subversion among the young, while lauding the innate superiority of white over blacks. Eventually he proved to be too right wing even for the Rhodesian Front.

Montrose had the rare distinction of being a member of two parliaments: having inherited his father's titles in 1954 he sat in the House of Lords as Earl Graham; four years later he was elected a member of parliament for Hartley-Gatooma in the federal assembly of the Federation of Rhodesia and Nyasaland. He served the government in Southern Rhodesia as minister of agriculture, lands and natural resources (1962-63) and minister of agriculture (1964-65). After UDI, Ian Smith made him minister of external affairs and defence (1966-68).

At his birth, James Angus Graham was heir to a series of ancient titles – Duke of Montrose, Marquess of Graham and Buchanan, Earl of Kincardine, Viscount Dundaff, Baron Aberuthven, Mugdock and Fintrie. He spent much of his childhood at Brodick Castle on the Isle of Arran, where he learned to speak Gaelic with which he was sometimes inclined to serenade fellow Rhodesians at late night parties in Salisbury years later. He was educated at Eton, where Lord Hailsham was among his contemporaries, and Christ Church, Oxford; and he boxed for both Eton and Oxford. After a spell in the RNVR he went out to Southern Rhodesia as an agronomist in 1931 and settled there, using the title Earl Graham.

On the outbreak of the second world war he rejoined the RNVR and served in destroyers involved in the evacuations of Greece and Crete. Later he commanded the *Ludlow* on convoy duty.

Back in Southern Rhodesia after the war he fought his first parliamentary election in 1953 for the Confederate Party, which was to the right of the right-wing Dominion party. He lost but was elected five years later under the auspices of the Dominion party, precursor of the Rhodesian Front. His attitude to Africans was clearly expressed in a document which he submitted to the 1960 Monckton

Commission enquiring into the constitution of the Federation of Rhodesia and Nyasaland, which he entitled "Factors Affecting African Psychology that should be Considered when Contemplating Widening Spheres of African Advancement". In this he wrote: "It is a common observation that the African child is a bright and promising little fellow up to the age of puberty, which he reaches in any case two years before the European. He then becomes hopelessly inadequate and disappointing and it is well-known that this is due to his almost total obsession, henceforth, in matters of sex. Whatever the reason for this most disappointing state of affairs, the phenomenon is recognised by practically every investigator."

With views such as these, Montrose had no difficulty in rising to political prominence in Rhodesia, joining the cabinet in 1962. Three years later, when Harold Wilson, then prime minister, visited Salisbury in an attempt to head off the independence rebellion, Montrose was called upon to entertain him at a dinner at Ian Smith's official residence. Recalling the incident in his memoirs, Wilson wrote: "I forbear recounting his story. Suffice it to say that it was about an American girl who was not a very good dancer, particularly in relation to the physical gestures with which she displayed her charms while dancing and her inability to master such a technique of the art as related to bumps, grinds and other advances of modern terpsichorean technology. How she was trained in these arts was dramatically recounted by Lord Graham who found it necessary to the point of his story to act the part in full with every gesture carried out by his enormous frame. Each time he went into one of the motions of the dance, he brushed his capacious frame against my face. Although I am normally tolerant, I found myself unimpressed by his performance."

Montrose himself maintained that he did not perform a solo dance – "though as a raconteur I no doubt swayed in sympathy with the lady's problems."

As a politician Montrose was regarded as unorthodox, even by Rhodesian standards. At a Christian crusade in Salisbury on one occasion he told his audience how the Beatles, international finance groups, colonial freedom movements and student agitators were all agents of a communist plot to achieve world domination. "Long before the Beatles and pop music began to affect our youngsters, I noticed how rhythm affects the Africans," he said. "Tired people, having worked all day in the fields, would be enticed into dancing to the beat of drums all night long until they were absolutely exhausted. This is the danger for young people. They can be completely confused by the power of rhythm. When they are exhausted almost anything can be planted in their minds."

Despite such views he insisted that he, and other whites in Rhodesia, had great faith in Africans, evidenced by the fact that they entrusted their wives and children to their care and lived among them in the remote bush.

But differences developed between them over the goal they were seeking. Montrose, together with William Harper, the minister of internal affairs, was opposed to Smith's proposal of a constitutional solution that would have involved an interim multi-racial parliament. He advocated an apartheid-style constitution which would have ensured white supremacy for all time. The Harper-Montrose proposals were narrowly defeated at the Rhodesian Front party congress in September 1968 and immediately afterwards Montrose resigned from the government citing his differences of opinion with the prime minister. His departure was seen as an attempt to crystallise opposition to Mr Smith from right wing elements but, although he was a respected and popular figure in the white community, he lacked the heavyweight political capabilities to mount a leadership challenge in his own right. In the event, the right wing threat to Ian Smith's leadership was doomed to failure. Montrose remained a member of the Rhodesian Front and a member of parliament until the next election. In 1972 he led a "palace revolution" at the Rhodesian Front party congress, on the grounds that it was undemocratic for one man to be both prime minister and party president. Right-wingers nominated him for the post of party president but, after satisfying himself that the majority of delegates were solidly behind the prime minister, he withdrew his name. During the 1970s Montrose made several attempts to visit Britain, particularly for the weddings of two of his children, but the government refused to lift the ban it had placed on him at the time of UDI.

In 1979, with majority rule and independence looming, he left Rhodesia to settle in Natal, South Africa. His 16-year exile from Britain finally ended in 1980 when he returned to celebrate his 73rd birthday in Scotland. Rhodesian Front rule having been replaced by majority rule in what was now Zimbabwe, the voices that had called for Montrose to be charged with treason were this time silent and he was able to escape the fate that befell the 1st Marquess of Montrose. Indeed he returned to the House of Lords and spent his last years peacefully in Kinross. He had a son and daughter by his first marriage to Isobel Sellar, which was dissolved in 1950 and two sons and two daughters by his second marriage in 1952 to Susan Gibbs. His heir is his eldest son, James Graham, Marquess of Graham.

b 2.5.07   d 10.2.92   aged 84

EARL SPENCER

Earl Spencer, LVO, DL, 8th earl and father of the Princess of Wales.

SOME men are born famous, others achieve fame, but few have it thrust upon them so forcibly as this amiable peer. His distinction reflected the fame of his immediate family.

Earl Spencer's daughter, Diana, became the Princess of Wales in 1981. It was his deportment, still affected by a stroke he had sustained three years before, on the day of her marriage to the Prince of Wales on July 29, 1981, that gave him a place in the hearts of the nation. Although weak and still unsteady on his feet, he conducted himself with courage and determination during a long and exhausting day of pageantry which involved him in escorting his daughter up the long aisle of St Paul's Cathedral and standing on the cathedral steps after the ceremony.

Contact with the Royal family was, of course, nothing new to Earl Spencer. In the 1950s he had been an equerry successively to King George VI and the Queen. As such he had accompanied the Queen on the Commonwealth tour which was one of the principal features of the early part of her reign. Some aspects of his family life did not give such unalloyed pleasure as his youngest daughter's marriage. His son, Lord Althorp, soon developed an impetuous public personality of his own and was rarely out of the newspapers.

His second wife, the novelist Barbara Cartland's daughter, Raine, was a powerful figure whose devotion to her husband from their marriage in 1976 never wavered, even if to outsiders it often seemed to be domination. That this devotion to her husband could be a force for his own good never reconciled her to her stepchildren. She saved his life in 1978 by procuring a new, untested drug to treat his stroke. Her redecoration and aggressive marketing of what might have been a steadily decaying stately home at Althorp in Northamptonshire brought it a new prosperity and dynamism. But this too increased family unhappiness at Lady Spencer's ascendancy, which became desperate as the couple began selling off family heirlooms, sales that reached what many conservationists considered a crisis in 1991.

Edward John ("Johnny") Spencer was the only son of parents whose families had long served as courtiers. Known as Lord Althorp until his father died in 1975, he was educated at Eton and Sandhurst and subsequently joined the Royal Scots Greys. Though his military career was brief, he was mentioned in dispatches during the second world war.

From 1947 to 1950 he was ADC to the Governor of South Australia. In 1950 he became equerry to George VI, continuing in the post until 1954 under the present Queen. He joined the Queen's Commonwealth tour of 1953–54 as equerry and acting Master of the Household. A keen amateur cameraman, he filmed many of the tour's events. On his return to Britain he showed the film around Norfolk with a running commentary of his own, raising £2,500 for charity.

In June 1954 he married the Hon Frances Roche, daughter of the 4th Lord Fermoy, and subsequently settled down to farm near Sandringham. In Northamptonshire, where Althorp is situated, he served as High Sheriff and Deputy Lieutenant. In Norfolk he sat on the bench and the local council. A more *outré* post was his chairmanship of the Schoolmistresses' and Governesses' Benevolent Institution from 1962, though it was appropriate in view of his youngest daughter's later employment at a Pimlico kindergarten. In 1969 the Althorp's were divorced. He obtained custody of the children and struggled to bring them up alone. His second marriage with Raine, divorced wife of Lord Dartmouth, followed their shared involvement in European Heritage Year in 1975.

Lord and Lady Spencer – it became impossible to regard their activities separately – threw themselves energetically into showing Althorp to the public. The guidebook was a joint effort: his remarkably professional photographs, her effusive text. They had already collaborated on a pamphlet entitled *What is Our Heritage?* with colleagues in 1975. They installed a wine mart at Althorp and introduced "own-label" wines. Attempts were made to attract Japanese package tours and conferences. The exercise was reminiscent of some of the Duke of Bedford's earlier commercial efforts at Woburn. While it had its purist detractors, such entrepreneurship is at least one way of ensuring that such great houses can survive in private hands.

But death duties as well as Althorp's upkeep remained a problem. The Spencers sold valuable paintings and other possessions, challenging those who believe that every house must be forced to retain all its existing works of art, irrespective of financial shortages. Art historians rate the Althorp collection highly, but it remains one of the finest in private hands and Earl Spencer's sales can hardly be described as catastrophic.

Earl Spencer's eldest daughter, Sara Lavinia, married in 1980, Neil Edmund McCorquodale; his second daughter, Jane, married, in 1978, Sir Robert Fellowes, KCVO, CB, Private Secretary to the Queen. His son and heir, who now succeeds him, married in 1989, the former model Victoria Lockwood; they have one daughter.

b 24.1.24   d 29.3.92   aged 68

GRAND DUKE VLADIMIR

Grand Duke Vladimir in Paris (1938)

Grand Duke Vladimir of Russia, head of the Romanov imperial family overthrown in 1917.

THROUGHOUT his life Vladimir Kirillovitch nursed the hope that one day he might be Tsar of all the Russias. A tall man with the bearing of a Cossack, he spoke fluent but old-fashioned Russian, having never set foot in the country of his royal forefathers until November last year, following the collapse of communism. It was then that he travelled to St Petersburg to attend the ceremonies marking the reinstatement of the city's Romanov name, describing the moment as one of "indescribable joy."

Vladimir Kirillovitch was the third child and only son of the Grand Duke Kirill Vladimirovitch and Victoria Feodorovna de Saxe Cobourg, a granddaughter of Queen Victoria. His father was a first cousin, and the closest surviving male relative of Nicholas II following the June

1918 massacre of the Tsar and most of the royal family.

A year earlier as the revolution was beginning, the Grand Duke Kirill had fled with his two daughters and his pregnant wife to Finland where Vladimir was born. In 1924, when it had been established to the satisfaction of all but a few diehards that the imperial family had been murdered, the Grand Duke Kirill issued a manifesto proclaiming himself head of the House of Romanoff and legitimate pretender to the throne of Russia, "Emperor of all the Russias".

The exiled family settled in Saint Briac, France, where at the age of 16, in accordance with Russian law, Vladimir came of age, swearing an oath of fealty to the Grand Duke. He was educated privately and then at Paris's Russian Lycée and London University and could speak fluent French, German, English and Spanish as well as Russian.

In 1938, on the death of his father,

Vladimir issued his own proclaimation laying claim to the throne although, unlike his father, he said he would not "for the present" use the imperial title, preferring to be addressed as Grand Duke. A year later he returned to Britain and began working in a machine factory near Peterborough "to experience personally the life of a factory workman." The job was arranged for him by Lord and Lady Astor and he worked under the pseudonym "Mikhailoff", the same name that Peter the Great had adopted while working in the royal shipyards in Deptford.

He remained in France throughout most of the second world war. At one time it was rumoured that he had received emissaries from Hitler attempting to negotiate his return to a puppet throne in Russia but the rumours were generally regarded as without foundation as Vladimir was fiercely opposed to Nazi policy towards Russia. Then, as the allied landings became imminent, he was obliged by the German authorities to move eastwards. At one time, he later recalled, he found himself in a village with the Soviet army advancing fast towards him. "The prospect of meeting them," he said "was most uncomfortable."

Instead, armed with a safe conduct pass from the German authorities, he motored down alone to a village in the westernmost tip of Austria. He remained there for 17 months until he was able to cross into Switzerland and from there travel to Spain where he settled.

In 1948 Vladimir married in Switzerland, Princess Leonida, the second daughter of Prince George Bagration-Mukhransky of Georgia. She had been married previously to Sumner Moore Kirby, an American who had died in a Nazi concentration camp in 1945.

For most of his life Vladimir was a full-time pretender. He once told an interviewer that he was busy most days dealing with his correspondence, adding, perhaps mistakenly, that he received about a dozen letters a day. He and his family lived in substantial residences in St Briac, Paris and Madrid enjoying a relatively luxurious life-style but he said the stories of a vast Romanov family fortune being salted away were untrue. Commenting on the claims of a woman called Anna Andersen to be the Grand Duchess Anastasia, a surviving child of Nicholas II, Vladimir said nothing would have given him greater pleasure than to believe that a daughter of the last emperor had survived. But the family had investigated the claim; his own sister, Kira, had visited the woman and it was 99.9 per cent improbable that she really was Anastasia.

Vladimir was an energetic man maintaining contacts with exiled White Russian compatriots and travelling widely. After a life in exile lived in parallel with the rise and decline of the Soviet regime, its demise gave Vladimir grim satisfaction moderated only by the desperate plight of the Russian people. He viewed the reforms in the Soviet Union instituted by Mikhail Gorbachev as hopeful ones and last year expressed his readiness to back Boris Yeltsin, the Russian president.

He remained determined that whatever happened in his homeland, the Romanov claim to the Russian throne would stay alive.

"It is something you cannot give up, because you are born with it," he said. He is survived by his wife and one daughter, the Grand Duchess Marie Vladimirowa, who was born in 1953. She married Prince Franz-Wilhelm of Prussia in 1976 and succeeds her father as head of the Russian imperial family.

The grand duke is also survived by a grandson, the Grand Duke George of Russia, aged 11.

b 30.8.17　d 21.4.92　aged 74

JIM JOEL

Jim Joel and Maori Venture

H. J. "Jim" Joel, race horse owner, breeder and member of the Jockey Club.

JIM Joel was a pillar of the racing establishment, albeit a most unassuming one, and was one of the last links, through family connection, with the more spacious and sporting Edwardian era of the Turf. That connection was reinforced by the fact that, with Edward VII (when Prince of Wales), Joel had the rare distinction of having owned both a winner of the Derby and of the Grand National.

Royal Palace, who had also won the Two Thousand Guineas in 1957, was his Derby triumph, trained by the late Sir Noel Murless and ridden by the Australian champion George Moore. He had bred the colt, a descendant of Picture Play, winner of the One Thousand Guineas in 1944, when she provided Joel with his first Classic success.

Joel was much admired for his sporting but unfashionable decision to keep his Derby winner in training as a four-year-old instead of following the standard modern practice of hustling him away to stud lest lack of subsequent success should devalue his worth as a stallion. The policy was both justified and richly rewarded when Royal Palace added the Coronation Cup, the Eclipse Stakes, and the King George and Queen Elizabeth Stakes to his former triumphs, netting a prize money total of £166,063.

There was no less admiration of this popular owner because of his staunch and enthusiastic support of National Hunt racing. The leading Flat owners are not generally noted for their support of the winter game. Joel's enthusiasm brought many rewards and his crowning moment came when Maori Venture won the Seagram Grand National in 1987.

The famous racing colours of "black, scarlet cap", were first made known on every racecourse in the land by Joel's father, Jack Barnato Joel, who had owned no fewer than eleven Classic winners and who, with his brother Solly, was a dominant and distinguished figure on the turf in the early years of this century. Their father (Jim Joel's grandfather) had kept the King of Prussia public house in the East End of London. It yielded only a bare living and, in their early twenties, and relatively poor, the brothers sailed for South Africa and the Kimberley diamond fields in order to join an elder brother, Woolf, and their uncle Barney Barnato.

Barnato (originally Barnett Isaacs: his adopted name derived from his early days on the music halls) became, with Cecil Rhodes, one of the most influential and respected figures in the diamond industry. Under his guidance and with their own financial acumen, the brothers were millionaires before they were 30 and extended their influence beyond diamond mines to many other businesses in South Africa including breweries and collieries. Barney Barnato, however, was drowned at sea in 1897, and two years later the elder brother was murdered. So, in 1899 Solly took over leadership of their huge enterprises, while Jack returned to England to represent their companies' interests in the City – and to pursue his Turf career.

He bought the Childwick Bury Stud near St Albans.

The stud showed an early return on investment when the homebred Picture Play won a wartime One Thousand Guineas in 1944, ridden by Charlie Elliott and saddled by Joel's private trainer, J. E. Watts at Foxhill. Picture Play traced to a mare called Absurdity who had bred two Classic winners for her owner's father. When Picture Play was retired to the paddocks at Childwick Bury, she herself became an outstanding broodmare. Of her direct descendants, three became Classic winners for her owner.

A further three were placed in various Classics: West Side Story, beaten by only inches for the 1962 Oaks by the French-trained Monade, but the best filly of that year both in England and Ireland; Photo Flash, runner-up in the One Thousand Guineas, 1968; and Welsh Pageant, third in the following year in the Two Thousand Guineas. Apart from Picture Play's produce, the Childwick Bury Stud provided many other first-class horses and other Classic near misses for Joel. Among the latter was Connaught who, in 1968, came near to giving him a second Derby in succession. Approaching the final furlong Connaught looked unbeatable, but was cut down by the acceleration of Sir Ivor, ridden by Lester Piggott. Major Portion was another homebred Classic runner-up, being beaten in the 1958 Two Thousand Guineas by Pall Mall, carrying the colours of HM The Queen. Later in the St James's Palace Stakes Major Portion reversed the placings.

This was but one of Joel's victories at Royal Ascot where he enjoyed phenomenal success with 26 victories over four decades.

The achievements of Joel as a breeder were complemented by those of horses he bought. He possessed keen judgement in the sale ring. Henry the Seventh, secured for 3,500 guineas at Newmarket Sales is a good example. Trained by Bill Elsey in Yorkshire, Henry the Seventh won four races in 1961, culminating in a dead-heat for the Cambridgeshire; then, the following season, he took the Zetland Gold Cup, the Rous Memorial Stakes and the Eclipse Stakes. Another purchase led to Predominate becoming, at an age when most Flat horses have retired, the most popular runner to carry the Joel colours.

Predominate was bought for hurdling; but despite having won over obstacles, he patently disliked them, so was put back to Flat racing. Trained by Ted Leader, Predominate then proceeded, between 1958 and 1960, to win the 2m 3f Goodwood Stakes three years in a row, then the following season was victorious in the even longer-distanced Goodwood Cup.

Jim Joel's quiet, unassuming manner earned him many friends in racing, the admiration of the public because there was never a breath of suspicion about the running of his horses, and the immense respect of his trainers and jockeys to whom he was unfailingly loyal.

b 4.9.94   d 23.3.92   aged 97

KITTY GODFREE

Kitty Godfree, née Cathleen McKane, ladies singles champion at Wimbledon in 1924 and 1926 and Olympic gold medal winner.

KITTY Godfree was twice Wimbledon singles champion when the prize was a five guinea gift token and tennis manners were more polite. But tennis was not her only game. She was badminton champion of Great Britain and was chosen to play for England against Scotland at lacrosse in 1918 only to find the match cancelled because of the war. She also pursued golf, cricket and skating, winning a medal from the Skating Association at the age of ten. In her nineties she was still playing tennis: a legendary heroine of British tennis, who remained a familiar figure at Wimbledon, not least in the sporadic parades of former champions.

Kitty was proud of one event in her life

even before her later sporting triumphs. Before she was ten she joined her parents, sister and governess on a 600 mile journey from High Street, Kensington, to Berlin by bicycle, an extraordinary feat for two young girls. Her father also took the family to see the winter sports at St Moritz. Open air activities and sport were their upbringing, particularly at St Leonard's School in St Andrews in fresh Scottish air. There were daily cold baths and a healthy life.

The first world war prevented her from playing serious tournament tennis until she was 22. Kitty Godfree was remarkable on at least three counts. She won Wimbledon twice during the era of two of the greatest players in the game's history, Suzanne Lenglen and Helen Wills. In 1926 she shared a unique mixed doubles triumph with her husband, Leslie Godfree. She was also the All England Badminton champion four times, and in 1924 she held the tennis and badminton titles at the same time.

When Godfree achieved her singles triumphs in 1924 and 1926, she also shared in both years the mixed doubles title, first with Jack Gilbert, and then, five months after their marriage, with her husband. Both her partners played for Britain in the Davis Cup competition. From 1923 to 1934 Godfree also represented her country. In the annual Wightman Cup contest with the United States she broke even in ten singles, and won two of her seven doubles. She also shared three doubles titles — two women's, one mixed — in the United States championships, and in 1925 was runner-up to Helen Wills in the singles. In addition, Godfree won an assortment of gold, silver, and bronze medals in the Olympic Games of 1920 and 1924. She competed at Wimbledon from 1919 to 1934, and her first singles triumph was remarkable in that she was drawn to play both of those great players, Lenglen and Wills. Lenglen had to scratch from their semi-final because of the after-effects of jaundice, and in the final Godfree came from behind to beat Wills, 4–6, 6–4,

6–4. Wills, then 18, and competing at Wimbledon for the first time, was champion on eight occasions. Godfree was the only player to beat her in the Wimbledon singles.

In 1926, the window of opportunity opened again — and again Kitty Godfree jumped through it. Wills was not competing and Lenglen, who was expected to win, scratched from the tournament in controversial circumstances — her temperament clashed with that of the referee over the peripheral details of scheduling — after having reached the third round. In the final Godfree, as in 1924, came from behind to win, this time against Lili de Alvarez, of Spain.

Kitty Godfree was one of Britain's finest, most tenacious competitors. Her footwork was good, and her game briskly aggressive. She had a powerful forearm and was one of the first players to use the volley to good advantage when moving up to the net. She was never an easy player to beat — and never wasted an opportunity to win.

She came to see big changes in the game. The strokes were pretty well the same but the ball was now hit harder, she said, the racket design increased speed of play and serving led the game. In her day the service just put the ball into play.

To show her joy of living, she used to play friendly mixed doubles at Wimbledon up to the age of 90, often partnering the Frenchman Jean Borotra. Kitty Godfree had a busy retirement up to the end. She flew to the Los Angeles Olympics in 1984 and was invited to Paris by the French to present the trophy to the women's singles champion Chris Evert.

But her greatest distinction came in June 1986. That was Wimbledon's centenary year and, as the oldest surviving champion of Wimbledon, she was invited to present the prize to the ladies champion, Martina Navratilova.

A widow for many years, she leaves two sons, David and Martin.

b 7.5.96   d 19.6.92   aged 96

REG HARRIS

Reginald Hargreaves Harris, world champion racing cyclist.

REG Harris brought courage to a natural talent for sporting achievement. He needed it in a life that was punctuated by adversity, both on and off his bicycle, and by controversy.

He was riding through the lanes of his much loved Cheshire only two days before his death when he was believed to have suffered a minor stroke. Heart problems had featured in the later years of his life but, true to character, he was at first reluctant to go to hospital. Finally he agreed, but there suffered a further stroke.

During his racing career Reg Harris won five world sprint championships, one as an amateur and four as a professional, and broke world records. He had set himself the highest standards and in retirement he was critical of the state of British sprint cycling. Indeed he felt so strongly that thirty years after he had won his first national amateur championship, Harris made a comeback. He proved his point by winning the British professional title at Leicester in 1974 at the age of 54.

Reg Harris grew up in Lancashire, the son of a shoemaker, and saved the money from his work at a local paper mill to finance his passion for cycling, which had started as a schoolboy. He was prepared to work seven days a week during the winter in order to cycle during the summer. During the war he served in the 10th Hussars and was considered lucky to have escaped from a blazing tank in North Africa after an encounter with the Germans.

Harris was always reluctant to discuss the background to his injuries. Instead, he demonstrated his great courage in setting about regaining the speed that had seen him selected for Britain's world track championship team in Milan in 1939. But, with war appearing to be just around the corner, the team was ordered home before the competition started.

Declared unfit for further military duties, Harris had returned to racing a year before his discharge and in 1944 won his first British amateur sprint title, his speciality. He was to continue an unbroken run of successes through to his last in 1947. By that time he had exchanged the scrawny legs of a teenager for two well-muscled adult pistons that drove him at 40mph in a finishing sprint.

Harris, once a railway ticket clerk, became the first of a group of young British riders to attempt to join mainland Europe's racing "circus" and, for many years, was the only one to succeed. His reputation was quickly established and at the back of his mind was the thought that, with so many of the top Continental riders passing into the autumn of their careers, the possibility of turning professional had greater attractions, especially financial ones, than remaining an outstanding amateur.

When Harris won his first world sprint title on the original Parc des Princes track in Paris in July 1947 he had succeeded in overcoming those wartime injuries and took Britain's first "rainbow jersey" (arc en ciel) since the victory of Harold Johnson in 1922.

Harris was fortunate in two respects at that time. He had an invaluable rapport with a Manchester Wheelers team colleague, Tom MacDonald, and he had also attracted the support of the country's foremost cycle manufacturer, Raleigh. But the lonely transition to the cash ranks (there were no other British professionals at the time) was suspended for another year.

Harris wanted to win the Olympic title at the London Games in 1948, knowing that it would enhance future contract money and make him an attractive asset to a sponsor. His build-up for the Games was disastrous. When the British track season started on the Good Friday with the traditional opening meeting at Herne Hill he was missing.

Driving to the venue Harris was involved in an accident serious enough to jeopardise his Olympic hopes and, possibly, his entire future as a champion cyclist. He had two broken bones in his spine and doctors were not optimistic about a permanent recovery. The courage of Harris was evident again. Within a month he was riding, albeit at a snail's pace, and in early May he returned to competition.

There was a further setback to overcome when, in one of his early races, Harris crashed, breaking a bone in his wrist. The Games were only a month away; Harris had been selected for the individual sprint and also to pilot Alan Bannister in the tandem event.

There were moments in the interim when Harris must have believed that he would never go to the line in the Olympic competition, becoming involved in a row with the then controlling body, the National Cyclists' Union, and losing his place in the team.

He had been required to complete his final training in London with the rest of the squad. But Harris, by now used to being a "loner" and preferring to make all his own arrangements, did not find the camp's facilities suitable and returned home to Manchester to train by himself.

The NCU removed him from the team. Peace moves lasted for days but eventually Harris, now mentally as well

as physically injured, was reinstated. His condition showed once the Games started. He lost the Olympic gold to Italy's newcomer, Mario Ghella, in the two-man final. It was again to be silver in the tandem sprint when all Harris's strength and courage were needed as his machine's front wheel punctured at high speed in the semi-finals. His handling of the tandem, keeping upright, saved him and Bannister from possible serious injury on the cement track. That display gained him some of the biggest applause of his career.

Harris had his first professional race in October that year. It was an inauspicious debut. He punctured and crashed in Brussels. But that memory was quickly wiped out. In 1949 Harris was firmly established as a professional and launched a brilliant run of four world titles (1949, 50, 51 and 54) to add to his 1947 amateur championship.

He was hailed as one of Britain's great postwar sports ambassadors at a time when our sporting achievement, weakened by the war, was distinctly poor and in 1950 he won the Sportsman of the Year award with a clear majority from the footballer Billy Liddell. Whenever Harris raced abroad he was appreciated not only for his cycling prowess but because he was articulate, spoke fluent French, was immaculate in dress and of impeccable behaviour.

Among the disappointments he felt in retirement was that national organisations did not take advantage of his experience, knowledge and contacts. He would have been a hard taskmaster as a team manager, but Britain's cyclists might have been persuaded to reflect his own golden days. Instead he became a successful businessman – and then he was persuaded to take up professional cycling again in his early fifties by his own doctor.

He married three times and leaves a widow, Jennifer.

b 1.3.20   d 22.6.92   aged 72

DENNY HULME

Denis "Denny" Hulme, Formula One world motor racing champion in 1967, died of a heart attack during the Bathurst 1000 saloon car endurance race in Australia.

THERE could scarcely by a more vivid contrast than that between today's publicity conscious and wealth-seeking motor racing champions and Denny Hulme, who won the 1967 Formula One World Championship in a Brabham-Repco, retiring to his native New Zealand seven years later.

Throughout his long career, which began in 1955 at the wheel of an MG TF and included eight grand prix victories between 1967 and 1974, two with Brabham and the remainder with McLaren, he was motivated solely by his love of race driving. Wealth was of little concern to him and he abhorred the publicity which came his way at the height of his fame, although in recent years he seemed to take quiet enjoyment at being celebrated as something of a "golden oldie" on his occasional return visits to Europe.

The most recent of these was last May, when he revisited Monaco on the twenty-fifth anniversary of his first grand prix victory there, but more important to him was his journey to Goodwood a few days later for the unveiling of a memorial stone to his former team-mate and close friend Bruce McLaren, who had been killed at the circuit in 1970 while testing one of the Can-Am sports cars.

During the 1960s, McLaren and Hulme had completely dominated the North American race series, where they were known affectionately as the Bruce and Denny show.

It was on McLaren's death that the calibre of Hulme was to be seen in painful vividness. Weeks earlier, his hands had become so badly burned in an alcohol fire at Indianapolis that he could scarcely touch a steering wheel for fear of exacerbating his wounds. Yet soon he was back in a McLaren cockpit, racing in agony and lengthening his recovery in a selfless effort to help restore the morale of his shattered team.

Hulme dismissed it all as "just a job that had to be done", much as his father, the late Clive Hulme, would do when questioned on how he won the Victoria Cross in Crete. Denny Hulme's formidable appearance earned him the nickname The Bear, which he rather enjoyed and at times pretended to live up to, usually with the help of a minimum of well-selected words.

In reality, he was a shy and modest man, and when he was not behind the wheel of a racing car, or in recent times even a racing truck, he was at his most content tending the restoration and operation of his collection of stationary steam engines.

Hulme was the only son of a haulage contractor. Soon after his birth, the family moved to a small town called Te Puke in the Bay of Plenty province, North Island. Never much of a scholar, he was fond of engineering and was a natural mechanic. He learned to drive at the age of eight, obtained his private

*Denny Hulme at the wheel of the McLaren Ford with Sir Dennis Blundell (centre)
and Bruce McLaren (1970)*

driving licence at 15 and a heavy traffic licence at 18.

On leaving school, he worked in a local garage repairing cars, tractors and even washing-machines before taking over the maintenance of his father's transport fleet.

Hulme made his motor sport debut in 1955 in a hill-climb, driving a new MG TF, and granduated through a series of sprints and club meeting to his first major victory at Ardmore in December 1957. From that moment he was determined to become a professional driver.

After an important victory in a Cooper Climax at the Vic Hudson Memorial Trophy at Levin early in 1960, Hulme and his compatriot George Lawton were jointly chosen by the New Zealand International Grand Frix Association to be sponsored for a season of European racing. Their promising progress was tragically cut short when Lawton was killed at Roskilde, Denmark in September. Hulme returned home for the 1960–1 season and won the New Zealand drivers' championship in a Yeoman Credit Cooper.

He came back to Europe in 1961 and started his long struggle for recognition in the tough Formula Junior category. In 1962 he went to work for Jack Brabham (word champion driver in 1959, 1960 and 1966) as a racing mechanic and there is no doubt that Brabham must take much of the credit for advising and moulding Hulme into world championship material. Hulme was a driver who lived, breathed and dreamed about racing cars and before long he was not only driving a works Formula Junior Brabham, but was rated one of the best and most ruthless drivers in Europe.

Brabham was pleased with his tyro's progress and entrusted him with a drive in the 1964 Tasman series, where he won at Pukekohe and had several other meritorious drives. With the advent of the new Formula Two category in 1964 (1000cc cars), Hulme really got into his stride and carried the Brabham marque to victory at Clermont-Ferrard and finished runner-up to Brabham himself in the French F2 championship.

Hulme made his Formula One debut in 1965 and drove a works-entered Brabham in six championship events, finishing fourth in the French and fifth in the Dutch grand prixs. He was also unbeaten in the Group 7.2-litre class with a Brabham BT8 and won the Tourist Trophy for the first time that year. He repeated this success in 1966.

It was in 1966 that Hulme really came to the fore with some electrifying successes with Sid Taylor's Lola T70: a fourth place in the drivers' world championships, second at Le Mans in the 24-hour race in a Ford, and many brilliant supporting roles to Brabham in the all-conquering Formula Two Brabham-Honda cars.

He won his first grand prix victory at Monaco in May 1967, driving the 3-litre Brabham Repco. This was the start of an excellent year. He was second to Brabham in the French Grand Prix, second to Clark in the British event but won the German race on the formidable Nurburging circuit.

He took a second in the Canadian GP and a third in the United States race at Watkins Glen. The world championship was not decided until the Mexican GP in October. Jim Clark won the race, Brabham came second and Hulme, needing only to get a place in the first five, finished third. He thus beat into second place his patron and team-mate Brabham,

the 1966 champion, by 51 points to 48.

The following year Hulme joined the Bruce McLaren team at Colnbrook, Buckinghamshire, and drove McLaren F1 and Can-Am cars. He stayed with the team for five seasons. He was placed third in world championship, winning the Italian and Canadian GPs and coming second in the Spanish GP. He also won the non-championship F1 *Daily Express* Trophy at Silverstone. He was Can-Am champion for the first time, winning the Road Amercian at Elkhart Lake, the Klondike Trail 200 at Edmonton and the Stardust GP, Las Vegus.

In 1969 he was placed sixth in the drivers' championship, winning the Mexican GP.

After McLaren's death in 1970, he took over as leader of the team and was fourth in world championship with a second place in the South African GP, third in the British, German and Mexican GPs and fourth in the Monaco, French and Italian GPs.

He was also Can-Am champion for a second time. In 1971 Hulme won at Mosport Park, Edmonton and Riverside, to become runner-up in the Can-Am series.

He is survived by his wife Greeta, whom he married in 1963, and their daughter Adele. Their son Martin was killed in a boating accident a few years ago.

b 18.6.36   d 4.10.92   aged 56

Jackie Stewart leads Denny Hulme at Brands Hatch (1970)

ARTHUR LEES

Arthur Lees, British Ryder Cup golfer four times between 1947 and 1955.

PROFESSIONAL golf, indeed the game as a whole, has lost one of its richest characters with the death of Arthur Lees. Lees played in four Ryder Cup matches soon after the war. It was an era when the United States made a habit of overpowering any British team, but Lees emerged with his head high. He scored four points out of eight and recorded Britain's only two victories at Pinehurst, North Carolina, in 1951. He was twice sixth in the Open championship, in 1947 and again two years later.

In 1950 he finished second to Match-Play champion Dai Rees in the year's order of merit and in 1956, while suffering from a sprained left thumb, he shattered the course record at Stoneham, Southampton, with 65 in the southern qualifying section of the Match-Play championship, winning the southern professional championship with 135 for 36 holes.

A burly, free-hitting golfer with an unspectacular method, typical of a natural player, Lees believed in maximum results rather than theatrical showmanship. His successes were built upon his exceptional ability with his irons and, on his day, he was a phenomenal putter. Lees began his golfing career as a boy caddie at Lees Hall, Sheffield, where, at the age of 14 in 1923, he came under the wing of J. H. Atkinson. He developed rapidly and after a seven year apprenticeship took an appointment at Marienbad, Czechoslovakia. From there he returned to Sheffield and from the Dore and Totley club became a golf world personality. He was a late choice for the 1947 Ryder Cup team but two years later was an automatic selection.

Lees's reputation ripened in later years when his Yorkshire accent remained undiluted by close proximity to fashionable Sunningdale, where he was the club professional from 1949 to 1977. "Nothing rubbed off on him", said Keith Almond, Sunningdale's secretary until last year. "And he was honoured for it."

He underwent an operation for cancer of the bladder 15 years ago and his life was in the balance, but an indomitable will carried him through and he survived several later crises.

Lees was an accomplished raconteur and if some of his stories seemed too tall at the time his exact repetition of them down to the last detail, year after year, testified to their authenticity. He seemed able to recall every golf shot ever played. He was never short of listeners as he held court in the Sunningdale club house or out on one of the two courses.

He was a wily opponent right up to 1989, when at last he had to put his clubs away. Even with a shortened swing he was something of a wizard around Sunningdale and was never known to refuse a bet.

A club stalwart remembered yesterday an occasion when Lees gave a four up start to Major Dolt-Henderson, an American amateur recently returned from a victory on the continent. All betting save for one shrewd punter was on the American. Lees then played the first nine holes of the Old course in 27 strokes and reached the turn three up. It was a bookies' bonanza.

When Lees joined Sunningdale soon after the war the club was in trouble, seriously short of members, whereupon Lees, a man very much in the Fred Trueman, Harvey Smith mould, became a self-apponted recruiting agent. Some of his initiates, were not, perhaps, typical of Sunningdale, as we now know it, but at least they helped the club to recover from the ravages of hostilities.

He was much sought after as a coach, especially by good golfers. Those who enlisted his help included Dai Rees and Norman Von Nida, the eminent Australian.

Lees, a widower, is survived by his son.

b 21.2.08   d 26.3.92   aged 84

IAN PROCTOR

Ian Proctor, yachtsman who was responsible for the Merlin Rocket, Osprey, Wayfarer and Topper dinghy designs.

IAN Proctor was Britain's most prolific small boat designer, and died while watching the world championship of one of his most enduring class designs, the Wayfarer. He produced more than 100 dinghy and small keel boat designs including the Topper dinghy, now 35,000 strong, and the Tempest, the two-man keelboat chosen for the 1972 and 1976 Olympic Games.

Although disabled by polio during the second world war, Proctor was also a first-rate helmsman, winning several national and world titles during an illustrious sailing career that spanned five decades. He learned to sail while attending Gresham's School, Holt, Norfolk, and bought his first boat, a sharpie, when he was 18. He later graduated to a National 12, bought by his

parents as a 21st birthday present in 1939, The year he was also elected as Rear Commodore of Aldenham Sailing Club.

Proctor's first career choice was a far cry from the sailing world and it was only the war that prompted him to give up medical studies to join the RAF's air/sea rescue service. By 1944 he had command of his own rescue patrol boat but he was then struck down with polio. The disease left him with a paralysed right arm and withered chest muscles. After a lengthy recuperation, he managed a boatyard at Portsmouth for a short period after the war until being invited to co-edit *The Yachtsman* magazine, a job he shared with Adlard Coles. From there he graduated to becoming yachting correspondent for *The Daily Telegraph*, a vocation he coupled for 12 years with designing racing dinghies and developing the first tapered metal masts.

Ian Proctor's first dinghy design was a Merlin Rocket which dominated the national championship in 1952. *Sirrus*, steered by the designer and crewed by Tony Norbury, won overall and a sister design, sailed by Tony Fox and John Oakeley, was second. The same year, he designed the Osprey dinghy to compete in the trials for a new two-man international class.

The Flying Dutchman, which has retained its Olympic status since the Melbourne Games in 1956, was given the nod, but Proctor's clinker-built Osprey won many admirers and developed into a thriving class of its own. The design was given further impetus when Proctor steered the prototype to a memorable one second victory in the 60-mile Coronation Round-the-island (Isle of Wight) race in 1953. The design was followed in 1956 by his 15ft 6in Kestrel, the first one-design class to incorporate glass fibre construction from the outset, and the smaller Gull. Later came the Wayfarer, the SigneT, launched by *The Sunday Times*, and the Jiffy, Minisail, Bosun and Topper dinghies.

Proctor was always an innovative designer. His first metal mast, produced in 1956, led to the formation of Ian

Proctor Metal Masts Ltd, a company that grew to dominate spar construction worldwide during the 1960s and 1970s. His Jiffy, a small tender, was the first dinghy to be built utilising a fully-mechanised moulding system and led to the mass-produced injection-moulded polypropylene Topper, a class now 35,000 strong and his most successful design.

In recent times, Ian Proctor had been busy developing a larger family version of the Topper, utilising a much cheaper injection moulding system developed to take advantage of a new high-impact plastic used to mould car bumpers and body panels.

Proctor was voted yachtsman of the year in 1965, won a Council of Industrial Design award in 1967 and Design Council award in 1977 and 1980. He also wrote several books on sailing including *Racing Dinghy Handling* (1948), *Racing Dinghy Maintenance* (1949) and most recently, *Sailing strategy* (1977).

Ian Proctor is survived by his wife, Betty, and four children.

b 12.7.18   d 23.7.92   aged 74

Ian Proctor sailing his Osprey, Fabulus, *in 1963*

PAT TAAFFE

Pat Taaffe on Arkle (1965)

Pat Taaffe, outstanding Irish jockey and partner of the legendary Arkle.

NO JOCKEY in National Hunt history, not even the great Fred Winter, rode more winners of important races than the long-legged, modest, soft-spoken Irishman Pat Taaffe. He was a champion many times in his own country where he rode no fewer than half a dozen winners of the Irish Grand National, but was also justly famous on this side of the water. In a professional career lasting 20 years his

triumphs included four Cheltenham Gold Cups, three of them on Arkle, two Grand Nationals (Quare Times in 1955 and Gay Trip in 1970) as well as every other big jumping race in the calendar.

Yet the term "jockey" requires qualification. Taaffe was first and foremost a superb and sympathetic horseman blessed with perfect hands, with a particular talent in the difficult art of presenting a horse to a fence. In a driving finish, however, his style, because he rode very short for his length of leg, was described politely as "untidy" but more realistically by the late Fred Rimell who, watching Taaffe in vigorous action approaching the winning post, remarked that it looked as if an unprintable assault was being carried out from the saddle on "a box of red hot tin tacks". Nevertheless, that did not prevent Rimell from engaging Taaffe to ride Gay Trip in the National when his stable jockey, Terry Biddlecombe, was injured.

Patrick Taaffe was born in Rathcoole, Dublin, the son of the trainer Tom Taaffe, and from childhood was brought up in the world of horses: showjumping, hunting and point-to-points being a natural preliminary to his becoming an amateur rider under National Hunt rules. He rode his first winner, Ballincorona, a chance ride, at Phoenix Park in 1947. In 1950 he became a professional and regular stable jockey for the great trainer, Tom Dreaper, for whose skill and considerate Irish logic Taaffe had the highest praise: "He never abused me for giving a horse a bad ride. The most he ever said was: 'Don't ride the same race you rode the last time.' "

It was under Dreaper, more than a decade later, that Taaffe's life became inextricably woven with that of the horse who is widely regarded as the finest chaser ever foaled: Arkle, owned by Anne, Duchess of Westminster. The effect of Arkle upon the racing scene, which he came to bestride like a Colossus, while attracting an enormous, devoted, public following, was as if a new and entirely superior breed of thoroughbred had suddenly emerged. His victories in the

Gold Cup three times, the Hennessy twice, the King George VI Chase, the Whitbread and the Irish Grand National form a record unsurpassed in racing history.

The role of Taaffe in shaping that record between 1963 and 1966 has never, perhaps, been given its fair measure of recognition. Yet there is no doubt that Taaffe was the perfect and unique partner, and that Arkle's reputation owes a considerable debt to the man who rode him as no one else could. Equally, Taaffe's association with him has tended to overshadow and obscure the jockey's noteworthy achievements with other outstanding horses of the 1960s also trained by Dreaper and who were formidable spearheads of the great Irish gambles of that decade, chiefly at Cheltenham.

Fortria, Flyingbolt and Fort Leney, winners between them of a total of 47 races for the stable, 42 of them ridden by Taaffe, were all stars in their own right. Fortria, winner of the 1961 Irish Grand National and twice runner-up in the Gold Cup, was really best at shorter distances, his victories including the Mackeson Gold Cup and the two-mile Champion Chase twice apiece. Flyingbolt, beaten in only two of 18 races in his first three seasons, won the 1966 Irish National but likewise shone in shorter chases as well as being a smart hurdler – finishing third to Salmon Spray in the 1966 Champion Hurdle only 24 hours after cantering home in the two-mile Champion Chase.

Fort Leney, meanwhile, was involved in 1968 in two desperate finishes: in the Gold Cup, a fourth triumph in the race for his rider, Taaffe drove him home by a neck. The following month he just failed, by the same margin, to beat Larbawn in the Whitbread. Among a host of Taaffe's other good horses Ben Stack, Muir, Straight Fort and French Tan must also be mentioned; as well as, early in his career, for the trainer Clem Magnier, that courageous performer Teapot II, third to Sir Ken in the 1953 Champion Hurdle,

winner two days later of the County Hurdle under top weight and within the next two weeks of a Rank Cup and the Liverpool Hurdle, both under punishing burdens.

Teapot II's prowess, in fact, well illustrates the courses at which Taaffe shone most of all: Cheltenham and Aintree. His "strike-rate" at the former was quite remarkable. From close on a hundred rides at Cheltenham, 30 per cent were winners and a further 25 per cent places. His four Gold Cups apart, he rode five winners each of the two mile Champion Chase and the Broadway Novices Chase, three winners each of the Cathcart Challenge Cup and Cotswold Chase, and twice each a division of the Gloucester Hurdle and the National Hunt Handicap Chase.

At Liverpool, aside from his two Grand National victories, Taaffe excelled over the formidable fences, winning the Becher Chase and Molyneux Chase twice apiece and once each the Grand Sefton and the Topham Trophy; while he also rode with considerable success over the smaller obstacles with two victories and two places in the November Handicap Hurdle and victories also in the Lancashire Hurdle and Liverpool Hurdle.

Taaffe retired from the saddle in 1970 after a season which provided an appropriate swansong. His four rides at Cheltenham produced three winners as well as a second on French Tan in the Gold Cup, and he finally went on to take the Grand National on Gay Trip. He then took up training and was successful almost immediately with Captain Christy, whose successes included the Irish Sweeps Hurdle, Scottish Champion Hurdle, the King George VI Chase twice and the 1974 Cheltenham Gold Cup.

Last year Taaffe successfully underwent a heart transplant operation. He leaves a widow, Molly, two sons and three daughters.

b 12.3.30   d 7.7.92   aged 62

MIKHAIL TAL

Mikhail Nekhemyevich Tal, former Soviet world chess champion.

WHO can tell what impact the brilliant Latvian chess grandmaster Mikhail Tal would have made on the history of chess, had he not been the victim of prolonged, paralysing and almost permanent bouts of ill-health? During the 1950s Tal's native talent blazed like a meteor amongst the stolid generations of chess grandmasters who had been brought up in the painstaking school of strategic accuracy promulgated by Botvinnik and Smyslov, those two great players whose

matches for the world chess championship had dominated the period from 1954 to 1958.

To almost universal surprise amongst the chess pundits Tal dethroned the olympian Botvinnik in 1960. En route to this world championship challenge, Tal had confused, smashed and obliterated the world's elite with a sacrificial arsenal, the like of which had never before been seen. The experts asserted that Tal's style of play, bold, brilliant and hair-raising as it was, could not be sound. Nevertheless, in the practical struggle no one could find the holes in Tal's play that the theorists claimed were present.

Professor Nathan Divinsky, the Canadian master and author of the *Batsford Chess Encyclopaedia*, reviewing Tal's style, wrote: "As Tal's successes increased, experts pronounced his sacrifices unsound and assured the chess world that the big three, Keres, Smyslov and Botvinnik, would destroy him. They were astonished to see all of the big three fall before Tal's furious onslaught, crumbling under the depth of the complexities combined with the time pressure of a real game."

After Tal had defeated Botvinnik and reached the pinnacle of what chess had to offer, becoming at the age of 23 the youngest world champion so far in the history of the game, the chess world now expected that future glories would soon await their newly-crowned hero. Unfortunately, fate dictated otherwise. Unwisely and proudly refusing to postpone the 1961 revenge match, to which Botvinnik, as defeated champion, was entitled by the rules then prevailing, a sick Tal went down to an unmitigated disaster at the hands of the ex-champion.

Since that time, ironically, the unfair revenge rule for a defeated world champion, though briefly revived for Karpov, has now been definitively dropped by the game's regulating body, the World Chess Federation.

Having been crushed by Botvinnik in this return match, Tal never again succeeded in his goal of qualifying for a title challenge. He did, though, remain a fierce tournament competitor, always likely to win first prize and in so doing demolished the very strongest of opponents with arcane sacrifices which baffled most expert observers.

Considering his ill-health, Tal's long run on the chess board was remarkable. In 1959 he enjoyed his greatest tournament triumph when he won by an overwhelming margin the Candidates' Tournament held in Yugoslavia, which swept him on to the challenge against Botvinnik. Twenty years later Tal achieved an almost equally remarkable performance at Montreal where, as the only undefeated player, he shared first prize with Karpov, ahead of the strongest Grandmasters of the day. Even in 1988 Tal was still able to display his lightning speed of reaction when he won the world Blitz Chess Championship in Canada, ahead of both Kaspanov and Karpov.

Born in Riga, the son of a doctor, the young Tal first showed an interest in chess when he saw the game being played in his father's waiting room. At the age of eight he became a member of the chess section of the Palace of Young Pioneers in Riga, but it was not until he won the Latvian championship of 1953 that Tal started to make serious progress. He was not a child prodigy in the sense that Paul Morphy or Bobby Fischer were.

In 1957 Tal won the Soviet championship at Leningrad and went on to repeat this performance in his home town of Riga a year later. He fired the opening shots of his campaign to seize Botvinnik's world chess crown by a clear victory at the Interzonal tournament of 1958, held in Portoroz, Yugoslavia. He then went on to his greatest tournament triumph, the Candidates' Tournament of 1959, again held in Yugoslavia at Bled, Zagreb and Belgrade. Here, out of 28 games Tal won the enormous total of 16 and lost only four. It was at this tournament that the Hungarian Grandmaster Pal Benko donned dark glasses for one of his games against Tal to deflect his alleged powers of hypnotism during play.

By winning this event Tal became the official challenger and in 1960 he defeated Botvinnik in Moscow by the score of six wins to two losses with 13 draws. Tal thus became the youngest world champion up to that time, but a year later Tal lost the return match, also in Moscow, by the even more devastating margin of five wins with six draws but no fewer that ten losses.

Tal immediately embarked upon a fresh challenge but at the Curaçao Candidates Tournament of 1962, instead of the anticipated race between the young lions, Mikhail Tal and Bobby Fischer, the tournament resulted in a narrow victory of attrition for the Fabian tactics of the ultra cautious Armenian Tigran Petrosian. During this tournament Tal's health collapsed and he had to withdraw well before the end. Never again, in spite of brilliant tournament victories, which included the Soviet championships of 1974 and 1978, or the Riga Interzonal of 1979, did Tal ever succeed in penetrating to a further world championship match.

Tal was born with one hand badly deformed and an excessively frail constitution. He suffered from chronic kidney disease, having one removed in 1969. His condition was exacerbated by his smoking and drinking to extraordinary excess.

Tal's love of chess, though, was paramount and he will go down as one of the all-time greats of the game. His record of six first prizes in Soviet championships has been equalled only by Botvinnik. Had his health been good Tal might have entered history as the greatest chess player of all time. Although a prolific journalist, Tal published just one book, a commentary of his victory in his first world championsip match against Botvinnik in 1960.

It was ironic that, just as Latvia achieved its ambition of playing once again as an autonomous state in the Chess Olympics in Manila, which finished last week, Tal, a Latvian, who had spent his whole life representing the USSR, was too ill to make the Latvian team.

b 9.11.36   d 28.6.92   aged 55

ROBERTO D'AUBUISSON

Roberto d'Aubuisson, founder of El Salvador's ruling Nationalist Republican Alliance party and alleged leader of right-wing death squads. A ruthless torturer, his nickname was "blow-torch Bob".

A FANATICAL anti-communist with the reputation of being a ruthless killer, Roberto d'Aubuisson had rugged good-looks and practised a swaggering, machismo style of politics that struck fear into the hearts of many Salvadoreans while winning the adoration of others. Although the allegations were never proved in court, he was widely believed to be the "Godfather" of the right-wing death-squads that murdered thousands of Salvadoreans suspected of harbouring left-wing sympathisers as El Salvador moved towards civil war in the early 1980s. He was publicly accused by Napoleon Duarte, the late, former Sal-vadorean president, and Robert White, a former United States ambasador to San Salvador, of masterminding the assassination of the Archbishop of San Salvador, Oscar Romero, who was shot in the heart as he said mass in 1980. White called d'Aubuisson "a pathological killer" but d'Aubuisson shrugged off the accusations with disdain.

Although his bid for the presidency failed he hand-picked his successful successor, Alfredo Cristiani and remained a powerful figure in the background.

D'Aubuisson was the descendant of a Frenchman who went to Central America to help build the Panama Canal. His father was a salesman and his mother a civil servant. He received a Roman Catholic education at a Jesuit-run school in San Salvador and then joined the National Guard.

He quickly became rabidly right-wing

in his political outlook and as a junior officer in the Guards' intelligence department became involved in compiling detailed records of thousands of Salvadoreans deemed to hold politically unacceptable opinions: liberal politicians, trade union officials, academics, student organisations and even some colleagues in the military. These files provided the raw material for the death squads which plunged El Salvador into a nightmare of political violence over the ensuing decade. The secrets they contained ranged from suspected connections with the country's emergent guerrilla movements to bank accounts, love affairs and drinking habits. Once a victim had been selected, off-duty troops and policemen did most of the dirty work. But d'Aubuisson gained a reputation as a ruthless torturer of suspected leftists which later led US embassy personnel to nickname him "blow-torch Bob."

By 1979 d'Aubuisson had become chief intelligence officer of the National Guard but became implicated in an attempted coup and when reform-minded officers staged their own coup he was cashiered. Some members of the new *junta* wanted him tried for treason but he fled to Guatemala. He spent 18 months in exile from where, with the backing of Guatemalan and Argentine paramilitary right-wing movements, he set about creating the Nationalist Republican Alliance party, known by its Spanish acronym Arena.

His belligerent anti-communist stance brought him support from El Salvador's right-wing business sector, wealthy landowners and military hardliners and his lean good looks and skin-tight shirts won him an adoring female following. He was a slight, wiry man, only 5ft 7ins tall but – having been wounded twice in unsuccessful assassination attempts – he exuded a tough, virile appeal. He thrived on a reputation of smoking and drinking heavily, playing poker and chasing women. He was also a spellbinding public speaker. A favourite gimmick was to hold up a watermelon and compare it with his rivals, the centrist Christian Democrats,

whose campaign colour was green. "Green on the outside," he would say. Then, slicing the melon open with a machete, he would spit contemptuously: "and red on the inside."

When he left his National Guard office, he had reputedly taken with him much of the damaging material he had accumulated on suspected leftists, together with a network of death squad contacts. And after establishing Arena, he capitalised on the right's horror of communism. In regular television appearances he would identify and denounce what he called "subversives", after which many would be killed by the death squads.

Arean won a majority in the National Assembly in 1982 and d'Aubuisson became president of the Assembly. Two years later he campaigned against Napoleon Duarte for the presidency, on an uncompromising platform of defeating the left-wing guerrillas on the battlefield.

The communists were not his only ogre. The US came a close second. The Carter administration had barred him from entry to the US and the Reagan administration, which was backing Duarte's Christian Democrats, was no warmer. He dismissed the significance of US military aid, saying if he was elected he would accept it only if it came without conditions – in effect rejecting US congressional demands for more attention to be paid in Salvador to the question of human rights.

In the 1984 election, however, he lost narrowly to Duarte. Afterwards d'Aubuisson appeared to mellow. He selected Cristiani, a conservative businessman, as Arena's candidate for the 1989 presidential elections and after Cristiani's victory apparently acquiesced when the new president moved away from the rabid anti-communism that had been d'Aubuisson's hallmark, introduced a series of economic reforms and entered into a dialogue with the left-wing rebels.

He is survived by his wife, Luz Maria, and four children.

b 23.8.43   d 20.2.92   aged 48

ANTHONY "FAT TONY" SALERNO

Anthony "Fat Tony" Salerno, boss of New York's powerful Genovese crime family.

LUCK ran out for Fat Tony Salerno in 1986, when he was finally identified by federal prosecutors as a senior member of "the commission" – the ruling council of the five member families of La Cosa Nostra, otherwise known as the Mafia. Arrested after FBI surveillance of a commission meeting, Salerno was the central figure in a dramatic trial that lasted for ten weeks.

It was the first time that the federal government had suceeded in bringing racketeering charges against the mob, and Salerno was sentenced to 100 years imprisonment at the age of 75. To make assurance doubly sure that he would never get out of jail, he was subsequently charged with a separate racketeering offence and sentenced to a further 70 years behind bars.

Fat Tony was a gangster of the old school. Not for him the flashy elegance of John Gotti, who paraded the streets in $1,000 suits. Despite his immense wealth – at the time of his trial he was rated by *Fortune* magazine as the most powerful and wealthiest gangster in America – Salerno frequently held council dressed in a fedora, T-shirt, and crumpled trousers.

He grew up on the streets of East Harlem, running numbers for the mob, and never strayed far from his power base. But as boss of the 200-member Genovese family his influence extended from the Miami waterfront to labour unions in Cleveland, and to rigging construction bids on Manhattan skyscrapers. His annual income from these activities – and from loan sharking, profit-skimming from Las Vegas casinos and a "Mafia tax" on building operations in New York – was estimated at tens of millions of dollars. He maintained a home in Miami Beach, a 100-acre estate in Rhinebeck, New York, and an apartment in the fashionable district of Gramercy Park. Yet he steadfastly maintained that all this came from the ownership of several small businesses.

It was not until the early 1980s, with the retirement of Philip Lombardo, that Salerno became boss of the Genovese family. But his rise in the hierarchy of the underworld had begun much earlier. In 1959, when he was already well known to the Manhattan district attorney as a "gambler, bookmaker and policy operator", an investigation into the Mafia's involvement in boxing found that he had secretly helped to finance a heavyweight title fight at Yankee Stadium between Ingemar Johansson and Floyd Patterson. But he was never charged with any offence. Nor was any action taken over his alleged control of Harlem's biggest numbers racket, which was said to be raking in as much as $50 million a year.

Salerno's first and only other criminal conviction came in 1978, when he was charged with federal tax evasion. His attorney, Roy M. Cohn, said that he was merely a "sports gambler", but Salerno pleaded guilty and was sentenced to six months imprisonment. Next time, in 1986, he was less fortunate.

When he died he still had 167 years of his sentence to serve but would have been eligible for parole in 1996.

b 1911 d 27.7.92 aged 80

LORD FRANKS

Baron Franks, OM, GCMG, KCB, KCVO, CBE, PC, former British ambassador in Washington, head of two Oxford colleges, academic and chairman of the Franks Committee which investigated the causes of the Falklands war.

A WHITEHALL civil servant not known for being lavish with praise said of Oliver Shewell Franks that he had "an alpha treble-plus mind." The judgment was just, but it was also insufficient. The name of Franks became linked with absolute integrity. Whenever a post of major responsibility came up, be it the editorship of *The Times*, the chancellorship of Oxford Univeristy or the next director-general of the BBC, then the name of Oliver Franks would be canvassed.

Surprisingly Franks was 77 before he accepted the post that was to give him most public prominence: the chairmanship of the inquiry into the Falklands war. Sir Robert Armstrong, as he then was, travelled to Oxford to make sure the Franks's faculties were as sharp as ever. He needed little persuading. Franks, steeped in years of public service with most of them close to the summit, accepted the job. In the summer of 1982 his committee was closeted with the evidence for six hours a day and Franks confessed that he used Braudel on the eastern Mediterranean as relaxing evening reading. After the witnesses had been called the report, which generally exonerated the government from blame in its reaction to Argentinian aggression, was delivered in mid-January 1983.

Perhaps Oliver Franks would have preferred to remain at Oxford: he always claimed that academe was his natural habitat. If so he was not going to say. He had, after all, long experience as a diplomat. He was an outstanding public servant, at different times British Ambassador in Washington, chairman of Lloyds Bank, the head of two Oxford Colleges, professor of moral philosophy and, at the end of the second world war, permanent secretary in the Ministry of Supply.

Any one of these positions, each of them requiring different gifts, would have been an achievement for most people. Franks conquered all of them, and served with distinction in them, because of an exceptional combination of that first-class intellect, administrative ability and a sense of discretion and balance in handling delicate public issues. Those who did not know him well found him an austere, even aloof, man. Jokes circulated around Oxford to the effect that once the ice was broken there was much cold water to be found below. But he nonetheless had a considerable capacity for human relations when he relaxed.

He began his career in the academic world, and it was to Oxford that he always liked to return, to the informal give and take of college life. But it was clear from early on that academic life alone could never be enough for him, and that led him to venture out into the world of public and international affairs.

His time in Washington as ambassador from 1948 to 1952 was perhaps the peak of his career, if, though, the Falklands assignment was to bring him more fame. Those were the difficult years after the end of the war, and he estalished a particularly close relationship with Dean Acheson, the secretary of state, which helped to lay the foundations of the postwar period. But he later made a distinctive contribution, as chairman of Lloyds Bank, to the City.

Franks was born of Noncomformist stock. His father, the Rev R. S. Franks, was for many years principal of the Western Theological College at Bristol. His family also had close associations with the Society of Friends, and these links were further strengthened by his marriage in 1931 to Barbara Tanner, whose father was a well-known Quaker in the business circles of the West Country.

After receiving his early education at Bristol Grammar School, Franks entered The Queen's College, Oxford, in 1923 as an Open Scholar in Classics. There his outstanding qualities soon established him as the leading undergraduate of his time. Apart from his academic successes – his distinguished Firsts in Mods and Greats, and later the John Locke Scholarship in philosophy – he participated fully in the general life of the college. He rowed for the college, and – though a teetotaller – he was elected to the select membership of the Eagle Club, which was dedicated to the pleasures of good food and wine.

After taking his Schools, Franks was elected to a fellowship and the praelectorship in philosophy at Queen's in 1927. After a year on the Continent, he began teaching in 1928 both for Lit. Hum. and PPE. His philosophical interests lay rather in the moderns than in the ancients, and after a time he stopped teaching and Aristotle. His lectures drew huge audiences by reason of their clarity and orderliness of presentation; while his tutorials provided a considerable stimulus to the undergraduates, especially the abler ones.

In spite of his academic distinction it is nevertheless doubtful whether Franks's real interests were primarily academic. It soon became clear that he was fascinated by the arts of administration and planning, that he loved to apply the analytic processes of philosophy to the problems of practical affairs. One of his earliest exercises of this kind was to conduct an inquiry into all the possible needs of the college, immediate and remote, and to assign to each its appropriate degree of priority. Another congenial task was the reorganisation of philosophy teaching at Chicago, where he spent a term in 1935 as visiting professor.

Franks had always made it clear that when he had completed 10 years as a don he would seek the first suitable post elsewhere. In 1937 he applied for the vacant chair of moral philosophy at Glasgow, and was successful.

But his active tenure of the chair was to be short. On the outbreak of war he joined the Ministry of Supply as a temporary civil servant and entered upon one of the most spectacular periods of his career.

His exceptional administrative talents

now found their full scope. His progress was meteoric and he finished up in 1945–46 as permanent secretary to the Ministry of Supply and Aircraft Production. The secret of his success, apart from his breadth of vision and his incisive intellect, was two-fold. First, he knew how to delegate and so reserve his energies for the major problems of policy. Secondly, when he had made the best desision that he could, he did not worry about it afterwards. This enabled him to bear the strain of his responsibilities wih a certain serenity, even during the worst days of the bombing. The award of a knighthood in 1946 was a recognition of his contribution to the war effort.

On retiring from the Civil Service, Franks was offered various posts of national, even international, importance. But it was no surprise to those who knew his love of Oxford that he chose instead to accept the vacant provostship of Queen's. This appointment gave him great happiness, but did not prevent him from acceding to Government demands for his services. During 1947 he was absent for a prolonged period as chief British delegate to the Paris Conference on Marshall Aid, where he received the irreverent nickname of "No Lolly Ollie". Then, in 1948, he announced that he was obliged to resign the provostship to become ambassador to the United States.

When Franks arrived in Washington at the end of May, 1948, the tide was running in his favour and he was the man to take it at the flood. It was as an economic expert that he was welcomed in the United States, as one who knew, to quote *The New York Times* when he landed, "as possibly no other man in Europe the aims, possibilities, and attendant national responsibilities of the Marshall European recovery programme". But he proved himself to be much more than that – "a fine diplomat", Truman called him.

Ernest Bevin, despite the very considerable difference in educational background, trusted Franks and listened to his advice. So did Sir Stafford Cripps. Truman and Acheson were well aware of

this, and it made him the more valuable to them, at the same time strengthening his own hand.

His task was made easier by the extraordinary understanding that grew up between Acheson and Bevin. But his own contribution to the consolidation of that understanding was important.

In his memoirs Acheson mentions an unorthodox proposal he put to Franks: "on an experimental basis I suggested that we talk regularly and in complete confidence about any international problems we saw arising". They met at the cocktail hour, unbeknown to their superiors in Whitehall and the White House. The experiment ran for four years. On many Sundays Franks drove his own small car to Acheson's country house in Maryland, unseen by journalists and unsuspected by Congressmen. The four-and-a-half years of his mission now appear to have been the golden years of Anglo-American cooperation. Understanding was probably deeper and serious disagreements fewer than during the war. Two great crises – the Berlin blockade and the Korean war – were met and surmounted in unity. The North Atlantic Treaty was drafted and the foundations of a European defence system were laid.

Franks's most valuable quality through those years was his lucidity. He had an extraordinary ability for clarifying complicated issues. More than once in his memoirs Truman refers to this quality: "Sir Oliver Franks, as he had done in previous meetings, proceeded to pull the threads of the conversation together. . . . Sir Oliver Franks. . . .skilfully summarised the discussion we had." These remarks were typical of Truman's justified admiration.

Wisely he did not try to outstay the Truman Administration. His experience with Dulles, who had been in the State Department as an adviser for much of his time, had not given him any great confidence in the new secretary of state as a colleague. And he knew that the Republicans would find it hard to trust anyone who had been so close to

Acheson. A new ambassador would have a better chance than he could have.

On his return it was known that he wished to be free of executive work for at least a year. Yet his qualities were so admired that in spite of this he was offered more than one important appointment, one being the editorship of *The Times*. In March, 1953, he was elected a director of Lloyds Bank and in June a deputy chairman. In November 1954 he succeeded Lord Balfour of Burleigh as chairman.

As chairman for eight years Franks brought a new and welcome dynamism in the City. His ability and determination to reason matters out on their merits, within the framework of tradition, rather than accept them on the grounds of tradition alone, was beneficial if at times a little startling to the City. His annual statements to shareholders and his much sought-after addresses to international gatherings, revealed and added to his international stature. He was a member of the Radcliffe Committee which inquired into the working of the monetary system and later as chairman of the Committee of London Clearing Bankers (from 1960 to 1962), presented the banks' evidence, cogently and comprehensively, to the Jenkins Committee on Company Law Amendment. He had the capacity to absorb a situation and reduce it to its extreme simplicities without getting involved in details.

During those years he lived in Oxford and occasionally took part in seminars. Such time as he could spare from the City was mainly devoted to acting as chairman of the board of governors of the United Oxford Hospitals (from 1958 to 1964). During that time he initiated a scheme of expansion and reform which took his successors more than a decade to put into effect.

In 1962, on giving up the chairmanship of Lloyds Bank, he became provost of Worcester College, where he remained until 1976. That same year he was made a life peer, and he subsequently took the Liberal Whip in the House of Lords.

Franks's predecessor at Worcester, J.

As British Ambassador arriving in Southampton 1950

C. Masterman, had presided over a period in which the college had established itself at the centre of university life and not just one with a good sporting record. Franks was able to consolidate that achievement. Masterman had been a rather remote figure, often tending to favour undergraduates from the better schools and the better sort of background. Like Franks he had been a civil servant in his time. But Franks's views were more liberal and he had his own characteristic way of interesting undergraduates and, to the surprise of some of the fellows, passed with flying colours the severest of all tests for a head of house, that of regaining the affection and regard of old members. He fitted easily and naturally into college life, with its equality in the common room and democracy on the governing body.

His most considerable service to the university was his chairmanship of the commission of inquiry into its working (from 1964 to 1966). Oxford was under some pressure to examine itself, and Franks's authority and reputation made him a good choice as chairman. He insisted that the commission should do as much of its work as possible in public, and many of the hearings attracted big audiences. The final report contained a wide range of recommendations which had considerable influence on the university among them, proposals for more undergraduates and post graduate students, for a higher proportion of women, for more emphasis on applied sciences and technology, for a reform of the administration, and for changes in the system of admissions.

In spite of his activities in Oxford Franks continued to play a part in various bodies elsewhere, such as the Welcome Trust, the Rhodes Trust and the Rockefeller Foundation. From 1962 to 1964 he was a member of the National Economic Development Council. In 1965 he was elected chancellor of the University of East Anglia.

In 1971 he was called on by Edward Heath, then prime minister, to be chairman of a departmental committee to look into the issue of official secrets. This issue had come to the fore as a result of the unsuccessful attempt by the Crown to prosecute the *Sunday Telegraph* under section 2 of the Official Secrets Act, 1911. The intention was to devise a more sophisticated secrecy statute which would be narrower in scope, but surer in action.

The Franks committee made proposals for a new Official Information Act which would aim to protect genuinely sensitive material related to such areas as defence and international security, foreign relations and currency. But because of differences at Westminster over the proper extent of liberalization it did not become law.

Franks returned to the issue at a Civil Service College seminar in 1978, when he suggested a House of Commons select committee on open government as being a constitutionally sound method of reconciling the conflicting impulses of confidentiality and publicity. But it was not acted upon.

In July, 1982, when Franks was already 77, he was called on to take on one of the most sensitive, and public tasks of his career, the chairmanship of the committee of Privy Councillors to review the background of the Falklands dispute. The issue was, of course, one of great political importance, because of the effect that any severe criticism of the Government's actions in the period leading up to the Argentine invasion would have had. In the event the committee formally exonerated the Thatcher administration, saying that it could not have foreseen or prevented the invasion, and concluding that "we would not be justified in attaching any criticism or blame" to the Government for the Argentine juntas's act of aggression. But at the same time the narrative section of the report, based on a wealth of diplomatic and intelligence documents, produced abundant material for accusations of ministerial and official neglect.

The upshot, presumably foreseen by Franks, was that the Government was able to make the most of the exonerations, and that, though there were accusations of a cover-up, with Mr Callaghan talking of "a bucket of whitewash", the issue of possible Government failings disappeared from public discussion.

Franks was elected a fellow of the British Academy in 1960, and was awarded the OM in 1977. He was an honorary fellow of Queen's, Worcester and Wolfson Colleges and of Lady Margaret Hall, Oxford, as well as of St Catherine's College, Cambridge. He also had honorary degrees from Oxford and other universities.

b 16.2.05   d 15.10.92   aged 87

AVRAHAM HARMAN

Former Israeli ambassador to Washington and president of the Hebrew University of Jerusalem.

PRESIDENT and later chancellor of the Hebrew University – "the university of the Jewish people" as he liked to call it – Avraham "Abe" Harman played a leading role in rebuilding and expanding the original campus of the Hebrew University on Mount Scopus after the Six Day War of 1967 and in attracting Jewish students to it from all over the world. His life was imbued with the course of Zionism and with forging links between Israel and the Jewish diaspora. As a youngster in London he played a leading role in the Habonim (youth) movement (which his older brother Philip helped to found) and alongside Abba (Aubrey) Eban, was an active member of the Federation of Zionist Youth.

In 1938, shortly after he earned a law degree from Wadham College, Oxford, he emigrated to what was then Palestine from where he was soon sent to South Africa as an emissary of the Jewish Agency. Later he headed the English section of the agency's information department, spearheading the infor-mation effort against British mandatory rule and for the establishment of a Jewish state.

Following the founding of the state in 1948 Harman was appointed deputy director of the press and information division of the ministry of foreign affairs and a year later became Israel's first consul general in Montreal. Then followed a series of diplomatic postings in North America, culminating in his appointment as Israel's ambassador to Washington in 1959. In 1967, when Arab armies massed on the Jewish state's borders and Israel prepared to take pre-emptive action, Harman played a crucial liaison role in the intensive contacts with Lyndon Johnson's administration and in the contacts and confrontations at the United Nations. He also helped prepare the ground for the ensuing close relationship in which the US became Israel's chief political and military supporter.

In 1968 he returned to Jerusalem to become president of the Hebrew University of Jerusalem. Israel's victory in the Six Day War had restored free access to the old university campus on Mount Scopus which had been denied since 1948 when the Jordanians captured the eastern part of Jerusalem; while in West Jerusalem there were 13,000 students on the Givat Ram campus.

Abe Harman turned his energies to the rebuilding and expanding of the old campus, travelling the world seeking funds and support for the tremendous task from Jewish communities everywhere.

He left that post in 1983 and was appointed university chancellor, a position he held until his death. Today the Hebrew University boasts seven faculties, 12 schools and 21,000 students on the Mount Scopus campus which Abe Harman brought back to life.

He is survived by his wife, Zena, a former member of the Knesset, two daughters and a son.

b 1914   d 23.2.92   aged 77

FRIEDRICH VON HAYEK

Friedrich Hayek, CH, the economist who was known as the "father of monetarism".

FRIEDRICH Hayek was the last, and among the most distinguished, of the Austrian school of economists. During a long and fertile intellectual life, his wide interests enabled him to organise his ideas into one of the most original and impressive of all systems of political thought. From a single fundamental principle, which he called "spontaneous order", Hayek sought to deduce the evolution not only of markets, but of law and knowledge itself. All the greatest human achievements, he believed, arose from unintentional activity, to which human design was nearly always inimical. His work embraced psychology and the history of ideas as well as economics and political theory. Though based firmly on empirical research, in the end Hayek's philosophy amounted to a vast systematic elucidation of man and society.

Hayek never held office; nor, with the exception of his best-seller *The Road to Serfdom*, did he engage in political debate. But he exercised a profound influence upon the climate of thought in Britain, his adopted homeland, in America and ultimately throughout Eastern Europe. His systematic defence of individual liberty, private property and the rule of law attracted countless victims of socialism. Hayek was loathed by those who advocated state intervention into social and economic activity in order to produce a certain outcome. His last book called this vain desire "the fatal conceit".

Hayek grew up in a recently ennobled Viennese family of Czech origin. His father was a professor of botany, and the Hayeks moved in a cosmopolitan milieu which Friedrich later described as philosemitic. As a young man he served in the Austrian army on the Italian front, where he met his distant cousin Ludwig Wittgenstein; the two had little in common.

At this stage Hayek was a moderate social democrat, much influenced by the leading economist and minister Friedrich von Wieser. Only when, in his mid twenties, he met Luwig von Mises, an uncompromising believer in the free market and the ideas of Adam Smith, did he abandon socialism. Having gained doctorates in both economics and law at Vienna University, Hayek worked as a civil servant. In 1927 he became director of the Institute of Economic Research, at which he wrote important papers on monetary theory and the trade cycle, published in book form in 1929.

By the time of the collapse of the Austrian banking system in 1931, Hayek was already sufficiently well-known for Lionel Robbins to invite him to the London School of Economics, where he became Tooke Professor of Economic Science and Statistics. But his fame as an economist dates from the lectures he gave at the LSE, published as *Prices and Production* in 1931. It was a brilliant, original, brief analysis which was highly relevant to a nation suffering from a severe deflationary slump. At the age of 32, Hayek was instantly established as a serious rival to Keynes, whose star rose as the helplessness of politicians became more evident with the formation of the National Government.

By 1932 Hayek was the champion of those who maintained, against Keynes, that state intervention in general, and demand management in particular, would be more likely to prolong the depression than to curtail it. Having published a detailed critique of Keynes's *Treatise on Money*, Hayek was dismayed to find that the Cambridge economist had already abandoned some of his main positions in that book before the review appeared. When Keynes published his *General Theory* in 1934, therefore, Hayek refused to attack it − a grave error, as he later acknowledged, for Keynesian economics thereafter speedily became dominant in Britain. The two men remained on good personal terms, however, and it was Keynes who ensured that Hayek was given rooms at King's when the LSE was evacuated to Cambridge during the war.

Meanwhile Hayek had not been idle.

He published a steady series of books and articles: *Monetary Nationalism and International Stability* (1937), in which he broke a lance for free trade and a substitute for the gold standard; *Prices, Profits and Investment*, which continued the argument of *Prices and Production*; and in 1941 there appeared what he hoped would be his *magnum opus, The Pure Theory of Capital*. This book, almost unnoticed amid the tumult of war, was the high watermark of Hayek's concern with technical economic theory. But the ascendancy of Keynes had given economics an empirical thrust, and Hayek was interested neither in macroeconomic policy nor in econometrics. Unlike Keynes, he did not welcome the opportunity to put his theories into practice offered by the quasi-socialist war economy.

Even before 1939, however, Hayek's work had taken a new turn, with his interest in the theory of centrally planned economies. Having demonstrated in debate with the left-wing economist Oskar Lange the impracticability of substituting a central authority for the decentralised decision-making of the market, Hayek began to develop his distinctive theory of spontaneous order. He also wrote a celebrated paper − not published until 1949 in the first of several important volumes of essays, *Individualism and Economic Order* − on the two traditions of rationalism, one (beneficient) deriving from the Scottish enlightment, the other (malevolent) from the French Revolution. In *The Counter-Revolution of Science* (1952) Hayek later developed this rich theme even further, into a critique of the "constructivist" rationalism popular among intellectuals, of which modern socialism was only one consequence.

During the 1939−45 war, however, Hayek had produced his one popular book, and the one for which he will always be remembered: *The Road to Serfdom*. It was not intended to be a prophesy, but to warn against the potential for creeping totalitarianism which Hayek saw hidden in the burgeoning welfarism of the Labour party after Beveridge. *The Road to Serfdom* has sold millions of copies, though Hayek, like many economists a poor businessman, never made a penny from royalties. But from the first it made him enemies. When Churchill picked up its attack on state intervention and planning in the 1945 election campaign, Attlee made a withering reference to "the Austrian Professor Friedrich August von Hayek" (Hayek had long since become a naturalised British subject). He was hurt more by Orwell's strictures: free competition would impose a tyranny "probably worse, because more irresponsible, than that of the State". Keynes called it a "grand" book, but stuck to his advocacy of "moderate" planning. For Hayek, the Labour landslide of 1945 presaged years in the wilderness.

In 1950 he therefore moved to Chicago, where his break with formal economics was signalled by his acceptance of a chair in social and moral science. It was a fruitful time, after his last unhappy years at the LSE. He published his theory of mind and the senses, *The Sensory Order*, in 1952; though ignored by most psychologists, it influenced the aesthetic ideas of his fellow-Viennese E. H. Gombrich.

In 1960 came his magisterial political treatise, *The Constitution of Liberty*, which took many years to establish itself as a modern classic. Together with *Law, Legislation and Liberty*, which appeared in three volumes between 1973 and 1979, *The Constitution of Liberty* represents Hayek's mature political thought. Hayek is no longer primarily concerned to refute socialism, whether in its democratic or undemocratic forms, but turns his attention to the characteristic corruptions of liberal society.

Hayek was uncompromising in his readiness to limit the meddling of politicians. His ideal was indeed mid-19th century England; he was suspicious even of J. S. Mill's egalitarian tendencies, though he edited Mill's correspondence with Harriet Taylor. He abhorred what he called "weasel words", widely used by

conservatives as well as social democrats, such as "social justice". All attempts to redistribute wealth were not merely inimical to the market, but to civil society itself.

In 1962 Hayek returned to Europe, this time to Freiburg in Germany, where he held a chair of economics until his semi-retirement in 1969. By this time his following around the world had grown. In Germany he had enjoyed considerable respect since Ludwig Erhard rose to power in 1948; he was close to the *Ordo* circle of liberal economists and jurists who influenced the Federal Republic's Basic Law. But Hayek always treated the "social market" as a propaganda tool for free competition.

When in 1974 Hayek was awarded the Nobel Prize for Economics, jointly with his old opponent Gunnar Myrdal, it was clear that the *enfant terrible* of the profession had become one of its grand old men. Another triumph was the election of Mrs Thatcher's government, which was strongly influenced by think tanks in which Hayek had played an important role, above all the Institute of Economic Affairs and later also the Adam Smith Institute. Hayek played no part in the British government, but he was treated with great respect and his books were once again quoted with respect. His bold ideas on the denationalisation of money were not taken up, but his strong views on inflation undoubtedly strengthened the government's resolve not to reflate the economy during the recession of the early 1980s. In 1984, at Mrs Thatcher's instigation, Hayek was made a Companion of Honour.

Hayek's last years were marred by illness, but he was able to finish *The Fatal Conceit*, his last book. He lived to see the collapse of communism in eastern Europe, and only in his final year or two did he lose touch with events. Hayek was twice married: to Hella von Fritsch (died 1960), by whom he had a son and a daughter, and to Helene Bitterlich. His second wife and his children survive him.

b 8.5.1899   d 23.3.92   aged 92

LORD JAMES OF RUSHOLME

Lord James of Rusholme, High Master of Manchester Grammar School, 1945–62, and the first vice-chancellor of York University, 1962–73.

ERIC James was an apostle of excellence, an unashamed elitist in an egalitarian age. From the perspective of having been a commercial traveller's son who became High Master of Manchester Grammar School (and set new standards of attainment) and then played a pivotal role in building the University of York into one of the best post-war institutions of higher learning, he argued, cogently, that in matters of the intellect and in judgments of value, the idea of equality was irrelevant. A culture would be debased, he said, if popular values were adopted in an effort to transmit that culture to ever greater numbers. One man's opinion was not necessarily as good as another's.

James was a Fabian socialist who believed in equality of opportunity; he favoured comprehensive education for small communities, but opposed it for large cities. And he said that the difficulties of the exceptionally gifted child could be met only by the existence of some highly selective schools. The elitist nature of the universities, he argued in 1978, could best be preserved by strengthening other types of higher education in polytechnics and colleges of higher and further education. That would leave the universities free to take only students committed to tough academic work and free them from the pressure to introduce narrow, vocational studies.

Eric John Francis James went to Taunton's School, Southampton, where his great intellectual promise was soon apparent. He became an exhibitioner, and afterwards honorary scholar, of Queen's College, Oxford, and having gained a First in the Chemistry Schools, he took his DPhil in 1933. That year he became an assistant master at Winchester and he was an instant success, both with boys and with his older colleagues. It was, for example, a singular compliment that that great but conservative housemaster, Malcolm Robertson, should choose him as his house tutor, James's avowed sympathies were with the left, but he had a directness of manner and a width of interest which won widespread commendation and which made him in those days an exceptional scientist.

In one of the highest forms on the science side he taught a group of science pupils who were to become leaders in their particular lines: Dyson the physicist, Longuet Higgins the chemist, Swan the biologist. The original inspiration of that great department was no doubt due to S. A. McDowell, but James was the most remarkable of his younger colleagues and, after McDowell's death, it was James who maintained and extended the tradition that the scientist should be a man of wide interests in philosophy, literature, and the arts.

As a bachelor he lived in the "Rough House", an institution whose abounding vitality in no way belied its name. Its stock in trade was the "imita", but the brilliant mimicry of their older colleagues practised by James and Ridgway had as its basis, in part at least, a real devotion to them. It was merciless, but succeeded in being at the same time affectionate, and was one of the great features of Winchester at that date.

James was obviously marked out for a headmastership, and when he applied for the High Mastership of Manchester Grammar School, one of his referees — a former colleague at Winchester who was headmaster of one of the London schools — commended him as likely to inspire in his pupils that intense personal admiration which was in the tradition at Manchester and which James had already been accorded by his Winchester pupils. In fact his great headmastership worked out differently. It was on staff and governors that the "Chief" made the strongest personal impact. His tremendous drive and lofty academic standards gave him a touch of ruthlessness which quickly reinforced the extraordinary reputation already enjoyed by the school. He sometimes made rather short work of parents. But Lancashire suited him, and he rapidly became one of

its outstanding figures. It was no surprise therefore when in 1949 he became a member of the University Grants Committee (a rare distinction for a headmaster) or when he was knighted in 1956.

He was a chairman of the Headmasters' Conference from 1953 to 1955, deriving his interest in education politics largely from his last headmaster at Winchester, Spencer Leeson — one of those whom he mimicked with devastating effect, but passionately admired. Unlike Leeson, he had little patience for the struggling "public" school whose one, dubious, asset was a certain social pretension. But headmasters knew exactly where they stood with him. They could rely on him to conduct the conference's business with outstanding ability and dispatch. And his pronouncements carried great weight in the educational world. He was concerned, above all at this time, to preserve the academic standards of grammar schools, which seemed to be threatened by attacks on the examination system, and by a tendency to narrow salary differentials between the honours graduates and the teachers with only a college of education certificate. Like most of the battles he fought, he won this battle also.

In 1954 it was confidently expected that he would go back to Winchester as headmaster; and it is believed that strong pressure was brought on him to do so. But he resisted it. The appeal of Lancashire (and perhaps the possibility of a university job) were probably the main factors in his decision. For four years from 1957 he was a member of the Central Advisory Council on Education.

A life peerage in 1959 as Lord James of Rusholme brought him to Westminster as the only — perhaps the first — headmaster baron. He sat on the cross benches, being disposed to support Labour on social issues while retaining his own educational views which made few concessions to the egalitarian tendencies of the Labour Party. In 1962 he became vice-chancellor of the new University of York, one of the institutions brought into being in the so-called Baedeker round of university foundation of the early 1960s.

The new universities were needed to inject new ideas, not simply to expand the number of university places. He brought to the job all his experience as a great schoolmaster, his devotion to high standards and the "responsibility of clerisy" which made him an unashamed elitist in intellectual matters. But he also took with him a style. It was said that he ran a school as if it were a university. So too, as a vice-chancellor he gave his colleagues unstinted support — "miles of rope" as one of them put it — and saw the job of the vice-chancellor as "one great enabling act".

He helped form the distinctive character of York, a small, collegiate university on a campus a few miles from the centre of an ancient city, and strove to protect it from those who were hell-bent on expansion or wanted to multiply its subject disciplines in such a way as to change its atmosphere. As founding father, he had a major role to play in the architectural plan. He worked closely with Sir Stirrett Johnson-Marshal, the architect, whose approach to educational building demanded constant and detailed responses from the university client, to produce buildings which more fully than most, expressed the university's total academic and social objectives.

York was modelled much on Oxford and Cambridge. James created halls of residence with the aim that they should be centres of social and academic life with tutors living in and he ruled that at least 50 per cent of the students should live on the campus. As a vice-chancellor he deployed brilliant talents as a chairman, including those relieving gifts of humour which can hold together conflicting opinions or at least accommodate them. Yet he was always an odd-man-out among his fellow university heads, often finding himself in a minority of one without wishing to be so.

He was an obvious candidate in 1970 for the chairmanship of the Departmental Committee on the Education and Training of Teachers set up by Margaret Thatcher, the then secretary of state for education and science. The committee recommended the creation of an all-graduate teaching profession, the ending of the links between colleges of education and universities, the introduction of a two year diploma of higher education and in-service training course for not less than one term in every seven years.

The committee's efforts had a catalytic effect on thinking about the future of teacher training — an effect fully seen in the White Paper *Higher Education — A Framework for Expansion* issued in 1972 which integrated plans for teacher education into a new structure for the public sector of higher education.

James opposed the demand for relevance in university studies and the emphasis of research at the expense of teaching. He argued that many studies apparently remote from the contemporary world brought students face to face with human experience and helped them to think clearly. For some students he said, the study of Aeschylus or medieval history or the theory of numbers could be as relevant to the quality of their lives and their contribution to society as courses in sociology or production engineering. But he warned that the quality of universities' teaching was often being endangered by the emphasis put on research. Although research was a fundamental activity of a university, it had to be recognised that most university teachers did not possess truly original minds and were better employed reflecting on and interpreting what was already known rather than adding to the body of new facts.

In 1939 he married Cordelia, daughter of Major General F. Wintour. There is one son.

b 13.4.09   d 16.5.92   aged 83

JOHN SPARROW

John Sparrow, OBE, Warden of All Souls College, Oxford, for some 25 years from 1952 until 1977.

FEW Englishmen of his generation had a more distinguished, gifted and lively mind than John Sparrow. If it was not deeply speculative or metaphysical it was capable of rapid mastery of any subject presented to it. As a young lawyer his approach had been nimble and shrewd rather than profoundly studious. Yet he had all the qualities of the first class scholar. In later life and as Warden of All Souls he paid court to none, and always had time for the creative, the independent, the clever and the brave. He himself had all those qualities except the first: he was once heard to say that to become a creative artist, he would cheerfully have forgone all else.

John Hanbury Angus Sparrow was the eldest child of Isaac Sparrow, a barrister who practised little and was comfortably off by inheritance. At Winchester John Sparrow shone both as scholar and as footballer. In 1925 he went up to New College, Oxford, as a scholar. He took in his stride a first in Honour Moderations in 1927 and the Chancellor's prize for Latin verse in 1929, but found the path to his first in Greats (1929) more arduous. However, Sparrow's classical proficiency and his flair for the rapid if somewhat superficial mastery of subjects quickly won him a fellowship after examination at All Souls College; and, rather against the advice of his close friend and mentor Maurice Bowra, the young dean of Wadham, who seems to have seen in Sparrow a born Mids don, he decided to enter the Middle Temple and read for the Bar in the chambers of Cyril Radcliffe.

From 1931 Sparrow was a fully engaged and notably successful junior, working under Radcliffe in all-round Chancery practice. If the law to him was a game rather than an avocation, his lucid elegance of diction and his bland cogency in argument came off well in court. This was a time when he first became a welcome guest at dinner-parties in London and house-parties in the country where his wit and intellectual sparkle — rather in the mode, even consciously, of

Sydney Smith – were specially valued. Winston Churchill was sufficiently aroused by him to growl across Venetia Montagu's table "I don't like young men who darken counsel." Ironically enough, however, Sparrow, who in the Fifties and Sixties was often tilted at by progressive journalists as "a pillar of the Establishment", made something of a mark in the late Thirties with his acute, if acerbic thrusts in *The Times* and elsewhere at the appeasement line of the National Government.

In those days he was a frequent and vivacious reviewer of novels and poetry for the weekly magazines: though no commission pleased him more than being sent to report the appearance (and, to his sorrow, defeat) of Major Buckley's famous Wolverhampton Wanderers at the Wembley Cup Final of 1939. By then he had also established a serious and lifelong reputation as a book-collector and bibliophile.

When war broke out Sparrow surprised both family and friends by enlisting, in a genuine flash of the spirit of T. E. Lawrence, as a private in the Oxfordshire and Buckinghamshire Light Infantry. There is no doubt that he found happiness in the ranks and intended to stay there; but the powers that be had other ideas and in 1940 Sparrow was commissioned in the Coldstream Guards and was soon made military assistant to the Adjutant-General, Lieutenant-General Sir Colville Wemyss. When in June 1941 Wemyss was made head of the joint staff mission to Washington, Sparrow went with him as ADC, coinciding for the next six months in the American capital with two other All Souls luminaries of his generation, Isaiah Berlin and John Foster.

By January 1942 he was back with a Coldstream battalion in training, but was soon summoned to assist General Sir Ronald Adam on the War Office's morale committee, a newly created and deeply influential organisation which was intended to by-pass the ordinary channels of military communication. The rest of the war Sparrow spent visiting the soldiers in training camp and in the front line in India, Persia, Italy and Germany. He became Deputy Assistant Adjutant General, Assistant Adjutant General, and was promoted to lieutenant-colonel and appointed OBE.

Return to the Bar after the war found Sparrow deeply divided within himself about his future. At 40 he knew that he had serious prospects of silk and the Bench; but the law seemed to him to demand only his expertise, and All Souls, where he had always been an active fellow, offered the chance of the scholar's life. A long-standing ambition was to write a definitive study of Mark Pattison (no one was more familiar than Sparrow with the Pattison MSS in the Bodleian); another was to contribute to Donne studies – and Sparrow while a schoolboy had published an edition of Donne's *Devotions*.

But in 1951 the Warden, B. H. Sumner, died and plunged the college into a hotly-contested election. Sparrow had few supporters to begin with; eventually he was one of the three to run forward from an over-large field to a tight and tense finish. Yet within nine months the somewhat reluctant victor, Sir Hubert Henderson, was dead, and Sparrow was now carried into office, on March 1, 1952, by an overwhelming majority of votes.

He did not make an eager start as Warden. He admired and appreciated fine scholarship; but he did not take university teachers altogether seriously. For the first dozen years of his wardenship, All Souls hardly took her full chance to play a vital role in the life of the university. But no one denied that he was a master of college business, a dexterous chairman, and a discriminating lover of the fabric and traditions of All Souls, who undertook the beautifying of the Codrington Library and the Old Library and the rebuilding of the Hawksmoor Towers.

Assuredly his wardenship gave him time to write; and it might have been thought that he would produce a major study of Pattison. But it was his nature to put off the *magnum opus*, and to settle for the brief, brilliant essays on "Mark Pattison and the Idea of a University", which were the Clark lectures for 1967. Sparrow was an effective essayist and reviewer. His prose was agile, graceful, ironic, although he never used his pen cruelly; and he had a taste for the anonymity long afforded by the front page of *The Times Literary Supplement*. Certain subjects drew him strongly; Donne, Pope, Tennyson, Housman, on all of whom he was a serious authority, and the poems of Bridges and his friend John Betjeman, which he edited. His general views on English poetry were expressed in *Sense and Poetry* (1934) and his Warton lecture "On Great Poetry" (1960): they may be termed both original and traditionalist, and betray an acute sensitivity to surface and texture in art.

His writings evince a delight in taking the unfashionable side, though more from a desire to make people think again than from pure mischief, and his unorthodox analysis of *Lady Chatterley's Lover* hugely inflated the sales of *Encounter* in 1961, evoked a pained uproar in many quarters and was never refuted. Some of the best of his occasional pieces were reprinted in *Independent Essays, Controversial Essays* and *After the Assassination*. They ranged from a spirited defence of the Warren report on President Kennedy's murder to severe criticism of what he called "the Revolting Students" of the Sixties. His specialist publications on aspects of Italian Renaissance Latin poetry and epigraphy and his collections in the six volumes of *Lapidaria* (1943-70), *Visible Words* (the Sanders Lectures, 1969), *Line Upon Line*, and *Grave Epigrams* of unusual epitaphs and inscriptions (some of them his own) were of scholarly value, the output of an accomplished Latinist.

In retirement Sparrow remained in Oxford in accommodation provided by All Souls. He was a frequent visitor to college where he witnessed substantial changes, the admission of women fellows, a greater emphasis on academic research and increased participation by All Souls in the mainstream of university affairs. Although the innovations were not all to his taste, he remained a courteous, if occasionally mischievous, dinner companion.

He was unmarried.

b 13.11.06   d 24.1.92   aged 85

APPRECIATION

I KNEW John Sparrow at Oxford from time to time, when he was emeritus warden and an hon fellow of All Souls. His favourite tale was at his own expense. The Prime Minister, Margaret Thatcher, invited him to a Sunday lunch at Chequers; and he warmed to the compliment, rather expecting he might be asked to chair a selcet committee. He drove over buoyantly one sunny summer's day.

On arrival he was introduced almost immediately to another John Sparrow, who was on secondment to the cabinet office as head of the central policy review staff (which soon earned him a knighthood). He saw at a glance that one of the two sparrows was not meant to make that summer, not at Chequers. He relaxed, realising that two may be called but only one chosen; so he enjoyed a genuine "free lunch".

Dom Alberic Stacpoole

INDEX

ACKNOWLEDGEMENTS

The publishers would like to thank the following relatives, friends and organisations for their kind permission to reproduce the following photographs in the book:

Baron (p 3), Ronald Grant (p 7), Thames Television (pp 19, 20), Kendal family (p 27), Roger Corbeau (p 34), London Weekend Television (p 36), Donaldson family (p 42), Ministry of Defence (p 46), Lady Grantham (p 47), J. N. Gillis (p 52), Mrs McMullen (p 55), Lincolnshire Standard Group (p 58), Martin Moore (p 60), Sir G. Jackson (p 63), Thames Television (p 65), Methodist Church Press (p 66), Young family (p 68), RNLI (p 73), ter Horst family (pp 74, 75), Andy Lane (p 76), Lady Loehnis (p 78), Brandt family (p 92), Trievnor & Moore (p 102), Colin Pershard (p 109), Parmar family (p 130), John Player & Sons (p 148, 149), Peugeot Cars (pp 152, 153, 154), Cunard, (p 155), Scottish and Newcastle Breweries (pp 165, 166), Luigi Baldalli (p 172), Metropolitan Commissioner of Police (p 173), G. Stream (p 186), Chris Pearcey (p 197), BBC (p 198), *Daily Express* (p 200), Yorkshire Television (p 220), G. Millais (p 228), Adel Rootstein Mannequins Ltd (pp 231, 232), *Sunday Telegraph* (p 235), Tate Gallery (p 254), Zimbabwe High Commission (p 259), Peter Cook (p 284), Eileen Ramsey (p 285).

THE CONTRIBUTORS

The publishers wish to acknowledge their gratitude for the co-operation and guidance of *The Times* team of obituaries writers Peter Davies, Peter Evans and Michael Knipe.

EDITOR'S NOTE

The obituaries reproduced in this book were chosen from those published in 1992 in *The Times* up until 3 November.